Feminist Philosophies *of* Life

Feminist Philosophies *of* Life

EDITED BY HASANA SHARP AND CHLOË TAYLOR

McGill-Queen's University Press

Montreal & Kingston · London · Chicago

© McGill-Queen's University Press 2016

ISBN 978-0-7735-4744-5 (cloth)
ISBN 978-0-7735-4745-2 (paper)
ISBN 978-0-7735-9926-0 (ePDF)
ISBN 978-0-7735-9927-7 (ePUB)

Legal deposit second quarter 2016
Bibliothèque nationale du Québec

Printed in Canada on acid-free paper that is 100% ancient forest free
(100% post-consumer recycled), processed chlorine free

This book has been published with the help of a grant from the
Canadian Federation for the Humanities and Social Sciences, through
the Awards to Scholarly Publications Program, using funds provided
by the Social Sciences and Humanities Research Council of Canada.

McGill-Queen's University Press acknowledges the support of the
Canada Council for the Arts for our publishing program. We also
acknowledge the financial support of the Government of Canada
through the Canada Book Fund for our publishing activities.

Library and Archives Canada Cataloguing in Publication

Feminist philosophies of life / edited by Hasana Sharp and
Chloë Taylor.

Includes bibliographical references and index.
Issued in print and electronic formats.
ISBN 978-0-7735-4744-5 (cloth). – ISBN 978-0-7735-4745-2 (paper). –
ISBN 978-0-7735-9926-0 (pdf). – ISBN 978-0-7735-9927-7 (epub)

1. Feminist theory.   2. Life.   I. Sharp, Hasana, editor   II. Taylor,
Chloë, 1976–, editor

HQ1190.F469 2016   305.4201   C2016-902262-5
                                        C2016-902263-3

Set in 11/14 Sina Nova with Mrs Eaves
Book design & typesetting by Garet Markvoort, zijn digital

for Zaius, Daphne, *and* Marigold

Contents

Acknowledgments

We gratefully acknowledge the innumerable nonhuman, energetic, and ambient powers that made this work possible. We thank the Social Sciences and Humanities Research Council of Canada for the Connection Grant that funded the Bios: Feminist Philosophies of Life conference in Banff, Alberta, in May 2013. We also extend our warm thanks to our research assistants, Kelly Struthers Montford and Mila Ghorayeb, for their work on this volume.

Why Life Now?

As we struggle to understand and prepare ourselves for climate change, the effects of globalized neoliberal capitalism, and violence (both governmental and extra-governmental) on a planetary scale, we also struggle to name what it is that we cherish and hope to foster and protect as well as what it is that, of itself, opposes the forces that may well destroy us. One of the words that has emerged in this context is *life*.

Philosophers do well to pay close attention to any concept that attains such centrality and exercises such power in our thinking, which is one reason to be grateful for the thinking collected in *Feminist Philosophies of Life* and for the editorial work that brought it together. The collection could not be more timely. Yet it is also puzzling, prodding a reader to wonder: What is it that brings these very different essays together? They all speak of life, but when they do so, do they speak of the same thing?

Editors Sharp and Taylor are aware of the question, and the answer they give has to do not so much with the thematic content of the essays but rather with their strategic intent. Something has changed in feminist thinking since the turn of the twenty-first century, and that change is reflected here, they suggest. Whereas so much feminist scholarship in the last century was dedicated to exposing "the tendency of discourses to normalize and exclude," as they write in the introduction, these essays strive to move beyond those discourses and imagine and cultivate new ways to speak, think, and act. And a necessary step in that project is "to ask what life is." No one essay answers that question or even addresses it directly. But the great value of the collection as a whole lies in its creation of an occasion for philosophical meditation on the question and its implications and possibilities.

I confess to skepticism regarding the ontological importance of the question; as a student of Foucault's work, I much prefer to treat powerful terms – which life most definitely is – as effects of and operators within historical and political forces. Nevertheless, I believe the editors are right to raise it as a general intellectual imperative. What is life? What is *life*? What is life doing here, among us, in our work, in this feminist philosophical moment?

In this collection – and in fact in much of the work now referred to as feminist new materialisms and posthumanism – the term life operates in a number of ways and has multiple meanings and effects. These are not necessarily contradictory or mutually exclusive – in fact, some functions and meanings reinforce or shade into each other – but there are differences. And it is important, I think, to consider these differences in their differences as well as in their overlappings and similarities. Although I would like to consider how life functions in posthumanisms and new materialisms in general, here I will simply identify and briefly explore a few of the divergences that occur in the present collection.

Herein life names, first and obviously, the course that one traverses between birth and death. Life is not a general phenomenon but an oft repeated – though never precisely replicated – particular one. It is my life, your life, the president's life, the life of the janitor who cleans my classroom. As Jane Barter writes (following Adriana Cavarero and opposing Giorgio Agamben), there is no such thing as bare life; there is always a "who," and a singular who at that. It is not clear to me whether Barter would attribute a who to the lives of nonhuman beings, but many contributors to this collection might well do so; not only my life and your life, then, but also those of the doe and the oak tree, and the twenty-one-day life of the evasively buzzing house fly. Each is particular, though we may not be able to discern it in its material and temporal particularity.

Related to this first way of employing the word life are the ways in which some of these authors use Gilbert Simondon's concept of individuating, Stephen D. Seely most overtly. For Simondon, as Seely explicates, life is or at least fundamentally involves the activity of individuation. This is not to say that any living being ever becomes a complete individual totally separated from all others, but that each emerges out of an indeterminate multiplicity in an ongoing process of differing from its own field of emergence. Particularity, or singularity, though not individualism, is affirmed; differentiation takes precedence over replication of the same. Life is this activity of differentiation, ever differing from "itself" – that is, from whatever is.

Another way that life functions in these essays is as a means to emphasize the occurrence of activity without total predictability, without epistemic or ontological certainty. Life is change – self-transformation (or perhaps a middle-voiced event of materially transforming itself, with no determined and determining *telos*). It points, therefore, at what always ultimately escapes the forces styled and ranged to catch it, manipulate it, direct it, and manage it – forces such as the carceral eugenic complex that Lisa Guenther identifies in chapter 11. Life "is" resistant to conceptualization and instrumental rationality. It names a material force that is, finally, unnamable and untamable.

Yet another function of life in many of these essays is to oppose the assumption of passivity in material existence. Understanding life as matter's self-organizing activity rather than as some kind of nonmaterial force added to or acting on materiality "destabilizes anthropocentric and humanist ontological privilege," writes Astrida Neimanis in chapter 2. Indeed, these authors assert, matter needs no external nonmaterial impetus or mentality; it is its own agent for change. A sort of Spinozist monism runs through much of this collection, a nonreductive materialism that celebrates matter as a (self-)organizing, structuring, transforming force – in other words, that celebrates life not or not only as particularities of becoming, but as a general phenomenon of material transformation of planetary and perhaps cosmic proportions.

Celebration, but also alarm, animates many of these essays. Life is what is most endangered; life is what must be protected; harm to life must be averted to whatever extent possible. Climate change, mass extinction, discrimination against the disabled, violence against queer people, murders of indigenous women of Manitoba, eugenic incarceration – all these forces assail not just individuals and classes but also life itself. For that reason, as well as others, these issues are of great feminist concern. Life as trans-formal phenomenon is not only valorized, therefore, but also powerfully desired and fearfully defended. Is life emerging here as another name for the good? At times, one might be justified in suspecting so. At other times, it can have no such metaphysical meaning. And that tense difference is worth pondering at length as feminists take up this work for further exploration and elaboration.

Life points in many directions in this collection, then: life as singular temporal becoming, life as nonteleological event, life as active material self-organization, life as to be desired and protected from harm. Life works very hard. But why? Why life, and why now?

Many feminists now search for ways to talk about ways of being that are not accommodated by – and in fact are largely inexpressible in – Enlightenment humanistic and liberal discourses. We witness a broad rejection, here and elsewhere, of atomized individualism and valorized mentality; of the purely spiritual; of hard distinctions between subject and object, self and other, Homo sapiens and our coevolving cohort of eukaryotes and even prokaryotes. But this rejection is not new to feminist thought. Feminist philosophy and cultural critique have taken Enlightenment Man as a major target for four decades. We need only remember the work of Genevieve Lloyd or Susan Griffin or Carolyn Merchant. Feminists have virtually always understood Cartesian dualism and liberal political theory, with its emphasis on rational self-mastery, to exclude the feminine, the effeminate, and anyone or anything that might be labelled as such, including "nature." Knowledge figured as the disinterested subject's mastery of the inert object is an old and well-treated theme. Critique of Enlightenment Man is not new among feminists, which has prompted many critics to suggest that there is nothing really new at all about the supposedly new feminist materialisms.

What may be new, as Sharp and Taylor suggest, is this particular concerted effort to leave Enlightenment Man behind, which here and elsewhere now often takes the form of an attempt to produce an ontology that simply excludes him. The Enlightenment Man is decentred – totally marginalized if not eradicated – in favour of an all-inclusive, down-to-earth, inherently self-overcoming concept of life.

This decentralization is a bold move beyond critique toward creation. It signals a break, albeit an incomplete one, with the feminist theory of the twentieth century, a decision to be done with the work of finding the fault lines in masculinist cultures, and to turn instead to the work of building new conceptual frameworks and systems for thinking. In that context, life is a versatile new building material – the twenty-first century's concrete or synthetic polymer – whose potential for conceptual formation and structuring is currently under exuberant exploration. What can life do? Where can thinking with life take us? These essays embody preliminary answers to those questions, even when they do not overtly state them: unlike man, life is inclusive of the nonrational; unlike man, life is immanent in and as the material world. And insofar as life differs in these ways from man, it enables thinking to diverge and venture.

But there are reasons to worry about all this. As Lynne Huffer warns, there are dangers in using life as our means of departure from Enlightenment thinking. In our time, she writes, life is a problem. She means this in a very specific Foucauldian sense: life is problematized; it is a site of interrogation, analysis, and struggle. Far from a happily neutral given, it is a particularly fraught and intensified node of power/knowledge.

Huffer offers a brief but very important genealogy of this notion of life, likening it to Foucault's description of sex in *The History of Sexuality*, volume 1. Sex is a product of biopower, according to Foucault, not the natural given upon which power seizes. Sex is the node formed where biopower groups together, "in artificial unity, anatomical elements, biological functions, conducts, sensations, pleasures, and it enabled one to make use of this fictitious unity as a causal principle, an omnipresent meaning, a secret to be discovered everywhere."[1] Huffer suggests that in both Judith Butler's and Elizabeth Grosz's work, life functions very much as sex functioned in biopolitical discourses of sexuality as they emerged in the late nineteenth century. Life is an artificial unity surreptitiously comprising disparate elements but posing as the common key to understanding ourselves and our world. If that is a plausible claim, the obvious danger is that life tends to operate as an allegedly transhistorical signifier; it purports to have no history and no political investments. But it does, and because it does, we feminists are not in control of how it operates through our discursive productions.

If life is to be a major force in organizing feminist thinking now, Huffer cautions us to be very deliberate and as clear as possible about life's histories and politics. We need a conception of life that is alert in its own manifestations of those forces and their contingencies. She suggests that the conception that Foucault offers is less apt to lead in directions that feminist materialists do not want to go than are less genealogically informed conceptions. Foucault's concept of life is unstable in that, as Huffer puts it, "the evidentiary matter that grounds our belief in something called life is, by definition, fragmented, incomplete, and shifting."[2] His genealogical approach – in particular his archival research – focuses on "material traces of lives" (note the plural) and thus "can break open the metaphysical frame of life itself that characterizes some feminist renaturalization projects."[3] Whether we use Foucault's techniques or others, we must take care to attend the materialities of singular lives, multiple and mortal, not life as a sort of universal presence.

The space of philosophical meditation created by *Feminist Philosophies of Life* is a crucial one, therefore. The project of thinking how to think – thinking thinking – without Enlightenment Man is among the most important facing us. We are rapidly living into an unforeseeable future that will demand of us a new ethos, new ethea. Will life help us imagine a path into it? Is that what life is doing here?

Ladelle McWhorter
August 2015

NOTES

1 Foucault, *The History of Sexuality*, vol. 1, 154.
2 Ibid., 122.
3 Ibid.

Feminist Philosophies *of* Life

Death is overrated.
— *Rosi Braidotti, "The Politics of 'Life Itself'*
and New Ways of Dying"

Introduction

HASANA SHARP AND CHLOË TAYLOR

With our title, *Feminist Philosophies of Life*, we signal the importance of distinctively feminist reflections upon matters of shared concern among living beings. Likewise, we point to the growing number of voices engaging in ontological inquiry and developing new idioms for describing the reality in which we find ourselves and within which we strive to realize feminist ambitions. The tools of feminist analysis have traditionally focused upon understanding and combating unequal distributions of power, responsibility, and vulnerability, structured as these are by the demands of gender and compulsory heterosexuality. While this volume reflects diverse perspectives, the various essays reinforce, on the whole, a long-standing dissatisfaction among feminists and Continental philosophers with the legacy of Enlightenment humanism, animated by the figure of the unmarked rational agent. They also share a growing appreciation of the involvement of our fates with those of nonhuman beings. Much of the history of Western ethical thought has been composed of debates about the bases of "the good life." It has typically been taken for granted that the good life is achievable only by (certain) human beings. Feminists and Continental philosophers have long challenged both the descriptive accuracy and the prescriptive hold of the idea of the human life whose goodness is under discussion. Beyond the normative demands implicit in the idea of the good life, or the properly human life, more and more philosophers now interrogate the question of life from within a broader frame.

For many contributors to this volume, it is not enough to expose the tendency of discourses to normalize and exclude racialized, feminized, differently abled, and gender nonconforming people, although such a task remains central to feminist theory and to many of the essays collected here. It is also necessary to ask what life is. What are the conditions under which life on earth is possible? To what extent do we share the struggles and needs of other living beings? What is it about living bodies that enables them to develop in so-called social or spiritual ways? What is life such that it can be social? A number of the following essays bring feminist attention to a broader range of phenomena and simultaneously reflect on the dangers of losing sight of core feminist concerns like sexual difference, gender, and racial oppression.

The need for a broader analytic of life has been long heralded by ecofeminists but reformulated more recently in feminist science studies, in an emerging family of discourses known as "feminist new materialisms," and in the recent work of Continental feminist philosopher Judith Butler. Ecofeminists insist that an analysis of sexist oppression is inadequate without an account of environmental degradation and exploitation.[1] In providing an account, for example, of sexist priorities within health care systems, it is imperative to consider how women's reproductive systems are distinctively vulnerable to pollution, and that those with greater exposure to, for example, toxic waste are also marginalized by virtue of race, class, nationality, and other factors. To understand the nature of the harm of groundwater pollution from toxic waste, then, one's perspective would be truer and more attuned to various injustices by an ecological analysis that would point to the shared concerns of sea life, those with female reproductive organs, children affected by toxins in utero, plant life, and so forth. An ecofeminist perspective illuminates how the exploitation of nature generates vulnerabilities specific to female bodies but connects them to a whole web of beings implicated in such phenomena.

Pioneers in feminist science studies like Donna Haraway engage in a critical reprise of ecofeminist literature to further complicate our species ontology. In her now classic "A Cyborg Manifesto," Haraway shows how deeply our existence is integrated with technology. For example, ever more sophisticated machines generate the images that populate our minds, like robot cameras on Mars and the invasive surveillance of Google Earth. Our subjectivities are ultimately indistinguishable from the technological devices that we have made and that in turn make us. This technology seems to divide us from nature, to divide us from nonhuman animals, and to transform us into nature's dangerous and despotic master. Yet, at the same time, technology makes possible not only certain forms of human life – such as those who use mobility devices or breathing technology – but also greater intimacy with nonhuman animals. Technology allows us to incorporate (and exploit) nonhuman animal bodies in new ways, allowing pig hearts to beat in human chests. It also allows for encounters with penguins and lantern fish, who reside in places hostile to human life. Thus, Haraway advocates a posthumanist ontology of the human for feminist theory. In her words: "By the late twentieth century, our time, a mythic time, we are all chimeras, theorized and fabricated hybrids of machine and organism; in short, we are cyborgs. The cyborg is our ontology; it gives us our politics. The cyborg is a condensed image of both imagination and material reality, the two joined centres structuring any possibility of historical transformation."[2] Rejecting either the neuter man or the romanticized woman as the starting point for philosophy, Haraway advocates an approach sensitive to our corporeal and subjective impurity. We are composed of flesh and machine and we dream with camera images. Likewise, as she later shows in *The Companion Species Manifesto*, we feel in community with companion species and develop with canine DNA.

The new materialist literature emerges from both science studies and feminist post-structuralism. Feminist new materialism consists of a creative and ambitious effort to reground feminist ontology. Stemming from dissatisfaction with radical "social constructivism" in which matter and reality threaten to become all the more elusive, it is nevertheless deeply influenced by the exemplary and pioneering work of Butler. She develops an account of the "materialization" of the gendered body. She endeavours to show how the performance of corporeal gestures reiterated over a period of time in conformity (or not) with gender regulations appears as the timeless substance of "sex." So while sex appears to cause gender, in fact a compulsory stylized performance of gender produces the appearance of sex. This occurs through a more or less fluid process of materialization over time, in response to historically, geographically, and culturally specific norms.[3] Famously, Butler describes gender as "performative," as a compulsory repetition of norms, which, rather than expressing a pre-existing sex, brings into being that which it is supposed to represent.[4]

Karen Barad, in her influential essay "Posthuman Performativity," stages a critical dialogue with Butler that presses the concepts of materialization and performativity into the service of a more general ontological inquiry. She develops an account of the doings of matter and nonhuman agencies in order to show how all phenomena come to appear through an unstable "enactment of boundaries."[5] Barad asserts that matter and nonhuman agencies are actors that contribute, along with social forces, to the shape of reality. She thus insists on specific material changes that affect "the shifting boundaries and properties that stabilize and destabilize ... what it means to be human," such that even discursivity cannot be founded on the distinction between the human and the nonhuman.[6] The tools of feminist analysis that emphasize how materialization is comprised of exclusionary practices, disciplinary normalization, and incitements of desire are thus driven deeper into domains of philosophy traditionally reserved for metaphysicians.

A decade ago, Butler published *Precarious Life: The Powers of Mourning and Violence* in response to post-9/11 US politics. She is concerned in this book with why some lives appear more real, and some deaths more grievable, than others. She contends that some deaths do not signify as grievable in the way that others do because the lives in question are never fully signified as lives. For Butler, the question of which lives "count" as lives and which are "derealized" is intimately caught up with the question of which are recognized as human: to be denied one's humanity – to be "dehumanized" – is, for Butler, to be derealized or denied a grievable life. Revealing this equivalence between having a (grievable) life and being (recognized as) human, she asks: "Who counts as human? Whose lives count as lives? And finally, *what makes for a grievable life?*"[7]

> Is a Muslim life as valuable as legibly First World lives? Are the Palestinians yet accorded the status of "human" in US policy and press coverage? Will those hundreds of thousands of Muslim lives lost in the last decades of strife ever receive the equivalent to the paragraph-long obituaries in the *New York Times* that seek to humanize – often through nationalist and familial framing devices – those Americans who have been violently killed? Is our capacity to mourn in global dimensions foreclosed precisely by the failure to conceive of Muslim and Arab lives *as lives*?[8]

For Butler, despite the fact that we differentiate between human lives – indeed, we seem to deny that some human lives count as lives, or as human, at all – it is still possible to "appeal to a 'we,'" as there is something that all humans share, and this is our exposure to loss.[9] Butler notes that vulnerability is a fundamental feature of the human condition, which means that we all have lost and will lose. By virtue of having bodies we are given over to the world not of our choosing, and are given over to others, making us interdependent and at risk. As she writes: "This disposition of ourselves outside ourselves seems to follow from bodily life, from its vulnerability and its exposure ... The body implies mortality, vulnerability, agency: the skin and the flesh expose us to the gaze of others, but also to touch, and to violence, and bodies put us at risk of becoming the agency and instrument of all these as well."[10] While vulnerability is differently distributed, for Butler the very fact that we are flesh makes humans relational subjects, dispossesses us, and renders us dependent on others prior to our choosing. We necessarily rely on others both to fulfill our social and bodily needs and to refrain from harming or killing us, and – or as a consequence – we are, in her words, necessarily "beside ourselves" in states of desire, rage, and grief for the other.

Although philosophers have long devalued such affects, for Butler these painful and ecstatic states of grief, desire, and rage provide not only onto-logical insight into the human but also a "normative reorientation for pol-itics."[11] Grief in particular can return us to a "sense of human vulnerability, to our collective responsibility for the physical lives of one another."[12] Unfortunately, we often find ways to refuse grief and the self-recognition as vulnerable that grief brings. Rather than grieve the violence that has been done to us, we may resort to acts of counterviolence, and rather than mourn the lives we exploit and kill, we may deny that those lives are griev-able. In these ways, we refuse the moral and political work of mourning and facilitate violence against those lives whose grievability we deny. Such a refusal is how Butler characterizes the US government's response to 9/11: violence quickly supplanted grief for American losses in order to reconsti-tute the nation's wounded sense of invulnerability, even while the grievab-ility, or humanity, of the lives that Americans took was denied.

As argued elsewhere, incarnation and thus vulnerability and inter-dependence are common (and differentially distributed) not only among humans but among all animals, and thus there is nothing about Butler's argument that explains the language of the human that she employs in *Precarious Life*.[13] Indeed, animals manufactured as "meat" are painfully clear examples of lives that never signify as lives, since they are, from the start, conceived as products. In turn, the deaths of these animals are never grieved since they are not recognized as deaths, merely as points in a process of unquestioned production. While Butler argues for the necessary abandonment of "United States hubris," and insists that "the notion of the world itself as a sovereign entitlement of the United States must be given up, lost, and mourned, as narcissistic and grandiose fantasies must be lost and mourned,"[14] arguably the narcissistic and grandiose fantasies of humanism must also be lost and mourned so that we can begin to recognize and grieve the animal lives we take. Ecologists attempt to unburden us of these fantasies when they note that humans are relative latecomers to this planet, that we have survived (and will likely only survive) for a short time compared to other species, and that if we were to go extinct tomorrow the planet would metaphorically breathe a sigh of relief.[15] In the context of Butler's critique of post-9/11 US politics, it might be said that with respect to other species, (most) humans have been Americans. That is, with some exceptions (such as some indigenous cultures), humans display toward other species the same kind of hubris that Americans display toward the rest of humanity, viewing "the world itself" as their "sovereign entitlement" and all the creatures in that world as mere resources, livestock, game, and prey. Perhaps climate change should have the role with respect to human hubris that Butler argues 9/11 should have had with respect to American hubris. As climate change reveals both the limitations of our power to control the world and the irreversible extent of the damage we have done, we have an opportunity to realize the precariousness of our survival and to abandon the dream that we ever had dominion over the world.

While in *Precarious Life* Butler focuses on the ways that Palestinian and Iraqi lives have counted for less than First World lives in post-9/11 US politics, in *Undoing Gender* she shifts her focus to the ways that queer, trans, and intersexed lives fail to be recognized as fully human and thus as legible and grievable. These transgressive or anomalous subjects call into question cultural grids of intelligibility, failing to signify as properly human or as proper lives. The epistemic disorientation that such subjects induce places them at risk of violence from those who would shore up what they know and insist on the impossibility of that which challenges their frames of reality.[16] Butler makes the Spinozist point that humans (although, we might insert, not only humans) wish to persist in their being, and the Hegelian argument that humans require recognition to survive. Thus we wish to persist as we are and be recognized as humans, rather than to change or be changed in order to achieve recognition. Finally, she adds the Foucauldian insight that norms of recognition are cultural and contingent.[17] The rights of the intersexed and of sexual and gender minorities thus demand not only protective laws, but more importantly that our grids of intelligibility change to recognize these subjects as fully human lives. As Butler writes, "we must learn to live and to embrace the destruction and rearticulation of the human in the name of a more capacious and, finally, less violent world, not knowing in advance what precise form our humanness does and will take."[18] She asks that we "learn to live in the anxiety of that challenge, to feel the surety of one's epistemological and ontological anchor go, but to be willing, in the name of the human, to allow the human to become something other than what it is traditionally assumed to be."[19]

Although Butler's argument that we must learn to live unanchored by oppressive norms or grids of intelligibility is appealing, certain kinds of violence continue to go unquestioned – and may even be reinforced – by her ongoing focus on the human. Butler writes: "On the level of discourse, certain lives are not considered lives at all, they cannot be humanized; they fit no dominant frame for the human, and their dehumanization occurs first, at this level. This level then gives rise to physical violence that in some sense delivers the message of dehumanization which is already at work in the culture."[20] We can question the equivalence that Butler makes here and throughout *Undoing Gender* between being "a life" and being "humanized," as well as the unquestioned inevitability of violence when a being fails to signify as human. Butler declines to challenge the ways that to be human is to be valued and to be other than human is to be subject to violence. For Butler, the solution to contemporary forms of political violence is to find ways to recognize all humans *as* human, but this disregards violence against those lives that simply are not and never will be human. Butler does not appear to be arguing that the category of the human should become so capacious as to include mice, whales, and bees, and so long as we fail to problematize the equation of dehumanization with violence, we cannot resist the pervasive violence that humans inflict on other animals.

Interestingly, while in *Precarious Life* Butler collapses the questions "what is life?" and "what is the human?," she opens *Undoing Gender* by worrying about just such a collapsing. She writes:

> What makes for a livable world is no idle question … Somewhere in the answer we find ourselves not only committed to a certain view of what life is, and what it should be, but also of what constitutes the human, the distinctively human life, and what does not. There is always a risk of anthropocentrism here if one assumes that the distinctively human life is valuable – or most valuable – or is the only way to think the problem of value. But perhaps to counter that tendency it is necessary to ask both the question of life and the question of the human, and not to let them fully collapse into one another.[21]

As in *Precarious Life*, however, Butler goes on to say that she would like to "start, and to end, with the question of the human, of who counts as human, and the related question of whose lives count as lives, and with a question that has preoccupied many of us for years: what makes for a grievable life?"[22] She thus immediately abandons her worry about anthropocentrism, and focuses from that point onward on the human alone. Despite her own precaution, by her second paragraph she has once more collapsed the questions of the human and life, or at least of lives that count as lives and are grievable. As in *Precarious Life*, however, when Butler defines what she means by the human, nothing about what she says excludes other animals or explains her humanistic language. She writes: "There is a more general conception of the human at work here, one in which we are, from the start, given over to the other, one in which we are, from the start, even prior to individuation itself, and by virtue of our embodiment, given over to an other: this makes us vulnerable to violence, but also to another range of touch, a range that includes the eradication of our being at the one end, and the physical support for our lives, at the other."[23] Other animals, like humans, are born embodied and in a world where they are dependent on and vulnerable to others in virtue of that embodiment. It seems that Butler's ethical and political arguments that build on this notion of corporeal vulnerability would thus hold for other species of animals as well. Stripped of the language of the human, Butler's suggestions for an ethics and politics of corporeal vulnerability and her interrogation of our differential recognition of lives as grievable is powerful and compelling, not least because it has the potential to avoid the speciesism and ableism that are entailed by philosophies of life that deem human lives good and valuable in virtue of their cognitive and linguistic capabilities. As animal ethicisists and critical disability scholars have argued, the traditional philosophical emphasis on reason and language is speciesist and ableist: it selects certain features deemed typical of humans (reason, speech) as morally valuable, thereby depriving nonhumans and many disabled humans of such value. As Stephanie C. Jenkins argues in chapter 10 in this volume, by highlighting instead the moral value of embodiment, vulnerability, grief, and grievability, Butler offers us an ethics and politics that has the potential to speak to the lived experiences of all humans – including the cognitively and linguistically disabled[24] – and, we can add, of nonhuman animals as well.

While in *Undoing Gender* Butler writes of human "grids of intelligibility" and "norms" that prevent the dominant gaze from seeing queer, trans, and intersexed lives as fully human, in her 2009 *Frames of War: When Is Life Grievable?* she does similar work by distinguishing between apprehension and recognition. Apprehension, for Butler, is the weaker term, and indicates that we register something without full cognition.[25] Recognition is the stronger term and is largely (though never entirely) determined by what Butler describes as historically contingent frames of recognition, such as speciesism and Islamophobia, which structure our ways of seeing life. These ways of seeing enable the destruction of lives that do not figure as lives within these frames of recognition, as well as the failure to mourn those lives. The challenge, then, for Butler, is to change our frames of recognition such that more lives will be recognized as lives, or so that we can "see" life more "democratically."[26]

In contrast to both *Precarious Life* and *Undoing Gender*, in *Frames of War* the language of the human has all but disappeared. Although Butler's focus in this book, as in *Precarious Life*, is intrahuman war, she goes so far as to acknowledge that "there ought to be recognition of precariousness as a shared condition of human life (*indeed, as a condition that links human and non-human animals*)."[27] A bit later she makes this point more forcefully:

> It does not ultimately make sense to claim ... that we have to focus on what is distinctive about human life, since if it is the "life" of human life that concerns us, that is precisely where there is no firm way to distinguish in absolute terms the *bios* of the animal from the *bios* of the human animal. Any such distinction would be tenuous and would, once again, fail to see that, by definition, the human animal is itself an animal. This is not an assertion concerning the type or species of animal the human is, but an avowal that animality is a precondition of the human, and there is no human who is not a human animal.[28]

Increasingly in this work Butler replaces "human being" with the species-inclusive "living being," writing, for instance, "precisely because a living being may die, it is necessary to care for that being so that it may live,"[29] and, "grievability precedes and makes possible the apprehension of the living being as living, exposed to non-life from the start."[30] Nevertheless, she resists having her discussion of precarious life taken up for animal activist ends, much as she resists having it taken up for pro-life political arguments.

As for Shannon Dea in this volume, and for many other feminist philosophers who are also animal ethicists,[31] the question of animal life appears caught up for Butler with the question of reproductive freedom and fetal life. Can we insist on the ethical nonvalue of fetal life on the grounds that fetuses are not yet fully developed humans or properly persons, even while we insist on the value of nonhuman animal life? Although she does not pose this question in quite this way, repeatedly Butler's discussions of reproductive freedom give rise to comments on nonhuman animal life, and repeatedly her comments on nonhuman animal life give rise to comments on reproductive freedom. *Frames of War* opens with Butler stating that her interest is in the epistemological and ontological framing of life: Through what frames do we come to recognize certain lives as lives (but not others), and through what framing devices is life constituted? Both of these questions are interwoven with questions of power, and Butler demonstrates this by raising the issues of reproductive freedom and animal rights. Who decides what life is, when life starts, or when life ends? Who speaks the discourses that define life and its parameters? Which definitions, in turn, are deployed to make life and death decisions? Butler immediately notes that these questions could be taken up to discuss issues of reproductive freedom,[32] and a few pages later notes:

> Indeed, we have ongoing debates about whether the fetus should count as life, or a life, or a human life; we have further debates about conception and what constitutes the first moments of a living organism; we have debates also about what constitutes death, whether it is the death of the brain or of the heart, whether it is the effect of a legal declaration or a set of medical and legal certificates. All of these debates involve contested notions of personhood and, implicitly, questions regarding the "human animal" and how that conjunctive (and chiasmic) existence is to be understood ... The fact that these debates exist ... implies that there is no life and no death without a relation to some frame.[33]

As the cases of animals and abortion arise in conjunction throughout the opening pages of *Frames of War*, Butler makes similar rhetorical moves with respect to each. In both cases she denies that the mere facts that a being is living and precarious are sufficient for those beings to have a right to go on living, or to evade our destruction of them. In rebutting potential animal activist interlocutors, Butler points out that "plants are living beings, but vegetarians do not usually object to eating them."[34] In rebutting potential pro-life interlocutors, she points out that "stem cells are living cells, even precarious, but that does not immediately imply what policy decisions ought to be made regarding the conditions under which they should be destroyed or in which they can be used."[35] For Butler, it cannot be the case that we, as humans, have an ethical obligation to try to protect all beings that are living and whose lives are precarious, for "processes of life themselves require destruction and degeneration,"[36] and so to be against all death would ultimately be to be against life. Moreover, Butler argues that for humans to attempt to prevent all death and degeneration would be the worst kind of anthropocentrism, a kind of fantasy that we are omnipotent and can dictate all comings into being and goings out of being on this planet.[37] In fact, life becomes and dies for the most part beyond our control, "there is a vast domain of life not subject to human regulation and decision,"[38] and we must recognize that most of the dying that takes place on this planet is simply a part of life and beyond our jurisdiction. Thus, Butler argues, the ethical imperative that her argument gives rise to is *not* a pro-life or radically species-egalitarian position that requires us to defend the "right to life" for all beings that live and whose lives are precarious. Rather, what her argument implies, she insists, is that we must "seek to minimize precariousness in egalitarian ways"[39] and to produce the conditions required for life to flourish. As she writes: "Our obligations are precisely to the conditions that make life possible, not to 'life itself,' or rather, our obligations emerge from the insight that there can be no sustained life without those sustaining conditions, and that those conditions are both our political responsibility and the matter of our most vexed ethical decisions."[40] These conditions that make life possible and which we have an ethical obligation to produce include "food, shelter, work, medical care, education, rights of mobility and expression, protection against injury and oppression."[41] Some may be human specific, and yet most of them are required by *any* animal to flourish.

Although Butler's point – that many lives come into being and die on this planet that are beyond human control – is undeniable, human decisions impact billions of nonhuman animal lives every day, and so we cannot simply dismiss it as anthropocentric to wish to intervene in those lives and deaths. As animal ethicists such as Sue Donaldson and Will Kymlicka argue, it is no longer plausible for animal activists to declare that we should leave even wild animals alone, let alone animals more generally.[42] Most obviously, the lives of billions of agricultural animals, laboratory animals, fur farm animals, entertainment industry animals, and companion animals are directly under human regulation and control. Beyond this, billions more feral and liminal animals live in our midst in urban and rural spaces, and wild animals continually traverse human-occupied parts of the globe in their migrations. Human activity encroaches ever more on wild animal territories, and climate change forces those animals to move further into human-populated areas in their search for food. Even animals humans rarely see, such as polar bears in the Arctic, are almost certainly doomed to extinction because of human activity that has impacted their environment. Although far from omnipotent, humans dramatically impact and thus are responsible for nonhuman animal lives whether we choose to be or not.

In some cases, moreover, Butler acknowledges that we do and should make decisions in which we intervene in other lives, and choose which lives to sacrifice in order to prevent harm, death, and destruction for which others. She writes, for instance, that "we can understand those modes of justifying stem-cell research when it is clear that the use of living cells may increase the possibilities for livable life. Similarly, the decision to abort a fetus may well be grounded in the insight that the forms of social and economic support needed to make that life livable are lacking."[43] Although one may be sympathetic to these examples, they raise the questions: when do we deem intervention in the workings of death and destruction an anthropocentric fantasy and when do we deem it an ethical imperative? More specifically, would Butler replace "stem-cell" with "animal" in her argument? Could her ethics justify *animal* research when such research increases the possibilities for livable life for other animals, most notably for humans? In the case of the fetus for which social and economic supports are lacking, are we obliged not merely to end that life but also to find ways to provide the social and economic supports that would have enabled it to flourish, such that others like it need not be aborted in the future? What do we say of those cases where the social and economic supports for the fetus to survive and flourish *are* present, yet the pregnant woman does not wish to continue her pregnancy because it is her considered desire to be childless? Can Butler's ethics defend that woman's reproductive freedom in this case as well? Finally, when Butler speaks of the conditions necessary for life to flourish, what does flourishing entail? Too often, as critical disability scholars and ecofeminists such as Chris Cuomo note, what is understood by flourishing includes health- and species-typical capabilities, which notions are themselves caught up with historically and culturally contingent ideas of normalcy.[44] Following disability feminist scholars, we might therefore ask: is it enough to insist upon women's right to have abortions without also insisting on the rights of certain women – such as disabled women and women pregnant with fetuses that are likely to be disabled – to have and to raise their children?[45] Is it enough to insist on women's right to have abortions without questioning the ableist norms that too often inform women's decisions to abort fetuses that are likely to be disabled? These questions indicate that while Butler offers us powerful new ways to think about the epistemological framing and ontological constitution of life, as well as suggestions for how we might live in order to secure the conditions for the flourishing of life, more work needs to be done to think through the implications of corporeal vulnerability for key feminist issues such as reproductive justice, intersections of gender and disability, and interspecies relations in times of ecological catastrophe. Many of the essays in this volume take up just such work.

New Feminist Perspectives on Life

Part 1 of this volume is titled "New Feminist Perspectives on Life." As with Butler's recent work, this part of the volume demonstrates that even when the primary object of investigation is not gender, feminist philosophy may give rise to new styles of thinking about what life is and how to live well in a fragile world. In chapter 1, "Matter, Life, and Their Entwinement," Elizabeth Grosz argues that it is precisely these new ways of thinking that we ought to appreciate as agencies proper to feminist politics. Whereas Barad mounts an argument for matter's historical agency in the co-constitution of reality, Grosz argues that thought acts in the world, *"it does something."* While inquiry into the agency of thought may seem remote from traditional feminist concerns, Grosz emphasizes that feminist politics and pedagogy have always been about the contestation of prevailing forms of thought. Thus, speculative philosophy, the study of the character of different forms of reality, remains of utmost feminist concern. Yet, we must not think that this return to the question of thinking – a traditional philosophical question if there ever was one – is a return to the human. Grosz endeavours to grasp thought as a natural force among other forces, acting in excess of subjectivities.

In chapter 2, "Thinking with Matter, Rethinking Irigaray: A 'Liquid Ground' for a Planetary Feminism," Astrida Neimanis takes up Luce Irigaray's most watery text, *Marine Lover of Friedrich Nietzsche*, in which she implores her interlocutor not to forget the waters that made him possible. Where our early twenty-first-century planetary waters are increasingly polluted, redirected for profit, and otherwise instrumentalized, Irigaray's plea seems all the more pressing. *Water is life*, we are repeatedly told these days – but thinking with Irigaray underscores that this life intimately connects our individual emergence from a maternal, watery womb to multispecies planetary survival. Beginning with a contextualization of Irigaray's work within feminist new materialisms, Neimanis explores the complex matter of living waters in Irigaray's work, and asks: Can concern for sexually different bodies *also* be curiosity and care for the waters that comprise and sustain them? Neimanis argues that thinking watery matters with Irigaray can bring together an embodied feminist ethics of sexual difference with broader ecological questions of shared aqueous embodiment across individual bodies, as well as times and species.

Chapter 3, "Ethical Life after Humanism: Toward an Alliance between an Ethics of Eros and the Politics of Renaturalization," is a dialogue between feminist philosophers Cynthia Willett and Hasana Sharp. In this conversation Sharp advocates for a "renaturalization" of feminist theory in order to more fully appreciate how deeply nonhuman forces constitute our powers and pleasures. Her approach emphasizes the nonvolitional forces that enable and constrain feminist efforts to constitute new futures, and thus calls for an ecological analysis. Willett is more wary of such an ontology: in her development of a feminist ethics of eros pertinent to nonhuman animals, she engages critically and sensitively with Sharp's proposed project of renaturalization. Willett is unconvinced by the attribution by Grosz and Sharp of agency to beings who are not subjects. Although she goes beyond other critics with similar concerns by insisting that nonhuman animals are ethical agents, she argues for ethics as a fundamentally "social drama" that plays out in "the flesh-and-blood call and responses of one creature to another." Sharp, meanwhile, is concerned that the language of "sociality" presents all of reality in the image of humanity (or man).

Lynne Huffer and Stephen D. Seely likewise raise concerns about the limitations of renaturalization and feminist new materialisms. In chapter 4, "Foucault's Fossils: Life Itself and the Return to Nature in Feminist Philosophy," Huffer finds fault with both Butler's social constructivism and also Grosz and Sharp's renaturalization for a "transhistorical" appeal to life itself. Despite the long tradition of feminist reliance on the historicization of concepts in order to question their ostensible givenness, Huffer suggests that the resurgence of the language of life might reflect rather than challenge modern biopower. She argues that Foucault's genealogical approach to the contingency of life brings a crucial historical lens to what Grosz calls a "new metaphysics" of life. Foucault's archival method enjoins us to rethink our contemporary age by engaging the historicity of matter from the past. Specifically, Huffer shows that the nonhuman historicity of nature emerges in Foucault's figure of the fossil in *The Order of Things*. Rereading the fossil record as "nature's archive," Huffer finds in Foucault's fossils a timely challenge to ahistorical conceptions of nature in an age of mass extinction where lives are threatened on every scale.

In chapter 5, "Does Life Have a Sex? Thinking Ontology and Sexual Difference with Irigaray and Simondon," Stephen D. Seely calls "new materialists" to task for their rejection of the ontology of "sexual difference" as incompatible with developments in biology and a Deleuzian metaphysics of becoming. Seely advances an interpretation of Irigaray's concept of sexual difference that is neither exclusively symbolic nor exclusively human. Rather, for Seely, sexual difference and sex, understood as informatics exchange with at least one other body, is something proper to life itself: the source of infinite becoming and diversification. Seely thus claims that, contrary to appearances, Irigaray's notion of sexual difference offers a more dynamic ontology, more susceptible to radical transformation. Nevertheless, rather than oppose the project of new materialists to reimagine agency in excess of the human, one might understand Seely to provide them with an overlooked resource.

Lived Experience

Part 2 of this volume, titled "Lived Experience," assumes the classical feminist position that personal, lived experience is inseparable from philosophy. That is, quotidian, embodied life experience generates philosophical insights, and philosophical practice is felt as (different kinds of) lived experience. Whereas early feminism drew insights especially from meditations upon domestic and maternal experience, the work collected here considers disability and dance, the collective activity of walking, and illness and temporality, and reassesses existentialism as a source of feminist reflections on the meaning of life.

Attention not only to our representations but also to the very component parts of our bodies shows that "we were never really human."[46] With insights like these, Rachel Loewen Walker, Danielle Peers, and Lindsay Eales describe the thinking animating their choreography and performance. In chapter 6, "New Constellations: Lived Diffractions of Dis/ability and Dance," they extend the idea of transcorporeality developed by new materialists indebted to Haraway "to the co-creative configurations of limbs, mobility tools, vectors, timings, stage floors, politics, and mobility strategies that make up different embodiments." The idea of transcorporeality points not only to how deeply humans depend on and affect one another (for better and for worse), but also to how profoundly we are constituted by the nonhuman world and our environment. Loewen Walker, Peers, and Eales's perspectives on dis/ability illuminate how technology and flesh can yield tremendous power. Likewise, they underscore the extent to which a city's infrastructure can amplify or minimize the access of dis/abled people to participation in social and economic life.[47]

In chapter 7, "Philosophy Comes to Life: Elaborating an Idea of Feminist Philosophy," Florentien Verhage argues that living feminist philosophy does not stay in academe but mingles and messes with our daily lives and personal narratives. According to Verhage, the philosophical becomes personal and the personal becomes philosophical because this life and these narratives cross into the theoretical work and, without a kosmotheoros, philosophy becomes muddied and comes to life. In this chapter, Verhage discusses what it means to say that "philosophy comes to life" by exploring three dimensions of doing alliance work: (1) collision and discomfort; (2) corporeal collusion; and (3) "ritualizing coalition" and revolution. Verhage argues that philosophy does not come to life to impose its theory on the lived body; instead, philosophy is enlivened when it is no longer thought of as separate from the personal and mundane. It comes to life in the intimate encounter with another while holding open the dynamic engagement of discomfort, hesitation, provocation, and the uncertain promise of a complex harmony.

In chapter 8, "Surviving Time: Kierkegaard, Beauvoir, and Existential Life," Ada S. Jaarsma makes the case for an explicitly existential account of life in late capitalism. Jaarsma reflects on two philosophical concepts – Kierkegaard's diagnosis of levelling and Beauvoir's affirmation of ambiguity – in order to explore their import for how we inhabit and understand the scripts of our present age, especially scripts about time, futurity, and progress. Jaarsma argues that scripts like those of cancer culture offer simulations of choice, individuality, and freedom, but also result in violence, suffering, and the deceptions of bad faith. According to Jaarsma, what is at stake is our capacity to inhabit our shared social space in ways that foster solidarity and cultivate passion. While Kierkegaard and Beauvoir each proffer methods by which to redress bad faith, Jaarsma examines the feminist resources that emerge from reading these two thinkers in light of each other. The resulting interplay points to the subjective as well as the intersubjective significance of how we navigate the temporal predicaments of embodied life.

In chapter 9, "Beauvoir and the Meaning of Life: Literature and Philosophy as Human Engagement in the World," Christine Daigle argues that philosophical reflections on the meaning of existence have not to date given adequate attention to Beauvoir, relegating her to the atheistic existentialist group of thinkers who claim that life in itself is meaningless and that it is up to the human being to render it meaningful. While this general claim may apply to what Beauvoir offers as an answer to the question of meaning, Daigle's investigation shows that Beauvoir's insights into the meaning of life are more sophisticated and intricate where they intertwine with her views on philosophy and the task of a writer. From Daigle's examination of *Pyrrhus and Cinéas* and Beauvoir's views on the philosophical endeavour, she demonstrates that Beauvoir's use of nonsystematic philosophizing alongside literature and autobiographical writings is how she performs her own moral and political commitments. In the process, Daigle shows how these commitments relate to Beauvoir's understanding of the meaning of human existence as transcendence, or the movement of the individual toward her self-assigned project(s).

Precarious Lives

Part 3 of the volume, "Precarious Lives," brings together essays that attend to lives that, to use a Butlerian term, are particularly precarious. While Butler focuses on the precarity of Muslim lives during the War on Terror, and of queer, trans, and intersexed lives in a gender-normative society, the essays here attend to the precarious existences of disabled people, prisoners, fetuses and pregnant women, indigenous women in Canada, and, finally, of life itself on a planet that is rapidly being impacted by climate change.

In chapter 10, "Defining Morally Considerable Life: Toward a Feminist Disability Ethics," Stephanie C. Jenkins explores the limits of the two currently dominant models of understanding disability: the medical model and social model. While the medical model locates the problem of disability in individual pathology, the social model identifies it in social exclusion, inaccessible environments, and discriminatory institutions. Jenkins notes that each model results in a different ethics: while the medical model corresponds with a "bioethics of disability," the social model corresponds with "disability bioethics." Jenkins builds on recent work in critical disability studies to identify and develop a third approach to disability, sometimes called the "impairment" model of disability, and to advocate for what she proposes as a corresponding ethics: a "disability ethics." This disability ethics challenges the negative ontology of disability, the framing of morally considerable life, and the naturalization of impairment.

In chapter 11, "Life behind Bars: The Eugenic Structure of Mass Incarceration," Lisa Guenther alerts readers to the fact that between 2006 and 2010, nearly 150 women were unlawfully sterilized in California prisons. Prison medical staff defended the procedures as a service to taxpayers, and even to the women themselves, as a way to prevent the birth of "unwanted children." Guenther situates this sterilization in the history of eugenics in the United States, as well as in broader patterns of racism, class oppression, reproductive injustice, and mass incarceration. Her central claim is that the current US prison system is not just implicated in eugenics at particular moments, but in its very structure, insofar as it systematically prevents certain groups of people – primarily poor people and people of colour, who are targeted for disproportionate police surveillance, arrest, and incarceration – from making basic decisions concerning their own reproductive capacity. Guenther concludes by considering the reproductive justice movement led by women of colour activists and scholars, arguing that this movement provides a framework for dismantling the eugenic structure of mass incarceration beyond the alternatives of pro-choice and pro-life.

In chapter 12, "Fetal Life, Abortion, and Harm Reduction," Shannon Dea also considers reproductive justice and argues that the simplistic dichotomy between pro-choice and pro-life positions is inadequate to the complexity of the issues. She argues that it is a mistake to characterize the abortion debate as a contest between two incompatible rights in which one must show moral concern for either the lives of women or the lives of fetuses, but not both. Dea insists that this is a choice we need not make, and one that rests upon a false dichotomy. On her view, anyone genuinely concerned with avoiding the loss of life, as well as with supporting quality of life, ought to support safe, accessible abortion. Indeed, the very best way to act on appropriate concern for fetal and maternal lives is to adopt a harm reduction approach to abortion. Dea sketches the history of harm reduction, offers criteria for the application of such an approach, and argues that abortion satisfies these criteria. She provides evidence that a holistic approach involving quality sexual health services, both clinical and educational, and access to legal abortions is the best available mechanism to reduce the harms – both maternal and fetal – associated with abortion.

In chapter 13, "Beyond Bare Life: Narrations of Singularity of Manitoba's Missing and Murdered Indigenous Women," Jane Barter examines the enactment of ontological reasoning on identity by families of murdered and missing indigenous women in Winnipeg. Drawing on the feminist ontology of singularity of philosopher Adriana Cavarero, and the revised indigenous essentialism of literary critic Craig Womack, Barter argues that the narrations of identity of the stolen sisters by their loved ones are a lived protest against the biopolitical identities ascribed to them by their assailants, media, and the justice system. Instead of identifying these women with bare life, family members insist on both their singularity and their common and specific victimization as indigenous women. Through an analysis of family members' testimonies in memorials, media interviews, and activist gatherings, Barter demonstrates the exemplariness of female family members as feminist and Indigenous activists, but also as those who demonstrate how identity might be reinstated without being reified in political action.

The volume concludes with Hasana Sharp's chapter, "Endangered Life: Feminist Posthumanism in the Anthropocene?" Here, Sharp considers Claire Colebrook's vigorous objection to the move in posthumanism and new materialisms to deflate and diffuse traditional conceptions of human agency. Colebrook claims that it is precisely anthropogenic climate change that exposes posthumanism as an escapist fantasy of human continuity with nature. Just as human agency becomes a geological force in its own right, posthumanists aspire to undermine the image of "sovereign man," calling attention to the role that nonhuman powers – such as impersonal social structures, technologies, nonhuman animals, and physical systems – play in enabling and constraining our capacities. Sharp finds that Colebrook's concerns about the deflection of human responsibility in an era of climate devastation are legitimate, but argues that a critical posthumanist ontology can nevertheless provide the best perspective on our current predicament, albeit not without difficulties. Posthumanism does not merely name an ontological project or a deconstructive exercise; it expresses the will for an alternative to society organized by the ideas of human exceptionalism, anthropocentrism, and the masculinist models of man they entail. Ecological catastrophe will soon require that we find new ways to live. Sharp contends that feminist posthumanism has a role to play in imagining how to live amidst the destruction wrought by masculinist humanism.

We thereby offer these feminist meditations on life that are not limited to human life. We affirm the move to deploy the critical resources of feminist thought in creative and new ways. Feminist thought will always be attuned to the particular vulnerabilities structured by the oppressive norms of gender and sexuality. This volume is one testament to how the insights and tools yielded by decades of dialogue about the character of gender domination can inspire anything from speculative philosophy to practical considerations at a time when the balance of life, for humans and nonhumans alike, is especially precarious.

NOTES

1 Warren, "The Power and Promise of Ecological Feminism."
2 Haraway, "A Cyborg Manifesto," 150.
3 This is a loose summary of Butler's position as it is articulated in her early works *Gender Trouble* and *Bodies That Matter*, which are the most influential texts for new materialists.
4 See especially Butler, "Phantasmatic Identification and the Assumption of Sex."
5 Barad, "Posthuman Performativity," 803.
6 Ibid., 818.
7 Butler, *Precarious Life*, 20.
8 Ibid., 12.
9 Ibid., 20.
10 Ibid., 25–6.
11 Ibid., 28.
12 Ibid., 30.
13 Taylor, "The Precarious Lives of Animals"; Oliver, *Animal Lessons*; Stanescu, "Species Trouble."

14 Butler, *Precarious Life*, 40.
15 Taylor, "An Ethics of Respect for Nature."
16 Butler, *Undoing Gender*, 35.
17 Ibid., 31–2.
18 Ibid., 35.
19 Ibid.
20 Ibid., 25.
21 Ibid., 17.
22 Butler, *Precarious Life*, 20; Butler, *Undoing Gender*, 17–18.
23 Butler, *Undoing Gender*, 23.
24 Jenkins, this volume, chapter 10.
25 Butler, *Frames of War*, 5.
26 Ibid., 6.
27 Ibid., 13 (italics added).
28 Ibid., 19.
29 Ibid., 14.
30 Ibid., 15.
31 Houle, "Making Animal Tracks."
32 Butler, *Frames of War*, 2.
33 Ibid., 7.
34 Ibid., 16.
35 Ibid., 18.
36 Ibid., 16.
37 Ibid., 18–19.
38 Ibid., 18.
39 Ibid., 21.
40 Ibid., 23.
41 Ibid., 22.
42 Donaldson and Kymlicka, *Zoopolis*.
43 Butler, *Frames of War*, 22.
44 Cuomo, *Feminism and Ecological Communities*.
45 Piepmeier, "The Inadequacy of 'Choice'"; Hubbard, "Abortion and Disability"; Lloyd, "The Politics of Disability and Feminism"; Saxton, "Disability Rights and Selective Abortion."
46 This is a play on Bruno Latour's phrase "we were never really modern."
47 See Jenkins, this volume, chapter 10.

PART ONE

New Feminist Perspectives on Life

I

Matter, Life, and
Their Entwinement

Thought as Action

ELIZABETH GROSZ

In this essay, I explore the intimacy between, indeed the inseparability of, thought and action – thought as action and action as thought.[1] This very abstract project has quietly fascinated me for years, since the work of the Marxist philosopher Louis Althusser, who invented an ingenious solution to the question of the status of theory in political practice: the concept of theoretical practice, namely the material practices involved in the production, circulation, and use of theory that invent or produce their own conceptual objects,[2] so I relish the opportunity to develop it a little more here. Theory – philosophy, to call it by its name – not only says something, but above all, does something. Theory, thinking, concepts, and ideas act. They are themselves a mode of action, but a mode of action among other thoughts, enhancing or diminishing them, transforming them or leaving them untouched. It is this insight that an entire, albeit under-represented, tradition has attempted to understand, from the work of the pre-Socratics, meandering through Spinoza, on to Nietzsche, Bergson, Deleuze, and Irigaray. For this traceable, sometimes subterranean, tradition, thought acts: it does things; it makes connections; it links to the world not directly but as a totality, through its effects on concepts and on thinking, and in the way in which it accompanies and always covers matter, objects, actions.

I address here a series of ontological questions that are indirectly feminist and political. These questions do not directly inform our feminist, antiracist, postcolonial, and queer struggles; but they are indirectly raised by these struggles, which must be as conceptual as they are practical. The struggle for identity, for a place within society as one of its valued members, is in part the struggle for how to think oneself and others, how to think one's immersion in the world, as much as how to change the world. It is because of the two-sided, or actually multisided, nature of concepts or thoughts and practices or actions, even the two-sided nature of matter and ideality, and of things and concepts, that political questions are also – and always have been – intellectual questions. Without this connection, all our words – and this is our profession, after all, words, teaching them, writing them, critiquing them, rewriting them – are untethered from their possibilities for acting, for having effects, and for making a difference. Having effects surely must be one of the goals of feminist theory and practice: to change ourselves and the world by changing how we think about ourselves and the world.

I address here the broadest questions of ontology, a domain that has been long inactive and has never really had a chance to direct questions, and action, through its feminist permutations: What is the nature of what exists, and the manner in which what exists coexists with a world of different entities? Ontology enables us to address how thinking thinks itself; how thought connects with and makes relations between other forms of thinking; and modes of material existence, whether entities, processes, or events. There is a dual intrication of thought with action, but also of action with thought, for action is often mistakenly considered spontaneous, unplanned, real, or direct. Thought acts, it does things, it enables things to happen and connections to be created with other thoughts, thoughts that even pretend that they are not thoughts but truths; above all, thought acts in the world not as application but as force, which is why it is so hotly contested and interpreted. We are the witnesses to the forces at work in the constitution of knowledges to the extent that we attempt to think differently, against the grain, according to different procedures and principles. For we whose activist work occurs at the site of learning and teaching, our politics is about the contestation of prevailing forms of thought, assumptions, techniques, and objects of analysis, with the hope of making a difference, even though it is never clear where or how. It is thus, as I argue, also about the contestation of bodies and their meaning, value, and operations. This is why this very abstract reflection on mind, matter, and power is nevertheless a feminist reflection, a form of feminist action.

The Substance of the Real

The question of what constitutes the real – what things, orders, or forms make the real – is one of the most fundamental questions of ontology, a question that seems very far from the concerns of feminist politics. Nevertheless, whether we focus on it or not, ontology and the question of what counts as real is one of the most fundamental questions of feminist politics. To address the relations between thought and action, to think about theory and practice in terms other than binary – in other words, to see the mutual entwinement of matter and concepts – we need to go back to before our conceptions of subjectivity were developed, that is, before Cartesianism was established as the model by which mind and body, thought and action, matter and soul, space and time, animal and human are considered in opposition to each other. We need to go back to Descartes's contemporary and challenger, Spinoza, whose effects on contemporary radical theory and politics cannot be neglected: back to an understanding of the ways in which substance itself, being, the real, the world – that is to say, in the terms of the seventeenth century, God – expresses itself equally, and always in parallel directions, through mind and body.[3] Spinoza provides the only alternative to the Cartesianism that links a series of bifurcated terms – mind, soul, time, and subjectivity in one series and body, matter, extension, and space in the other – through their alignment with concepts linked to femininity, women, and all other forms of minoritarian existence on the one hand, and through becoming identified with masculinity and privilege on the other. Spinoza, in other words, provides one of the conceptual frameworks that may become intellectually useful in feminist challenges to how we think subjects, objects, epistemologies, and ontologies, even though he barely addresses feminist interests directly. If I am right about the intimate connection between thought and action, it may be that thoughts that seem quite far from the actions we want to under-. take are in fact, by virtue of their apparent independence, sometimes the necessary condition under which we act in particular ways. Thought may not direct action, but it always accompanies it and gives it a new dimension and complexity.

Spinoza has come to define a counterhistory of Western philosophy, a history of repressed texts and concepts that have undergirded and supported the key texts and terms of phallocentric philosophy. Feminist or not, his work, along with that of other repressed or minoritized figures in Western thought (like the Presocratics and especially Nietzsche) provide strategic concepts for the critical and constructive use of feminist thought and action.

For Spinoza, mind and body are never in a causal relation with each other, for ideas can affect only other ideas, and bodies can affect only other bodies. This commitment to what philosophers call "psychophysical parallelism" implies that not only are there no causal connections between these two series, there also can be no primacy of the one over the other, no reduction of one to the other, and thus no elimination of their separation. "The body cannot determine the mind to think, nor the mind the body to remain in motion, or at rest, or in any other state."[4] If traditional morality seeks to subordinate the bodily passions to the dictates of reason (as Descartes and Kant suggest), Spinoza in *Ethics* by contrast affirms that any activity or passion of the mind or soul is also simultaneously and irreducibly an activity or passion of the body. There can be no question of the mind's control over the body; the mind and the body are two forms of expression of one and the same thing, the substance of the world, nature, the real. The mind must be understood, for Spinoza, as the idea of the body, as two parallel and equal expressions of a singular substance that itself exists in an infinity of forms beyond mind and body. Mind and body, thought and action, are the limited ways in which we, as humans with our finite corporeality and conceptuality, grasp the complexity and irreducibility of the real. In this sense, the mind and the body are the same thing, two modes of expression of one and the same substance, two parallel languages across which there can be no translation but that are equally capable of articulating reality.

Spinoza defines a body as "that mode which expresses in a certain determined manner the essence of God in so far as he is considered as an extended thing";[5] and correspondingly, an idea as "a conception of the mind which the mind forms by reason of its being a thinking thing."[6] The body is thus a mode of extension while the mind is a mode of thinking. The mind and the body, equally, and in parallel, express the essence of God insofar as God is extended and thinking. These are two irreducible perspectives of one and the same thing, two attributes that, distributed into modes, become definite "things" with their material and conceptual parallels. The complexity of mind parallels that of the body, and accompanies it wherever there is body, whether the body is conceived as living or as inert materiality. Mind or thought do not reflect on the body, nor does the body express or articulate what is mind or thought: rather each operates in its own sphere, but according to the same principles, according to the same laws, and with the same order of consequences.[7] Thought engages with and transforms itself through its various encounters – good or bad, joyful or sad – with other thoughts just as body engages with and transforms itself through its encounters with other bodies. Each is autonomous in its operations, though each remains attached to, and carried by, the other.[8]

There can be no body without thought, however simple, just as there can be no thought without body. Neither controls, directs, contemplates, or acts on behalf of the other. Yet each accompanies the other and can be regarded as a form of expansion or opening out of the other, even if in fact thought never directs action and action never gives itself up to reflective thought. Bodily action acts among other bodily acts, and among things, objects, processes, living or not; thought, though itself a body, thinks among other thoughts that either enhance it or diminish it, with which it can make entire frameworks or only flickering ideas. Each moves in the infinity of its milieu, encountering events that enhance it – joyful encounters – or that diminish it – sad encounters. This means that those who experience life – the dynamic and nonmechanical organization of a temporarily sustained body and its correlative thought – have no particular privilege over the nonliving or the human over the nonhuman. All beings, all extended things and processes, all finite things, have a kind of life, or consciousness, or thought, as rich and complex as their material existence and behaviour. Both body and thought seek to continue their existence, to be themselves, they yearn, they are oriented to being themselves and connecting themselves through those relations, with other bodies and other minds, which enhance them. There can be no master, no control of thought by bodily appetite (appetite's conceptual parallel or translation is, for Spinoza, desire), no regulation of body by mind's discipline or control. Each comes together with its other, as (one of) its other side(s), but operates in its own sphere, with only those forms that can affect it, for only bodies can affect bodies and only ideas can affect ideas. As two sides of one coin, they can never connect, but always coexist and function together, inseparably, each expressing the same thing – the glory and the complexity of the world and the infinity of substance's attributes – in its own way.

Spinoza has made it clear that the real, what constitutes the universe – which he calls God though it has long been recognized that his nonpersonal immanent God could just as easily be called Nature – is both material and immaterial, both bodily and conceptual, both action and thought. The real is always at least two, though it is also capable of more attributes, perhaps even infinite attributes that we – limited humans – cannot access, expressed in at least two irreducible ways, entwined in at least two different directions – acting and thinking. Being acts, but it also thinks. Matter is thus always connected with ideality, a process of belonging together. Perhaps this is what draws Irigaray to Spinoza?[9]

Will to Power

If Spinoza represents an opening at the very horizon of modern thought that makes the human only one example of, and not the very condition for, the eruption of mind or thinking in and through corporeal existence, his work opens out on to the writings of a number of other theorists, some of whom are explicitly Spinozan (like Deleuze, Althusser, or Macherey) while others (like Nietzsche, Bergson, Simondon, Ruyer, and Irigaray) seem less enthralled by Spinoza's substance and are instead interested in a continuity or belonging together of thought and action. This latter group at least continues, elaborates, and develops Spinoza's insight of the belonging together of action and idea. Nietzsche, for example, affirms that all matter, even the most inorganic, has an inner will, an orientation, a mode of "thought" appropriate to it, and a will to power that empowers and acts through every object. This is not an animism that attributes to the material world the qualities of life. Rather, it is the reverse: a genealogy of the emergence of the animal from the impersonal forces of self-expansion that mark materiality, which wills even for matter not just Spinozan conatus, the perseverance of one's being, but an increase of power and even the maximization of one's power, that is, the will to power. This will disdains mere survival or persistence and seeks expansion. The plant and the animal, the human or the nonhuman, the atom, the molecule, and the objects that are made from them are not eruptions of a different order than materiality but are, like matter itself, incapable of a merely mechanistic interpretation, which always acts to reduce the dimension of ideality to the automatism of closed-system, calculable, mechanical material relations. They contain an inner will, an internality that originates with all the forces of the nonliving world: "The connection between the inorganic and the organic must lie in the repelling force exercised by every atom of force. 'Life' would be defined as an enduring form of processes of the establishment of force, in which the different contenders grow unequally."[10] If the will to power, if willing itself, belongs to every being and process – not to mention if it constitutes the contradictory impulses that make up all things and processes – then willing, having an aim, a goal, an intent, an idea, a mode of interpretation is not something that only life, let alone only self-conscious life, attains. Every force, no matter how apparently elementary and simple, interprets its milieu and strives to make the most of itself in whatever way possible, even if doing so requires an apparent obedience to external forces or a transformation of its milieu. Every action has intent, a conceptual component, an inner will. But equally, every concept or idea is a weapon, a mode of interpretation, a mode of seizing hold of something as a will to power. The will to power, neither material nor immaterial, is the condition through which they each serve the other, and the condition under which thought acts and actions interpret or think. Neither can action be without idea, intent, direction, or orientation, nor can thought be without force, energy, or the impulses to command or to obey. There can be no thought without its own actions (on other forms of thought and on the bodies that carry thought through its intent), and there can be no action without intent, without activity rather than mere reactivity. Action, to be active, must act out its forces as it can, and direct itself to its own command of itself and its intent. Action must thus have at least two dimensions: one corporeal (though never reducible to mechanism that only ever grasps a force from outside) and one conceptual (its intent or orientation, its trajectory or accomplishment). It is not only living beings that act, and it is never only material objects that react: Nietzsche's accomplishment is to complicate this relation so that its terms are the inversion of dualism. All being, from the smallest element of matter (remembering that the atom itself is a fiction of a calculating rationality)[11] to the most complex social and epistemic engagements of humans with each other and the world, function on the same level, function in the same way, operate through and through according to the logic of the will to power, a logic that links thought and action in a two-way relation. There is only this force, working through matter and concept equally, enabling each to outdo itself, and especially to expand itself, through the encounter with what is other than itself. This is the will to power: the will to overcome, to incorporate other wills outside itself, to become through such encounters more than itself. This will characterizes not only every object, element, or quality in the world, but also the eternal recurrence of every alignment and arrangement between objects and qualities.

The Logic of Sense

In this quick overflight of nonfeminist or prefeminist philosophers, whose work may help us to rethink the relations between theory and action, theory and practice, and thus open up a new and more inclusive way of understanding feminist politics and theory in their intimate interrelations, we can discern that thought and action belong together. Instead of seeing theory as what one may at best apply to situations that theory predicts, or practice as the application of a preexistent plan, the quirky tradition of philosophy I invoke here gives us a way to conceive a much more complex, open, and creative relation. If thinking engages with or enters into joyful or sad encounters with other forms of thinking, and if actions are augmented and complicated by their involvement in other actions, this is because each is always carried with the other; each addresses its own concerns, but always through the inherent connection of each order with the other. Feminist theory opens up the relations of power and privilege that have marked the ways in which dichotomous terms are characterized. Where thinking, in for example Platonism or Cartesianism, is privileged over materiality, it is invariably associated with masculinity and its qualities, and the subordinated term, body, matter, is invariably associated with femininity and its qualities. These are not neutral characterizations, but the consequences of a long history of thinking that has privileged one category of human – "civilized" white masculinity – over others, one mode of thinking – the syllogism, logical or deductive thought – over others, and one particular order – mental rather than material – over others. Cartesianism provides the framework through which modern Western philosophy comes to think the world, and its subjects, through the neutralization of any specificity. This is perhaps why feminist and other forms of critical social movements require an overthrow of these dominant concepts of reason, knowledge, and the real, for we require a different trajectory than that which has directed thinking for the last several hundred years. And this is why feminists may find something of interest and relevance in the work of Spinoza, Nietzsche, and, perhaps more than any other male theorist in the present, Deleuze; not something that is explicitly feminist, but a way of thinking that can complicate and problematize the alignment of the mind/body relation with the oppositions between masculinity and femininity.

Deleuze, of course, is in many ways the culmination, and also perhaps the latest provocation for more, of the tradition I have been elaborating; a thinker whose materialism brings with it a tinge of idealism, and whose concept of the concept is nevertheless embedded in various kinds of practice and labour that operate on the plane of consistency. Although he has, through all his works, developed a peculiar kind of materialism that was always interested in the nonmaterial resonances of repetition and difference from his earliest work on Hume through to his final writings with Guattari, it is primarily in *The Logic of Sense*, his most intense and obscure text, that we come to understand the peculiar immersion of concepts and material objects and processes as the force and the lining of events. In elaborating a philosophy appropriate not to objects conceived in their stillness, but to the strange status of events – which are as it were midway between things and processes, and contain elements of both as well as an excess that is not explicable solely in material terms – Deleuze calls this excess "sense," among other things (he also calls it the "incorporeal"), a dimension of ideality, the becoming event, that accompanies and infuses all matter.

He opens *The Logic of Sense* with a return to the Stoics and their conception of an ontology and an ethics of the event. Just as Spinoza's work might act as a kind of antidote to the Cartesian bifurcation of mind and matter, so a rereading of the Stoics may well provide an alternative to both the Platonism and Aristotelianism that dominate philosophy as its very (Western) origins. For the Stoics, Deleuze claims, there are two orders of being, two forms of cohesion: the world of causes, which is the world of bodies and their "tensions, physical qualities, actions and passions, as the corresponding 'states of affairs,'" a material world of interconnected things and relations; and a world of effects, "properly speaking, 'incorporeal' entities [that] are not physical qualities and properties but rather logical or dialectical attributes [that] are not things or facts, but events."[12] These two orders, like Spinoza's psychophysical parallelism, never touch but accompany and enable each other, incorporeals, or as the Stoics call them, "the intelligibles"[13] functioning as a thin film that covers the surface of the thickness of material bodies, "like a mist over the prairie."[14] Bodies act and are acted on: only they can be either active or passive. Reason is considered a body that acts; and matter is a body that is acted upon. Each is a body that encounters another body. The incorporeals or intelligibles are inactive, unable to act or be acted upon, for they are "either wholly inactive and impassive media, such as place, space, or the void, or they are the expressibles which are stated by a verb and which are the events or external aspects of the activity of a being – in a word, all that is thought in connection with things, but not things."[15] The incorporeals are divided into four categories: time, or rather, eternity, the infinite, what is never present but always past or future (Aion); place; the void; and the lekton (or sense, the sayable). In other words, the incorporeals accompany or express beings, reason, or matter, without being either matter or reason themselves. These incorporeals accompany bodies and their qualities, whether these bodies are words, acts, or events. If words are construed as bodies, their incorporeal sense, or their lekta, are the intangible film that covers words to make them comprehensible, and let them have linguistic, extra-material effects. The lekton is the event that adheres to the surface of bodies and their qualities and that clings to the proposition as its sense and enables propositions to refer to bodies and their qualities. If everything in the world is material, a body – even reason, even propositions – then nevertheless this materialism is peculiar, perhaps even queer, to the extent that it requires an excess that cannot be material, which enables material things, bodies, to function in their various modalities, that provides fields within which things acquire their functioning.

This means that the dualism the Stoics develop, unlike the mind-body opposition that tends to dominate Greek thought, involves a distinction between bodies and states of affairs on the one hand and effects or incorporeal events on the other. Bodies, qualities, and processes are conceived as substances or causes; while incorporeals or intelligibles, which have "extra-being," are effects that inhere in their causes as those causes persist. Events are more than bodies and states of affairs, for they carry with them, at their surface, the incorporeals that never exist as such in the present, but are past or yet to come, that inhere or subsist in corporeality. Events are the coming together and inherence of the incorporeal in the present arrangements of objects and qualities. Events involve bodies, qualities, and their relations – active and passive – but also incorporeals, sense, the lekton, that inhere in these relations. Bodies and their qualities belong to the present (they are ordered in Chronos, chronology, history); but the sense that clings to these bodies, that lines the surface of events, is always already past or yet to come (they function according to Aion).

This can be illustrated with one of Deleuze's own examples, the battle, which is "the Event in its essence."[16] In its material forces, the battle consists in various actions of soldiers, weapons, bodies, tactics, cries, wounds, swords cutting flesh, but cannot be identified with any of these actions or with objects such as weapons, bodies, animals, humans, the land on which they struggle. The battle does not consist in any of these objects, but it consists in them all. While bodies and things are wounded, killed, or destroyed, the battle itself as pure event is bloodless; bodiless; incorporeal; hovering over all the objects but incapable of localization in any or all of them; indifferent to the individuals involved, to the particularities of the struggle, to who lives or dies.[17] It is an impersonal, anonymous process, never present, always about to occur or always having happened:

> The battle hovers over its own field, being neutral in relation to all
> of its temporal actualizations, neutral and impassive in relation to
> the victor and the vanquished, the coward and the brave; because
> of this, it is all the more terrible. Never present but always yet to
> come and already passed, the battle is graspable only by the will
> of anonymity which it itself inspires ... Hence, the most important
> book about the event is Stephen Crane's *The Red Badge of Courage*,
> in which the hero designates himself anonymously as "the young
> man" or "the young soldier."[18]

The world of incorporeal effects, which rides on the surface of things that exist in depth, is the world of sense, or the event, or the incorporeal, or the virtual, or thought. This world – not a self-contained one, but a self-subsisting one – makes language possible, which may explain why Deleuze considers that perhaps fiction, even nonsense, is the most direct access to the world of sense. This world draws sounds and sights from actions and objects, making language a thin degree of distance from the body's sound effects and vision effects, making these body effects resonate with the incorporeal sense that they could not have before the emergence of language. It is the incorporeal or sense that enables bodily practices to signify, to denote, to express without actually changing themselves: "Without it [sense], sounds would fall back would fall back on bodies, and propositions themselves would not be 'possible.' Language is rendered possible by the frontier which separates it from the things and from bodies (including those which speak)."[19] The incorporeal event lying on the surface of things and states of affairs, and the sense that inheres in a proposition are not two parallel phenomena, but rather are one and the same thing. This is why sense lies between things and propositions, neither the one nor the other, but the very possibility of the emergence of a proposition about things. Language itself is only possible because sounds can be incorporeally separated from the bodies that emit them, compacted into words that then can express events. Language is the effect of an emergence out of a metaphysical surface of sense and the physical surface of the body.

Deleuze addresses the Platonic opposition between matter and idea and the Cartesian transfiguration of this opposition into extension and reason through seeking an alternative history of philosophy, another plane of immanence, that not only affirms matter against its privileged other, "mind," "reason," or ideality, but also makes it clear, contrary to how he is commonly read, that matter always carries ideality with it, the corporeal is always bound up with the incorporeal. Deleuze is not a materialist, if by that we understand the privileging of one of the terms of a binary opposition. Instead, he shows that a materialism limited to simple objects and the mechanisms of determinism that regulate relations between objects not only is unable to understand the conceptuality that all objects carry with them, but is above all incapable of addressing the complexity of events.

Events require an excess of sense over materiality. Restoring matter in its various entwinements and forms to the ideality from which it has been severed is the condition under which thought, philosophy, knowledge, expands itself to touch the real without necessarily referring to or designating it as such. The event is always enshrouded in sense, and it is sense that enables propositions to be formed about events. It is sense, the incorporeal, or the lekton that connects propositions to the events they express and it is sense that enables objects to be more than themselves and thus expressible. Bodily actions (and the passions they require) generate and are generated by the thoughts that attend them, the orientations or directions within them, and the excesses of the infinite they carry with their present consequences.

Politics, and feminist politics in particular, is about addressing not only the finite history that has constituted the patriarchal framework against which we struggle, but, above all, what is to come, the future that we make rather than the past which we inherit. We make the future, whether it is invested in feminist politics or not and whether we conceptualize what we do or not. A feminist future entails that we conceptualize not only the points of vulnerability within patriarchy, but, above all, other ways to undertake practices, new ways to do things, and new ways to make sense.

NOTES

1 A version of this essay was delivered to the Thought as Action conference organized by Ellen Mortensen in Bergen, Norway, 16–18 August 2012.
2 Althusser, *Lenin and Philosophy and Other Essays*.
3 For a discussion of Spinoza's relation to and critique of Cartesianism, see Deleuze, *Expressionism in Philosophy*.
4 Spinoza, *Ethics*, part 3, proposition 2.
5 Ibid., 2, def. 1.
6 Ibid., 2, def. 3.
7 Sharp addresses Spinoza's parallelism and its significance for feminist theory in *Spinoza and the Politics of Renaturalization*. She makes it clear that his ontology of the inseparability of matter from mind challenges the pervasive philosophical assumptions of both human exceptionalism (the Cartesian privileging of mind as the mind only of humans, speaking beings as the only

thinking beings) and of the elevation of nature as an ethical norm: "Spinoza's 'parallelism,' whereby mind and body do not interact, sets the stage for a radical renaturalism that redefines human existence and agency in several ways: (a) thought is irreducible to matter, and yet does not have a unique spiritual logical that distinguishes it from (other attributes of) nature; (b) mental life is not confined to human, rational, or spiritual beings; and (c) thought and extension, mind and body, are not involved in a struggle for control" (3).

8 Deleuze claims that thought and body are doubly connected. Thought is the thought of a body and as such it is also that which participates in the engagement and interaction of ideas, whether attached to a particular body or not. And extension is connected to a particular body but also to the relation that all bodies have to each other: "Since the individual has an essence, the individual mind is constituted first of all by that which is primary in the modes of thinking, that is, by an idea ('Ethics,' 2, ax. 3, and proposition 11). The mind is therefore the idea of a corresponding body. Not that the idea is defined by its representative power; but the idea that we are is to thought and to other ideas what the body that we are is to extension and to other bodies ... Each thing is at once body and mind, thing and idea." Deleuze, *Spinoza: Practical Philosophy*, 86.

9 See Irigaray, "The Envelope."

10 Nietzsche, *The Will to Power*.

11 Ibid., 334. Nietzsche argues, in a section called "Against the Physical Atom" (#624): "To comprehend the world, we have to be able to calculate it, we have to have constant causes; because we find no such constant causes in actuality, we invent them for ourselves – the atoms. This is the origin of atomism. The calculability of the world, the expressibility of all events in formulas – is this really 'comprehension'?"

12 Deleuze, *The Logic of Sense*, 4–5.

13 Bréhier, *The Hellenistic and Roman Age*, 45.

14 Deleuze, *Logic of Sense*, 5.

15 Bréhier, *The Hellenistic*, 45.

16 Deleuze, *Logic of Sense*, 100.

17 Sextus Empiricus gives the example of the scalpel cutting flesh. The scalpel is a material body; the flesh it cuts is a material body, but the predicate, "being cut," is immaterial, a process that subtends the bodies joined momentarily together. Being cut is, for the Stoics, an order different that the body and the scalpel that cuts it, it exists or inheres even if the scalpel and body do not come together. It is an incorporeal state, never present, always already having happened or always about to happen.

Long and Sedley, in *The Hellenistic Philosophers*, 340, claim:

The alternative was presumably to say that thanks to the scalpel one body, uncut flesh, ceases to exist and is replaced by a new body, cut flesh. But that would imply that no body persists through the process, so that there is no body in which we can say that the change has been brought about. Since the object changed must, normally speaking, persist through the change ... it proved more palatable for them to say that the effect is not a new body but the incorporeal predicate "is cut" which comes to be true of the persisting flesh.

18 Deleuze, *Logic of Sense*, 100–1.
19 Ibid., 166.

2

Thinking with Matter,
Rethinking Irigaray

A "Liquid Ground" for
a Planetary Feminism

ASTRIDA NEIMANIS

So remember the liquid ground.
— *Luce Irigaray*[1]

In Luce Irigaray's most watery text, *Marine Lover of Friedrich Nietzsche*, she implores her interlocutor not to forget the waters that made him possible. Where our early twenty-first-century planetary waters are increasingly polluted, redirected for profit, and otherwise instrumentalized, Irigaray's plea seems all the more pressing. *Water is life*, we are repeatedly told these days – but thinking with Irigaray underscores that this is a life that intimately connects our own individual emergence from a maternal, watery womb to multispecies planetary survival. My main aim in this essay is thus to explore the complex matter of living waters in Irigaray's work, and the ways in which these bring together an embodied feminist ethics of sexual difference with broader ecological questions of shared aqueous embodiment across individual bodies, as well as times and species.

For Irigaray, water is paradoxically a "liquid ground" – both essential to life and also always shifting. Water is at once the originary matter of life, but also its force of differentiation and wellspring of unknowability. Indeed, the multivalence of Irigaray's liquid ground epitomizes the notable difficulty many commentators have had in classifying her work within feminist philosophy according to terms such as "essentialist" or "constructivist," particularly on the question of the materiality or nature of sexed bodies. Before turning to the specific matters of Irigaray's waters, then, I begin by examining the recent so-called material turn in feminist theory and philosophy. I suggest that this turn provides a helpful frame for understanding Irigaray's complex relation to sexually different bodies and elemental matter – one that we can understand as "thinking with matter." On such a reading, the elemental stuff of biological or physical life eschews containment within reductive essentialisms or as brute and inert matters. Rather, matter is recast as a meaningful collaborator – that is, something to think *with*, rather than about. Moreover, while thinking Irigaray's waters within a feminist new materialist frame provides a productive way to understand the ambiguity of Irigaray's elemental matters, it also helps to clarify the stakes of feminist new materialism as an ethico-onto-epistemological project. The deep ethics at the heart of Irigaray's work reinforces the need for feminist new materialisms not to forget the ethics of difference that Irigaray's philosophy has so carefully staked. In turn, considering Irigaray's liquid ground in the context of more-than-human life reminds us that such an ethics of difference cannot end with human sexual difference, but must also facilitate a feminist ethics of responsivity toward our planetary waters. In the concluding section of this essay, I work in this emergent space of a feminist more-than-human ethics of difference. While Irigaray's work may only be suggestive in this sense, it nonetheless opens a path for thinking through life as not only our own, but also distributed through, indebted to, and facilitative of lives that reach far beyond the bounds of our skin. In a specifically global or planetary context, such an opening might be just what we need to hone an ethics of responsivity toward waters both common and different, and toward bodies that are intimately close but also distant and dispersed.

Thinking with Matter: New Feminist Ethico-Onto-Epistemologies of Life

The recent so-called turn in feminist philosophy and feminist theory more generally toward the *matter* of life has been met with mixed reactions – none perhaps stronger than those articulated around the idea of new materialism.[2] Admittedly, that term has proved a contentious signifier: even if the post-structuralism that dominated feminist theory in the 1990s might have put the emphasis elsewhere, feminist interest in materiality – in fleshy, material bodies, in the material effects of immaterial processes, in "nature" that too often served as a foil to "culture" – has remained steady. A concern for materiality – if that is all this turn means – is hardly new. Such a misnomer might be corrected with alternative terms like "feminist materialisms" or "posthuman feminisms," but even these names do not swiftly alleviate concomitant concerns about the feminist turn to matter. Characterized as primarily ontological, and drawing increasing attention to the nonhuman or more than human and the biological and ecological dimensions of life matters, this turn also elicits questions about the focus of feminist theories. Does this materialist concern undo or otherwise discount the shaping of "what matters" through language, discourse, and representation? Is this turn's espoused reorientation toward ontology a dismissal of epistemology as a site for groundbreaking feminist contributions to philosophical scholarship? Or even more troublingly, is it a disavowal or forgetting of the ethics that have grounded feminist concerns as a key (the key?) raison d'être? Or more specifically: What does concern about nonhuman or more-than-human matter have to do with the ethical and attendant political projects of feminism? In this turn, have we not, so to speak, lost the feminist plot?

Such concerns provide an opportunity for feminist new materialist or posthumanist philosophers to clarify their terms. While this turn does not introduce matter as a feminist object of thought, perhaps there is nonetheless something new going on within these posthuman, materialist philosophies of life[3] – not new as in previously unthought, but new as in a shift in patterns of thought as a way to reconfigure what was already there, already thought. One such new patterning of thought, I propose, could be articulated as a refusal to think merely about matter, and instead an attempt to think with it. A feminist thinking with matter, then, might be a way to name a busy new conversational space within feminist theory and philosophy that collects diversely nuanced but similarly oriented ways to turn and return to the question of matter. This "new" gathers both possible pasts and potential futures; it not only collects feminist thinkers from diverse types of inquiry, but also acts transversally, unfolding both backward and forward, and gathering thinkers from different (nonlinear) times.[4]

For new feminist engagements with matter, "thinking with" is not a meditation "on," but an engagement or conversation "with." This speaks to the specific ontological orientation of the so-called turn toward matter; in these theories, matter is rethought as lively in a way that destabilizes anthropocentric and humanist ontological privilege. Understandings of matter (including nonhuman nature and the biological substrata of human life) as something that "feels, converses, suffers, desires, yearns, and remembers,"[5] "reads and writes, calculates and copulates,"[6] or attempts to "question, solve, control, calculate, protect, and destroy"[7] all suggest that matter is in fact agential. While this claim is not uncontroversial (as it may risk diluting feminist conceptions of moral agents), it importantly reminds us that when matter moves us (or moves other matters), this is not a brute causal determination. Agency, in the new materialist and posthumanist sense, is quite basically about "changing the possibilities of change."[8] All matters take part in this agency as a doing, where possibilities for change emerge in ongoing intra-actions of matters that are never completed. Rather than a dilution of agency as applied to humans, new materialist agency invites us to consider how nonhuman bodies or matters might contribute to their own actualization or demand a response.[9]

Considerations of matter as agential in fact substantially contribute to why feminist thinking with matter is not only an ontological but also an epistemological and ethical concern. Such epistemological stakes are highlighted, for example, when Karen Barad reminds us that "there is an important sense in which practices of knowing cannot fully be claimed as human practices, not simply because we use nonhuman elements in our practices but because knowing is a matter of part of the world making itself intelligible to another part."[10] Even if the matters we think with inspire us to think in new ways, we never think alone. Put otherwise: if we understand nonhuman matter as agential, then we must also give up an impetus to mastery. Thinking with matter thus draws on feminist epistemological critiques of total knowledge, resonant with what Donna Haraway calls "situated knowledges"[11] and Rosi Braidotti calls an epistemological position of "embeddedness and embodiedness."[12] Thinking with matter is not a return to self-evident realism or empiricism. At the same time, this recuperation of matter's liveliness does not mean that issues of language and representation are overwritten or effaced. Thinking with matter also foregrounds thinking. Important insights into representation and discursive constructions are not eschewed, but rather understood as entangled in matter's own expressive limits. According to Iris van der Tuin, a rejection of dualisms (matter *or* meaning; empiricism *or* linguisticism; the real *or* the constructed, etc.) is a defining feature of these (in van der Tuin's words) "third wave" materialisms.[13] Self-evident materiality does not trump discursivity, any more than ontology would epistemology;[14] feminist "thinking with" is always and inextricably "onto-epistemological," to invoke Barad's term.

Still, in the context of these onto-epistemologies a question remains: "Was this turn (whatever we want to call it) an ethical turn?"[15] While key thinkers in this area of feminist thought, such as Barad and Braidotti, consistently outline the ethical implications of turning to life matters, these, like the epistemological dimensions, tend to be overshadowed by an emphasis on new ontologies. Yet Cecilia Åsberg provides an excellent synopsis of the ethics at stake in the new feminist turn to materiality: "Posthumanist ethics, entangled with onto-epistemologies of worldly 'intra-actions' [Barad], emerge as efforts to respect and meet well with, even extend care to, others while acknowledging that we may not know the other and what the best kind of care would be."[16] The ethical commitments of thinking with matter do not come from a "normative morality;"[17] ethics here do not comprise intentional "right actions," moral universalisms, or an extension of human ethical programs (e.g., human rights) to the nonhuman world.[18] Because this ethics is inseparable from the ontologies and epistemologies that condition it, it must also reject human mastery. We may not know who or what the other we encounter is or needs, but, forever entangled in these relations, we must negotiate the ethics of these meetings and their collaborative matterings. As such, this ethics demands that we remain open, attentive, and curious toward the other and what she asks of us.[19] As Åsberg is keen to underline, even as this ethics provides no checklist of right action, it is still fundamentally about care, respect, and concern.[20] Barad calls this an ethics of responsivity: it is "about responsibility and accountability for the lively relationalities of becoming of which we are a part."[21]

Not only do these posthumanist, new materialist ethics expand a feminist conception of how ethics might be construed, they also beg the difficult question of toward whom or what a feminist ethics should be directed.

Might we join thinkers such Val Plumwood, Braidotti, and Claire Cole-brook in understanding "a critique of masculinism [as] intertwined with a concern for the nonhuman"?[22] If the deep structures of power and oppression are a feminist issue, then these concerns do not stop at the human skin. At the same time, and crucially, such an expression of care and concern for the nonhuman is not a homogenized or "flat" ethics: within a feminist cartography of power, difference still always matters.[23] A relationship of *re-specere* toward the nonhuman does not erase differences between humans and nonhumans, or among differently situated humans. In fact, an ethics of responsivity, never knowable in advance, pointedly underlines such differences: how am I responsible to *this* body, *this* time, in *this* encounter? A feminist thinking with matter is not a negation or erasure of a feminist genealogy of ethical thinking, but its very embrace and further development. Onto-epistemology is always already ethico-onto-epistemology.[24]

Yet to fulfill this ethical promise, feminists thinking with matter must resist instrumentalization at all levels; we must remain vigilant in our refusal to reduce these life matters to their use-value for the thinker. Here, this includes a refusal to treat these matters as mere fodder for our intellectual products, and a refusal to simply recruit matter as metaphor or concept.[25] Even (or especially) as we call on nonhuman matter to ignite our theoretical, creative fires as our collaborators, "we must find another relationship to nature" – or nonhuman matter more broadly construed – "besides reification, possession, appropriation, and nostalgia."[26] As Åsberg notes, more-than-human matters such as animals, microbiomes, neurologies, and climates "are not of concern as merely instruments of theory, but because our lives also affect them."[27] Life is made up not of these individual bodies, but of the ongoing intra-actions and relations in which all of these bodies provisionally emerge. In the context of the ethics of responsivity that Barad outlines, we must insist that the matter of life, in all of its nonhuman and more-than-human guises, is more than a "co-labourer," doing all the grunt work for little or nothing in return.[28] The ethics at stake here are thus not just in general, to be learned from these matters, but specifically an ethics to be directed specifically toward these matters we "think with." "Thinking with" in a feminist context must remain committed to holding on to this "with," even once the heavy thinking is done. These matters give us insights and theories (publications, jobs, livelihoods), but what do we give back? How do we honour these matters and their gifts? In this sense, an acknowledgement of the ethics implicated in the material turn is as much provocative as it is descriptive.

Rethinking (with) Irigaray Thinking with Matter

Using these new materialist or posthumanist orientations as a frame, my aim in this essay is to rethink the waters that animate Irigaray's writings. Not simply an amniotic trope of feminine-maternal gestation, these waters become a differentiating life force that flows across bodies, species, and times. Rethinking Irigaray's liquid ground in this way moreover demands that we attend to an ethics of responsivity toward nonhuman matter – in this case, water. Doing so, I propose, can also open Irigaray's work to a specifically more-than-human ethics of difference. In order to reconsider the waters that flow through Irigaray's writings, however, it is necessary first to understand how she "thinks with" bodily matter in relation to the natural or elemental matter of the world more generally.

Irigaray's contributions to a feminist thinking with matter arise most obviously in her attention to body-morphological phenomena as distinctly material. Her philosophy of embodiment notably includes deep descriptions of the materiality of women's genital lips, mucous, womb and intrauterine space, placenta, amniotic fluid, saliva, and breath. Yet on these questions in particular, Irigaray is famously difficult to classify. Any appeal to bodily matter might read as a biologically reductive gesture (essentialism?). Yet at the same time, Irigaray is distinctly committed to an unknowability – a woman to come, a body multiple – that clearly counters any impulse of predetermination (radical constructivism?). While Irigaray's writings predate feminist new materialism as a named theoretical orientation,[29] this emerging ethico-onto-epistemological frame provides a helpful reference for understanding natural and corporeal matters in her work without having to fall back on either dichotomized position. Instead, matter in Irigaray can be appreciated as dynamic and facilitative.[30] The being and becoming of bodies in her work are indebted to what Barad would call the agential realism of matter, whereby matter is a lively participant in the "worlding" of the world.[31] Such worlding, or unfolding, does not occur in a teleological or deterministic sense, but rather through intra-acting with other entities to generate new possibilities and bodies, never fully knowable in advance.[32] The cultural meaning of woman is not arbitrary – it is certainly worlded through her biological matter, such as the genital lips or the placenta. But absolutely crucial is the fact that this meaning is not locked or fixed. It is precisely because of the open possibilities afforded by this specific biological matter (e.g., the placenta's gestation of life in the plural; the erogenous flesh that enables woman to "touch herself all the time"[33]) that woman remains ultimately unknowable. In other words, bodily matters are vital collaborators in the unfolding meanings of what "woman" is and what she could be. This aligns with Irigaray's overarching position that woman is not only a subject in the present but also always still unsignified and still to come. The matter of the body is not a static trap but an opportunity and a generative force; "certain properties of the 'vital,'" Irigaray reminds us, "have been deadened into the 'constancy' required to give it form."[34] In this way, Irigaray can be read as a key contributor to new materialist ontologies of embodiment.

Irigaray's attention to matter, however, is not limited to the human body. She is also explicitly interested in elemental phenomena – such as air, water, the earth, and the sea. More accurately, we could say that Irigaray's attention to bodily matters is also an attunement to the matter of our elemental milieus – which, as we will see, are both deeply co-implicated in life. At some points Irigaray does seem to suggest that the connections of our human bodies to other natural bodies are metaphorical – for example, when she describes how the sexual difference of bodies mirrors the nature of weather, plants, animals, and the elemental more generally.[35] Yet we can also trace in her work a contiguity or continuity (rather than analogy) with the elemental. For Irigaray, human bodies are neither impermeable nor discrete: "A body becomes a prison when it contracts into a whole ... When a line is drawn around it, its territory mapped out."[36] She writes moreover that "we are made up of these elements [air, water, fire, and earth] and we live them"; she reminds us that the gift of breath comes not only from human bodies but from vegetable bodies as well.[37] Her descriptions of fleshy human corporeality in terms of "elemental passions" can be read as an extended material metaphor that is effective precisely because our physiological reality is intimately connected to a meteorological and geophysical one. Irigaray's is "a body of air filled by palpitating blue," "eating the sun"; a body "animated throughout" and "changed by a cloud"; a body that is an "atmosphere of flesh."[38] Like all other bodies of water, human bodies drink the rain and feel the drought; the winds that bend tree branches strengthen and make supple our own swaying spines; the warmth of the sun encourages our growth, as it does algae on a pond's surface or seeds germinating in the soil. To use a term recently propounded by material feminist Stacy Alaimo, Irigaray's ontology of embodiment is also fundamentally *transcorporeal*, where "the substance of the human is ultimately inseparable from 'the environment.'"[39] The matters of the body overlap with and transit through a more expansive elemental milieu.

Irigaray's philosophy of nature is compellingly explored elsewhere,[40] and (re)thinking her work in transcorporeal terms would be a lively complement to these discussions. Here, however, I return to my more modest aim, namely of asking how Irigaray's thinking with matter might help us rethink the relation of human bodies to more-than-human waters. Given that we humans are composed mostly of water, it seems imperative to ask how our theories of embodiment might foster (or hinder) care, concern, and responsibility toward the diverse planetary bodies of water that sustain us. Before proceeding, one caveat is necessary: Irigaray's theory of embodiment is also fundamentally one of sexual difference, yet the theory of watery embodiment we might extract from her writing will not seem, at first glance, to foreground this crucial and probably inalienable aspect of her work. Indeed, a study of sexual difference in relation to elemental waters deserves a deeper exploration than I can engage in here, particularly as it suggests, to my mind, a rich opening for thinking about sexual difference in Irigaray in distinctly posthumanist terms. Despite my backgrounding here of an explicit concern with sexual difference, Irigaray's evocation of waters – which are themselves sexually different, and which also gestate sexual difference – sketches a certain membrane logic that is imperative for understanding her ontology as also an ethics. Attending to membranes – that is, zones and processes of differentiation – within transcorporeal flows prevents the amorphous homogenization of water's intricate biodiversity. This ineradicable alterity that is also sustained and gestated by an aqueous commonality is, I propose, what rethinking Irigaray's bodies of water can help us to imagine. I return to these questions in my conclusion.

Marine Lover and Bodies of Water

Marine Lover is an amorous dialogue between the textual avatars (presumably) of Irigaray and Nietzsche. In it, Irigaray illuminates how Nietzsche's conception of the eternal return betrays a fear and terror of the watery element to which his birth is nonetheless indebted, and how, because of this fear and disavowal, the eternal return will never be able to return difference *as* difference. By refusing to acknowledge the feminine watery abyss from which he has come, nothing but the self-same will be continually reborn for Nietzsche, leading only to entropy and death. Alternatively, Irigaray calls for the fluvial gestational feminine – that which is different from the self-same – to engender creative reproduction of something new.[41]

In this text, as in others, Irigaray invokes multiple "women" that operate on different strata. We encounter women as beings in the present, that is, the specular woman of Nietzsche's eternal return who is refused admittance into his "echonomy."[42] We also encounter a woman in the future, whom we do not yet know and who is to come – a woman who will demand a different potentiality than that the eternal return of the self-same offers her. And, we encounter some sense of a "first woman," a maternal primordial feminine who engenders and gestates sexual difference – a connection underscored in the original French by the homonymic relation between "mer" and "mère." This multiple woman is then diffracted through the multiple ways in which fluid, water, and the sea figure in *Marine Lover*, as these move between descriptions of waters that are feminine, waters in which the feminine lives, and womb-like waters both feminine and maternal. The rapturous sea that moves about endlessly is described in feminine terms,[43] as are the maternal waters out of which the Overman and the masculine are born, and whose depths they now fear.[44] The waters that man uses, unacknowledged, for sustenance, and which he attempts to solidify in his image, are also feminine. So, on the one hand, we see how water marks off the qualitative difference of woman and the feminine. While in man's world, "it is always hot, dry and hard,"[45] the feminine sea is multiple, flowing, gestating, sustaining.

Yet, on the other hand, water is undeniably a part of the masculine as well, even in his fearful forgetfulness. In these pages we glimpse how the masculine variously emerges from water, is afraid of and repulsed by water, depends physiologically upon water, and is returned to water. While clearly the masculine comes from and is indebted to the forgotten sea/ the fluid feminine, no clear moment of separation of the masculine from his "immemorial waters" and no clear renunciation of his watery beginnings is offered, for the masculine returns there, too; as phallogocentric fisherman, as a drowning man engulfed by waters he cannot escape, as a swimmer-to-come once he stops resisting the flow.[46] The sea is both danger and saviour, threat and buoy. And to complicate the watery figuration further, the narrator describes the masculine as not only *in,* but *of* water. She acknowledges the saliva in his mouth that enables him to speak, even as it/she is forgotten once speech is underway,[47] and asks, "Where have you drawn what flows out of you?"[48] While it is the sea to which the masculine must return for sustenance, this sustenance not only immerses him, but saturates him as well – even when he would prefer to "freeze rather than flow."[49] And, similar to her remarks in "Mechanics of Fluids" (the title of one chapter in *This Sex Which Is Not One*) where Irigaray considers the fluid potentiality of sperm that has been coopted and reified in a logic of solids,[50] in *Marine Lover* her descriptions of a frozen and solidified masculine implicitly ponder the masculine's fluidity in the future: What might the ethical and political potentiality of the masculine be if a phase change of water were to occur – and if this water were acknowledged rather than disavowed and feared? While what Irigaray's interlocutor thinks he fears is drowning, Irigaray reminds him that what he should really fear is thirst.

These descriptions underline how Irigaray's bodies of water can be read in new materialist or posthumanist terms as both material and discursive. Irigaray is certainly carefully attuned to the ways in which meaning configures matter and how, as such, the feminine fluid participates in a very specific signifying economy (which she attempts to resignify). At the same time, she accounts not only for the discursive limits of bodily mattering, but for the material limits as well. Cultural meanings of feminine morphology are not arbitrary, but flow from actual "mechanics of fluids" – that is, from the physical properties of water as a material substance, as well as the biological or chemical water-related processes in which many female bodies participate. But similarly, no signifying economy could dehydrate a male body completely: he also experiences life as a composition of blood, bile, tears, saliva, perspiration, ejaculate, urine, and breathy vapour.[51] No matter what disavowal is enacted, water comprises and is required of all life for maintaining our cell structure, facilitating necessary chemical reactions, physically transporting nutrients and oxygen through the body, and enabling waste elimination. It is thanks to water that we move, grow, live, or have a body at all.

Irigaray's descriptions of aqueous feminine and masculine bodies acknowledge that the waters these bodies comprise are agential, lively, and potentially generative. The nature of these waters is neither static nor "biologically essentialist." The fluid feminine is not a corroboration of the body as prison; her elemental waters are, rather, an engine of becoming. The sea/mother/woman "instantly perishes when taken away from her shifting bed" in/as watery milieu; "torn away from the place which gives place to her" she is "deprived of the permanence of her becoming."[52] These agential, facilitative seas support a new materialist reading of Irigaray's ontology of bodies, but they also importantly suggest that waters in this text might be more than human. The masculine *and* the feminine are both of water, but water also comprises the gestational element between or beneath the masculine and feminine. "Between you and me, me and you," *Marine Lover*'s narrator laments, "you want me to make a dam."[53] Here, Irigaray suggests a different flow of water, one that is vital both for the maintenance of sexual difference in a respectful relation, and also for the continued fecundity, development and growth of all bodies. While we are bodies "of" water, in the material, constitutive sense (i.e., we comprise it), we are also always "of" water, in the gestational sense (i.e., we emerge from it).

Of course, water as the gestational element distinctly overlaps with the feminine waters described above. But importantly, this element is not reducible to human maternal amniotic waters. Thinking with matter transcorporeally, amniotic waters are not like our planetary waters, but continuous with them. Irigaray, for example, asks her interlocutor in *Marine Lover* whether his "most dangerous beyond" is not in fact "the unexplored reaches of the farthest ocean."[54] Hence she asks us to consider the maternal waters in which we are created and nurtured as a part of the greater element of water that continues to sustain us and protect us, both extra- and intercorporeally, after we emerge from these wombs. As Irigaray notes elsewhere, the fecundity of gestation is not limited simply to human gestation and the moment of birth, but is rather an ongoing regeneration.[55] Our gestational milieu might thus be understood as the contraction of a greater ocean into a tiny one, and our birth as the passage from a smaller womb back to a larger one. Yet this passage enacts neither severance nor separation, but rather diffusion, evaporation, condensation, and incorporation. The passage from body of water to body of water (always *as* body of water) is never synecdochal or merely metaphoric; it is radically material. These complex and shared cyclings – body to body to body – comprise our planetary hydrocommons.

Moreover, these abyssal, unknowable depths that gestate us – "that dark home where you began to be once upon a time. Once and for all"[56] – also posit a transcorporeal stretching of waters and watery species across planetary times. Despite Nietszche's rejection of Darwinism, the evolutionary tones of *Thus Spoke Zarathustra*, referenced by Irigaray in *Marine Lover*, are well noted. As Penelope Deutscher puts it, Nietszsche "evidently appreciated the image of the human as a composite interconnecting genealogically with a plurality of animal forms and fragments."[57] When Irigaray asks her interlocutor, "Why leave the sea?" and chastises Zarathustra for his penchant for terrestrial companions, bridges, solid ground, and lofty heights,[58] she also reveals the continuity between maternal and evolutionary waters in her interlocutor's "forgetfulness of birth."[59] "The fluid world [he] once inhabited"[60] might be a maternal womb, but could also be the primordial evolutionary soup that gestated us all. Right back to the first signs of life on earth at least 3.9 billion years ago, when small organic proteins likely interacted with their habitat to produce the first bacterial life forms, water has been necessary for the proliferation of life in the plural. Granted, the evolutionary undertones are subtle in Irigaray's text, and she certainly isn't an "evolutionist."[61] Her references to our evolutionary debts nonetheless invite us again to understand gestationality in her work in terms beyond the human maternal womb. The watery habitat that gave the planet life is also the water that the first land-bound species in turn folded inside themselves – a process that scientists Mark and Dianna McMenamin describe as "Hypersea."[62] On land, the life sustenance that was passively accessible in a marine environment had to be actively facilitated through increasingly complex networks dependent on symbiosis, physical connection, and proximity. In other words, like all species, we carry the gestational milieu of our evolutionary waters with us; our own species-bodies become gestational milieus for new species and new proliferations of life. In evolutionary terms, water is the primary mechanism not only for survival, but for the gestation and further pro-liferation of other life, too.[63] In her reading of *Marine Lover*, Deutscher avers that Irigaray "favors elemental and avoids animal analogies,"[64] but, like Deutscher, I agree that Irigaray's criticisms of Zarathustra's prefer-ence for terrestrial animals might nonetheless open to a thinking about evolution in terms of species genealogies. Thinking in terms of Hypersea corroborates Deutscher's suspicion that elemental and animal analogies cannot be "secured from one another."[65] And Irigaray seems to agree: she notes that "as a companion" her interlocutor never chooses "a sea creature. Camel, snake, lion, eagle, and doves, monkey and ass, and … Yes. But no to anything that moves in the water. Why this persistent wish for legs, or wings? And never gills?"[66] By gesturing toward our evolutionary soupy, even fishy, beginnings, Irigaray suggests that transcorporeal cycles of ges-tationality echo not only across human bodies and maternal wombs, nor only between human bodies and watery habitats, but also across species, symbiotic becomings, and evolutionary times. This transcorporeality, dis-turbing the discrete boundaries of the human, again positions Irigaray im-portantly within a post-human, post-anthropocentric, and new materialist orientation toward bodies and matter.

The proliferation of life in the plural brings us back to the question of difference. In *Marine Lover*, Irigaray's narrator asks, "Where does differ-ence begin? Where is it (elle)? Where am I? How can one master that dark place where you find birth? Where you begin to be."[67] With these ques-tions, Irigaray infers that difference begins in the (maternal, planetary, evolutionary) seas: I (the feminine) begin in the sea; you (the masculine) begin in the sea; and difference/it (elle) also begins in the sea. As lively matter, engaged in the unfolding of the world, water also differentiates. Again, we can find here resonances with contemporary new materialist ex-plorations of matter and difference. In Barad's terms, difference is thought in terms of "agential separability";[68] in matter's ongoing intra-actions, cuts are made. These cuts continue to produce bodies of difference, not "once and for all," but always contingently and changeably so. Similarly, for Iri-garay, difference isn't something that "is," but rather something that is ges-tated – here, beginning in the sea. Anticipating Barad's concept of agential separability, Irigaray's figuring of waters that make a difference also sug-gests that there is always a membrane that separates the gestational body from the body it proliferates ("between me and you"). This membrane is not a divisive barrier, but an interval of passage: solid enough to differentiate, but permeable enough to facilitate exchange. Moreover, the water that one body gives up through gestation and facilitation of another watery being is never directly or symmetrically returned. Such debt is only repaid through the diffuse cyclings of differentiating waters. The very asymmetry of these relations is what accounts for the necessary difference between bodies and the active proliferation of life that accompanies their relation. Watery transcorporeality does not collapse all bodies into an undifferentiated mass. As always transcorporeal – taking from and giving to other bodies – bodies of water reject discrete individualism, but the membrane logic of gestation also safeguards difference. As gestational, waters are always becoming different/ce. *Water both connects us, and makes us different. As water we are connected, we are different.*[69] As I show below, this element of Irigaray's transcorporeal ontology is also the source of its ethics.

Of course, difference for Irigaray is ineluctably a question of sexual difference; it is *sexual* difference that seems for her to begin in the sea. As noted above, in this sense Irigaray's philosophy of aqueous embodiment certainly has implications for thinking through sexual difference specifically, which requires a study of their own. Very briefly, these implications include the suggestion that sexual difference might also be thought beyond the human. As we saw above, rethinking sexual difference according to broader terms of gestationality refuses a synonymous or entirely overlapping relation to the feminine-maternal. The maternal seas are *diffracted through* a more elemental gestational milieu (rather than overlaid in a one-to-one relation). This might enable us to untie sexual difference from sexually dimorphic, heterosexual bodies and reproductions – a question that continues to trouble many readers of Irigaray. Sexual difference as gestationality could suggest instead a queer, multispecies, posthuman, and elemental proliferation of life in the plural. I do not intend to suggest that Irigaray offers us a fully developed theory of gestationality in this sense, but by inviting us to think about our own bodies of water in the context of deeper, more-than-human gestational waters, where the human body of water is contiguous with rather than analogous to these gestational species-seas, neither does her philosophy refuse this possibility.[70]

This opening toward unknown and future possibilities for sexual difference also underscores the epistemological significance of the relation between gestational waters and unknowability in Irigaray's work. Significantly, she describes both the sea and the maternal womb as abyssal, un-knowable depths – a bottom that "has never been sounded."[71] Like the depths of the sea, the maternal origin always in some way eludes us; there is no clear beginning of beginnings. Just as Irigaray suggests an inability to contain or definitively represent the "mystery"[72] of the feminine, the abyssal depths of the watery elemental suggest a similar resistance to definitive representation. As she comments elsewhere, we do not *see* our first beginnings in our amniotic habitat,[73] and the moment at which this watery world passes from the realm of the concealed to the realm of the revealed for us will always be ambiguous. Similarly, there is no way to illuminate, fully or definitively, the material abyss of the seas. Over 60 per cent of the earth is covered by ocean more than a mile deep, which makes it by far the largest habitat on earth; yet what lies beneath the surface of these oceans remains less charted by humans than the moon. In this sense, Irigaray's transcorporeal aqueous ontology of bodies is also necessarily an onto-epistemology, in Barad's terms. Irigaray's waters caution against the epistemological mastery of matter. Just as our watery origins will always elude our full knowledge, the ongoing proliferations of watery differ-ence will continue to elude our full control. Such a thinking with water refuses both a brute empiricism that would claim matter to be causally deterministic, as well as the idea that matter is fully controlled by human intention. The membrane logic that always differentiates bodies of water also reminds us of the impossibility of subsuming/knowing/consuming the other *who or which is also flowing through us*. The unknowable watery origins are matters that we (literally) *em*body and *in*corporate, of which we always carry traces, and by which we continue to be sustained. In other words, the generativity of matter is one that we continue to participate in and enact, but this generativity is always beyond what we could know or control. This unknowability or nonsubsumability is a key dimension of matter's mattering.

Plural Waters in a Planetary Hydrocommons: Toward an Ethics of Responsivity

Thinking with Irigaray opens to thinking with bodies of water as transcor-poreal, across watersheds, species, and times. As water evidences, our lives are here and now, but they also gather pasts and anticipate futures; they are distributed and circulating, and part of many other lives beyond what we narrowly consider our own.

But we recall that thinking with matter should also be attentive to the matters that help us think – to those matters that offer up their lively materiality in collaborative conversation. Irigaray recognizes this relation of indebtedness between matters of life and matters of thought (while knowing these are hardly separable). "*Matter*," she notes, is what "always begins anew to nourish speculation, what functions as the resource of reflection" – but she also acknowledges that matter in turn becomes reflection's "*waste*" or "discard."[74] More directly addressing matter's instrumentalization, she wonders: "And in order to speak the meaning of the earth, is it necessary to exhaust all her stores?"[75] These espousals raise the question: How can Irigaray's suggestion of transcorporeal watery embodiment also lead to an ethics of responsivity – of curiosity, care, and concern – not only for sexually different human subjects, but also for the diverse waters of our planet, currently threatened in myriad ways?

Our planet's life-proliferating and life-sustaining gestational milieus are wounded. Aqueous habitats – in the Gulf of Mexico, in the Alberta tar sands, in the Niger Delta – are sacrificed to human petroleum dependency, while rain and snow become poisonous messengers to Arctic food chains. Ancient aquifers are pumped, bottled, and sold for profit. We slake our consumerist thirst with melting glaciers, to end up rowing lifeboats down the middle of our flooded streets. Monolithic megadams displace humans and other animals, destroying once-lively riparian ecosystems. New islands of plastic rise out of the sea. Understanding how water has reached this state of degradation and exploitation demands a new materialist, material-semiotic understanding of water. As geographer Jamie Linton puts it, "water is what we make of it;" what water "is" cannot be disentangled from what we imagine it to be.[76] It is not a static thing, but an entanglement of matter and meaning. To illustrate this, Linton details how waters that were once full of social and spiritual content, and always attached to specific times, places, and functions, have been reduced for the most part in the contemporary West to modern water.[77] "In essence," writes Linton, "modern water is the presumption that any and all waters can be and should be considered apart from their social and ecological relations and reduced to an abstract quantity ... Through this discourse, all water is made known as an abstract, isomorphic, measurable quantity that may be reduced to its fundamental unit – a molecule of H_2O – and represented as the substance that flows through the hydrological cycle."[78] Moreover, Linton claims that modern water is also global water. Detailing a "new global water regime" that includes everything from quantifying water volumes at a global scale to creating management regimes for global waters, Linton describes how water has also been abstracted from its inherence in place. Like modern water, global water's abstractions are artificial and misleading: "A paradigm with such universal ambition," he notes, "suffers a critical breakdown when brought to bear on specific water issues."[79] Disembodied and displaced, global water – like Haraway's epistemological "God Trick"[80] – is everywhere and nowhere, and thus difficult to respond to according to an ethics of curiosity and concern.

While Linton's diagnosis is more nuanced than I can elaborate here, the important point is that how we treat water is fundamentally linked to our changing understanding of this matter. It follows that a hegemonic imaginary of abstract, modern water makes it fully ripe for instrumentalization and exploitation. Caring for water, it seems, will require thinking with water's rich biodiversity; a concern for this matter we think with will require an acknowledgement of waters as plural, specific, storied, situated, spirited, and always more than just brute matter – a technical problem to be solved. The question then remains: can Irigaray's bodies of water – as gestational, transcorporeal, and differentiating – offer an antidote to the problem of abstract and global water as diagnosed by Linton?

On first glance, we might wonder whether Irigaray's waters might not be just another articulation of global water in a feminist philosophical guise. We might even worry that the notion of transcorporeal aqueous embodiment *extends* the reach of global water even further, amalgamating waters across times and other species as well. Yet, although Linton rightly expresses concern over the reduction of all waters into a homogenous, amorphous chemical compound, the transcorporeal waters circulating in Irigaray's writings suggest that global (diffuse, interpermeating, flowing) water is not anathema to specific waters situated in particular configurations of power. In fact, Irigaray's work presents an opportunity to articulate a feminist ethics – an ethics of responsivity, in new materialist terms – whose specific work is to insist on difference and specificity within iterations that are planetary in scope and deep in time.[81]

After all, a global or planetary imaginary of water is *also* a collaboration with certain facets of water's materiality. Ocean currents, weather systems, and even ongoing transfer of biological water between globally circulating bodies all evidence waters that are profoundly mixed and hybrid – not interchangeable, but certainly interacting and changing. In our contemporary context, this planetary connectivity is amplified in material terms (through proliferating technologies, communications, and transits), but it is also produced in discursive terms by our proliferating global imaginaries (planet-scaled discourses of climate change, or the universal right to water, for example). Water materializes as global in both material and semiotic intra-actions. Even as Linton expresses concern over the abstract, modern, and global water that conditions our current water crises (and our inability to adequately address them), it is imperative to ground our ethics in where we are now – that is, in the discourses by which we currently live our lives. An ethics necessarily grounded in the local, specific situatedness of water must be joined by a way to think about the globalized waters that are our current reality. We are embodied and embedded as both localized and globalized subjects, caught up in planetary flows of all kinds. A planetary ethics of responsivity needs to account for this. The water that we have in part "made," as Linton argues, may be particularly open to exploitation and instrumentalization, but we need an ethics that recognizes and responds to these planetary implications.

Thinking with matter with Irigaray suggests that one way to do so is to vigilantly attend to the ineradicable difference and membrane logic that the waters in her writings evidence. Irigaray nurtures the conviction that even as planetary waters flow at considerable distances from our individualized lives, species, and times, we are implicated in these dispersed waters, too – but to respond to them demands also acknowledging their difference. Within planetary flows, waters still pool and puddle. Common waters are cut through with eddies and currents. Phase changes continually transform waters that we think we know into something (somewhere, sometime) different. We are all bodies of water, but in an aqueous paraphrase of Adrienne Rich, *we are all bodies of water that are many, and that do not want to be the same.*[82] Just as Rich reminds us that we must account for the specificity of our own locations within our common feminist struggles, a transcorporeal ethico-onto-epistemology of water reminds us that transits of gestational waters through a global hydrocommons are still always transits that safeguard and even proliferate difference.

Irigaray's waters facilitate an attention to sexually different bodies and their relation to water as continguous with, rather than separate from, care and concern for rivers, glaciers, and aquifers. For example: industrial pollution in a local riparian system connects to clouds that carry contaminated precipitation across continents, and connects to the poisoning of women's bodily waters, such as breast milk and placental blood, by polychlorinated biphenyls and other toxic substances. It also connects to glacial melt, connects to habitat loss for nonhuman species, connects to social and economic upheaval of Arctic cultures. And the mutating fish of that river connect backward and forward to watery species already lived, and queer, Hypersea proliferations still to come. Somewhere in these entanglements is the pressing question of women's oppression and well-being, but what is the "proper object" for a feminist ethics, swimming in these transcorporeal seas? Can concern for sexually different bodies, in its richest sense, be also curiosity and care for the waters that comprise and sustain them? Surely a truly feminist ethics of life must recognize difference as an engine of life,[83] and the pressing need to care for those different bodies that facilitate difference. *We, bodies of water that are not all the same.* An invitation to think our planetary waters as both extensive and intimate, as both common and different, as multispecies and multigenerational, may be precisely what we need to world a specifically feminist ethics of responsivity for our time.

NOTES

1 Irigaray, *Marine Lover of Friedrich Nietzsche*, 37.
2 Ahmed, "Imaginary Prohibitions"; Sullivan, "The Somatechnics of Perception and the Matter of the Non/Human."
3 I deliberately use a variety of monikers loosely and somewhat interchangeably to signal two things: first, even if definitions and criteria have been offered, no accepted or authoritative definition brands any one of these labels. Second, I am not interested in a particular school of feminist thinking as much as in a general trend toward the question of matter and the material, in various feminist guises. Strictly speaking, a new materialist orientation might not be posthumanist, yet, at least for the principle conversations within feminist new materialisms, this orientation includes a specific attention to nonhuman matter as ontologically, ethically, and epistemologically significant – which resonates strongly enough with feminist posthumanisms to justify a loosely synonymical relation. Detailed exegesis of the overlaps

and departures between these two directions in feminist thought requires a study of its own.

4   Van der Tuin and Dolphijn, "The Transversality of New Materialism."

5   Barad, "Matter Feels, Converses, Suffers, Desires, Yearns and Remembers."

6   Kirby, *Quantum Anthropologies*, 95.

7   Wilson, "Gut Feminism," 82.

8   Barad, *Meeting the Universe Halfway*, 178.

9   A more detailed discussion of the relation between a posthumanist or new materialist conception of agency, in light of other feminist conceptions of agency, is not possible here, but is clearly important. See Barad's discussion in *Meeting the Universe Halfway*, 175–9. Moreover, a new materialist focus on differentiation underlines that even a "flat" new materialist ontology does not erase difference, but rather produces it. Thus, a focus on the difference of bodies invites rather than forecloses a discussion of what is specific about human moral agency that might not apply to other kinds of bodies. At the same time, this should not be taken to mean that agency is a matter of degrees (178), but rather that there are different possibilities for "changing the possibilities of change" for different bodies. For example, human agency might pose different questions and require different criteria than the agency of water. Finally, a hesitation about this broad use of agency should also be formulated in relation to a masculinist valorization of activity.

10 Barad, *Meeting the Universe Halfway*, 185.

11 Haraway, "Situated Knowledges."

12 Braidotti, "Affirming the Affirmative."

13 Van der Tuin, "Deflationary Logic," 415.

14 See for example, Barad's challenge to "the common-sense view of representationalism" that "positions us above or outside the world we allegedly reflect on" in *Meeting the Universe Halfway*, 133, where she reworks Butler's account of performativity to more thoroughly pay attention to the limits of matter.

15 Åsberg, "The Timely Ethics of Posthumanist Gender Studies," 7.

16 Ibid., 8.

17 Puig de la Bellacasa, "Ethical Doings in Naturecultures."

18 Braidotti, *The Posthuman*, 190.

19 The resonances here with a Levinasian ethics of the other, but in a more-than-human context, are explored in Barad, *Meeting the Universe Halfway*, 391–6, and Chandler and Neimanis, "Water and Gestationality."

20 For Puig de la Bellacasa, such an ethics relates strongly to a feminist ethics of care; see "Ethical Doings in Naturecultures."

21 Barad, *Meeting the Universe Halfway*, 393.

22 Colebrook, "Feminist Extinction," 72.

23 Braidotti, *The Posthuman*.

24 Barad, *Meeting the Universe Halfway*, 185.

25 MacLeod makes this potent argument in relation to the commodification of water and water metaphors in "Water and the Material Imagination."

26 Haraway, "Otherworldly Conversations, Terran Topics, Local Terms," 126.

27 Asberg, "Timely Ethics," 8.

28 Neimanis, "On Collaboration (for Barbara Godard)."

29 Such claims are difficult because new materialism, as noted above, is not exactly new: key figures such as Haraway were writing as Irigaray's contemporaries. Nonetheless, it is relatively uncontroversial to suggest that Irigaray's writing did not emerge out of this area of thought. To suggest that Irigaray is an early (even anachronistic) feminist new materialist, as I do in this essay, underlines that feminist new materialism is not amenable to linear narratives, but rather gathers possible pasts and potential futures in an ongoing unfolding.

30 Braidotti in *Metamorphoses* and Grosz in *The Nick of Time* and *Time Travels* inspire a rethinking of Irigaray in a new materialist vein, as they both find in her writing a strong resonance with process ontologies of becoming, and a productive elaboration of sexual difference as an engine for the material proliferation of life in the plural. Similarly, Kirby in *Telling Flesh* expresses an early dissatisfaction with the dualistic treatment of material bodies in commentaries on Irigaray's work. While none of these commentaries explicitly situate Irigaray's work within new materialism or posthumanism, they significantly contribute to our understanding of the multivalent and transversal genealogy of feminist new materialism and posthumanisms.

31 At the same time, Irigaray's work could be read to take issue with the emphasis on "activity" and "agency" (versus passivity, facilitation, and gestation) that seems to dominate the language of new materialist and posthumanist feminist approaches to matter. See Chandler and Neimanis, "Water and Gestationality," where we argue that despite devastating challenges to "nature versus culture" and "human versus nonhuman" binaries, the "passive versus active" binary has not been adequately challenged within posthuman or new materialist thought. A more careful working out of this terminology within feminist thinking with matter is still necessary.

32 Barad, in *Meeting the Universe Halfway*, 179, writes: "Intra-actions are nonarbitrary, nondeterministic causal enactments through which matter-in-the-process-of-becoming is iteratively enfolded into its ongoing differential materialization."

33 Irigaray, *This Sex Which Is Not One*.

34 Ibid., 115.

35 See Stone, "The Sex of Nature"; Stone, *Luce Irigaray and the Philosophy of Sexual Difference*.

36 Irigaray, *Elemental Passions*, 17.

37 Irigaray, *Sexes and Genealogies*, 57; Irigaray, *Between East and West*, 51.

38 Irigaray, *Elemental Passions*, 39, 43, 99, 24.

39 Alaimo, *Bodily Natures*, 2.

40 For example, Stone, "The Sex of Nature"; Stone, *Luce Irigaray*; Fielding, "Questioning Nature."

41 Oliver in *Womanizing Nietzsche* and Lorraine in *Irigaray and Deleuze* both provide helpful comments on Irigaray's *Marine Lover*, and both suggest that she does not adequately consider how Nietzsche's philosophy of the eternal return might also admit the return of difference. Both nonetheless find Irigaray's critical attention to Nietzsche's elision of the maternal and sexual difference compelling and insightful.

42 Lorraine, *Irigaray and Deleuze*, 66.

43 Irigaray, *Marine Lover*, 13.

44 Ibid., 52, 67, for example.

45 Ibid., 13.

46 Ibid., 48, 66–7, 37.

47 Ibid.

48 Ibid., 38.

49 Ibid., 33. Water, of course, has other phase states in addition to the fluid, which Irigaray acknowledges. We should be careful of simple substitutions of fluidity and water in Irigaray's work (and more generally): these terms are not synonymous.

50 Irigaray, *This Sex*, 113.

51 Lingis, in *Foreign Bodies*, richly describes the economies of male fluids and their connection to, rather than discrete separation from, both the fluid feminine and the wetness of the vegetable or geological strata: breast milk, penile ejaculate, and the sap of the aerial roots hanging from the trunks of the pandanus are all part of the Sambia social economies of fluids and bodies that sustain and proliferate the vitality of their culture.

52 Irigaray, *Marine Lover*, 48.

53 Ibid., 56.

54 Ibid., 38.

55 See for example Irigaray, *An Ethics of Sexual Difference*, 5; Irigaray, *Je, Tu, Nous*, 15; Irigaray, *Between East and West*, 128.

56 Irigaray, *Marine Lover*, 57.

57 Deutscher, "Animality and Descent," 64.

58 For example, in *Marine Lover*, Irigaray's narrator tells her interlocutor, "Into the sea you are returned," at the same time as she asks him, "Why leave the sea?" (12).

59 Irigaray, *Marine Lover*, 12.

60 Ibid., 67.

61 Direct reference to Darwinian thought in Irigaray's work is rather uncomplimentary, for example. In *Je, Tu, Nous*, Irigaray criticizes a "Darwinian model" of behaviour that she characterizes as life's struggle against both the external environment and other living beings (37).

62 McMenamin and McMenamin, *Hypersea*.

63 Chandler and I make this argument more extensively in "Water and Gestationality."

64 Deutscher, "Animality and Descent," 71.

65 Ibid.

66 Irigaray, *Marine Lover*, 13.

67 Ibid., 67.

68 Barad, *Meeting the Universe Halfway*, 176–7.

69 For a more detailed reading of the "difference and repetition" of water in a Deleuzian sense, see Neimanis, "Bodies of Water, Human Rights, and the Hydrocommons"; Chandler and Neimanis, "Water and Gestationality."

70 As noted above, Chandler and Neimanis develop a posthuman theory of gestationality in "Water and Gestationality."

71 Irigaray, *Marine Lover*, 60–1.

72 Ibid., 40.

73 See Irigaray, "The Invisible of the Flesh."

74 Irigaray, *This Sex*, 151.

75 Irigaray, *Marine Lover*, 18.

76 Linton, *What Is Water?*, 3.

77 While modern water is a hegemonic orientation in the West, more complex material-semiotic understandings of water flourish in other cultural and subcultural contexts.

78 Linton, *What Is Water?*, 14.

79 Ibid., 217.

80 Haraway, "Situated Knowledges."

81 Drawing on a critique of the "global" articulated by Spivak in *Death of a Discipline*, we might say that Irigaray's waters are not global (plottable, interchangeable, knowable) as much as they are planetary. While the global

"allows us to think we can aim to control it," planetarity is what we inhabit and comprise, even as it is "inexhaustible" and "in the species of alterity" (72). Unpacking these nuances for Irigaray must be the subject of another essay; here, I invoke "global" and "planetary" somewhat interchangeably to signal a circulation of matter beyond an individualized or localized reach.

82 Rich, "Notes towards a Politics of Location." The original reads: "We who are many. We who are many and do not want to be the same" (451).

83 Grosz, *Nick of Time*; *Time Travels*.

3

Ethical Life after Humanism

Toward an Alliance between an Ethics of Eros and the Politics of Renaturalization

HASANA SHARP AND
CYNTHIA WILLETT

In this essay, we aim to ground an alliance between Cynthia Willett's theory of an ethics of eros[1] and Hasana Sharp's argument for a politics of renaturalization.[2] Both approaches seek a vocabulary and practices for ethical life that the requirement of rationality does not circumscribe. Traditionally, ethical and political theory have as their starting points the idea of rational man as the aspirant norm. While it is acknowledged that no one is born rational – indeed, the empirical necessity of childhood is a kind of obsession and anxiety throughout the history of political thought – many agree that political and ethical principles should follow from what a reasonable individual would choose if unencumbered by the particular demands of his sensuous life. Feminists have long questioned both the desirability and possibility of this abstract notion of the autonomous man making decisions that do not reflect the particularity of his attachments, desires, and needs. If ethics and political institutions reflect what this imaginary figure would hypothetically choose, it is hard to see how they respond adequately to the texture and diversity of human lives.

Many feminists call for an ethics that reflects and respects our lives as desiring, needy beings implicated in a complex network of attachments and relationships.[3] Moreover, they call attention to how our desires and needs generate not only vulnerability and dependency but also the communal infrastructure through which our lives become meaningful and our bodies and minds become powerful.[4] We are not just affected by our sensuous involvement with others, we *are* that involvement. We join the feminist call for an ethics and politics that follows from a profound acknowledgement of life as a rich network of relations.

The relations to which an ethics of eros and renaturalization must attend include social relations – the tender ministrations of mothers, lovers, and friends that sustain and nourish (and sometimes threaten) each of us. Our lives, bodies, and minds, however, are also deeply involved with the non-human environment. Our existence depends on air, water, bacteria, shelter, and infinite other nonhuman beings. Our desires and needs include a habitable environment and, arguably, the indulgence of "biophilia," what E.O. Wilson describes as a basic attraction to life and lifelike processes.[5] The increasing fragility of our ecosystems suggests that there is more need than ever for an ethics that goes not just beyond man – although that is certainly an ongoing project – but beyond the human.[6] This essay is an attempt to ally our approaches in the feminist effort to produce a broad basis for ethics, allowing for a robust consideration of nonhuman nature. This effort will likely raise more questions than it answers, but we hope others will join us in the project of developing a feminist, posthumanist ethics of desire.

Eros ethics, in contrast with logocentric moral philosophies, foregrounds desire as the source for a compelling vision of life. Yet eros as desire is also not reducible to subjective preference. The use of the ambiguous Greek term eros indicates that its meaning is not fully determinate, but interpretative and perhaps even mythic in import. In his eros dialogues, *Symposium* and *Phaedrus*, Plato portrays eros as a daimon that overpowers the soul with a drive toward transcendence, generating images of life's meaning and purpose. Even more, the logocentric emphasis on the individual cultivation of capacities for reason and control over subjective desires occludes not only transcendent but also nonconscious and communal dimensions of erotic existence from substantial consideration in philosophical thought. This occlusion begins with Plato's own logocentric turn and culminates in Kant's development of a moral system based on universal laws found in pure reason. Hegel modulates this rationalist legacy by embedding the modern moral individual in the traditions, rituals, and practices of ethical life. In the *Phenomenology of Spirit*, he interprets the individual not primarily in terms of rational control over wayward subjective impulses – although this feature of philosophy's rationalist heritage does play an important role – but as a struggle for recognition. Self-consciousness is first and foremost a desire, which is not to be understood as an interest in survival but as a desire for the desire of the other, and is, thus, at root social. Even if Hegel would aim finally to locate the practices or institutions that might subdue desire through logos, his dialectic of self-constitution turns on the real-life drama of intersubjectivity. For Hegel, this drama – the master/slave dialectic – begins with misrecognition, social conflict, and ontological alienation, but aims for reconciliation. The self emerges through the figure of the master, who gains an illusion of recognition for his spirited courage, at the expense of another who yields to his show of bravado and submits to a life of servitude. As Hegel insists, the coercion and subordination at the heart of the master/slave relation renders the master's claims to selfhood and recognition fraudulent. However, Hegel can only envision the overcoming of this fraudulent recognition through the rise of the rational citizen in the modern nation-state. He fails to question the ideology of servitude against historical accounts of ancient debt bondage or sexual and race-based slavery.[7] He fails to question the disciplining practices that pose basic drives and vulnerabilities as asocial or savage and in need of rational suppression. And he fails to question the ethnocentric or humanist boundaries of the modern state.

By the twentieth century, it became clear that the Western canonical thinkers had in many ways set philosophy as a moral discipline on the wrong path. In response to the Holocaust, Levinas rejects the ethnic bonds of the nation-state and the figure of the master in the configuration of desire and ethical life, and establishes instead the ethical priority of the vulnerable and stranger. His "alterity ethics" – also known as "response ethics" or even as an "ethics of eros" – exposes the inhumane blindness that can warp considerations of rational and moral law or patriotic duty, and regrounds ethics in sheer generosity to the Other.[8] In fact, eros ethics recuperates a critical tradition that Enrique Dussel traces back further than Jewish traditions or even the West.[9] Along with a critique of the West as the centre of a dominating world system parasitic on Latin America and other peripheral regions, Dussel develops this ethics of eros as a liberatory political project. Reaching back to pre-Western ethical writings, he adds a radical moral component and an expansive political critique of neocolonialism to Herbert Marcuse and the Frankfurt School's critique of bureaucratic discipline, instrumental reason, and capitalism as a system of exploitation and domination.

However, it is Audre Lorde who first takes eros ethics to its radical feminist – if still humanist – edge with her analysis of oppression as an appropriation of erotic energy.[10] Only by freeing this erotic energy's creative play principle, and reasserting agency in its terms, can oppressed people tap into life's vital core. Luce Irigaray reimagines eros as a lyrical song and gesture of love between a couple, effectively displacing Hegel's rendition of mutual recognition and yet also insisting on desire as an intersubjective dynamic.[11] Toni Morrison and Patricia Hill Collins explore further eros's social force in essays on communal belonging and connection across the Africana diaspora and on history's rough force.[12] Finally, Donna Haraway's research on companion species and the symbiotic relationships of multispecies communities opens eros beyond humanism to encounters with other creatures.[13] Eros ethics attends first of all not to principles, duties, pleasures, autonomy, or reason, but to encounters now understood as interspecies.

Eros ethics first aims not to measure utilities, lay down the moral law, or establish duties, but to heed to the exigencies of these encounters. Rather than moral systems, it engages communal and cosmopolitical practices of reconciliation, forgiveness, consolation, festive celebration, and the avoidance of assaults on relationships, or what the old tragedians termed hubris. Its critical edge, ranging from the anarcho-communitarianism of Occupy Wall Street to erotic bonobo social politics, combats – through negotiations, alliances, and solidarities – such oppressive, eros-draining structures as found in factory farms, finance capital, and the tyranny of alphas.

The politics of renaturalization draws its inspiration from the philosophies of Benedict de Spinoza and Elizabeth Grosz.[14] Spinoza's ontology maintains that each and every being – human or nonhuman, animate or inanimate – strives to persevere in being and, when possible, to enhance its existence. This ethics understands all finite, singular things as "conative," exerting effort to be the things that they are, and seeking to endure and expand their power of existing whenever possible. This is as true of human beings as it is of thought formations, social networks, and, as he explicitly affirms, stones.[15] Thus, rather than grounding ethics and politics (a subspecies of ethics, for Spinoza) in a feature of human nature imagined to be unique to our kind, Spinoza takes as his first and guiding principle what must be predicated of any being whatsoever, a yearning to be what one is as potently as one can muster. Insofar as we are conscious of this striving (*conatus* in Latin), it is desire: the desire to live and to live well.

Such a point of departure supports Grosz's effort to wrest feminism from the impulse to denaturalize every aspect of human existence.[16] Although feminist and antiracist critics have irrevocably transformed our understandings of sex, sexuality, race, gender, ability, and more by revealing how these terms conceal histories of warring wills, Grosz and Spinoza ally to supplement and challenge this approach with an understanding of how human life is shaped by so much more than human volition and struggle. Grosz's feminist turn to the idiom of nature stems from her conviction that every humanism implies a masculinism, and seeking to include women (or nonhuman animals) within its terms confines us to a perpetually reactive stance in relationship to patriarchal imagination. Seeking inclusion risks leaving in place the masculine norms against which women, nonhuman animals, corporeality, and non-Europeans always appear deficient. Whereas traditional humanism stipulates a particular feature universally found in man and never found in nature as the ground of ethical responsibility, renaturalism seeks local sites of freedom and power without recourse to the figure of an exceptional human faculty, be it reason, moral sensibility, the capacity for autonomy, or even Hegel's desire for recognition. Grosz philosophizes absent the figure of man, while also transforming oppressive representations of nature as the ground of immutable essences, indifferent to the emancipatory strivings of incipient forms of life.

Combined also with inspiration from Haraway's appreciation of complex human hybridity that is both animal and technological as well as Spinoza-inspired anticapitalist theories (Louis Althusser, Gilles Deleuze and Felix Guattari, and Antonio Negri), the politics of renaturalization apprehends human desire as thoroughly permeated by its animal, machinic, social, and historical involvements. Spinoza maintains that we remain unfree as long as we continue to imagine that human existence is somehow different in kind from that of anything else – the idea that "man in nature" is "a kingdom within a kingdom." When we affirm that we are the history of our affective, corporeal, and intellectual involvements, we learn that it is only through transforming a whole network of relations that we can hope to live differently. Such radical rethinking of the human is as necessary for human liberation as it is for enabling new and better ways of living with (and as) nonhuman nature. Both approaches, in other words, find in desire an index of our psychic and corporeal involvement with others and our yearning toward a future in which those constitutive relationships are more nourishing, enabling, and satisfying. Desire, conative and erotic, is a desire not just to preserve our being, but to liberate it.

The two approaches diverge on just what desire is and for this reason offer contrasting visions of emancipation and freedom. For eros ethics, desire is a social drama, attended by an interplay of subjectivities. A stone or mechanical process could not enter into this interplay of social life, and hence would not be thought of as having ethical agency in the relevant sense. In a Spinozist project of renaturalization, agential networks cross boundaries and extend to any existent. Not only do cats and dogs join with humans in agential communities, but so do software systems, power grids, and sewage systems. The diverging ontologies of desire shed light on deeper questions regarding what these two traditions might offer and how they might conflict and complement each other, or raise questions that may or may not find any resolution.

Eros turns on subjectivity, which is anything but a settled notion. It is not clear which creatures have parallel or related modes of subjectivity or what subjectivity even is. Willett offers a four-dimensional model of ethical agency to capture some of the complexity of ongoing research, but the range and import of this creaturely ethics resists any systemization. The four dimensions are as follows: (1) the subjectless subjectivity that may be transmitted as waves of affect such as panic or calm; (2) affect attunement and companionship between individual creatures who seem to have some sense of self; (3) multispecies communal structures or clustering phenomena that carry a sense of home; and (4) ethical compassion for the stranger or other elevated spiritual demeanor.

1 Waves of laughter or panic and fear spread across populations, sometimes even across species, indicating a subjective response in the context of a biosocial scene.[17] Singular creatures, varying along

lines of irritability or resilience, may respond to these waves in their unique fashion. Still, these affect waves may not involve conscious striving or intentionality. One infant in a nursery cries, and there goes virtually the whole room. These infectious waves indicate an ethos of subjective response and an ethical climate prior to what ordinarily might be called the emergence of a self or a subject. The emotional contagion traces the subjectless subjectivity of creaturely life that forms a basic layer of striving as biosocial, or eros. These responses may have a cognitive component as intelligent responses to a complex situation. But these affect cognitions cannot rely on rational reflection – not if, say, a synchronized flock of birds are to flee quickly and safely in unison from an approaching predator. Similarly, microexpressions of disgust (a gape mouth in humans) may spread across a group to indicate the need to withdraw from some foul pollutant or unwanted parasite.[18] These expressions – often, like mood change in music, a matter of tempo or key – can prompt a shared group response below the level of awareness. Some of the most ancient social rituals and modern media techniques invoke cathartic practices to alter or compose social moods. Arguably, the American neoconservatives who declared the post-9/11 war on terror manufactured waves of panic and fear supportive of US hegemony in what Dussel calls the world system. Affects can charge a political climate by fuelling ethnophobias and reinforcing rigid boundaries between insiders and outsiders, but affect waves can also traverse ingroup-outgroup or even species boundaries, and destabilize hierarchies. As Lorde insists, eros is also a warrior's ethic.[19]

2 A second, and more complex, dimension of ethical interaction might be said to naturalize aspects of what Kelly Oliver terms, after Levinas, the ethics of "response-ability."[20] For Levinas, the Other is encountered through a transcendent aspect of facial or linguistic expression that testifies to the presence of another creature and her urgent need. This Other in their singularity eludes understanding or empathy, and, in their vulnerability, solicits an infinite response akin to what various religious traditions term spiritual compassion or love. However, Levinas's transcendent ethics opens an abyss between humans and other animals as natural creatures that is difficult to challenge, at least if we are faithful to his dichotomous

metaphysics. In what could be called a renaturalized eros ethics, the encounter with the Other occurs originally not through the metaphysical appeal of some fleshless face or soundless speech, but through the flesh-and-blood call and responses of one creature to another. Rather than the vertical vector of a sacred appeal from an unfathomable stranger, these horizontal encounters across varying sensory modes reveal that we humans dwell in multispecies communities. Companionship may transmit signals across diverse media and mixed forms of expression, as in the dog's bark to human vocalization or face-to-crotch interaction, but nonetheless constitute, through these sensory rich stimuli, a creative basis for a social relationship in playful reciprocities.

3 Eros ethics features the affective waves and social drama of relationships rather than the self-organization of autonomous agencies or atomic individualism. For a multitude of creatures, these relationships are, to varying degrees, oriented beyond one-on-one encounters and clustered in groups or situated in a sense of place we might call home. Uprooted elephants transported to zoos or pushed into new lands, and effectively stripped bare of communal structure, experience the trauma of lost connectivity.[21] Their symptoms of a lost sense of home are eerily similar to human modes of social alienation or deracination, and can pass tragically from one generation to another. Pain and loss are the destiny of mortal creatures, but the ritual grieving for losses found among mammals and birds bestow meaning through a shared sense of belonging.[22]

4 This sense of belonging to something larger than a self-organized unit of subjectivity may take a vertical turn, orienting creatures toward moral or spiritual experiences of transcendence. Various creatures are now known to extend assistance to strangers within or even outside of their species with no expectation of reward, or even of the communal and political pleasures of a continued friendship.[23] Utilitarians and deontological thinkers argue that only an appeal to reason, claimed as a universal capacity unique to humans, can explain acts of kindness or a sense of obligation that breaks from any kind of expectation for reward. However, critical race theorists and feminists warn that these allegedly impartial or objective stances of "universal reason" are in fact inflected with implicit bias due

to the inevitable impact of social position, cultural traditions, and emotions. Meanwhile, some nonhuman creatures exhibit a capacity for ethical concern that transcends family or species boundaries. This transcendent capacity to come to the radical Other's assistance does not break from biosocial eros but is one of its most rare achievements. Here we find the spiritual naturalized, and nature spiritualized. Or perhaps, eros ethics eludes the natural/spiritual binary altogether.

In comparison to the ethics of eros, which evokes our sensuous experiences of erotic attachments, Spinozism and the recent philosophy of Grosz can seem cold and abstract. They begin with the most basic metaphysical categories like being, body, time, cause, effect, force, and expression. Yet, they start from the ground up as a kind of tonic for our imaginations. If we begin with the contention, for example, that every person only comes to be who she is because she is nourished by a mother's placenta and emerges from her body to be held and cared for, we affirm something profoundly true and often forgotten in the history of ethical and political thought.[24] Yet it is hard not to lean on our culturally and historically specific ideas of motherhood and fatherhood, and thus to export these ideas when considering the tragedy, for example, of a mother sow pinned to the factory floor, unable to provide her young anything but the nutrients necessary to sustain the barest of lives. It is probably right to see in the sow an unfathomable sadness, and a savage crippling of her conative desire in not being able to teach her babies to play and live in the ways characteristic of pigs. Yet, the strategy of the politics of renaturalization calls for a radical revision of our ontology from the ground up to interrupt the nearly irresistible tendency to anthropomorphize the totality of nature, to see the sow as a mother analogous (and yet inferior) to our own (or to an aspirant) ideal of motherhood. This urgency follows not just from a Copernican ambition to decentre man but from the conviction that our notion of *anthropos* is both profoundly mistaken and destructive.[25]

Although Spinoza's ambition certainly was not to exorcise the masculinism that permeates our idea of humanity, his approach lends support to such a project. Because Spinoza uproots any antinaturalism and exceptionalism whatsoever in our conception of humanity, he opens the way to a radical redefinition of human agency. He is concerned that our idea of human beings as exceptional – i.e., as the only beings (other than God and perhaps angels) that are not subject to the natural laws of cause and effect – foments resentment. He contends that his denial of a free will, immune to the push and pull of cause and effect, "contributes to social life insofar as it teaches us to hate no one, to disesteem no one, to mock no one, to be angry at no one, and to envy no one."[26] In other words, the very human emotions that preoccupy Hobbes and become central to classical liberal political theory are, on this account, amplified rather than assuaged by conceiving society as the outcome of free human volition. In contrast to social contract theory, Spinoza rejects the notion that we freely desire our subjection to a sovereign authority, for we are not the kinds of beings equipped with a faculty of unconstrained will. According to his diagnosis, on our interpretation, the desire to see oneself and be recognized as free fuels an economy of resentment and a culture founded on misanthropy. Thus, although Spinoza would affirm Hegel's descriptive account (indebted to Hobbes) that we seek recognition, he rejects the normative aspiration to be recognized *as freed from the determinations of nature*. Although feminists since Simone de Beauvoir have seen in Hegel's doctrine a liberating rejection of natural determinism and an affirmation of our historically constituted limitations,[27] the renaturalist perspective worries that the cost of this critical perspective is that we – albeit a complex and constrained "we" – are held morally accountable for our own subjection. As a result, we will continue to hate ourselves and each other because we strive to be apprehended by others as exceptionally free, exceptionally minded, and even exceptionally desiring.

Renaturalism promotes what Hegel thinks of as a "primitive" portrait of an animate totality in which all beings are radically interdependent and ensouled. Spinoza urges us to be suspicious of any feature that provides a metaphysical explanation for our distinctiveness, including subjectivity. Indeed, the substantive "consciousness" does not appear in his philosophy. The ontological flattening of his system flies in the face of experience. Certainly there is something distinctive about our kind, for better and for worse. We seem boundlessly diverse and creative. We find so many ways to live and to find meaning, so many distinctive modes of cultural and artistic expression. We are likewise capable of what seem to be the profoundest forms of cruelty and widespread destruction. Yet, the critical edge of renaturalization razes the props so familiar in the tradition of Western thought so as to operate unconsciously. Renaturalization urges us to affirm ourselves as bound and similar in some way to every other existent. It exhorts us to affirm common ground with everything from squirrels to celestial gases to cyborgs. In an age that threatens ecological catastrophe, it is more important than ever to see our fates intertwined with the universe itself.

Yet this threat also demands that we discern which beings, actions, and passions are undoing the characteristic relations that make our lives possible. We are the beings that we are because our strivings are integrated with those of other natural beings. We are in delicate symbiotic relationships with plant life, myriad micro- and macro-organisms, technologies, and infinitely many other powers that compose our ecosystems. Our practices and desires come together with others in magnificent ways, but are also in tension with the network that makes life on earth possible. The politics of renaturalization appeals to the need for massive structural reorganization of human desire, such that we cannot be induced to destruction whether we are "guided by reason or passion."[28] That is, the denial of free will or given rationality means that change does not follow from an intersubjective appeal to act rightly or an intersubjective claim to be seen and treated in more eros-affirming ways. Likewise, it is not a program of information dissemination or a project of disinfectant through sunlight.[29] It begins with the notion of systematic constraint and seeks to reorient constraint in more enabling ways. If capitalists are now constrained to exploit workers, shareholders, and the environment to the greatest extent possible in order to remain in business, they cannot but desire the means of such exploitation, no matter how their reason or conscience may irritate them. We need to tie ourselves to masts to avoid the sirens' calls. We need radical structural transformation. Renaturalization names the view that we can only hope to foment this kind of change when we cease to see it as following from exceptional human agency (e.g., "political will"), including an erotic drive toward mutual reconciliation.

One may wonder, however, from where the seed for this redetermination comes. Is there some notion of a transcendent urge lurking within this naturalist liberatory ethics? How do we decide to get the rope? Who do we enjoin to tie us to our masts? Spinoza, Filippo Del Lucchese argues, denies the possibility of "bare life," mere existence without yearning to act and to enhance one's life.[30] Indeed, Spinoza affirms that "the mind strives to imagine only those things which posit its power of acting,"[31] and in this imagining, it "rejoices," which further amplifies its power. All beings, to the extent that their natures allow, seek a milieu in which they can apprehend themselves as actors and thereby rejoice in their existence. And the more others enjoy us – be those others infants, friends, animal companions, thriving vegetation, or buzzing power grids – the more we enjoy ourselves.[32] Since others enjoy us to the extent that we please them, we seek to please others to please ourselves, generating an erotic economy of, in the best circumstances, mutual empowerment. If we want to insist on identifying this urge to experience ourselves as actors in a distinctively subjective drama proper only to moral agents broadly construed (humans and many nonhuman animals) and not to stones or electrons, it may not be descriptively problematic.[33] The renaturalist perspective worries, however, that marking off moral from causal agency excites the nearly irresistible urge to both exceptionalism and finalism, to which the ethics of eros appears to succumb insofar as it grounds itself in a basic impulse toward harmonization, reconciliation, and recognition. Although Spinoza elaborates the ontological possibility of mutuality, cooperation, and ethical harmonization, our erotic natures do not drive us toward a horizon of unity. He does insist on a basic determination to affirm one's existence, driving finite life. Yet this is not transcendence. It is the fundamental vitality of material existence, operative everywhere – in cybernetic systems, ideologies, and toxins, as much as in the palpable yearnings of human and nonhuman animals.

Eros ethics, on the other hand, is born of struggle and alliance. To be sure, it shares with Spinozist renaturalization a suspicion of free will as a metaphysical shroud over the real politics of oppressive social structures. However, oppression calls up outrage (as an active form of slave resentment) and sets in motion social movements for solidarity and change. These movements share a sense of communal or social burden experienced across a range of animal species but not in striving stones. Freedom is found in lifting the heavy clouds of fear or despair that weigh down the ensouled creature; in mending the intersubjective dynamic warped by subjection and servitude; in reweaving disrupted communal bonds or, as

G.A. Bradshaw depicts among elephants, a haunted sense of home.[34] If the Greek word eros can serve to name the multidimensional connectivity that creatures seek, then the violation of vital relationships might be said to commit acts of overreaching, and sometimes appear as an unchecked power of acting.

Eros ethics would not aim to convert tragic loss to festivals of joy, or not at least without recognizing real suffering through rituals of mourning that reaffirm belonging. Elephants and dolphins demonstrate signs of depression over their losses, and like birds perform burial ceremonies to remember their passing. These losses are remembered because they occur among friends. Forms of friendship and communal attachment occur across a broad range of animal species. Marc Bekoff even observes friendships between animals who normally would operate in a predatory relationship.[35] The biosocial drama of eros ethics appears first and foremost in the particular attachments and communal drives and their renegotiation or challenge. Social practices such as consolation, forgiveness, reconciliation, or the rebuilding of alliances and the deposing of harsh leaders or exile of tyrants appear to various degrees across species in the animal kingdom.

In this context of desire, freedom signifies not first and finally self-actualization or self-expression, although it includes these elements. It is foremost intersubjective and communal engagement, or what in the post-Hegelian tradition is termed "social freedom." Of course, in modern liberal traditions, freedom is more typically understood in negative terms as freedom from external interference or as the positive freedom to act in accordance with rational choice. In these modern traditions, both negative and positive concepts of freedom reinforce aspects of individual autonomy. Social freedom, in contrast, as the aim of an emancipatory project, is found in the drive of a social animal to thrive through symbiotic relationships of belonging. Here belonging does not signify possession, as when property relations are central to freedom's meaning, but stems from dimensions of affective sociality and intersubjective agency. Through these multiple dimensions of agency, freedom appears as freedom from fear and panic, as limits to power and the tyranny of elites, and as the meaningfulness of attachment expressed through companionship and communal bonds. Freedom is not finally a concept of self-ownership, self-organization, actualization, or expression, but it may entail aspects of these freedoms. Freedom as a biosocial ethic is an interspecies practice of environmental belonging.

Renaturalization affirms social freedom as well, but perhaps on different grounds. In the Hegelian tradition, social freedom is a liberating form of ethical life that a spiritual collective establishes and through which it comes to experience and know itself as spiritual, as the overcoming of nature. Although an interspecies eros ethics critically reappropriates the Hegelian tradition, it still draws a deep line between animate and inanimate beings, and thus locates ethics in an exceptional – if multilayered – form of agency. As a matter of practice, Spinoza contends that human beings do and should privilege human relationships as the greatest source of power and pleasure available to us. This means that he, too, exhorts us to form powerful affective bonds across human differences, reorganizing those features of social life that engender sad passions, like fear, panic, and anxiety, and seeking out those joyful encounters that most spur us to think and act. Yet, if the normative guides by which we determine whether our relationships need mending or whether forgiveness is called for invoke the distinctiveness of either subjective or spiritual agency, we fall into an erroneous and disabling self-understanding that ultimately undermines our social relations, as well as our relations with our nonhuman others.

Maybe stones cannot love us in the way that we love them, and maybe they do not mourn the destruction of magnificent mountains the way humans and some nonhuman animals might. Yet, in our effort to challenge our human exceptionalism and to appreciate the vast network of beings necessary to our subsistence, we should ask why this line between animate and inanimate is so important. When we act we cannot avoid selecting some relations, some beings, and some models of life as more valuable to us than others. Line drawing between ethically relevant and less relevant others is practically necessary but always dangerous. Spinoza himself succumbs to it. Although he mounts perhaps the most powerful critique of human exceptionalism in the Western tradition, he insists on the prudential requirement to prefer humanity above all, which, for him, entails excluding the needs and desires of nonhuman animals. Although Spinoza has specific, historical, and ideological reasons for his insistence on prudential human provincialism, he overlooks the liberating force of our involuntary affective community with nonhuman animals.[36] He was not a romantic naturalist who saw in our biophilic urges a propensity to connect with vital and necessary sources of power and pleasure. Thus, renaturalization seeks to radicalize Spinoza's denial of human exceptionalism and to challenge his ethical provincialism. Feminist eros ethics shares with Spinoza the importance of acknowledging the distinctively empowering character of the human bond – love of those who have similar minds, bodies, and capabilities – but the alliance of eros and renaturalization must push us further beyond species provincialism and toward an interspecies ethics.

Eros ethics rejoins with a reconstructed Spinozist politics of joy to affirm the sometimes-mysterious affective community between humans and other life forms. For reasons we do not entirely understand, humans live longer, think better, and feel happier when they enjoy friendships with nonhuman animals. Perhaps the thrill that children manifest in the presence of nonhuman animals points toward the importance of contact and affective communion with our beastly kin? Although Spinoza feared that our agency would be undermined by the affective contagion between human and beast,[37] he never would have imagined the interaction a *National Geographic* contributing photographer describes between himself and a wild leopard seal in Antarctica. The photographer, Paul Nicklen, entered the water to photograph one of the predators, which can weigh in at 600 kilos. The seal thought that he might be hungry and offered him a penguin. Nicklen did not take it, and so the seal tried to teach him to eat.[38] The large predator was concerned with taking care of this other animal who was not a very impressive swimmer but otherwise seemed sufficiently intelligent and similar to herself. There are many ways in which nonhuman animals care for us, even if we often imagine that they depend on us. To see how we may be their charges, it is all the better for us is to acknowledge that our ethical agency is nurtured and sustained by much more than human social relations.

There may be even less obvious affinities and forms of connection between humans and our animal kin. Jane Goodall suspects that the ecstatic dances of African chimpanzees occasioned by waterfalls and violent gusts of wind "may be stimulated by feelings akin to wonder and awe."[39] Michael Tobias witnesses immanent spirituality swimming in the ocean among whale sharks: "These sharks exhibit bliss, the ultimate state of meditation and indwelling referred to by such diverse luminaries as Buddha and Thoreau."[40] Katy Payne discovers meditative moments among elephants.[41] Barbara Smith learns the baboons in Gombe National Park display signs of reverence and awe in their communion at the still pools along the path to the sleeping trees. And Smuts finds a spiritual connection similar to baboon sangha with her dog, Safi, in a respite from a game of fetch played by a stream, where Safi caught Smuts's gaze and elevated her melancholic mood: "She held her position and my gaze for about twenty minutes and then quietly approached and lay down next to me. My dark mood vanished. This was my first lesson in meditation."[42] These spiritual experiences may partake not only of nature's beauty but also of the sublime nature of its incomprehensible force.

And, of course, we can discern cross-species ethical compassion that does not involve us. Consider Kuni, the bonobo who assists a feathered stranger who lands in her cage, and whom she is destined to never see again, to a freedom that she will never know: "Kuni picked up the starling with one hand and climbed to the highest point of the highest tree where she wrapped her legs around the trunk so that she had both hands free to hold the bird. She then carefully unfolded its wings and spread them open, one wing in each hand, before throwing the bird as hard as she could."[43] Kuni's concern for the bird does not rest on any ordinary expectation for intimate attachment or friendship's eventual reciprocities. This act of compassion suggests a capacity for generosity that is unbound by any normal interest or attachment desire of any kind. Moral theory traditionally treats this capacity as a pure form of altruism, but more can be said. Unanticipated and limitless expressions of biosocial eros reveal to us the myriad forms of ethical community and agency that escape the masculinist anthropocentric imagination.

Despite their differences, we ally our projects in an effort to cultivate a receptivity to the nonhuman eros by which we are already nourished and to expand the possibilities for new connections and relations in our fragile worlds. Beyond man, beyond the human, and perhaps even beyond the animal kingdom, we call for a liberatory ethics that affirms and transforms our erotic and philic relations to maximize the possibilities for tenderness, collaboration, and joy.

NOTES

1 Willett, *Maternal Ethics and Other Slave Moralities.*
2 Sharp, *Spinoza and the Politics of Renaturalization.*
3 See the influential tradition of feminist ethics of care. For a somewhat recent example, Kittay, *Love's Labor.*
4 Butler, "Beside Oneself."
5 Wilson, *Biophilia,* 1.
6 For a good overview of this critical tradition, see Braidotti, *The Posthuman.*
7 On debt bondage, see Graeber, *Debt.* On Hegel's failure to question race-based slavery as well as Frederick Douglass's renaturalization of the dialectic from the slave's point of view, see Willett, *The Soul of Justice.*
8 Chanter, *Ethics of Eros.*
9 Dussel, *Ethics of Liberation.*
10 Lorde, *Sister Outsider,* 53–9.
11 Irigaray, *Sexes and Genealogies.*
12 Morrison, "Home," 7; Hill Collins, *Black Feminist Thought,* 166. On freedom in this tradition, see Weir, *Identities and Freedom,* 11–17.
13 Haraway, *When Species Meet.*
14 This summarizes some core principles Sharp develops in *Spinoza and the Politics of Renaturalization.*
15 See Bennett, "The Agency of Assemblages and the North American Blackout."
16 See especially *Time Travels.*
17 Here, the exchange of affects, or affect attunement, is understood to characterize social animals generally, which is an extension of my analysis of the biosocial significance of touch as a socially erotic drive between infants and mothers (a locus of presubjective sociality). Willett, *Maternal Ethics and Other Slave Moralities.*
18 Kelly, *Yuck! The Nature and Moral Significance of Disgust.* While he theorizes disgust as unique to humans, his general remarks on affect transmission should apply to any species that experiences the affect.
19 Lorde, *Sister Outsider,* 41.
20 Oliver, *Animal Lessons.*
21 Bradshaw, *Elephants on the Edge.*
22 Bekoff, *The Emotional Lives of Animals.*
23 De Waal, *Primates and Philosophers,* 31.
24 See Simms, "Eating One's Mother: Female Embodiment in a Toxic World."
25 See ch. 6 of Sharp, *Spinoza and the Politics of Renaturalization.*
26 Spinoza, *Ethics,* part 2, proposition 49, scholium.

27 Beauvoir's Hegelianism, however, is a complex and critical reappropriation. There has been a great deal of analysis of her deployment of the master-slave dialectic and so I point only to one essay that I found particularly illuminating: Mussett, "Conditions of Servitude."

28 Spinoza, *Political Treatise*, ch. 1, para. 6.

29 This is not to say that normative appeals do not shape human activity. Simplistically, it means that such normative appeals and the transformations provoked by new information is the tip of a very big iceberg and thus has little explanatory power, causally speaking.

30 Del Lucchese, *Conflict, Power, and Multitude in Machiavelli and Spinoza*, ch. 3.

31 Spinoza, *Ethics*, part 3, proposition 54.

32 Ibid., part 3, proposition 29.

33 Krause in "Bodies in Action" advances a compelling objection to the new materialist affirmation of distributed agency beyond the human. Willett's eros ethics in *Interspecies Ethics* shares Krause's suspicion of the attribution of agency to inanimate nature, but, in contrast to Krause, admits robust agency in nonhuman animals.

34 Bradshaw, *Elephants on the Edge*, 67.

35 Bekoff, *The Emotional Lives of Animals*, 17.

36 For further analysis, see Sharp, "Animal Affects."

37 See Spinoza, *Ethics*, part 4, proposition 68, scholium.

38 A wonderful video can be seen on National Geographic Live, "Face-off with Deadly Predator," https://youtu.be/Zxa6P73Awcg.

39 Goodall, "Primate Spirituality."

40 Bekoff, "A Gentle Heart," 173.

41 Payne, "On Being," originally aired 21 March 2013, http://www.onbeing.org.

42 Smuts, "Encounters with Animal Minds," 306.

43 De Waal, *Primates and Philosophers*, 31.

4

Foucault's Fossils

*Life Itself and the
Return to Nature in
Feminist Philosophy*

LYNNE HUFFER

For me, speech begins after death ... Writing is a wandering after death
and not a path to the source of life ... The axis of my writing does not run
from death to life or from life to death, but rather from death to truth and
from truth to death. I think that the alternative to death isn't life but truth.
— *Michel Foucault*[1]

Over the past three decades, feminist philosophers have increasingly
turned to the natural sciences to ask new questions about the body, materiality, nonhuman animals, affect, the biosphere, and the forces that animate the physical world. This renaturalizing trend has dramatically shifted
the broader landscape of feminist theoretical inquiry away from social
constructionism, subjectivity, and epistemology, and toward ontological
and metaphysical concerns about nature, the form/matter relation, the
limits of the human, and the question of life itself. Elizabeth Grosz writes,
in *Becoming Undone*: "We need a humanities in which the human is no
longer the norm, rule, or object, but instead life itself, in its open multiplicity, comes to provide the object of analysis."[2] Her comment reflects larger

interdisciplinary initiatives over the past three decades to link humanistic inquiry with the natural sciences and, especially, the health sciences. These efforts have materialized in the form of bioethics centres, joint faculty positions in health and humanities, and a proliferation of workshops, institutes, and research incentives designed to integrate what C.P. Snow once called the "two cultures."[3]

What are we to make of these posthumanist configurations? More specifically, what happens when we bring a Foucauldian genealogical lens to feminist renaturalization as life philosophy? And what are we to make of the explicitly ethical claims that are grounded in the feminist return to life? If, as Grosz puts it, renaturalization means that we need an "ethics internal to life itself," how can we avoid the dangers of a biopolitics in which, as Foucault puts it, "the life of the species is wagered on its own political strategies"?[4] If we agree with Foucault that modern biopower is characterized by "the entry of life into history" and the bringing of life and its mechanisms "into the realm of explicit calculations,"[5] how are we to assess the value and the danger of the contemporary feminist investment in that life?

Importantly, the new feminist ethics of life is not confined to renaturalizing thinkers. Indeed, the most influential feminist philosopher of *de*naturalization, Judith Butler, increasingly relies on life as an anchor for the ethical theory she develops in her later work. Both Grosz and Butler – a renaturalizer and a denaturalizer – stake their ethical claims on life itself. But is the vital matter of *life itself* a given? Or might life itself, like sex itself, be what Foucault calls an "artificial unity," a fictive ensemble that emerges in our own time as a speculative ideal, "a causal principle, an omnipresent meaning, a secret to be discovered everywhere"?[6] When Jane Bennett writes at the end of *Vibrant Matter*, "I believe in one matter-energy, the maker of things seen and unseen," ought we to wonder about such vitalist creeds for would-be materialists?[7]

I argue in this essay that life itself is a problem of our time: like sex in Foucault, life is "an especially dense transfer point of power"[8] that emerges at a particular historical moment, namely the contemporary moment of our biopolitical present. Beginning with life as a problem of our time, I explore how a genealogical approach to life itself can open up new questions about its celebration in contemporary feminist renaturalizing philosophies. In doing so, I insist on the importance of the epistemic conditions for the possibility of what Foucault calls games of truth. Although theorists like Grosz assert that it is time to turn away from epistemological questions, such a proclamation masks the conditions of possibility that allow her to make this or any assertion. To call for a new metaphysics and a new ontology, as Grosz does, evades the paradox of what Foucault calls in *The Order of Things* the historical a priori: that we are both bound and unbound by the temporal contingencies through which epistemes emerge and topple.[9]

My analysis proceeds in three parts. First, I offer a brief overview of the renaturalizing move in feminist philosophy, with a particular focus on Grosz's work. Second, I examine Butler's work as the Foucauldian, denaturalizing foil for the new feminist return to nature in order to demonstrate that feminist renaturalizers and denaturalizers alike make ethical appeals in the name of life itself. Third, I turn to Foucault to show how genealogy and the historical a priori give us a method and a concept for engaging life as historically contingent. In that turn, I suggest that the genealogical problematization of life we find in Foucault offers a nonvitalist alternative to life philosophy's vitalization of matter. Foucault's historically contingent, emergent conception of life forces us to engage with the materiality of the traces of the past through which we construct our present understanding of ourselves. Those traces include not only the archive of human lives struck down by power, but also the fossilized traces of nonhuman lives. This archival fossilization of matter opens what Charles Scott calls the recoiling movement of the question of ethics.[10] The fractured ground of such a question acquires material form in the figure of the fossil. In Foucault's reading of the monster and the fossil in *The Order of Things*, the condition for the possibility of the fossil's emergence is not life itself but a Foucauldian speech after death where, as my epigraph suggests, the alternative to death is not life but truth.

Feminist Renaturalization

The renaturalizing move in contemporary feminist philosophy reflects a broader shift away from feminism's decades-old engagement with questions of epistemology and subjectivity, from standpoint epistemologies to postmodern feminisms of various kinds. The rise of animal studies, posthumanism, critical science and technology studies, object-oriented ontology, and affect theory marks a displacement, if not outright rejection, of both the sociological foundationalism of standpoint theory and the psycholinguistic antifoundationalism of feminist post-structuralism. As part of this larger shift, feminist renaturalization has mounted an important challenge to the denaturalizing moves that dominated feminist thought in the second half of the twentieth century. The philosophical reprivileging of nature and the biosphere has produced new ways to imagine life, from innovative scientific and phenomenological accounts of corporeality to trans-species political theories to new cosmologies of space and time.

To be sure, the contemporary feminist return to nature is not a return to the kinds of naturalist ontologies that have traditionally been used to justify gender inequality, the marginalization of sexual deviants, or the perpetuation of European colonial conquest and white racial privilege. Today's feminist renaturalization projects challenge those ontologies along with the culture-nature, mind-body dualisms that support them. They tend to rethink binarism itself, reconceptualizing human agency as part of nature or matter rather than in opposition to it. Shifting their focus away from antiessentialist critiques of woman as nature, renaturalizers have turned toward animals, the cosmos, subatomic particles and waves, the brain, and the energetic pulse of biological life as objects of feminist concern.

A few salient examples serve to delineate the contours of the renaturalizing move in feminist philosophy. In her influential *Meeting the Universe Halfway*, Karen Barad offers an agential realist account of an intra-active matter where meaning and mattering are inextricably connected. New attunements to intra-active matter in all its complexity allow us, Barad says, to "hear nature speak" in the entangled webs of what she calls spacetime-matterings.[11] From a slightly different perspective, Hasana Sharp elaborates what she calls a "philanthropic posthumanism" for a "new universal," a vital, flourishing assemblage of humans, animals, rocks, and trees whose unity as nature is derived from Spinoza's geometric account of the universe as substance and modes.[12] Finally, in her later work, Grosz develops a Darwinian understanding of nature as dynamic and self-differentiating to articulate what she calls in *Time Travels*, "a more politicized, radical, and far-reaching feminist understanding of matter, nature, biology, time and becoming – objects and concepts usually considered outside the direct focus of feminist analysis."[13]

These thinkers obviously have important differences, and I do not mean to efface those distinctions: each has her own particular set of methodological and conceptual tools for redressing what she views as a dominant antinaturalism in feminist theory. I offer these examples as broad brushstrokes to sketch out a renaturalizing scene. Most crucially, I want to focus on how the feminist return to nature presents itself, on empirical grounds, not only as a more complete and more accurate description of the world than that provided by social constructionists, but also as more ethically and politically promising. Barad, for example, devotes the final chapter of her book to questions about our accountability to matter's intra-action; she ends with an ethical call for greater responsibility in our relation to the complexity of matter.[14] Sharp concludes her book on Spinoza with an ethological ethics that can promote the flourishing of all beings in the biosphere through the cultivation of joyful affects. And in *Becoming Undone*, Grosz expounds on the value of the language of the bees as an "insect ethics"[15] internal to life itself.

Grosz's reflections on life in particular have generated a burgeoning field of exciting and innovative feminist work. Under the banner of new materialisms, feminist science studies, or feminist renaturalization, these contemporary feminist returns to nature provide an important corrective to previous repudiations of scientific data in feminist constructivisms of various kinds. But what are we to make of Grosz's repudiations of the possible epistemic frames that might situate her claims about life? "Linked to the preeminence of the subject and of concepts of subjectivity," Grosz complains, "is the privileging of the epistemological (questions of discourse, knowledge, truth, and scientificity) over the ontological (questions of the real, of matter, of force, or energy)."[16] Rejecting feminist theory's long-standing obsession with subjectivity and epistemology, Grosz turns toward ontology and even metaphysics as the philosophical ground for her new materialism. "Feminist theory," she writes, "needs to welcome again what epistemologies have left out: the relentless force of the real, a new metaphysics."[17]

From a Foucauldian perspective, Grosz's metaphysical claims presuppose a Darwinian naturalism whose epistemic ground is specifically Victorian and therefore historically contingent rather than self-evidently true in all times and places. Indeed, Grosz's Darwinian life is the one "We

Others, Victorians," as Foucault calls us, take to be the truth of nature.[18] To be sure, Grosz departs from traditional Darwinian humanisms: as a posthumanist, she sees Darwin as a bridge between the "determinism" of "classical science" and "the place of *indetermination* that has been so central to the contemporary, postmodern forms of the humanities."[19] Reading Darwin as "the most original thinker of the link between difference and becoming, between matter and its elaboration as life, between the past and the future,"[20] Grosz finds in him an antifoundationalist critique of essentialism and teleology.

Importantly, Grosz highlights sexual difference as central to a Darwinian understanding of life itself. In *Time Travels*, she argues that the three evolutionary principles – individual variation, the proliferation of species, and natural selection – explain the "dynamism, growth, and transformability of living systems, the impulse toward a future that is unknown in, and uncontained by, the present and its history."[21] Grosz focuses on the third principle – natural selection – to bring out the crucial role of sexual selection as a sub-branch of natural selection. She then rereads Darwinian sexual selection through the Irigarayan lens of sexual difference. Darwin, Grosz argues, confirms "the Irigarayan postulation of the irreducibility, indeed, ineliminability, of sexual difference."[22] Thus sexualization – as Darwinian sexual selection, as Irigarayan sexual difference – constitutes the mechanism of deviation through which other differences are produced. As Grosz explains, sexual selection aesthetically "deviates" natural selection's principle of preservation to form what she calls "an ingenious [Darwinian] temporal machine for the production of the new."[23] Crucially, this ingenious machine produces, in Grosz's view, an ontological equivalence between sexuation and life itself. Refracting sexual selection through an Irigarayan lens, Grosz thus reclaims sexual difference as "one of the ontological characteristics of life itself, not merely a detail, a feature that will pass ... Sexual difference," she asserts, "is an ineliminable characteristic of life."[24]

In *Becoming Undone*, Grosz expands the Irigarayan-Darwinian frame of *Time Travels* to include the life-affirming philosophies of Gilles Deleuze, Henri Bergson, and Gilbert Simondon. Drawing on Bergson in particular, Grosz describes life as a "fundamental continuum,"[25] a "movement of differentiation that elaborates a multiplicity of things according to a unity of impulse or force."[26] Expounding on this Bergsonian conception of life as élan vital, Grosz articulates an "ontology of becoming"[27] to be found in the dynamism of things: an "affirmation of the vibratory continuity of the material universe as a whole."[28] This continuity is not only spatial but also temporal. As Grosz puts it: "Life ... becomes something other than its (species or individual) past while retaining a certain continuity with it."[29] The resulting "symbiosis" between living life and nonliving matter[30] occurs because life contains "virtualities" within itself. As Grosz puts it: "Life carries becoming as its core. It is because life is parasitic on matter that life carries within itself the whole that matter expresses."[31]

In *Becoming Undone*, Grosz incorporates sexuality into the same ontological frame that equates sexual difference with life itself. Gayness or straightness, Grosz argues, "is not produced from causes ... nor is it the consequence of a free choice." Rather, it is "the enactment of a freedom," the expression of sexuality as "an open invention."[32] This understanding of sexuality as a self-differentiating force coextensive with life itself has political implications. As Grosz explains, the political problem for sexual beings who have been oppressed or excluded by our sexual order is not the juridical achievement of more recognition, more rights, or more voice; rather, it becomes "how to enable more action, more making and doing, more difference."[33]

Grosz further argues that in order to facilitate this sexual élan vital of freedom or open invention, feminist theory needs to renaturalize itself: it "needs to turn, or perhaps return, to questions of the real ... questions of the nature and forces of the real, the nature and forces of the world, cosmological forces as well as historical ones."[34] That nod to history notwithstanding, Grosz's arguments are largely transhistorical. Decrying the shortcomings of a feminism obsessed with epistemological questions, Grosz's renaturalizing appeal is a call for a return to metaphysics. She frames this metaphysical turn, like the return to nature, as a return to the new: "a new metaphysics."[35] Again, Grosz finds her most consistent feminist support for this turn in Irigaray's "new metaphysics," where she finds "a new account of the forces of the real and the irreducibility of a real that is fundamentally dynamic."[36] For Grosz, that Irigarayan dynamism is driven by the division of being into "two irreducibly different types."[37] "Nature itself," she asserts, "takes on the form of [a] two[ness]"[38] that transcends historical contingency: "Whatever historical circumstances are conceivable," Grosz asserts, "there is no overcoming of sexual difference."[39] "The future," she continues, "will always contain and express sexual difference."[40] Indeed, sexual difference is "the very measure of creativity itself."[41] Without sexual difference there would only be "sameness, monosexuality, hermaphroditism," the "microbial reproduction of the same."[42] "Without sexual difference, there could be no life as we know it,"[43] "no life on earth."[44] Thus Grosz extracts sexual difference from the epistemic conditions of possibility that allow it to appear as a positivity out of what Foucault calls the contingent site, the "mute ground" or background[45] of our knowledge. So doing, she transforms what Irigaray calls sexual difference as a problem of "our time" into a transhistorical substance called "life itself."[46]

Butler's Ethical Turn to Life

Contemporary feminist philosophers of life often present Butler as the denaturalizing foil to feminist renaturalization. Barad, for example, praises Butler for performatively disrupting feminist social constructionism's unacknowledged conception of sex as a blank, mute, corporeal substance onto which culture makes its mark as gender. But ultimately she finds fault in Butler's insistence on a discursive materiality that cannot account for the nondiscursive aspects of matter. In linking what she views as Butler's flawed humanism to a "failure to theorize the relationship between discursive and nondiscursive practices,"[47] Barad articulates a common renaturalizing critique of Butler.

Like Barad, Sharp is critical of the anthropocentric humanism that undergirds Butler's work, particularly in its ethical phase. Sharp is especially wary of the death-driven, mournful ethics of sad passions Butler derives from her Hegelian spin on Spinoza. Contra Butler's somewhat heretical Spinozism, Sharp argues for a feminist politics of renaturalization that "begins with the denial of human exceptionalism."[48] Contrasting her own Spinozist "posthumanist view of agency"[49] with Butler's subjectivist, "antinatural concept of the human,"[50] Sharp affirms the value of a "vitalistic" metaphysics – the "conative striving" of "living organisms" as "a desire for life"[51] that exists whether we recognize it or not – as an ethical and political alternative to Butler's melancholy Hegelian project "of perpetual dissatisfaction."[52]

Although Grosz is less concerned than Barad or Sharp with Butler's anthropocentrism, her critiques of Butler are similar in their focus on the problem of Butler's discursive conception of matter. For Grosz, Butler represents "an entire tradition of 'postmodern,' 'constructivist,' or 'performative' feminism in devaluing matter, or in transforming it from noun ('matter') to verb ('mattering') and in the process desubstantializing it."[53] According to Grosz, in Butler "the body itself dissolves, the real always displaces itself by being written on, and matter disappears in the process of mattering, of being valued."[54] And while Grosz applauds Butler's attention to the question of value, she contends that "the process of mattering cannot be cut off from *what matter it is*," namely "biological or organic matter."[55] Most important, Grosz grounds her renaturalizing critique of Butler in an ethical claim. Grosz argues that because nature, and not culture alone, is "continually subjected to transformation, to becoming, to unfolding over time, ethics would itself dictate that the natural be owed the debt of culture's emergence, insofar as it is precisely the open-ended incompletion of nature itself that induces the cultural as its complexification and supplement."[56]

Despite their differences, these renaturalizing critiques all challenge Butler's *discursive* repudiation of what Grosz describes as "what matter is": "biological or organic matter," or "life itself." And indeed, in defending the materiality of the bodies she invoked in *Gender Trouble*, in *Bodies That Matter* Butler ultimately reinscribes corporeal matter as discursively produced. As Butler puts it, matter is "a process of materialization that stabilizes over time,"[57] where materialization is defined as "a forcible reiteration of norms."[58] Not surprisingly, most of her readers regard this reiterative, normalizing linkage between matter and intelligibility as an "antinaturalistic" account of matter. As Pheng Cheah puts it, Butler's synthesis of Foucault and psychoanalysis ends up conflating "an ontogenetic condition of possibility with an empirical cause" to produce a conception of matter as an epistemic object that is always in quotation marks.[59]

However, in Butler's later work, beginning in the late 1990s, those quotation marks give way to a conception of life that seems to evade discourse and legibility. What is this life of *The Psychic Life of Power*, *Precarious Life*, *Undoing Gender*, *Frames of War*, and *Parting Ways*? Like Grosz, Butler tends to use the irreducible terms "life" or "life itself" to refer to something nondiscursive: an irrepressible force that cannot be contained within meaning's frames. Importantly, Butler's turn to ethics corresponds with her turn to life: life's inherent capacity to contest intelligibility or meaning seems to be one of its key ethical features. In *The Psychic Life of Power*, for example, Butler poses "the ethical as a question" about "life."[60] Here, life appears as an enigmatic, psychoanalytically inflected energy, "drive," *Trieb*,[61] or instinct that turns back on itself, tropologically, to produce self-conscious-ness, conscience, and the psyche according to Hegelian, Nietzschean, and Freudian logics. Loosely aligning the Hegelian body with Nietzschean will and Freudian instinct, Butler suggests that there is something irrepress-ible about this bodily, instinctive drive, or life.[62]

In *Precarious Life*, life emerges again as a force that is not only insist-ent and irrepressible but also precarious. In Grosz we saw an ontological equivalence between sexuation and life, and in early Butler we saw the matter of sex as "a regulatory ideal whose materialization is compelled," "an ideal construct which is forcibly materialized through time."[63] But in her turn to ethics, Butler displaces her early ontological questions about sex, gender, and sexuality in favour of a Levinasian preontological ethics of the face that values the vulnerability of nondiscursive human life. To be sure, life's preontological status as human vulnerability differentiates Butler's humanist ethics of life from posthumanist feminist ethics. But it is also worth remembering that Butler's Levinasian humanism is not the same as traditional humanisms: following Levinas, she asserts the importance of human relations even as she destabilizes ontological or metaphysical assumptions about human nature. For Butler, as for Levinas, there is a rift at the origin of the human, and that rift is ethical. This hardly makes Butler a posthumanist, despite her assertion in *Frames of War* that there is "no firm way to distinguish in absolute terms the *bios* of the animal from the *bios* of the human animal."[64] As the title of that book suggests, Butler continues to insist throughout her work on the inextricable relation between specifically human epistemic frames and questions of ontology and ethics. "There is no life and no death," she writes, "without a relation to some frame."[65] "A life," she insists, "has to be intelligible *as a life*, has to conform to certain conceptions of what life is, in order to become recog-nizable."[66] By contrast, Sharp and Grosz assert that life exists whether we recognize it or not.

Despite this key difference between Butler's new humanism and renatur-alizing posthumanisms, I want to focus on the fact that both camps invoke life to anchor their ethical claims. As Butler puts it in *Precarious Life*: "To respond to the face, to understand its meaning, means to be awake to what is precarious in another life or, rather, the precariousness of life itself."[67] And even though, in *Frames of War*, she hedges on "life itself," invoking biopolitics and various critiques of vitalism, she continues to link the precariousness of life to something that exceeds the epistemic frame: "Precariousness itself," she writes, "cannot be properly *recognized*."[68] According to Butler it is precisely that which exceeds recognition in precariousness that "imposes certain kinds of ethical obligations on and among the living."[69] Importantly, the precarious life Butler invokes here is explicitly linked to what she calls life's precarity: life's social and political conditioning. So if, in *Giving an Account of Oneself*, Butler harnesses her ethics of the other to a Spinozist desire to persist that "is," she writes, "life itself,"[70] in *Frames of War* she rethinks the term life itself to include sociality as life's condition. In doing so she differentiates her conception of life from Spinoza's *conatus*, which she says "can be and is undercut" by our boundedness to others.[71] Thus she argues in *Frames of War* that if all lives are precarious, life's conditions make some lives more precarious than others. Precarity – the politically induced, differential susceptibility of certain populations to injury, violence, and death – comes to qualify the precariousness of life itself to which it is nonetheless inextricably connected. In *Parting Ways*, Butler concretizes this ethics of obligation to a precarious other as an ethics of dispersion by considering the precarity of Jewish and Palestinian lives. Such obligation, she writes, constitutes "the condition of a politics of diasporic life."[72]

As this trajectory suggests, Butler's insistence on the epistemic and sociopolitical frames out of which life emerges ultimately makes her conception of life somewhat different from those of the renaturalizers. And yet, the Levinasian, preontological, consistently "ecstatic"[73] frame of her ethics of the other requires that Butler implicitly ground her claims in an excess, an ineffable alterity, what Foucault calls in the first volume of *The History of Sexuality* the "something else and something more"[74] that is sex. While Butler articulates that something else and something more as precarious life, Foucault calls that life "'sex' itself":[75] "a causal principle"[76] whose "agency" is not "autonomous" but, rather, "an imaginary point... that each individual has to pass in order to have access to his own intelligibility."[77] What was once "madness" is now "our intelligibility"; what was once perceived "as an obscure and nameless urge" now gives us "our identity" and "the plenitude of our body" through the distributional, calculative, statistical rationality that characterizes biopower.[78] Many have asked why, in her turn to ethics, Butler turns away from the questions about gender and sexuality that dominate her early work. I want to suggest that in her ethical turn, Butler resignifies sex as life. Genealogy exposes the grid of sexuality that incites, intensifies, and proliferates Butlerian sex as life itself: the precarious life that Butler places at the heart of her ethics.

Fossil and Archive: Not Life but Truth

Foucault's genealogical approach to biopower, or power over life, brings a genealogical lens to the feminist ethics of life itself in both its renaturalizing and denaturalizing dimensions. Foucault famously argues in *The Order of Things* that life itself was invented in the nineteenth century. If biology was unknown in the eighteenth century, he writes, "there was a very simple reason for it: that life itself did not exist. All that existed was living beings."[79] According to Foucault, with the nineteenth-century invention of history, historicity was introduced into nature. The historicity of nature differentiates the mode of being[80] of the modern period from the tabulated, "vegetal values"[81] of the Classical Age by making the animal being's privileged form.[82] In modernity, being "maintains its existence on the frontiers of life and death"[83] in the form of the animal. Historicity introduces life as the "sovereign vanishing point"[84] that replaces the royal sovereign of the previous episteme. This shift is reflected in the rise of biology: the *bio-logos* or science of life whose focus is the developmental organism with its hidden structures, buried organs, invisible functions, "and that distant force, at the foundation of its being, which keeps it alive."[85] With life comes death, as Foucault puts it: "The animal appears as the bearer of that death to which it is, at the same time, subjected; it contains a perpetual devouring of life by life ... Life has left the tabulated space of order and become wild once more."[86] Life becomes "the root of all existence" and the "non-living, nature in its inert form" becomes "merely spent life."[87] "The experience of life is thus posited as the most general law of beings; the revelation of that primitive force on the basis of which they are; it functions as an untamed ontology," and "this ontology discloses not so much what gives beings their foundation as what bears them for an instant towards a precarious form and yet is already secretly sapping them from within in order to destroy them."[88] Crucially, life takes on a central role in the rise of the human sciences over the course of the nineteenth and twentieth centuries: the invention of life and the invention of the human go hand in hand. As Foucault puts it, before the nineteenth century, "man did not exist (any more than life)."[89]

In the 1970s, Foucault reworks this archeological understanding of life and the discourse of the human sciences through genealogies of sexuality in *Abnormal* and *The History of Sexuality*, volume 1. Here, life emerges as sexual instinct: the "dark shimmer of sex"[90] or "fragment of darkness that we carry within us."[91] Bringing together *eros* and *thanatos*, modern power-knowledge transforms the concept of an instinct of life into a drive toward death in a "Faustian pact" that "exchange[s] life in its entirety for sex itself."[92] Picking up on the logic of a "continuous gradation"[93] that in *Discipline and Punish* Foucault describes as a "great carceral network,"[94] in *The History of Sexuality*, volume 1, he rearticulates that network as a biopolitical dispositif of power-knowledge-*pleasure* that, in the late nineteenth century, sexualizes existence as life itself. Pleasure transforms and intensifies the dispositif that, earlier in the century, had invented life as natural, biological, and reproductive. As "the economic principle intrinsic to sexual instinct,"[95] pleasure uncouples sexual instinct from fertilization[96] and unhitches sexuality from the procreative kinship system Foucault calls "alliance."[97] Pleasure makes sexual instinct dynamic, self-differentiating, "an open invention,"[98] as Grosz might put it. Importantly, pleasure-driven sexual instinct "overflows its natural end" – heterosexual copulation – "and it does so naturally."[99] It therefore becomes "natural for instinct to be abnormal."[100] In Foucault's rendering, the natural deviation that Grosz celebrates in Darwin describes the sexological dispositif of proliferating perversions that incite and implant bourgeois sexuality as life itself. Finally, this pleasure-driven expansion of a gradational ontology of sexual deviation is intensified by the "interplay of truth and sex."[101] The economy of pleasure that defines life as sexual instinct reproduces itself through the invention and intensification of a new pleasure: a "pleasure in the truth of pleasure," the "pleasure of analysis"[102] that is "immanent in this will to knowledge."[103]

Importantly, Foucault further explains in *Abnormal* that this new logic of sexual instinct as the deviant nature of life itself *depathologizes* the abnormal. Although many thinkers have conflated Foucault with Georges Canguilhem's analysis of the normal and the pathological, Foucault departs from Canguilhem by demonstrating a modern shift away from the pathologization of the abnormal.[104] Foucault argues that the invention of sexual instinct and the naturalization of perversion gives rise to psychiatry as "a medicine that purely and simply dispenses with the pathological."[105] This allows psychiatry to become "a medically qualified power that brings under its control a domain of objects that are defined as not being pathological processes."[106] It is the "depathologization" of naturally deviant sexual instinct that allows for the "generalization of psychiatric power";[107] concomitantly, biomedicine expands and intensifies the points of access through which it orders both individuals and populations, shifting its target from mere disease – the pathological – to public health and nonpathological forms of life.[108] This shift is crucial to the logic of biopower and its modes for ordering and intensifying life itself through the measurement, monitoring, and control of populations. The biopolitical norm is internally derived from populations to produce a calculus of distribution that plots variation or deviance as a function not of an externally imposed ideal, but of their actual occurrence. This statistical logic of the norm as normal curve reduces the social world with its leaky, dying bodies "to the objective figure of the line, the curve, the histogram's alleged indifference, the purity of number."[109] In the "statistical panopticism"[110] of this scalar method, we as living social beings come to understand ourselves through the "detour" of a "numerical amalgamation of all – a ligature so ontologically alien to the social world that it fails to qualify as a relation at all."[111]

Life itself, then, is the biopolitical outcome of this shift from disciplinary power-knowledge into an ever-expanding grid of regulatory power-knowledge-pleasure. Like sex itself, the "imaginary element" that is life itself is increasingly constituted by the statistical tracking and manipulation of populations "as something desirable."[112] And again, as Foucault puts it with regard to sex, "it is this desirability" of life "that attaches each one of us to the injunction to know it, to reveal its law and its power."[113]

Foucault's description of the sexualized life of biopower is echoed in Grosz's description of life itself as a vital force at the heart of a new metaphysics and a new feminist ethics of sexual difference. But in Foucault's description of biopower, life is massified as population through a technology of statistics that redistributes life around a norm within a field of gradation. It is that massification that intensifies life in its aggregation as population or, as Nikolas Rose shows, on the smaller scale of cells and genomes.[114] And because, as I showed earlier, that intensification operates through the interplay of truth and pleasure, the will to knowledge that drives the disciplinary desire for individual identity and intelligibility also participates in a sexualizing feedback loop of power-knowledge-pleasure whose regulatory pole is the ordering norm of the indifferent histogram.

How, then, might Foucault's genealogical perspective on life itself help us to rethink the return to nature in contemporary feminist thought? Contra the renaturalizers' transhistorical conceptions of life itself, Foucault offers an unstable conception of life that remains bound to the disintegrating forces of temporal change. Specifically, in Foucault, the evidentiary matter that grounds our belief in something called life itself is, by definition, fragmented, incomplete, and shifting. In bringing our attention to the rift-restoring matter of time's traces, Foucault allows us to rethink life not as a timeless metaphysical substance whose features are derived from modern biology, but as the strangeness of lives we might "think differently"[115] in shifting interplays of space and time. That rethinking involves not structuralism's linguistic abstractions, as so many of Foucault critics claim. As a genealogical epistemology and method, thinking differently requires contact with the material traces of the past. "My object," Foucault says, "is not language [le langage] but the archive."[116] It is this Foucauldian archival approach to rethinking the material traces of lives that can break open the metaphysical frame of life itself that characterizes some feminist renaturalization projects. Specifically, if, as Foucault argues in *The Order of Things*, the spatial ruptures of eighteenth-century European thought transformed natural history into the historicity of nature and, with it, the possibility of life itself, the spatial continuity that defines our contemporary age might be ruptured through a radical rethinking of the archival traces of lives in time.

To be sure, an obvious posthumanist objection to this archivally based claim about the temporal dissolution of our epistemic ground might be that Foucault's archives track human discourse rather than the nondiscursive, nonhuman matter of nature. Does my attempt to trouble the epistemic presuppositions of a concept of life itself rely on a specifically discursive archive, thereby landing me back in our episteme's humanist trap? Or, alternatively, might it be possible to rethink Foucault's archival method as the contact of thinking with a discourse that is other than human and other than life? Might we reconceive that discursive materiality as a fossilized nature that suspends the human and life itself? And might we, in that rethinking, approach the archive as a fossil record? Might we, in so doing, allow the human and its life to become monstrous?

In *The Order of Things*, Foucault offers clues as to how we might reread the archive as a fossil record whose monstrous background provides conditions for the possibility of this suspension. In "Monsters and Fossils," at the heart of *The Order of Things*, the fossil emerges against the "background noise" that is "the endless murmur of nature."[117] Like a form from sediment once covered by oceans, the fossil is a figure for the emergence of intelligibility out of the undifferentiated murmur of unintelligibility. *The Order of Things* describes those frames of intelligibility as the epistemic conditions that give rise to the human sciences in the modern age. In that context, we might read *The Order of Things* as paleontology: each episteme, we might say, is like an untimely fossil dug up from the "endless murmur of nature."[118]

What then might we say about the fossil record as a nonhuman archive that makes the human monstrous? Rethinking the archive as a nonhuman fossil record requires resituating *The Order of Things* in relation to the desubjectivating movement of *History of Madness*.[119] If, as Foucault writes in the preface to *The Order of Things*, "the present study is, in a sense, *an echo of* ... a history of madness,"[120] can we, remembering *History of Madness*, rehear its story about the emergence of the Western subject as an echo of life's emergence in *The Order of Things*? In that hearing, might we also rehear *History of Madness*'s archive as a monstrous echo of the nonhuman fossil record we find in *The Order of Things*?

These questions point to the reverberating repetitions through which a history of madness is inverted as the scientific order of the human sciences. Importantly for my aim to destabilize the humanist presuppositions that subtend standard conceptions of the archive, I want to highlight here the repeated figure-ground structure that *The Order of Things* and *History of Madness* share. Just as fossils emerge from the murmuring "background noise"[121] of monstrosity in *The Order of Things*, so too in *History of Madness* positivities emerge from the murmuring "background noise" of unreason.[122] Like the books and documents Foucault encounters in his visits to the archives of madness, so too do these fossil forms bear traces of creatures "who lived and died."[123] Humanist historians decipher the archival traces of madness for a positivist project of knowing. So too with the fossil record: scientists read "thousands of forms" through a humanizing lens that translates the imprint of a shell as the beating life of "the human heart."[124]

But rereading the fossil record through the lens of *History of Madness* interrupts that human rhythm of life itself in a syncopated relation to the archive of the rational subject's emergence through the objectification of madness. Fossils may feel familiar to us in our Victorian thinking – Darwin devoted many pages to them in *On the Origin of Species*[125] – but Foucault makes the fossil strange by rendering it as "the privileged locus of a resemblance"[126] out of sync with its own space and time. This out of syncness makes it appear as a monstrous strangeness within the epistemic frame of our own space-time. Like the madman and the poet whose logic of similitude places them "on the outer edge of our culture," Foucault's fossil fractures the now in which lives are made intelligible as biological life.[127]

As other-than-human forms of "speech after death," Foucault's fossils thus expose what he calls "the exotic charm of another system of thought" and "the limitation of our own."[128] From the middle of *The Order of Things*, fossils emerge as if from the ocean floor in the shape of "ear, or skull, or sexual parts, like so many plaster statues, fashioned one day and dropped the next,"[129] as the cast-off parts of a human; the logic of resemblance peculiar to the fossil recasts those human parts as sea shell, bird, or worm. Rather than indicating the evolutionary triumph of life in man, Foucault's rendering of this part animal, part mineral, fragmented evidence of the spatial disruption of temporal continuity returns evolutionary human parts to another space-time as other-than-human characters in a taxonomic table we cannot fully know. In that return, the background monstrosity of temporal continuity out of which the fossil forms as spatial disruption becomes another kind of nature: not nature as a principle of life, but nature as an abyssal murmur which, like the murmur in *History of Madness*, can only be heard as "a dull sound from beneath history."[130] Rendered strange as an untimely relation to monstrosity, Foucault's fossils "reside in that uncertain frontier region where one does not know whether one ought to speak of life or not."[131] Thus Foucault leaves us to read the fossil in a dislocated space-time, where the fossil lingers as a strange remnant of life within a frame where life as we know it cannot be thought. In this sense, the fossil becomes a kind of nonhuman writing whose unintelligibility as discourse breaks the frame of life itself.

In its echoing relation to *History of Madness*, the fossil record thus offers a path toward the undoing of subjectivity and life itself at the site of humanism's heart: the archive. Showing the way in his 1977 essay "Lives of Infamous Men," Foucault returns to those archives – Charenton, Bicêtre, Salpêtrière – out of which he wrote *History of Madness* in the late 1950s. Like "Monster and Fossil," "Lives of Infamous Men" describes the Classical episteme and traces the emergence of form as the appearance of lives out of a murmuring, monstrous background. If fossilized nonhuman lives appear as stone, Foucault's infamous human lives appear as ashes or dried plants and flowers organized in a herbarium as an "anthology of existences."[132] And just as fossils appear as pictorial poems in the sedimented archive of nature, so too do archival "poem-lives"[133] appear in asylum registers and police reports to mark the passage of beings: sodomite monks and feeble-minded usurers. Further, Foucault tells us, their matter matters: unlike literary characters, he says, these beings "lived and died,"[134] and appeared to him only in their death, as a fossil would, in the form of petrified insect, fish, or worm. To be sure, unlike the fossil, the poem-life appears to us because of an encounter with power that, in striking down a life and turning it to ashes, makes it emerge, like a flash, out of the anonymous murmur of beings who pass without a trace. Foucault's conception of lives in his 1977 essay thus reflects his shift, since *The Order of Things* where the fossil appears, to a focus on knowing as it is traversed by power. But if we read the fossil in the 1966 text retrospectively, through the lens of "Lives of Infamous Men" and biopower, we can see quite clearly that to "animate" the fragmented remains of the past – the fossilized lives in the archive of nonhuman nature, the poem lives in the police archive of the human – is to create a biopolitical continuity called life itself that fills in the gaps of a discontinuous matter with a transhistorical substance. Indeed, Darwin himself worried about how the "imperfection" of the fossil record destabilized the foundations of his evolutionary theory of life. So too with the archive: in Foucault's hands, the poem-lives of madness emerge, like fossils, as the aphoristic remnants of an other-than-human, monstrous world.

Foucault's genealogical approach to life thus serves to remind us that when we invoke life itself we not only universalize our present world, but also render that world as if we could fully know it. Echoing Foucault in his comments on madness, we might say: "The experience of [life] is made in the calm of a knowledge which, through knowing it too much, passes it over."[135] Indeed, to know life is to kill it. As Foucault puts it in *Speech Begins after Death*: "I'm speaking over the corpse of others."[136] In knowing the human and life itself, we speak over corpses: the fossils and poem-lives in the graveyards of our knowledge.

Confronted with corpses, positivist historians and biologists alike flirt with fantasies of resuscitation, what Foucault calls in "Lives of Infamous Men" "the dream to restitute [the] intensity [of those lives] in an analysis."[137] Is the positivist's dream also the dream of the life philosopher: to resuscitate the fossil within the continuum of biopower, to chase the "good feelings of bio-energy,"[138] as Foucault puts it in *The History of Sexuality*, volume 1? And isn't this dream of giving life precisely the dream Foucault describes as the *ars erotica* of our *scientia sexualis*, where the greatest pleasure is "pleasure in the truth of pleasure" to be wrought from "a great archive of pleasures"?[139] Foucault diagnoses that pleasure as the force of intensification that motivates sexual subjects to play our games of truth in biopower. But in his genealogical thinking, he also enjoins us to problematize life itself along with the humanist subject spawned it its wake. In so doing, he offers us an ethics of something other than life – something other than human – that wanders not from death to life but from death to truth and from truth to death. Foucault's archive, like the fossil in *The Order of Things*, is the "*matière*" or "stuff" that grounds Foucault's ethical thinking.[140] Breaking our frame, the archive is to the modern episteme as the fossil is to the Classical Age: its mad logic of resemblance ruptures the grids that make us intelligible to ourselves, spawning other-than-human truths. Those truths hover, like monsters on old maps, in the murmuring background of a thinking about life that "ought to make us wonder today."[141]

NOTES

1 Foucault, *Speech Begins after Death*, 44–5.
2 Grosz, *Becoming Undone*, 16.
3 Snow, *The Two Cultures*.
4 Foucault, *The History of Sexuality*, vol. 1, 143.

5 Ibid.

6 Ibid., 154.

7 Bennett, *Vibrant Matter*, 122.

8 Foucault, *The History of Sexuality*, vol. 1, 103.

9 Foucault, *The Order of Things*, 157.

10 Scott, *The Question of Ethics*.

11 Barad, *Meeting the Universe Halfway*, 382.

12 Sharp, *Spinoza and the Politics of Renaturalization*, 219.

13 Grosz, *Time Travels*, 32.

14 Barad, *Meeting the Universe Halfway*, 361.

15 Grosz, *Becoming Undone*, 22.

16 Ibid., 85.

17 Ibid.

18 Foucault, *The History of Sexuality*, vol. 1.

19 Grosz, *Time Travels*, 32.

20 Ibid., 18.

21 Ibid., 19.

22 Ibid., 31.

23 Ibid., 25.

24 Ibid., 31.

25 Grosz, *Becoming Undone*, 46.

26 Ibid.

27 Ibid., 51.

28 Ibid.

29 Ibid., 53.

30 Ibid.

31 Ibid.

32 Ibid., 73.

33 Ibid.

34 Ibid., 85.

35 Ibid.

36 Ibid., 100. While I agree with Grosz that Irigaray is elaborating a new ontology, I disagree that this elaboration is "a new metaphysics." Irigaray's explicit indebtedness to Heidegger's dissolution of the metaphysical foundations of ontology is at odds with Grosz's claim.

37 Ibid.

38 Ibid., 104.

39 Ibid., 111.

40 Ibid.

41 Ibid., 101.
42 Ibid.
43 Ibid.
44 Ibid., 104.
45 Foucault, *The Order of Things*, xvii, 155.
46 Irigaray, *An Ethics of Sexual Difference*, 3.
47 Barad, *Meeting the Universe Halfway*, 63.
48 Sharp, *Spinoza*, 121.
49 Ibid., 139.
50 Ibid., 153.
51 Ibid., 133.
52 Ibid., 152.
53 Grosz, *Time Travels*, 78.
54 Ibid.
55 Ibid.
56 Ibid., 79.
57 Butler, *Bodies That Matter*, 9.
58 Ibid., 2.
59 Cheah, "Mattering," 115.
60 Butler, *The Psychic Life of Power*, 65.
61 Ibid., 22.
62 Ibid., 57.
63 Butler, *Bodies That Matter*, 1.
64 Butler, *Frames of War*, 19.
65 Ibid., 7.
66 Ibid.
67 Butler, *Precarious Life*, 134.
68 Butler, *Frames of War*, 13.
69 Ibid., 22.
70 Butler, *Giving an Account of Oneself*, 44.
71 Butler, *Frames of War*, 30.
72 Butler, *Parting Ways*, 31.
73 Ibid., 12.
74 Foucault, *The History of Sexuality*, vol. 1, 153.
75 Ibid., 156.
76 Ibid., 154.
77 Ibid., 155.
78 Ibid., 156.
79 Foucault, *The Order of Things*, 127–8.

80 Ibid., 276.
81 Ibid., 277. I have modified the translation of "valeurs végétales" in the French original from "vegetable values" (277) in the published English translation to "vegetal values." See Foucault, *Les mots et les choses*, 289.
82 Foucault, *The Order of Things*, 289.
83 Ibid.
84 Ibid.
85 Ibid.
86 Ibid.
87 Ibid., 278.
88 Ibid.
89 Ibid., 344.
90 Foucault, *The History of Sexuality*, vol. 1, 157.
91 Ibid., 69.
92 Ibid., 156.
93 Foucault, *Discipline and Punish*, 299.
94 Ibid., 298.
95 Foucault, *Abnormal*, 286.
96 Ibid., 286–7.
97 Foucault, *The History of Sexuality*, vol. 1, 106–8.
98 Grosz, *Becoming Undone*, 73.
99 Foucault, *Abnormal*, 278.
100 Ibid., 280.
101 Foucault, *The History of Sexuality*, vol. 1, 57.
102 Ibid., 71.
103 Ibid., 73.
104 For a more detailed account of the important differences between Foucault and Canguilhem in the context of sexuality and biopower see Mader, *Sleights of Reason*, 62–5.
105 Foucault, *Abnormal*, 308.
106 Ibid., 309.
107 Ibid.
108 For an example of how biopolital health projects and neoliberalism work together by targeting women through reprogenetics, see McWhorter, "Darwin's Invisible Hand."
109 Mader, *Sleights of Reason*, 65.
110 Ibid., 45.
111 Ibid., 65.
112 Foucault, *The History of Sexuality*, vol. 1, 156.

113 Ibid., 156–7.

114 Rose, *The Politics of Life Itself*.

115 Foucault, *The History of Sexuality*, vol. 2, 9. Foucault's aim, he writes, is to "free thought from what it silently thinks, and so enable it to think differently." Rethinking "life itself" can be seen as contributing to that aim.

116 Foucault, "On the Ways of Writing History," 293.

117 Foucault, *The Order of Things*, 155.

118 Ibid.

119 Foucault, *History of Madness*. For a book-length analysis of this movement of desubjectivation in *History of Madness*, see Huffer, *Mad for Foucault*.

120 Foucault, *The Order of Things*, xxiv (italics added).

121 Ibid., 155.

122 Foucault, *History of Madness*, xxxii.

123 Foucault, "Lives of Infamous Men," 157.

124 Foucault, *The Order of Things*, 156.

125 See especially "On the Imperfection of the Geological Record" (chapter 9) and "On the Geological Succession of Organic Beings" (chapter 10) in Darwin, *On the Origin of Species*.

126 Foucault, *The Order of Things*, 156.

127 Ibid., 49, 50.

128 Ibid., xv.

129 Ibid., 156.

130 Foucault, *History of Madness*, xxxi.

131 Foucault, *The Order of Things*, 161.

132 Foucault, "Lives of Infamous Men," 157.

133 Ibid., 159.

134 Ibid., 160.

135 Foucault, *History of Madness*, xxxiv.

136 Foucault, *Speech Begins*, 40.

137 Foucault, "Lives of Infamous Men," 238.

138 Foucault, *The History of Sexuality*, vol. 1, 71.

139 Ibid., 71, 63.

140 In this sense we might say, as Foucault does in a different context, that the archive is the ground for thinking "the freedom of the subject and its relationship to others – which constitutes the very stuff [*matière*] of ethics." Foucault, "The Ethics of the Concern for Self as a Practice of Freedom," 300.

141 Foucault, *The History of Sexuality*, vol. 1, 159.

5

Does Life Have a Sex?[1]

Thinking Ontology and Sexual Difference with Irigaray and Simondon

STEPHEN D. SEELY

Nature has a sex. Always and Everywhere.
— *Luce Irigaray*[2]

Within the so-called turn (or return) to ontology, realism, materialism, nature, and the sciences in recent feminist theory, and continental philosophy more generally, questions of sexual difference are rarely addressed in any sustained way. And yet, since at least the 1980s, Luce Irigaray has frequently made the controversial claim that sexual difference is ontological, natural, universal, irreducible, and real.[3] There is thus an interesting double rejection of Irigaray's work in much contemporary feminist theory: on the one hand, the early critiques of phallogocentric economies of representation are said to be exclusively focused on language, discourse, and the "epistemological," while on the other hand, the affirmative ontology of sexual difference presented in the later works has been read as, at best, naïve anthropomorphism or romantic naturalism and, at worst, indicative of a deeply problematic heteronormative and conservative essentialism. In this essay, I not only defend Irigaray's argument that sexual difference is fundamental to life, or nature, "itself" and suggest that her thought is absolutely indispensible to the ongoing rethinking of ontology in feminist theory, but also argue that her philosophy of sexual difference offers a far more dynamic account of sexuate becoming than performative gender theory, queer theory, or "new materialist" feminist theory. To make this argument, I reassess Irigaray's insistence on the ontology of sexual difference alongside Gilbert Simondon's philosophy of individuation to develop an account of sexual difference that is constitutive of life, without being binaristic, anthropomorphic, or closed, as well as to insist that sexual difference is a fundamental and irreducible philosophical problem.[4] If, for whatever reason, the contemporary moment is an occasion to think anew about ontology, the real, nature, and the sciences, then to ignore – or, worse, dismiss – sexual difference is a great detriment to both feminist philosophy and politics.

Sexual Difference, Life, Ontology

Through her elaboration of an ontology of sexual difference, Irigaray seeks to radically rework the relationship between Being and life or nature that has characterized the Western metaphysical tradition, including within the thought of Martin Heidegger himself. To help clarify this, it is worth looking at two common misunderstandings of this project, both of which conflate "ontic" (to adopt a Heideggerian parlance) or empirical claims with ontological ones. The first involves those who read Irigaray as suggesting that "man" and "woman" are fundamental categories of Being. Judith Butler, for example, famously rejects Irigaray's ontology of sexual difference because, for her, man and woman are performative productions – regulatory psychosocial formations that only congeal into the *illusion* of Being. As she puts it in *Gender Trouble*: "That the gendered body is performative suggests that it has *no ontological status* apart from the various acts that constitute its reality."[5] Yet, for Irigaray, the opposition between man and woman would constitute an ontic or anthropological distinction, as it would for Heidegger, produced within the phallocentric economy of the One (which for Irigaray is coterminous if not synonymous with what Heidegger and Derrida name the "metaphysics of presence").[6] Butler and Irigaray would thus agree that this distinction – that between man and woman – is not inscribed at the level of Being; however, in positing sexual difference as only a performative effect rather than an ontology, Butler participates in the same neutralization of Being that, according to Irigaray, characterizes the history of European metaphysics. In other words, for Butler, Being (ontology) remains neutral or empty, and sexual difference is reduced to the effect of a performance by an ontologically neutral or empty subject – what amounts to a purely existential question. In their respective approaches to the question of sexual difference, then, Irigaray and Butler effectively reproduce the disagreement Heidegger expressed with Jean-Paul Sartre in his well-known "Letter on Humanism."[7] Namely, the causal reversal between "essence" and "existence" in existentialism (or, to put it the idiom of Butler's theory of performativity, "the illusion of a sexed essence" and "gender performances") remains a metaphysical proposition, fully inscribed in the history of Western philosophy, that enacts the annihilation of Being as that which precedes the very division between essence and existence and makes it possible. For Irigaray, to be sure, Being "itself" is sexed – which is to say, sexual difference *is* ontological – but this cannot be thought within the oppositional anthropological (ontic) terms of man and woman. To fully explicate this point would require carefully working through Irigaray's rigorous engagement with Heidegger, which I do not have the space to do adequate justice to here.[8] However, one of Irigaray's principal critiques of Heidegger is that the supposed forgetting of Being takes place on the basis of an even prior forgetting; that is, even Heidegger forgets that *what gives* is not Being, but nature or life. For Irigaray, on the contrary, the ontology of sexual difference is given (*Es gibt*) by life itself or by nature. As she puts it in *I Love to You*, "Sexual difference is an immediate natural given, and it is a real and irreducible component of the universal."[9] Yet, here is where the second problematic slippage can occur: in deriving a *natural* ontology of sexual difference, several readers assume that Irigaray seeks to ontologize the empirical or biological categories of male and female. Again, such empirical "facts" would constitute ontic distinctions for Irigaray as they would for Heidegger, and Irigaray's argument about nature's sexuation must be understood *ontologically* rather than empirically or scientifically. Irigaray's philosophy of nature or life is thus different from the claims made about it by physics, chemistry, or biology – which is not to say unrelated, but not of the same order, not subject to the same practices of empirical observation, verification, or falsification. Her ontology of sexual difference thus ontologizes neither the man/woman nor male/female binaries, but rather means, quite simply, that what makes *beings* possible, or *what gives* – i.e., Being (or more accurately for Irigaray, life or nature) – is itself sexuate: that "nature" or "the real" is always more than one ("at least two"). As such, Irigaray offers a thinking of life, nature, and sexual difference that is not biological or anthropological, and an ontology that is not founded on a nihilistic or neutered metaphysical abstraction but is instead grounded in life as a sexuate process of becoming.

Yet, despite Irigaray's reformulation of fundamental ontology as (sexuate) life or nature itself, several new materialist feminist theorists, most notably Myra Hird and Luciana Parisi, argue that Irigaray's conception of ontological, irreducible sexual difference is fundamentally incompatible both with contemporary technoscientific understandings of sex and with open-ended, "nonlinear" philosophies of becoming such as those presented by figures like Charles Darwin and Gilles Deleuze.[10] Luciana Parisi, for example, argues that the ontology of sexual difference presented in both Irigaray and Elizabeth Grosz is a "biomaterialist" ontology of the "two," that is, in the end, reducible to the biological forms of male and female. According to Parisi, this is ultimately a form of anthropo- or zoocentrism that simply ignores that "all forms of sex – bacterial sex, endosymbiosis, sexual reproduction, parthenogenesis, algorithmic sexes, engineered cloning, nano and synthetic sexes – are events that expose sexual difference to a multiplicity of actual sexes, ontologically irreducible to the model of the two."[11] Similarly, Hird draws on contemporary biology to suggest that there is such a wide diversity of sexual exchange throughout the natural world that any coherency of sexual difference is impossible, citing the example of fungi that supposedly have 28,000 sexes.[12] Indeed, in her recent work, Hird goes so far as to posit metabolism as a foil for sexual difference, arguing that sexual difference as a "framework" is too closed, anthropomorphic, heteronormative, and repro-centric to be of value either to feminist theory or politics. Because, as she argues, metabolic processes, and not sexual difference, constitute all living forms, Hird offers it as a replacement: "Given [metabolism's] immanence to the origins of life on earth and its centrality to *all* life, we might propose metabolism as ontology – an 'ontology of metabolic difference' if you will. In other words, perhaps a substitution is in order, namely, metabolism for sexual difference."[13] I will return shortly to some of these claims, but for now, I want to emphasize that one of the major problems with Irigaray's philosophy, according to these thinkers, is that it seems anthropocentric, static, binaristic, and closed. If Being is life, and life is always already sexuate, how can Irigaray account for the immense diversity, and especially the emergence, of forms of sex across the evolutionary spectrum? Is it possible to think life's or nature's sexuation without an anthropomorphic projection of masculinity and femininity onto nonhuman forces, elements, material forms, or living beings? How can Irigaray's ontology respond to scientific documentation of the extraordinary plethora of sexuality throughout the natural world? On these questions I turn to Simondon's philosophy of individuation. Simondon provides an account of the dynamic processes of individuation that considers everything from the emergence of inorganic physical matter to the production of contemporary technology without ever positing an undifferentiated origin or participating in the annihilation or neutralization of Being, or what *gives*, that is characteristic of the phallogocentric metaphysics of presence.[14]

According to Simondon, Western philosophy has always taken the individual as an ontological a priori, and has only attempted to consider processes of individuation retroactively from the position of the existing individual. As such, and in resonance with Heidegger, Simondon argues that philosophy has "given an ontological privilege to the constituted individual," considering it either as an already-given substance or as a hylemorphic merger of matter and form.[15] Against this view, Simondon elaborates a philosophy of individuation in which he reconceptualizes Being as a "pre-physical" and "pre-vital" "metastable system that is filled with potentials: *form, matter and energy pre-exist in the system*," from which all beings, or "individuals," are generated.[16] This metastable system is the "preindividual field," out of which individuals are produced through "interactive communication" between divergent levels of emergence, or "orders of magnitude." For Simondon, this process occurs in both nonliving and living matter, with the added difference that "the living conserves within itself a permanent activity of individuation."[17] This capacity for ongoing individuation is the result of the fact that a living individual carries a certain "load" of preindividual metastability, giving it the capacity to fall out of phase (*déphaser*) with itself and, thus, to individuate itself further. The living individual, in other words, retains a permanent relation to the field of individuation – the preindividual – that enables its perpetual becoming. In the living, the process of individuation never stops; rather, the individual "resolves problems ... by modifying itself, by inventing new internal structures."[18] Indeed, this capacity for resolving internal tensions through further individuation is itself the mark of the difference between living and nonliving matter – life, here, is the capacity of certain coagulations of matter, force, and energy to become otherwise through internal processes of self-organization and individuation.

The process of individuation, moreover, takes place at increasingly complex orders of magnitude as the individual encounters higher-order problems: from vital individuation to psychic and collective individuation to technical individuation.[19] Life, for Simondon, prolongs physical and chemical processes of individuation by carrying internal metastability (the preindividual) into more and more complex forms; likewise, psychosocial individuation prolongs biological processes, and so on. This movement between the levels of individuation is what Simondon calls "transduction," or the "operation – physical, biological, mental, social – by which an activity propagates itself from one element to the next."[20] Transduction describes the relations each individuated being maintains to the preindividual and to the other levels of individuation, and is what allows "communication" between them; indeed, properly speaking, the individual is nothing but a node of communication or relation between disparate orders of magnitude. This process of transduction, moreover, is nonlinear; that is, there is no direct or smooth translation from one level of individuation to the next and the process is not unidirectional. "Higher" life forms (especially humans), then, exist only and always between preindividual metastability (which Simondon occasionally calls both "Being" and "Nature") and "transindividual collectivity," in which the physical, biological, psychic, and social are all linked, and where each level facilitates the emergence of the next, but in no simple linear way.[21] Because the process of individuation is never complete, Simondon proposes to replace a static ontology of Being with a perpetual *ontogenesis* of becoming.

The Ontogenesis of Sexual Difference

Simondon's theory of individuation is of immense importance in conceptualizing an ontology, or rather an ontogenesis, of sexual difference. Indeed, the few pages in Simondon's untranslated *L'individuation psychique et collective* in which he discusses sexuality resonate with Irigaray's work in many important ways. For Simondon, sexuality is one of the "innate psychosomatic dynamics and structures that constitute a mediation between the natural (pre-individual phase) and the individuated."[22] Rather than a type of subjectivity or property of the individual, "being sexuate is part of individuation."[23] Sexual difference, in other words, is part of the very process of individuation itself; it "molds the body and soul of the individuated being, [and] creates an *asymmetry* between individuated beings as individuals."[24] Importantly, Simondon locates sexuality at "an equal distance between the *apeiron* of pre-individual nature and limited and determined individuality."[25] Because the preindividual contains all the conditions for the emergence of living and nonliving matter, and thus cannot be said to be itself living, it is not sexed. Yet, for the very same reasons – that is, because the preindividual contains all the conditions of the living and the nonliving – it must contain the conditions of sex, and thus of sexual difference, within it. There is no law of the excluded middle or of noncontradiction in the preindividual that would otherwise render these two claims logically incoherent.[26] Thus, following Deleuze's usage of Simondon's work in *Difference and Repetition* and so using language that is not precisely Simondon's, we could say that the preindividual is *virtually sexed* as it is *virtually living*.

With this in mind, Simondon's theory also helps parse Irigaray's frequent and provocative statements, like, "Without sexual difference there would be no life on earth. It is the manifestation of and the condition for the production and reproduction of life," as well as the epigraph with which I began this essay.[27] Indeed, these are precisely the kind of assertions that draw the ire of the feminist science studies scholars like Parisi and Hird. Here, however, it is worth briefly reconsidering the work of the influential microbiologist Lynn Margulis, who both Parisi and Hird draw on extensively in their rejection of Irigaray's ontology of sexual difference, in light of the ontogenesis of sexual difference I propose here. According to Margulis and her coauthor Dorion Sagan, life, even down to the level of bacteria and archaea, is "sexual," or, as they put it at the start of *Origins of Sex*: "The story of sex starts with an account of the earliest life on Earth."[28] According to them, sex (at a biological level) consists of informatic exchange between at least two different individuals.[29] If we accept this, then "*a* sex" or "being sexed/sexuated" (the French adjective *sexué* that both Irigaray and Simondon use) would be here defined as an affective capacity: the capacity to engage in (informatic) exchange with another body.[30] This process occurs at multiple levels within multicellular organisms such as a human body, in which there is perpetual exchange between cells, viruses, and micro-organisms in ways that constitute sex from a biological perspective but that far exceed what we typically think of as a sexual relation. While Parisi and Hird both use Margulis's work in their refutation of Irigaray's claims about sexual difference, and insist that Irigaray's ontology of sexual difference is ultimately grounded in the reproductive binary characteristic of a form of sex particular to only a small percentage of living forms, I suggest that it is actually they who make this mistake. Margulis and Sagan write: "Sex confuses us not only because it literally has to do with the mingling of [at least] two distinctly different beings, opening us up to each other in the deepest way, but because we tend to make mistaken extrapolations about sexuality's importance. Our own biologically parochial existence as sexually reproducing beings does not mean, for instance, that there is only copulatory, genital-based sex or that sex has anything necessarily to do with reproduction."[31] While Irigaray's work might initially appear as the apotheosis of such a mistaken extrapolation of sexuality's importance, in fact it seems to be Parisi's and Hird's own mistaken conflation of sexual difference and reproduction that causes their hesitance to admit that nature is sexed. They would only rush to deny Irigaray's claims about nature's sexuation, in other words, because some organisms *reproduce* without sex, but Margulis and Sagan are quite clear that this does not mean that such organisms do not or cannot engage in sexual exchange, and therefore that they are not sexuate. Simply stated, there is no living matter that is not always already more than one (or as Irigaray frequently puts it, at least two).[32] In fact, none of Parisi's or Hird's examples negate the existence of sexual difference; indeed, any form of sexual exchange between at least two individuals, from bacteria, to viruses, to fungi, to nanotechnology, requires an interval of difference – sexual difference. And it is this capacity for sexual exchange – sexuation or sexuate individuation – at the organic level that is transductively propagated or prolonged at the psychic and collective levels.[33] Moreover, that nature is sexually differentiated and possesses the capacity for sexual exchange is a major condition for both the continuation and the continuing creativity of life itself, as both Irigaray and Grosz, but also Margulis and Sagan, contend.[34]

Yet, for both Irigaray and Simondon, this becoming has its own internal limits, which are, precisely, the limits of *already individuated sexual difference*. Simondon argues that in sexually reproducing species, "the adherence of sexuality to the individual being *creates an inherent limit of individuation within the individual*."[35] Indeed, according to Simondon, organisms that require sexual reproduction (i.e., most multicellular organisms) contain inherent limitations to their individuation due precisely to that sexuation. An organism that reproduces by binary fission or cloning such as bacteria, for example, might carry a full load of the preindividual within itself – that is, the individual organism *itself* constitutes a metastable system that can individuate into two individuals – and therefore does not require the fusion with another individual for reproduction. Meiotic organisms, however, are sexed, with sex serving as a cut into the preindividual carried by such organisms, requiring a relation with another individual in order to achieve the necessary metastability that can produce another individual.[36] Therefore, in all plants and animals, the preindividual virtuality that might be actualized is forever limited by sexual difference. A sexuate individual cannot, in other words, individuate beyond the forms of sexuation inherent to it as a specific living form. Likewise for Irigaray, nature's sexuation means that "limits are therefore inscribed in nature itself," and such limits are the conditions of life and the possibility of relationality.[37] Thus, as living beings continually individuate in response to increasingly complex "problems," the limit or interval of sexual difference is one that, as Irigaray says, "would never be *crossed*."[38] And yet, we do not – and cannot – know where that limit resides, or even how many limits exist. In humans, the fact of one's being sexuate is simultaneously physical, biological, psychic, social, and technological, and thus one must be able to attend to one's sexuate individuation at all of these levels. Sexual difference, as both Irigaray and Simondon insist, will always remain a problem for the living, but is also the condition of its future becomings in that this problem perpetually requires creative responses.

Virtual Sex and the Becomings of Sexual Difference

This account of sexuate individuation leads to an ontology that is more than one and to a philosophy of sexual difference that is beyond the reproductive binary. As Simondon argues, the preindividual persists alongside and within all individuated beings, and this preindividual contains all of the conditions of future emergence. The conditions for the emergence of sex, for example, were virtually present in bacterial forms prior to their actualization when two bacteria first exchanged genetic material. All living matter, then, carries with it the preindividual conditions of emergence that have generated all forms of life thus far and will generate all forms of life to come.[39] Thus, as Margulis and Sagan show, with the first emergence of sexual exchange, sexual difference becomes a condition of all living matter that provides the resources life has for its future becomings. The preindividual, then, is virtually sexed and contains all of the – perhaps infinite – forms of sexual difference that life may take; however, because the preindividual (or virtual) is forever transformed and, in a sense, determined by individuated (or actual) forms, once sexual difference emerged it became an ineradicable condition of life and all of its future forms.[40]

Thus, because we contain the *virtual* sexes of preindividual "nature" coeval with our actual sexuation(s) due to our ongoing connection to the preindividual as living beings, we are virtually sexed in countless and unknowable ways.[41] Actual human sexual difference draws on the virtual preindividual conditions of sex, which always persist, and this means that the actualizations of sexual difference from a virtual (preindividual) reserve are always in process. As Simondon puts it, "sexuality could be considered as a psychosomatic immanence of preindividual nature in the individuated being. Sexuality is a *mixture of nature [the preindividual] and individuation*."[42] This virtual or preindividual sexual difference, however, is not reducible to Freud's polymorphous perversity, Aristophanes's myth of the originary unity of sexed forms split into sexed individuals, Heidegger's "neutralization," or androgyny. On the contrary, it is the very condition of possibility of any individuated and knowable forms of sexual difference at the physical, chemical, biological, psychic, or collective levels. But, as Irigaray and Simondon insist, this actualization is not infinite and always takes place within certain limitations. We become, that is, only through sexual difference in its actualized forms, even as we continue to draw on its virtuality. The question of what forms sexual difference may take in the future is an open-ended one, but this becoming takes place only in and through the – differently sexuated – bodies of the beings that carry it. In humans, this means that organic sexual difference, for example, is carried by the two sexed gametes, but also opened up through them, as in the case of intersexuality, which may well constitute additional sexes.[43]

This is not to say, however, that sexuate individuation is only limited by the natural limits formed by the living body. Indeed, for Simondon, while technological individuation is a way of prolonging psychosocial individuation and further "communicating" between orders of magnitude, certain technical forms manipulate or arrest vital and psychosocial processes of individuation. I suggest, following Foucault, that the "*dispositif* (or apparatus) of sexuality," as outlined in the first volume of *The History of Sexuality*, functions precisely as such a technology operating at the biological, psychic, and collective (i.e., "population") levels to give an "artificial unity" and intelligibility to disparate phenomena such as "anatomical elements, biological functions, conducts, sensations, pleasures."[44] Such a technology of sex, in both its regulatory and disciplinary modalities, functions *orthopedically* – literally forcing one's physical, chemical, biological, psychic, and collective sexuations to line up "straight" and coherent under the sign of "sex." This orthopedics of sex is also known as phallogocentrism. Returning to Irigaray's so-called critical period, then, we can see that the phallocentric technology of sex has not only foreclosed the actualization of forms of sexuate individuation beyond a heterosexual reproductive dimorphism, but also greatly limited the becoming of feminine sexuality in particular. According to Irigaray, feminine (not "female") sexuality always has greater access to sexual multiplicity than does masculine. This could be because, to use Simondon's terms, it seeks, at least less than the masculine, to cut itself off from the reserve of preindividual or virtual sexual difference: that is, it is more in touch with the dispersion of sexual difference throughout the body. On the other hand, the phallocentric preoccupation with rigidity, calculability, solidity, and self-identity ensures that the masculine sex is positioned as *the* sex. In its attempt to position itself as fully individuated – best represented in the phallic One – it has reduced the feminine (particularly configured as the maternal) to the preindividual, undifferentiated ground against which the solidity and identity of man can be defined and measured.[45]

Of course, no sexuate individuation is ever fully complete, masculine or otherwise. As Deleuze describes the process of individuation, building on both Simondon and Bergson, the preindividual constitutes a virtual plane, or "intensive spatium," from which individuation generates differentiated extensive bodies and assemblages.[46] Individuation is thus an intensive process that is the condition for extensive differences between entities. If being sexed is a mode of individuation, as it is for Simondon, then this process occurs at an intensive level in the move from the virtual to the actual before it manifests at the extensive level. The bulk of sexual difference, then, remains virtual and intensive; only aspects of it are locatable in extension. And as Irigaray rigorously points out in her work on fluids, the phallocentric representational economy has only ever attempted to capture sexual difference as extended substance. Because of the external-ity of the penis, the feminine's multiple and diffuse sexuality has been reduced to nothing. This privileging of the male organ as the model of sex has subsequently led to an ontological privilege of the type that Simondon critiques: the primacy of visualization, measurement, and the counting of static substances at the expense of other fluid processes that cannot be seen, measured, counted, or located. Thus, to assume that when Irigaray speaks of sexual difference she speaks merely of penises and vaginas is to ignore the bulk of her work that challenges the very possibility of locating sexual difference (we might here release Hird from the onerous task of counting 28,000 fungal sexes). Coupling this critique of the phallic econ-omy with Deleuze's and Simondon's accounts of intensive and extensive differentiation, we might say that for Irigaray sexual difference is an inten-sive process even as it is also an extensive difference.[47] Sexual difference is an ongoing mode of individuation and becoming, a qualitative rather than quantitative difference that cannot be quantified without changing its very nature. We can, and in fact must, represent sexual difference as quantifiable in order to address it empirically and politically, but Irigaray points out time and time again that sexual difference always exceeds these representations.

In his brief review of Simondon's *L'individuation psychique et collective*, Deleuze points out the ethical significance of Simondon's philosophy: "Ethics," Deleuze writes, "follows a kind of movement running from the pre-individual to the trans-individual via individuation."[48] Given that the preindividual from which all life has emerged is the very condition of fu-ture becoming, ethics depends on staying open to both this preindivid-ual fund and to transindividual collectivity, so that future individuations remain possible. An ethics of sexual difference from this perspective would thus demand an openness to the sexuate individuation of the other(s) – that is, sexuate transindividuality – as well as to the forms of sexual difference to come – sexuate preindividuality. Thinking Simondon and Irigaray together on the ontogenesis of sexual difference therefore allows us to see that at every level of life – biological, psychic, collective, and technical – sexual difference is at work and forms a natural limit or interval. Yet, sexuation, for both thinkers, is not merely an *effect* of individuation – it is not merely a physicochemical, biological, psychological, social, or technical fact subject to empirical investigation. If ontogenesis is a better way of thinking about the ontological difference between Being and beings, then Simondon enables us to see how sexual difference *is* ontological without reducing it to a static oneness. In other words, if, as Simondon suggests, Being or "nature" is the preindividual metastability of form, matter, and energy and if, as Irigaray insists, "nature has a sex [a]lways and everywhere," then we are presented with an ontology – an ontogenesis – of sexual difference that is neither static, binary, or anthropomorphic; that is engaged with but not *grounded* the claims of techno-science; and that is inherently ethical. Perhaps this is why, for Irigaray, an attunement to sexual difference *as difference* both requires and constitutes "the necessary foundation for a new ontology, a new ethics, and a new politics,"[49] and why, I insist, Simondon and Irigaray offer the most provocative contributions to the ongoing attempt to rethink life, nature, and ontology within contemporary philosophy.

NOTES

1 The content of this essay has been through many incarnations and owes much to many people. For their invaluable input on various aspects of the project presented here, I must thank (among others): Luce Irigaray, Elizabeth Grosz, Drucilla Cornell, Ed Cohen, Hasana Sharp, Chloë Taylor, Lynne Huffer, Rebecca Hill, Mary Rawlinson, Gail Schwab, Louise Burchill, Yvette Russell, Max Hantel, Carolina Alonso Bejarano, Julian Gill-Peterson, the participants in the 2012–13 Rutgers Institute for Research on Women seminar, the participants in the 2013 Luce Irigaray International Symposium, my fellow panelists and audience at the 2013 PhiloSOPHIA annual meeting in Banff, Canada, and the

audience and organizers at the 2014 Luce Irigaray Circle annual meeting in Melbourne, Australia.

2 Irigaray, *Sexes and Genealogies*, 108.

3 See, most prominently, Irigaray, *An Ethics of Sexual Difference*; *Sexes and Genealogies*; *Thinking the Difference*; *I Love to You*; and *In the Beginning, She Was*. See also Grosz, "Irigaray and the Ontology of Sexual Difference."

4 I use the word "problem" here in a decidedly Deleuzean fashion, as that which impinges upon us from the outside and demands the development of creative responses or concepts. See Deleuze and Guattari, *What Is Philosophy?* Colebrook addresses the problem of sexual difference from a Deleuzean orientation in "Is Sexual Difference a Problem?" Remember also that Irigaray famously opens *An Ethics of Sexual Difference* with the claim that "sexual difference is one of the major philosophical issues, if not *the* issue, of our age" (5).

5 Butler, *Gender Trouble*, 173. To be clear, this claim comes not in the critique of Irigaray but rather as part of her well-known appropriation of Nietzsche's "no doer behind the deed." Butler reiterates her opposition to Irigaray's ontologization of sexual difference in the famous interview with Cheah, Grosz, and Cornell ("The Future of Sexual Difference").

6 See Irigaray, *Speculum of the Other Woman*. See also Derrida's essay on sexual difference in Heidegger, "Geschlecht."

7 See Heidegger, *Basic Writings*.

8 For Irigaray's most sustained engagement with Heidegger, see *The Forgetting of Air in Martin Heidegger*. For the elaboration of an affirmative ontology of sexual difference, and the transition piece between these two texts, "From *The Forgetting of Air* to *To Be Two*."

9 Irigaray, *I Love to You*, 47.

10 Interestingly, both Hird and Parisi studied in the laboratory of Margulis and both use her work to argue against an Irigarayan ontology of sexual difference as I present in this essay. Both Hird and Parisi also strongly critique Grosz for her long-standing and highly influential attempts to bring an Irigarayan understanding of sexual difference and a Darwinian or Deleuzean ontology of becoming together, going so far as to suggest that Irigaray is fundamentally incompatible with the work of Darwin and Deleuze. I do not have the space here to treat these claims with the focus that they deserve, but am doing so in a work in progress. While these ideas can be found throughout both Hird's and Parisi's work, they are articulated most explicitly in Hird, "Digesting Differences," and Parisi, "Event and Evolution."

11 Parisi, "Event and Evolution," 163.

12 Hird, *Sex, Gender and Science*. Indeed, the project of counting 28,000 sexes seems overly ripe for an Irigarayan critique of the phallocentric logic of quantifying sexuate difference.

13 Hird, "Digesting Differences," 216.

14 While none of Simondon's complete texts have been translated into English, the most commonly referenced is probably the book on technics, *Du mode d'existence des objets techniques*. Simondon's ontology of individuation is laid out in *L'individu et sa genese physico-biologique* and *L'individuation psychique et collective*. An excerpt from the latter text has been translated into English as "The Position of the Problem of Ontogenesis."

15 Simondon, "The Position of the Problem of Ontogenesis," 4.

16 Ibid., 7. There are important points of resonance between Heidegger and Simondon, which are beyond my scope in this essay. The critique of the metaphysical conflation of individuals with processes of individuation shares much with that of the annihilation of the ontological difference between beings and Being. For Simondon, the preindividual cannot be known, represented, or grasped as such. Even while Simondon does make it less "mystical" than Heidegger's Being (especially as it is presented in Heidegger's later writings), by understanding it as metastable systems of form, matter, and energy, the preindividual, like Heidegger's Being, is not amenable to scientific observation and precedes the distinctions between "things" that can be measured, quantified, and represented.

17 Ibid.

18 Ibid.

19 These "orders of magnitude" are not substantially different, nor teleologically ordered as in a Hegelian dialectic; they are, rather, *potential* phases of Being.

20 Simondon, "The Position of the Problem of Ontogenesis," 11.

21 Simondon describes subjectivity as the effect of psychic individuation in which the living being attains a sense of unity and "represents its actions through the world to itself as an element and a dimension of the world." Yet this gives the living being a sense of place *within* that world by incorporating it "in a system made up of world and subject," enabling its participation at a collective level with other beings. Psychic and collective individuation are thus inextricably linked and psychosocially individuated matter is an interface between inside and outside, psychic and collective. Simondon's theory of subjectivity thus makes living matter both the "agent and theater of individuation" (8).

22 Simondon, *L'individuation psychique et collective*, 200. The following translations from Simondon are my own. The original French reads: "Il existe des structures et des dynamismes psychosomatiques innés qui constituent une

mediation entre le naturel (phase pré-individuelle) et l'individué. Telle est la sexualité."

23 Ibid., 200. "Le fait, pour l'individu, d'être sexué, fait partie de l'individuation; et en fait la sexualité ne pourrait exister si la distinction psychosomatique des individus n'existait pas."

24 Ibid. "La sexualité modèle le corps et l'âme de l'être individué, crée une asymétrie entre les êtres individués en tan qu'individus."

25 Ibid., 201. "La sexualité est à égale distance entre l'ἄπειρον de la nature pré-individuelle et l'individualité limitée déterminée."

26 See Simondon, "The Position of the Problem of Ontogenesis," 10.

27 Irigaray, I Love to You, 37.

28 Margulis and Sagan, Origins of Sex, 2.

29 Sex, according to Margulis and Sagan, is "any process that recombines genetic information in an individual cell or organism from more than a single source." What Is Sex?, 235.

30 Thinking a sex as an affective capacity calls forth Spinoza's famous definition of a body as capacity to affect and be affected. This might be an interesting way to rethink Irigaray's frequent use of the term "body-sex."

31 Margulis and Sagan, What Is Sex?, 17.

32 Indeed, supposedly "asexual" organisms such as bacteria should not be seen as unsexed or unisexual, but rather as nearly infinitely sexed. These organisms, in other words, have the most complex forms of sexual difference, rather than the least.

33 In other words, the reason why sexuation is a psychic and collective problem is because it is "prolonged" from the biological level via processes of transduction.

34 A condition for the continuation of life, insofar as sex allows for the transmission of genetic memory with survival information. A condition for the continuing *creativity* of life, because sex is one way that the emergence of both new organisms and new organic structures takes place within life. According to Margulis and Sagan, sex began with bacteria and evolved into meiotic sex in protists. Meiotic sex is then what enabled the continued evolution of more complex levels of organic differentiation. *Origins of Sex*, 5. Furthermore, they position the capacity for sexual exchange as an engine not only of organic evolution, but of the development of human art and technology as well. See *What Is Sex?*, 201–12.

To be clear, I am not attempting to ground the ontology of sexual difference in bacteria or in the biological sciences. To say that forms of individuation at the physical, chemical, or biological levels are propagated across the psychosocial level is not to make them into an ontological ground. In the case of Margulis and Sagan, biology, as a scientific discipline, can help to understand how the organic level of ontogenesis is sexuate all the way down and that psychosocial levels, which are prolongations of the organic, are therefore necessarily also sexuate. The ontogenesis of sexual difference, however, emerges from the *pre*-physical and *pre*-vital preindividual (which itself makes the biological possible), meaning that "the biological" cannot be an ontological ground.

35 Simondon, *L'individuation psychique et collective*, 201. "L'adhérence de la sexualité à l'être individuel crée l'inhérence d'une limite d'individuation à l'intérieur d'lindividu."

36 Ibid. It may be helpful to remember that, according to Margulis and Sagan, reproduction is an increase in the number of individuals in a population or species. Sex is the exchange of information between two individuals. For species that sexually reproduce, then, production of another individual of the species requires exchange between two individuals. In asexually reproducing species, reproduction and sex can be independently occuring processes.

37 Irigaray, *I Love to You*, 35. As she puts it in *In the Beginning She Was*, 126: "To be living needs a certain surrounding world ... To be someone really living also calls for limits. Limits are provided by the necessities of life itself, among other things its surroundings, but also by relations with other living beings, in particular, those of one's own species. Relational limits between humans are provided through genealogy and sexuate difference."

38 Irigaray, *An Ethics of Sexual Difference*, 14.

39 This is what Bergson describes in his metaphor of the cone, in which the entire past of the cosmos is carried with the present at varying degrees of dilation and contraction. For Bergson, in *Matter and Memory*, the past provides the only resources upon which the future can draw. Margulis and Sagan, in *What Is Sex?*, 220–8, also argue something similar with specific reference to sex, suggesting that all forms of sex (up to and including cybersex) draw on the three billion year history of sex every time.

40 When I say that the preindividual is determined by individuated forms, I mean that while the preindividual (or virtual) may be limitless, the individuals or actual forms that it generates are limited. And given that further actualiations or individuations depend on the actual forms that carry the preindividual, the limited individuals that have been actualized give at least some determinate limitations to what the virtual can later do.

41 This seems to me to be what Derrida tries to address in his controversial notion of a "dispersed" sexual multiplicty beyond or "prior" to duality. As Derrida, in "Women in the Beehive," puts it in distinguishing between sexual

difference and sexual opposition: "Opposition is two, opposition is man/woman. Difference, on the other hand, can be an infinite number of sexes ... [This is not] sexual in-difference, but ... a sexuality completely out of the frame, totally aleatory to what we are famliar with in the term 'sexuality.'" Deleuze and Guattari also infamously speak of this sexual difference or multiplicty beyond what they call the "anthropomorphic representation of sex." In alluding to "nonhuman sex," they refer precisely, I suggest, to this virtual (preindividual) sexual difference that "precedes" any of its actualizations as the very condition for individuated sexes. They refer to this sexual difference variously as "*n* sexes," "molecular sex," and "a thousand tiny sexes." Like Derrida and Irigaray, they also make it very clear that the dual or oppositional model of sexual difference is a phallocentric production: "Castration is the basis for the anthropomorphic and molar representaiton of sexuality." *Anti-Oedipus*, 295.

42 Simondon, *L'individuation psychique et collective*, 201. "La sexualité peut être considérée comme une immanence psychosomatique de la nature préindividuelle à l'être individué. La sexualité est un mixte de nature et d'individuation." For Deleuze, Simondon's individuation is part of the actualization of the virtual; see *Difference and Repetition*.

43 This is one way that I suggest one can be both Irigarayan and Deluzean simultaneously. Most simply put: whatever open-ended virtuality bodies carry (Deleuze), the actualized bodies that carry that virtuality are always differently sexuated (Irigaray). On intersexuality, see Fausto-Sterling, *Sexing the Body*.

44 Foucault, *The History of Sexuality*, vol. 1, 154.

45 This explains the ubiquitous reduction of female sexuality to the maternal body, and the reduction of all of feminine sexuality to the womb, or void, out of which man sees himself as emerging as a complete individual, and to which man seeks to return to validate this self-identity. See nearly any of Irigaray's work for a critique of this logic, but particularly *This Sex Which Is Not One, Speculum of the Other Woman*, and *In the Beginning She Was*.

46 See Deleuze, *Difference and Repetition*, 252; Delanda, *Intensive Science and Virtual Philosophy*.

47 This intensive sexual becoming might explain Irigaray's claims that feminine sexuality is perpetually touching itself from *within*, and that the other is always already inside. See *This Sex Which Is Not One*.

48 Deleuze, *Desert Islands and Other Texts, 1953–1974*, 89.

49 Irigaray, "The Question of the Other," 19.

PART TWO

Lived Experience

6

New Constellations

Lived Diffractions of
Dis/ability and Dance

RACHEL LOEWEN WALKER,
DANIELLE PEERS, AND
LINDSAY EALES

The stage is bathed in a rich, dark red as seven seated bodies raise their hands above their heads. The light diffracts around them to create shadows upon the stage: shadows that stretch the bodies beyond themselves. They are reflected, but they are different. Recognizable figures are transformed into unrecognizable creatures; new life is created in the fuzzy shadows.

In physics, to diffract is to bend or change shape around an obstruction. The ring of light that surrounds the sun is a diffraction of particles. A dancer's hip meeting another can be a diffraction of energy as the movement is redirected and dispersed through the body of another. A dance performance can bend and amplify the lived experiences and theoretical musings of a scholar changing the shape of future scholarship and lived engagement. Think of two pebbles dropping into a still body of water. The disturbance in the water around each produces a series of ripples that progressively move outward. The ripples from one pebble eventually overlap with those of the other as they bend and shift around new obstacles. The changing ripples produce new patterns from the differences in amplitude and phase between the wave components. This overlap is called interference or a diffraction pattern. Contrary to apparatuses of reflection – such as mirrors, which produce faithful images of objects – apparatuses of diffraction "produce patterns that mark differences in the relative characters of individual waves as they combine."[1] A shadow is never an exact replica of its referent body; its irregularities and gaps reveal the varied densities at play, and the rupture of light and matter as they create a new pattern of life.

Diffraction has also been enlisted as a methodological term, first by Donna Haraway[2] and more recently by Karen Barad.[3] Barad takes diffraction to signify a method of reading ideas and insights through one another, and of attending to relations of difference between them, including "how different differences get made, what gets excluded, and how those exclusions matter."[4] Like others within feminist and queer theory,[5] Barad is hesitant about the process of "critique" that characterizes modern philosophy, and instead wants to shift her focus toward the production of new theories and the development of alternate ways to understand a changing political and social (and postmodern) climate. Diffraction contrasts with reflective or even reflexive analyses, which read things comparatively, looking for similarities and contradictions, or as Haraway writes:

> Reflexivity, like reflection, [as a critical practice] only displaces the same elsewhere, setting up worries about copy and original and the search for the authentic and really real ... Diffraction [on the other hand] is an optical metaphor for the effort to make a difference in the world ... Diffraction patterns record the history of interaction, interference, reinforcement, difference. Diffraction is about heterogeneous history, not about originals.[6]

Barad then explains how not only waves exhibit diffractive patterns, but also matter – electrons, neutrons, and atoms – sometimes exhibit diffractive patterns as well. This discovery enables a shift in the study of phenomena such that diffraction experiments can be used to learn either about passing through the diffraction grating or about the grating itself. A diffraction grating is the mechanism, lens, or frame through which diffracted particles or waves pass. Therefore, as Barad draws on it, the grating is understood as itself a contributor to the ways that we understand things.[7] Like the interferences between waves, the use of a diffractive methodology within philosophy can read the disturbances, or the ripples; that is, the way that practices of knowing themselves have consequences for what constitutes experience. Put another way, a diffraction grating reveals the ways in which matter actively constitutes its environment.

A diffractive methodology enables a process of inquiry that explores the ways that boundaries have been made across fields and the ways that these boundaries are the products of "material-discursive boundary-making practices that produce 'objects' and 'subjects.'"[8] Acting both as a reorientation and also as a paradigmatic shift in the way that truth, knowledge, and meaning are conceived, Barad's diffractive methodology offers fertile ground for an analysis of how diffraction (change, or transformation) can serve as a rupture in understanding.

Taking this cue, this essay uses diffraction as a lived methodology. It is a journey through the ways our lives and our scholarship, as authors, have diffracted in the wakes of each other. Our method then, is not only to share this diffraction but also to amplify it. Just as the ripples of pebbles dropped into a still pond eventually overlap, sparking patterns of interference and co-creation, we each drop a storied pebble into the swell, letting the event of their rupture amplify not only our understandings of dis/ability, but also the very movements and lived realities of multiple bodies in various dis/abling environments. Through this practice we work to de-colonize and de-stratify the lines between dis/ability, feminist theory, and dance performance, and to open up an affective engagement with each other and our audience.

Three Pebbles

A Choreographer's Pebble

I am hunched over, my breath bouncing off the floor and back into my face. Stars of red light pierce my eyes and reflect off of the back white wall, but my body is still washed in the cool darkness on stage. The air thickens with the call for movement. The breath of the six dancers next to me is syncopated as we carve the space with angular limbs. The music swells, stirring butterflies in my gut. The lights blaze, casting hot sunbeams on my lips and cheeks. As thick ribbons flick and ripple around me, I grab one from the floor: black broadcloth, bunched up in my sweaty palm. I pause for a beat to fill out the music, then snake-hop-kick-roll to the floor with the ribbon cascading behind me. A large metal washer sewn into one end of the ribbon weighs it to the ground until another dancer retrieves it. I wrap the ribbon around my wrist and knee, and together we pull the ribbon taut. Anxious anticipation pounds in my belly as the deeply familiar musical notes call for other dancers' movement. I catch a slightly framed dancer at the centre of the stage sweeping her arms up and then folding over at a musical turn that sends shivers through my body. My wrist is tugged as other dancers push and pull against the ribbons that enmesh the stage space. The ribbons are ripped from my body and crash to the floor with a metallic clang.

As the music shifts, I vacantly saunter to the other side of the stage and lie face down on the floor, peeking through my elbow at the rolling interlocked flesh-metal of four dancers, on and around a wheelchair, as they sweep across the front of the stage. The hum of a powerchair dragging another dancer towards me prepares my body to spring off the ground. I curl to stand up, connecting my hip with hers as a third dancer swings her leg over the chair and we spin. My hand connects with the dancer as she maneuvers her powerchair to drive me backward. We share a brief moment of eye contact and both break into a chest-exploding grin. I linger in joy for a second before my thoughts self-consciously flicker to the audience.

Lindsay drops a pebble: she choreographs, co-creates, and performs in *New Constellations* without knowing where its ripples will lead. *New Constellations* is an eight-minute performance staged in January 2012 by an integrated dance group now known as CRIPSiE.[9] Integrated dance is a physical art form performed by people with a wide range of embodiments and capacities, and specifically includes dancers who experience disability and those who do not.[10] The lived aesthetics of difference are central to CRIPSiE's choreographic and political engagement: dancers shop movements, themes, and aesthetics from their lives and bring these to the dance; dancers borrow movements, aesthetics, and strategies from dance and engage these in their daily lives. *New Constellations* was created out of the life experiences of its fourteen dancers. It is not a literal reflection of a singular story, but rather a diffraction formed in the overlapping wakes of fourteen lives: an abstracted and amplified shadow of inequity, possibility, and community. The performance was an event shared between the dancers and live audience, but it also reaches beyond that specific time and place through its online presence[11] and in the uptake of its continued audience.

A Crip Pebble

I first saw New Constellations as a member of the audience on opening night and I was completely lost in the movement. Ominous black ribbons unfurled onstage. Wheeling and ambulating bodies found themselves, and each other, caught in the cross(ing) threads. They wove their stories of survival across the stage: ducking under, pulling through, rolling over the web; leaning on, lifting up, holding close to each other through celebration and struggle.

It was not until the onstage movement had died down that I became aware of, and confused by, the ways the dance had moved me. I found tears welling up in my eyes, my chest full, and my thoughts wandering without explanations or tropes to anchor them. What did this dance mean? Why did it mean so much to me? I am generally distrustful of the swelling affect that rushes after and upon disability in motion. I am always suspicious that the emotional movement enables a political and discursive stillness. I suspect that when one breaks down into tears of inspiration, it serves to further fix the trope of pitiful broken bodies in need of fixing. And yet I cry, watching New Constellations, I cry out of a place and a feeling I can't yet name. Perhaps I cry in part out of a sense of resonance: my own lived realities amplified in the movement wake of some of these non-normative silhouettes. Perhaps I cry because of the unfamiliarity of it all against the daily backdrop of disabling ubiquities: moved by the unfamiliar relationships, the unimagined possibilities, and the unexpected beauty. I am destabilized and yet buoyed by the dance. For days after, I find myself reconfiguring my politics and theories, much like the bodies reconfigured disability and connection on that stage.

Danielle is in the audience to watch and video-record *New Constellations*. The ripples overwhelm her. They diffract with the post-structuralist and crip disability theories she is studying and with her lived experiences of dis/ability. She understands disability not as a problem of bodies, but as phenomena produced through social structures (e.g., architecture, discourses, policies, diagnostic techniques) that subject, isolate, and devalue individuals and populations who exhibit socially disfavoured variations in embodiment and capacities.[12] *New Constellations* resonates with this understanding of dis/ability but also embodies and materializes it in ways that exceed these theories. In the wake of the dance, Danielle feels her struggling breath take on a more intensely theoretical charge, and resonate with a more consciously crip aesthetic. This diffraction ruptures old understandings and creates new imaginings and experiences of dis/ability in her daily life. Danielle, so moved, drops another pebble: she emails the video to Rachel.

A Feminist Materialist Pebble

Watching a dance performance, I am taken in by the movement of bodies. At times angular and sudden, other times quiet, imperceptible. Red leotards catch the eye, transmogrifying into legs and arms as they move in and out of view. The dark fabric of a skirt slides forward and backward, keeping its own counter-rhythm to the movement of a body. A web of thick ribbon is pulled across the stage. I can feel its tactility as the tension of the constraint pushes and pulls the dancers. Suddenly the room feels heavy. I am claustrophobic, but on stage the dancers move with the ribbons, and cut new paths with and through the fabric. A simple piano waltz, clear and straightforward, counterposes the complex movement on stage. How is it that we believe movement is at all straightforward or simple?

A dancer takes to the stage, her metal wheels glint off the stage lights. She glides effortlessly, one steady, slow line until she meets her partner. The second dancer takes hold of the arms of her chair and balances in the air. The chair holds her up firmly, without sway. They turn together, the three/two/one of them, entangled as a dance apparatus. Suddenly there are many spinning, turning, intensive wheelchair multiple-bodied apparatuses. The deep blue stage lights silhouette these strange creatures, these compelling configurations of long arms, power wheelchairs, and torsos without legs.

The performance is electric. It pulls the hairs on my arms, tingles my spine. Bodies transform themselves; movement is enabled, disabled. These are the becomings, intensities, and creativities of matter.

Immersed in new work on feminist materialisms, Rachel takes a break to watch *New Constellations*. The piece reverberates through the texts piled up around her and brings life to their pages. Feminist materialisms stretch feminist theory into the material, whereby matter becomes more than the "little bits of nature, or a blank slate, surface, or site passively awaiting signification."[13] Instead, matter is the lively "emergent, ultimately unmappable landscapes of interacting biological, climatic, economic, and political forces."[14] This materialism, therefore, is coproductive. It cannot be the passive backdrop, or the material that we shape into political and economic life, for it constitutes these politics. A key component of such scholarship is that life is always already a fully material process. Contrary to thinking of life as a particular entity or closed system, the life of matter is such that mutual interdependencies share a reflexive relationship of force as they move, create, and influence one another.

All three of our starting points offer important insights into the extra- and contra-human operations of differently abled bodies, matter, and lives. As *New Constellations*, crip theory, and feminist materialisms amplify one another, they destabilize our familiar patterns of movement, our antici- pations of what differentially abled bodies do. In so doing, they make in- telligible the multiple forms of life at work on any transcorporeal stage. Through this collaborative and entangled practice we are able to work out a kind of language of the event, whether of the event of the dance or of any event that has an impact on our lived experiences. Rather than thinking of the event as any particular static occurrence, we can understand it in rela- tion to its diffractive effects, that is, as an opening up to life: a co-creative encounter between memory, matter, expectation, and possibility.

New Constellations: The Event(s)

For the choreographer, those in the audience, and those who saw it in the years that followed, CRIPSiE's *New Constellations* was an event: an import- ant happening, an occurrence locatable in time and space. We can think of it in relation to a before and an after; we can consider it to have a causal relationship with the range of feelings and ideas the performance sparked. In this sense, it acts as a sort of advent or origin point. But such a view of the event does not account for the material intensities that linger after (and before) the specific time-space occurrence of the performance; it doesn't quite get at the affective force of the piece. Gilles Deleuze stated in an interview that the event is a "philosophical concept, the only one capable of ousting the verb 'to be.'"[15] This means that an event is actually much more than that happening, that occurrence, or that locatable entity, and instead serves as a caesura: a pause or an instant that can never be present. An event is a cut, through which "the before and the after spring forth at the same time."[16]

To speak of CRIPSiE's performance as a Deleuzian event, then, is to speak of it as a set of multiple relations that occur through our familiar systems of language and meaning, as well as those virtual systems of "emotional investment considered in abstraction from the bodies that carry them."[17] The bodily configurations run through (and occur because of) the familiar structures of ability, dance, and movement, at the same time that they create open-ended possibilities for the body in motion. Likewise, the event moves us in unpredictable ways. It does not serve as a purely original occurrence (for example, the birth of a singular disability politics); instead, it is a convergence of multiple, preexisting ideas, bodies, structures, and forces as each of these diffract around and through one another. To watch *New Constellations* is to contract every single other dance performance witnessed in a lifetime. It is to anticipate what the bodies on stage can do – for in fact, normative expectations no longer work as they have in the past. And this is precisely the plurality of the event as it bursts onto the past. It rewrites one's habituated encounter with the National Ballet of Canada's *Nutcracker*, for example, a performance that has left traces of itself in a memoried understanding through years of television specials, conversations, and personal experiments with movement. So to comprehend any event, we must not try to categorize, locate, or idealize, but instead ask, "What are the [material] conditions that make an event possible?"[18]

The Web: Barriers, Connections, and Dis/ability

Cast in shadows, and backed by a brilliant red glow, seven dancers rise from the stage floor. These are thin, svelte dancers bursting with athleticism – "able" bodies? Black ribbons streak across the stage to weave a web of barriers, trapping one of these dancers inside. She struggles, but cannot get free. Gradually infiltrating the web is a fluid hand on wheel, a swaggering limp, a fluttering spasm, and a joy-filled stigmatized face, each navigating the web of barriers in their own, practiced ways. Disabled? One wheeling dancer approaches the first struggling ambulatory dancer, and lowers her head onto her lap. They navigate together, as one. A tall shadow emerges from backstage and beautifully staggers through the web, collapsing it with every non-normative step.

The web falls as the lighting turns purple, then bright blue. Bodies emerge out of silhouettes.

Two dancers excitedly arrive at a human rights conference, deflating as they find it is inaccessible. Defeat turns to rage, which turns to creative spark. The web emerges as a choreographic metaphor of the constant daily barriers that they and others face. In rehearsal, dancers are asked to engage with the black ribbons that make up the web, and demonstrate how they each navigate the distinct barriers in their lives. They are asked to hold the web: exploring how they participate in constructing barriers for others. One dancer, Kasia, flails desperately and beautifully in the centre of the web. She is caught. She is a recent immigrant, fighting to stay in Canada. Able-bodied? Disabled? Lived experiences of structural oppression bend around and through CRIPSiE's politicized dance aesthetic and practice. A distinctly crip politic[19] permeates CRIPSiE's performance, and yet the performance also seems to amplify and bend strands of crip theory to create new cathartic, activist, and artistic ways to engage.

Crip theory, practice, and aesthetics emerge in response to the perpetual forces of normalization and containment exercised on the bodies and communities of disability and queerness.[20] Whereas some movements seek to make disability more acceptable, normal, and seemingly manageable, crip engagements "generate visions of the body and desire and community that are in excess of attempts to contain and manage us,"[21] often through identifying and mocking the compulsive reproduction of able-bodied norms and ideals. Central to academic engagements with crip theory is Robert McRuer's[22] concept of "compulsory able-bodiedness": a concept that reveals able-bodiedness as the default frame of reference, and the performance of able-bodiedness as both an imperative act and an inevitable failure. No body can successfully and consistently perform able-bodiedness, and it is precisely this inevitable failure that makes able-bodiedness, and the ability/disability binary, all the more compulsively enacted.

Dance is a perfect example of institutionalized compulsory able-bodiedness. The archetypal dancer is molded and sculpted with mechanical precision into a body that can perform requisite configurations of strength, flexibility, endurance, and athleticism.[23] This expectation perpetuates the systemic exclusion of dancers with a range of different bodies, capacities, and forms of mobilization.[24] Dance also, however, inevitably excludes the hyper-able dancers it forms and exalts. The process of producing able dancers also produces acute and chronic injuries that lead dancers to fail at performing the flexible able-bodied subjects required for the largely inflexible world of dance performance.[25]

Simply expanding the compulsory able-bodied institution of dance to include some historically excluded (usually hyper-able) dis/abled dancers is not a crip enactment. As McRuer argues, the inclusion of dis/abled subjects in ableist cultural locations can reproduce rather than transform structures that systemically exclude and devalue alterity.[26] The inclusion of readable disabled subjects, that is, those who fail to perform able-bodiedness in explicit and visible ways (e.g., by using mobility tools), can be reassuring to a normative viewer because they can provide a foil against which the more subtle failure of the viewer and other dancers can be effaced. In effect, inclusion can reproduce and reify the abled/disabled binary. Such a reading also demonstrates the epistemological force of able-bodiedness; the way we understand movement according to a supposed origin or standard (and look for its reflection) rather than recognizing that the lens through which we comprehend (the diffraction grating) is itself the normalizing practice. What is crip about *New Constellations* is that it does not simply include dis/ability through adapted and derivative dance techniques and aesthetics. Rather, it crips dis/ability and dance in ways that potentially destabilize, deterritorialize, and denaturalize both areas. In essence, dis/ability, dance, and crip theory are shifted and amplified through the performance, or at the very least, through the event of these authors attending (to) the performance.

One example of this deterritorialization of dis/ability is in the destabilization of binaries through certain seemingly able-bodied dancers "coming out crip" – not declaring an essential disabled self, but rather "coming out to a political and cultural *movement*" where dis/ability is explicitly and collectively reshaped.[27] The first few minutes of *New Constellations* read, to an unaware audience, as a typical performance by nondisabled dancers. This assumption is undermined when some of the seemingly able-bodied movers find themselves caught, along with their more obviously non-normative counterparts, within the web of disabling barriers. As dancers struggle and mutually support each other through a range of non-normative relationships, the line between disabled and able-bodied dancers becomes increasingly hard to delineate. This choreographic move undermines the dis/abled binary and makes visible the failures that undergird politically dangerous compulsions to pass as able-bodied. In so doing, *New Constellations* renders visible the diffraction grating, the disabling social conditions, and the unique and creative strategies that structure the lives of many dancers whose non-normative ways of learning, thinking, remembering, feeling, or bending to standardized temporal expectations are constantly targeted, yet not readily readable on stage. In showing ambulatory dancers coming out crip, and in demonstrating how more obviously non-normative dancers strategize their navigation of the web and support their peers, the dance hints at what various scholars identify as the crip possibilities of failing or refusing to pass.[28] Shildrick and Price, for example, argue that crip theory and practice "can shift the problematic to a more productive phase that embraces, rather than denies, the inherent instabilities and vulnerabilities of the embodied self that disability can so readily exemplify ... [it can] mobilise a productive positivity that overcomes normative binaries, breaks with stable identity, and celebrates the 'erotics of connection.'"[29] In other words, crip theory and practice, in all its wonderful and difficult failure, excess, and messiness, can destabilize (though never entirely get rid of) the compulsion to perform able-bodiedness. In so doing, it can open up possibilities for new ways to act, identify, connect, and dance. As itself a diffraction grating – an alternate framing of movement – the web demonstrates that dancing failure and dancing dis/ability otherwise can open up whole new constellations of possibility.

This productive positivity is epitomized in *New Constellations*'s cripping of dance performance. Rather than selecting, disciplining, and eventually breaking down only the most flexible able-bodies within inflexible dance choreography and technique, CRIPSiE's technique and aesthetics focus on flexible and porous choreography that bends around dancers' shifting capacities. For example, ubiquitous unison choreography in dance is an inflexible construct that not only bends bodies to uniformly fit its pre-specified shapes, vectors, and timings, but also highlights and devalues those bodies that even minutely fail its compulsory performance by either accident or derivative adaptation. By contrast, *New Constellations* includes collective movements derived through translation. The communal feel of unison choreography is achieved by dancers translating a particular gesture (e.g., a circular motion to the left; joy) into movements and timings that work with their capacities and desires at that moment. This translation is the rupturing force of the piece: its excessive and expansive, rather than derivative and inclusive, engagement with aesthetics, practices, and bodies of dance and dis/ability. It is productive, and explores new possibilities for political, embodied, and aesthetic movement(s). In this way, *New Constellations* is not merely a crip application or exemplar, but rather an amplification of crip aesthetics, politics, and dance. It is a lived, and perhaps even living, crip engagement. It is an event.

The Lift: Interdependence, Generosity, Care-Sharing

A dancer slides out of her wheelchair onto the floor, and rolls herself under the web with stunning ease and fluidity. She meets two other ambulatory dancers on the floor, both of whom have also differentially navigated the web. The three dancers intertwine, melting into and rolling over each other. Each body supports and encourages the others' movement. The two ambulatory dancers rise to their feet, one of them clasping hands with the dancer still on the floor: together they pull toward the empty wheelchair. All three dancers reach high in the air, then the two standing dancers sweep their arms and bend to embrace: one ambulatory dancer supporting the second; the second dancer bending to embrace the third dancer, still on the floor. They revel in a slow rocking hug. In a move of great mutual strength, the second dancer stands, supported by the first. The third dancer pulls her weight up off the floor through her embrace of the second dancer. Once upright, the second dancer opens her arms, demonstrating the third dancer's great strength and agency. The three move together, as one, toward the wheelchair and bend until the third dancer is in her chair. She lets go.

In rehearsal, Sarah slid from her chair to move beautifully across the floor, inviting others to explore this rolling and sliding movement with her. She asked if another dancer could give her a bear hug to help lift her into her chair. Kaylee volunteered. Including this lift in the choreography incited criticism from some of the dancers, who were worried that it could appear to the audience as though Sarah was passively disabled and Kaylee was an independent able-bodied helper. This response led to two choreographic changes: first, Angela joined the human sculpture – helping the helper and showing that none of us lives without support; and second,

Kaylee was asked to open her arms mid-lift, showing Sarah's choice, trust, and strength in the lift.

Both the performance of and the context surrounding this lift illustrate Alexis Shotwell's claim that "subjectivity, shaped by gender, race, ability and more ... is always a coproduction."[30] This coproduction can be deepened by the concept of transcorporeality, which Stacy Alaimo describes as a new imagining of human corporeality, one where, rather than thinking of the human body as a distinct, autonomous entity, we realize that the human is "always intermeshed with the more-than-human world," and always "inseparable from 'the environment.'"[31] At the same time, Shotwell's work on interdependency reminds us that in many cases, the comment that things are embedded or transcorporeal does not always get us to really think about ability or movement. Transcorporeality invites us to reread coproduced subjectivity as it extends beyond the human subject. We extend it to the co-creative configurations of limbs, mobility tools, vectors, timings, stage floors, politics, and mobility strategies that compose different embodiments.

To think about the workings of interdependency and coproduced subjectivity through dis/ability, we are all the more faced with the impossibility of the autonomous subject, and this is an impossibility not to be framed in the narrative of humanist vulnerability, but rather as a precarity that makes palpable the ways in which all bodies take part in rich and varied systems of care, prosthesis, technology, and ability. In fact, as *New Constellations* unfolds, the lines we are used to drawing around "a body" shift. We watch the becoming-movement of a human body who sometimes uses a chair alongside a bipedal body and somehow the notion of the body *in* a wheelchair, of flesh plus machine/metal/technology, does not quite capture what is happening on that stage, in the event that we see before us, or in the performers' daily lives.

This sense of a body amplifies crip critiques of independence: perhaps one of the greatest discourses, technologies, and myths of compulsory able-bodiedness. Rather than celebrating the hyper-ability of a dancer who can independently return to their chair (or remain independent through remaining in their chair), *New Constellations* echoes and amplifies Shildrick and Price's sense of crip corporeality. Rather than trying to make disabled people read as "coherent and autonomous subject[s]," crip embodiments can help us to imagine all bodies as "flows of energy that bring together part objects – both living material and machinic – to create surprising new assemblages."[32] The lift does not make a body do for itself or do as it should, but rather explores new possibilities and multiplicities around what a body can do.

The Assemblage Machines

The blue light showers down on dancers as they gather themselves into four moving sculptures, the coming together of limbs, tools, and vectors making complex and creative embodiments. Each in turn, these new machinic assemblages glide across the stage with a speed, intensity, and quality drawn from, and forever shifting, their component parts. The sense of connection and creative possibility is palpable.

Each machine was entirely generated from the dancers, tools, and ideas that chose to group together during rehearsal. The choreographer helped only to orchestrate the timing and direction of the moving machine-statues in the final piece: the broader assemblage connecting each smaller machine. But each machine emerged out of the creativity, capacities, and connections of its constituent parts. Each machine's capacities were the amplified outcome of shared weight, flesh, thoughts, and time.

New Constellations works on us because it is not a repetition of the same; it is an enactment of difference. The machines bring the differentiations of movement to bear on the audience – co-participants in this event – in a manner that remakes past understandings of movement, and opens on a future where one's anticipatory regimes have been deterritorialized. When we witness *New Constellations* we encounter the metal arms of a wheelchair and the wooden planks of a dance floor, as well as the skin, bone, and sinew of a human body. We also catch our breath in the long ring of a piano note, and the carefully directed shaft of stage light. Each of these *makes* the event, but they alone do not create it. The intimate, interactive, and intensive sites of contact between these contributors burst forth from the instant. We are moved because a trio of arms pushes up as the music swells; because dancers and tools join together to form a new bodily configuration; because the material entanglements blur the lines around what it means to be a body. These qualities invite us to rethink ability through forces and movements that are clearly already engaged in multiple sites of possibility.

To really take in the dance encounter we might want to begin from the shaft of blue light that silhouettes the dancers: how does it bring a particular image of movement into view (and concurrently obscure another)? How does its glow temper the emotive impact of the performance? Or we may take heed of the space-time relations that contribute to our unique understandings of dis/ability: what architectures enable and disable movement of the body? What echoes of ability linger in the wooden planks of that stage? What memories of dance, art, and movement act on this moment?

Fittingly, a new constellation implies a reframing, rearranging, and reimagining of configurations and languages that have always been there, not unlike the work of feminist materialisms that reveal patterns of thought and patterns of life that are already there/here/becoming. Such patterns are often obscured due to the preeminence of other, more dominant constellations or apparatuses of thought, namely compulsory able-bodiedness and compulsory heterosexuality. Hence, the CRIPSiE community blurs the line between body and machine, able and disabled precisely through its refusal to *think*, *move*, and *act* within expected frames. But the event emerges out of more than mere refusal. Like the lift described above, the machinic assemblages of *New Constellations* reimagine transcorporeality. Like the web, it crips dis/ability binaries and the aesthetics of dance. As the performance closes, the audience, dancers, and choreographer are less able to distinguish between disabled and able than we were only seven minutes earlier. We have felt the artifice of what we had imagined real, and felt a material realness of possibilities we had previously failed to imagine.

Ripples and Tears

The dancers rush toward the front of the stage. For the first time in the piece, each dancer repeats a similar sequence of movements that they translate to fit their unique movement range, quality, timing, and speed. The dancers draw together in the centre of the stage. The group supports and exalts in each other's movements before collectively and raucously pumping their fists in joy and celebration. The group migrates to the right in a large sweeping circle made up of fourteen separate, wildly varying circular movements. The energy of the group swells in a swarm of flickering limbs, which is then grounded by each dancer painting their own bodies and the bodies of the other dancers. The warmth and connection between dancers is palpable. They then turn toward the audience, not only to project this warmth, but also to acknowledge and implicate those watching. We are pulled into the assemblage.

The dance brings a scholar to tears, and as she retells the event, she moves the choreographer to the same. Another is taken in by the shared intensity of the dance and retelling experience. We amplify one another, the three/two/one of us an entangled writing apparatus. The exchange electrifies the air; ideas transform themselves and their speakers, imaginations/constellations are enabled and disabled. These are the diffractions of understanding.

People cry when they watch CRIPSiE *dance. They tell us we are inspiring. I fear that these tears translate as pity: that their expressions of inspiration stem from believing that some of us are broken, tragically lacking, triumphantly overcoming, while others of our group are selflessly including, and benevolently helping. But sometimes when I am on stage, I stare directly back into the audience, and a dark faceless expanse of projected energy rushes at me. I am warmed by this pulse. I beam. This feels like community.*

What if tears are not that tidy? What if they cannot be traced to a single story? What if their tears – our tears – like our movements and our lives, are pulled from somewhere disjointed, expansive, messy, connected, and diffracted? What if the tears are but the beginnings of yet another pebble: a new constellation emerging?

NOTES

1 Barad, *Meeting the Universe Halfway*, 81.
2 Haraway, "The Promises of Monsters."
3 Barad, *Meeting the Universe Halfway*.
4 Ibid., 30.
5 See Rosi Braidotti, *Metamorphoses*; Coole and Frost, *New Materialisms*; and Grosz, *Time Travels*.
6 Haraway, as quoted in Barad, *Meeting the Universe Halfway*, 71.
7 For example, the discovery of DNA was accomplished through an analysis of the diffraction grating in order to understand the structure of the substance in question. Barad, *Meeting the Universe Halfway*, 84.
8 Ibid., 93.

9   CRIPSiE (Collaborative Radically Integrated Performers Society in Edmonton; http://www.cripsie.ca) was, at the time of this dance, performing under the name iDANCE Edmonton Integrated Dance.

10 Benjamin, *Making an Entrance.*

11 A video recording of the dance is available at http://www.cripsie.ca/integrated-dance.

12 McRuer, *Crip Theory*; Tremain, "On the Government of Disability."

13 Barad, *Meeting the Universe Halfway*, 151.

14 Alaimo, *Bodily Natures*, 2.

15 Deleuze, *Negotiations*, 141.

16 Zourabichvilli, *Deleuze*, 40.

17 Williams, *Gilles Deleuze's Logic of Sense*, 1.

18 Deleuze, *The Fold*, 86.

19 McRuer, *Crip Theory.*

20 Peers, Brittain, and McRuer, "Crip Excess, Art and Politics."

21 Ibid., 149.

22 McRuer, *Crip Theory.*

23 Cooper Albright, *Choreographing Difference.*

24 Ibid.; Cooper Albright, "A Detailed Analysis of DanceAbility's Contribution to Mixed-Abilities Dance"; Smith, "Shifting Apollo's Frame."

25 McRuer, *Crip Theory.*

26 Ibid.

27 Ibid., 88.

28 McRuer, *Crip Theory*; Peers, Brittain, and McRuer, "Crip Excess"; Shildrick and Price, "Deleuzian Connections and Queer Corporealities: Shrinking Global Disability."

29 Shildrick and Price, "Deleuzian Connections," section 3.

30 Shotwell, "Open Normativities."

31 Alaimo, *Bodily Natures*, 2.

32 Shildrick and Price, "Deleuzian Connections," section 20.

7

Philosophy Comes to Life

Elaborating an Idea of Feminist Philosophy

FLORENTIEN VERHAGE

As soon as one considers a system abstractly and theoretically, one puts oneself, in effect, on the plane of the universal ... That is why reading ... is so comforting. I remember having experienced a great feeling of calm on reading Hegel in the impersonal framework of the Bibliothèque Nationale in August 1940. But once I got into the street again, into my life, out of the system, beneath the real sky, the system was no longer of any use to me ... and again I wanted to live in the midst of living [human beings ... which] proposes no evasion.

— *Simone de Beauvoir*[1]

Elaborate an idea of philosophy ... It is not above life, overhanging. It is beneath.

— *Maurice Merleau-Ponty*[2]

We need to give up the notion that there is a "correct" way to write theory.

— *Gloria Anzaldúa*[3]

Simone de Beauvoir urges philosophers not to remain in the detached safety of libraries abstractly considering a system of thought, but to keep *coming to life* in order to let it mingle and mess with our daily routines and our personal narratives, and in order to recognize how our lives intrude into philosophy.[4] In this essay I discuss what it means to say that "philosophy comes to life." Maurice Merleau-Ponty suggests that philosophy can no longer be "above life" and that "it cannot be a total and active grasp, intellectual possession."[5] Instead, philosophy is beneath life: it is no longer separate from nonphilosophy (that which is, for example, "only poetry, sociology, personal memoir, or politics"[6]) and thus it becomes *a-philosophy*.[7] Over the course of this essay I further explain how a philosophy that comes to life moves away from "proper" philosophy and consequently is out of place and potentially disruptive. I elaborate this especially in the context of doing feminist philosophy.

As feminist philosophers who come to life, we stumble not just over small or large details of a theory, but over and upon one another's *lives*. As an example of such an enlivened feminist philosophy that is out of place, in this essay I refer to the rich and productive work done by "feminist visionary spiritual activist poet-philosopher fiction writer"[8] Gloria Anzaldúa in order to trouble "philosophy proper." I argue that an enlivened philosophy might indeed not be philosophy done properly: "We need to give up the notion that there is a 'correct' way to write theory ... [and] formulate 'marginal' theories that are partially outside and partially inside the western frame of reference (if that is possible), theories that overlap many 'worlds.' We are articulating new positions in these 'in-between,' Borderland worlds of ethnic communities and academies, feminist and job worlds."[9] Taking my lead from Anzaldúa, to further understand philosophy as the complicated intertwining of lives and theory I discuss a philosophy of the in-between, or a marginal philosophy. Anzaldúa's marginal philosophy helps understand a philosophy that comes to life as one that is continually painfully and joyfully "in collusion, in coalition, in collision"[10] with the different worlds it inhabits and the lives lived within them. Philosophy that comes to life, I conclude, is no longer proper philosophy but is instead the right way to do, think, enact, and live philosophy.

Moving Away from Philosophy Proper

If, as I say, philosophy is in need of being reconceived, what then is this philosophy from which we need to move away? In a most broad sense one could say that someone doing proper philosophy claims to operate in the universal domain of "a transhistorical, neutral, and apolitical truth"[11] that is removed from its specific embodiment and its historical location and becomes, as Merleau-Ponty writes, a "total and active grasp,"[12] a "pure look," a "ray of knowing ... [that] arises from nowhere."[13] He critiques such totalizing position taking and elaborates a new idea of philosophy in which philosophy is no longer divorced from life but closely situated in it. For example, in *In Praise of Philosophy*, Merleau-Ponty argues that philosophy is fragile because it is not autonomous from the concrete circumstances that underlie it,[14] and thus "philosophy limps. It dwells in history and in life."[15] As much as he might desire it, the philosopher cannot soar at a great height overlooking the complexities of life and constructing a systematic order out of its chaos. Instead, Merleau-Ponty writes, the fragility of an interhuman history and the particularity of life's concrete circumstances keep pulling the philosopher down from an inhuman summit of neutral universality. This means that the philosopher limps and stumbles because he both tries to pull himself away from particularity in order to take a position at a distance and is continually relocated from that position to find himself closely tied to his own situation. But, Merleau-Ponty continues, it is precisely because of this limping that we should praise philosophy, because "the limping of philosophy is its virtue."[16] He elaborates: "At the conclusion of a reflection which at first isolates him, the philosopher, in order to experience more fully the ties of truth which bind him to the world and history, finds neither the depth of himself nor absolute knowledge, but a renewed image of the world and of himself placed within it among others."[17] Through his phenomenological reconception of philosophical experience, Merleau-Ponty shows that a so-called proper philosophy is always already in a productive and limping tension with what could be called a philosophy "propre." By using the French term *propre*, I refer to Merleau-Ponty's own use of this term in *"le corps propre* [my *own* body],"[18] by which he describes a body that is lived as a particular subject in the world. A philosophy propre, as opposed to a proper philosophy, can thus also be described as a particularly lived philosophy, or a philosophy that comes to life in a particular historical and social world.

Carefully interpreting Merleau-Ponty's revision of philosophy into a-philosophy, Mauro Carbone suggests that a-philosophy is a philosophy that has arrived at its own limits[19] and "scoffs at [proper] philosophy."[20]

Carbone uses the notion of *conceptus* to further explain what such a-philosophy is. He writes that "concavity, or hollowness, is ... a crucial feature of the basic meaning of *conceptus*," which really means "to be pregnant ... receiving something into one's spirit."[21] Along Merleau-Pontian lines, Carbone interprets conceptus as evoking a "gesture of 'welcoming' rather than [a] gesture of 'grasping.' Rather than the attitude of 'subjecting,' it evokes the attitude of 'complying with.' According to the meaning of *conceptus*, 'to conceive does not mean to take possession of anything, but rather to create space for something.'"[22] A-philosophy does not grasp but instead conceives its subject matter and brings it to life, which means that it willingly and compliantly receives its object of study in openness and that it creates space for it as if one were a pregnant woman who does not grasp that which takes place inside her, but still welcomes it. Consequently, when philosophy is reconceived as a-philosophy, it is characterized by a letting go of the desire to be positioned at the abstract and universal centre of absolute knowledge. A-philosophy as conceived by Carbone is presented as yet another way to describe a philosophy propre in which the fecundity of ideas stands continually in relation to life.

These all too brief comments on Merleau-Ponty's elaboration of a new idea of philosophy and Carbone's interpretation of it set the stage for a discussion of the meaning of such living and welcoming philosophy, especially when considered in the context of doing feminist philosophy. In the following section, I explore this feminist welcoming in more depth. I argue that (1) by virtue of its inclusion of topics and subjects that might first have been considered nonphilosophical, feminist philosophy is already a-philosophical; however, I worry that (2) the notion of philosophical conception as complying, creating space, and welcoming it is not yet enough to elaborate a new idea of philosophy because (3) in order to truly let philosophy come to life we need to put more emphasis on how the philosopher is being pulled away into the margins and into the complexities and particularities of the lives that are lived there, and (4) Carbone's interpretation of Merleau-Ponty does not sufficiently capture the difficulties of such welcoming and responding. Instead, I stress that the feminist reconception of philosophy is not just about complying with and welcoming that which first was cast out; it also requires this philosophy itself to be cast out into the margins. Anzaldúa's notion of developing new *teorías* will prove helpful when elaborating this final point.

Welcoming the Cast-offs and Casts-outs of Philosophy/
Walking Together with Others

I look up from my work and notice a poster in my office featuring a design of two red comfortable shoes. The poster urges its readers to engage with life by participating in a community activists' walk. It reads: "WALK. Live a simple life. Support community enterprise. Reject exploitative lifestyles. Respect our neighbors & our earth. Laugh. Sing. Dance. Drink tea. Be gentle." As much as I like and support its message, I discover that this poster has begun to unsettle me because of its niceness and evasiveness: its being so very gentle, comfortable, calm, and safely welcoming. In addition it presents the act of walking as a metaphor of the simple life. But not everybody can simply and without complications join a walk. For example curb-cuts, barricades, and stairs might get in the way of those of us who rely on wheelchairs or canes from participating in the seemingly smooth movement of a protest march; or a protest march might be misrepresented as a riot when black and brown people walk together. Consequently the poster does not sufficiently take into account the real life difficulties we face when we try to give shape to a collective theory, a collective voice, or a collective movement.

One can invert the earlier question ("what is philosophy properly understood?") and ask: "What is *cast out* from philosophical propriety in order to sustain and secure the borders of philosophy"?[23] Judith Butler asks this question in the context of discussing the materiality of bodies. I use this question more loosely to discuss two related rejections that take place when proper philosophy expels philosophical impropriety from its theorizing: (1) women are cast out from being proper philosophers, and (2) they may "philosophize" only about those ideas that proper philosophy has cast-off itself. Michèle Le Doeuff writes: "We are the little sisters who get the broken toys, the worn-out ideas, and the signs that are being discarded."[24] For example, when a discussion of intuition loses its philosophical appeal, women are free to own it and write about it, but by taking up what has been discarded women philosophers show why they are rightly cast out from the place of proper philosophy.[25] In response, feminist philosophy aims to welcome back into the philosophical borders both the cast-offs and the cast-outs of philosophy. The aim is twofold: (1) to place at its centre women, gender, the material body, life, race, social discourse, intuition, affect, and many other philosophical ideas that proper philosophy considered nonphilosophical and thus expelled, and (2) to welcome women back into philosophical propriety and give them access to the whole of the philosophical field.

By expressing a welcoming gesture, the feminist philosopher is already a kind of a-philosopher, receiving and conceiving in her "womb" that which was earlier not welcome. Notwithstanding this focus on inclusivity in feminist philosophy and the ties the feminist philosopher has with life, I argue that in order to genuinely become a-philosophical it is not enough to welcome into (or near) the centre those who have been cast out if those who open up their ranks to let them in do not truly respond to the newly included and previously cast-off theories and theorists.[26] The welcoming in which a feminist a-philosophy engages should not merely consist of widening the philosophical boundaries to create space for something new; it should perturb the previous centre of proper philosophy and question the very division into what is proper philosophy and what is not. Furthermore, what is at issue here is the well-known fact that even though feminist philosophers have claimed to speak for *all* women, of *all* races, *all* classes, and *all* abilities, the voice at the centre of feminist philosophy has predominantly been a middle or upper-class, able-bodied, white woman's voice. Analouise Keating argues that by creating a "pseudo-universal category 'woman,'"[27] feminist philosophers do not truly comply with and respond to their nonwhite marginalized sisters but instead hold them in a totalizing and possessive grasp by, for example, repeating what was done to them: throwing them their cast-off ideas without really letting go of their own control over the "purity" and authority of the field. Thus the same (white) feminist philosophy that aspires to "intervene, thwart, interrupt, and expose" is also complicit in and responsible for some of the injuries done.[28]

Again I am distracted because Anzaldúa's words ring in my ears. She writes: "The world is not a safe place ... We shiver in separate cells in enclosed cities, shoulders hunched, barely keeping the panic below the surface of the skin, daily drinking shock along with our morning coffee."[29] Thinking about the poster in my office calling me to "Laugh. Sing. Dance. Drink tea. Be gentle," I realize that drinking tea or coffee together with other women will not be enough to undo oppression as long as some of us are forced to drink shock alongside it. Anzaldúa insists: "No, I will not make everything nice. There is shit among us we need to sift through. Who knows, there may be some fertilizer in it."[30] *A philosophy that comes to life should step away from making nice and making pure and engage in the demanding work of disentangling fecund arguments from injurious ones. Anzaldúa urges the feminist philosopher to continue this difficult work of putting "history through a sieve" so as to "rupture with all oppressive traditions of all cultures and religions"*[31] *and to work at this "in collusion, in coalition, in collision."*[32]

In order to really come to understand the radical challenge that a philosophy coming to life poses for us, it is important to understand such philosophy not only as a conceptual *welcoming*, but also as a true dynamic *coming* to life of philosophy, i.e., involving movement. Elaborating an idea of (feminist) philosophy thus means that it is conceived of as a transformative and responsive philosophy, as a philosophy that shifts, and as a philosophy that is out of place, and thus we need to listen better to Anzaldúa because "*necessitamos teorías* that will rewrite history using race, class, gender and ethnicity as categories of analysis, *theories that cross borders, that blur boundaries* – new kinds of theories with new theorizing methods."[33] In what follows, I use Keating's notion of *re(con)ception* and Kavitha Koshy's elaboration of it in order to shed light on a kind of theory making that does more than merely and compliantly welcome the cast out. In particular, I wish to hold Carbone's notion of *conceptus* in contrast with Keating's notion of re(con)ception in order to elaborate an idea of philosophy that is a continual dynamic, difficult, and risky movement away from the former centre of philosophical propriety.

Both Keating and Carbone emphasize that there is a link between conception (as birth and as theorizing) and reception (as welcoming), but, more so than Carbone, Keating emphasizes the role of radically re-conceiving ourselves in the process of such theorizing and welcoming. I worry that Carbone's particular account of a-philosophy suffers from a naïve understanding of pregnancy and from taking away agency from the a-philosopher herself. When a-philosophy is mostly about pregnantly complying with and giving space to something or someone else, what is forgotten is that not every pregnancy is welcome or received unambiguously. Instead most pregnancies, even welcome ones, involve struggle and joy, exhaustion and energy, anticipation and resistance. Merleau-Ponty's own elaboration of an actively limping philosophy does not shy away from such tensions and includes the important discord of someone who is trying to clearly grasp and understand life, while also being pulled away into the complexity of particular situations and a particular history. By interpreting *conceptus* mainly through *compliance*, Carbone's account reads as too passive, too nice, and too uncomplicated.

In contrast, in her excellent discussion of a transformational identity politics, Keating analyzes Anzaldúa's work and speaks about the continual complication of trying to re(con)ceive the Other.[34] This re(con)ception, she stresses, involves a "painful rebirth" of both self and other.[35] The crux of her argument about re(con)ception revolves around Anzaldúa's claim that we need to "leave the permanent boundaries of a fixed self ... and see ... through the eyes of the other."[36] When we see ourselves through the eyes of the other, Keating elaborates that "we recognize the others in ourselves and ourselves in the others. We, too, enter threshold spaces where transcultural identifications ... can occur."[37] This account fits well with a Merleau-Pontian account of intersubjectivity, in which one always finds that the self and the other cross-over into each other and are found in one another (*Ineinander*).[38] Nevertheless, we need to be careful about how we use this notion of "seeing through the eyes of the other" and "finding the other in ourselves." While the problem of other minds is not as effusive as traditional philosophy of mind has made it,[39] we would be naïve to think that we could simply pretend to take the other's place, imagine seeing ourselves through her eyes, and change ourselves accordingly. The final sentence of Keating's quote helps us understand the more complicated position that she and Anzaldúa take: in order to be able to see through the eyes of others, we need to enter the threshold space between ourselves and others. Thus, the challenge is not to pretend to become her but instead it is to find a way to enter the space that is in-between me and her, which is that space where we extend into one another and overlap (to speak with Merleau-Ponty[40]), or that borderland where our worlds grate against each other (to speak with Anzaldúa[41]). Koshy explains further: re(con)ceiving oneself through the eyes of the other means that one goes through the difficult work of learning to make visible one's own and other "multiple realities and simultaneous, contradictory standpoints that ... contradict simplistic notions of difference" and fixed identities.[42] I am always already an ambiguous subject who is fragmented but often presents herself unified, who is complicit in the very social hierarchies that she opposes, who is not fully transparent to herself, and who is always already in a colluded, colliding, co-allied relation with others.[43] Meeting in the borderland means that we need to begin to be aware of such fragmentation, complication, and inconsistency of selves and the relationships between selves. Thus, what is crucial for letting philosophy come to life is to attend to philosophy's and our own *limping*. This means that we should both be aware of our colluded aspirations to remain at the centre of our theorizing, our worlds, and ourselves, and also feel the pull away from the centre into the complexities, ambiguities, and collisions of a life shared with others. Thus: "We need *teorías* that will enable us to interpret what happens in the world, that will explain how and why we relate to certain people in specific ways, that will reflect what *goes on between* the personal 'I's and the collective 'we' of our ethnic communities."[44] How in practice such a move to the in-between is accomplished differs by particular circumstance. There is no clear guideline for border crossing, no recipes for freedom and liberation; "one can merely propose methods."[45] Fortunately, a wide range of work by diverse theorists helps us gain insight into some potentially helpful practices and methods for entering in-between spaces. To name some examples: (1) Anzaldúa, in her wonderful and very personal essays "Now Let Us Shift ... The Path of Conocimiento ... Inner Work, Public Acts" and "Bridge, Drawbridge, Sandbar, or Island," explores several of the difficult paths, stages, and tactics that lead her to finding a home in the in-between borderlands where change and community is possible and where former outcasts can come to voice.[46] (2) María Lugones and Elizabeth Spelman address the dominant white feminist's voice and tell her: "You need to learn to become unintrusive, unimportant, patient to the point of tears, while at the same time open to learning any possible lessons. You will also have to come to terms with the sense of alienation, of not belonging, of having your world thoroughly disrupted, having it criticized and scrutinized from the point of view of those who have been harmed by it, [and] having important concepts central to it dismissed."[47] (3) Jessica Cadwallader importantly speaks about the need of all of us to be open to letting sedimented practices be stirred into unease and discomfort and she highlights the importance of experiencing the anxiety (she calls this dis-com-fitting) of feeling that one's own easy, habitual, and so-called normal being in the world is disrupted.[48] (4) Finally, Alia Al-Saji helpfully writes about the importance of developing a hesitating vision that interrupts racializing habits of perception.[49] These thinkers are a few examples of feminist philosophers engaging in the difficult work of reconceiving philosophy by letting it come to life (through shifting its focus, welcoming others and choosing at times to withdraw from them, learning to be patient and letting oneself be disrupted by new visions, dealing with discomfort, and hesitating and interrupting harmful habits). They also illustrate that the movement into the borderlands is not accomplished but is an ongoing and complicated process – and an often-painful one, because it requires a difficult move into a place where borders between selves and others are simultaneously blurred and also vividly felt.[50] When philosophy comes to life it attends to such coalition, collusion, and collision, and works in many different ways to interrupt the evasive and privileged effortlessness of convention, complicity, and complacency.

And it occurs to me that underneath my poster's friendly invitation lies a much more difficult task. The call to laugh, sing, dance, and drink tea together, is not easy because "alliance stirs up intimacy issues, issues of trust, relapse of trust, intensely emotional issues."[51] To genuinely reject exploitative lifestyles and respect one's neighbours and the earth is not something that happens through a simple and kind welcoming gesture because it takes us out of the calm of an open and compliant space and into the difficulty and ambiguity of real life, "beneath a real sky ... in the midst of living [human beings ... which] proposes."[52] And I wonder, how can I, a white, able, middle class, European woman and immigrant, learn to mobilize together with another and be co-allied with her without evading such difficult issues of intimacy and ambiguity?

I am particularly interested in Anzaldúa's characterization of coalition work as taking place not only through a necessary communication with others, not only through reading and writing effective feminist philosophy, not only through participating in important work such as consciousness raising and reflective (self-)analysis, but also through *ritual*: "What is needed is a symbolic behavior performance made concrete by involving body and emotions with political theories and strategies, rituals ... group activities that promote a quickening, thickening between us."[53] And, I wonder, might it be the case that developing such new performative rituals would be one of the new theorizing methods that a philosophy that comes to life should begin to embrace? Should philosophy include nonphilosophy to the extent that philosophy includes performance or performance can be philosophy?

Ritual as performance is a deliberate shaping and repetition of actions and words. The repetition of a new ritual helps sediment it in our bodies, in our thoughts, and in our practices as a new way to live and to see. As such, it indeed might be a way to interrupt and replace the hurtful sedimentations and unthinking practices of the habit body. This does not mean that ritual uncritically always works to undo oppression; many deliberately and unintentionally repeated rituals are precisely in the service of an oppressive society.[54] Ritual is thus not a flawless response to oppression, but this is also not what Anzaldúa claims. Instead, she suggests that rituals should be sorted, such that injurious rituals are cast out, productive rituals are kept, and, most importantly, new productive rituals are conceived.

In the context of this essay, I focus in particular on the ritual of coming together in a collective protest (such as in the call for a communal walk that has kept interrupting my writing). Hasana Sharp emphasizes the importance of collective gatherings of activism. While such moments might not immediately and completely undo one's own inhabited rituals of oppression and complicity, the coming together in a particular (ritualized structure of) protest can forge "connections pregnant with unknown futures" that can produce "the basis of new forms of shared power," and, in Foucault's words, that can engage subjects in "'an art of not being governed quite so much' in their everyday lives."[55] In such protests one might, for example, reenact a ritual of communally reciting a speaker's words (Occupy), or take to the street banging pots and pans (Casseroles), or partake in a traditional round dance (Idle No More), or silently lie on the ground in a die-in (Black Lives Matter); in short, walk, talk, sing, laugh, or be silent together.

These examples of a coming together that releases the bonds of inhabited oppressions are particularly interesting because they are not primarily characterized by difficulty, collision, guilt, or evasion, but instead by a particular kind of *joy*. Sharp speaks about the joyful connections that are forged in such gatherings, i.e., about moments where one is better able to witness the intersubjective overlap between subjects, where there is no strong feeling of separation between subjects, but instead, I add, where one truly lives in the interhuman space (the borderland) that this particular protest has enabled. These connections "pregnant with unknown futures"[56] speak about the potential that situations and lives might shift, that futures might be open and are not yet determined or prefigured, and thus that a genuine freedom for all is possible.[57]

The joy that accompanies such moments of communal border dwelling need not be uncomplicated, shallow, or evasive, and it need not refer to the immobility of the complicit happiness of someone who is condemned to a comfortable stagnation (e.g., the housewife who claims she is happier than the worker).[58] Indeed, such joy need not be opposed to collision, guilt, and pain. Joy can be something different than the happiness that is immobility. Beauvoir writes: "In order for the idea of liberation to have *concrete* meaning, the *joy of existence* must be asserted in each one, at every instant; the movement toward freedom assumes its *real, flesh and blood figure* in the world by thickening into pleasure, into [existential joy]."[59] Here Beauvoir connects her demand for living in the real world among the multitude of concrete, particular human beings[60] and the demand that the idea of liberation be given concrete meaning to what she calls the thickened *joy of existence*. This joy, I suggest, is more than a fleeting and thin layer of pretense and it is also more than a fixed unmovable happiness of convention. Instead I would liken such joy to the thickness of blood that connects us to others, blood that gives life but whose flow can also be a sign of pain or woundedness, blood that rhythmically sustains us and also slowly drips, flows, and changes. With this reference to joy as blood, I want to say: (1) Joy is not always uncomplicated happiness; instead, joy can be felt in having a complicated and difficult conversation with another. (2) Joy is not always about feeling in comfortable control; instead, it can accompany a feeling of unease and discomfort.[61] For example, when such unease and discomfort signals the possibility of an open future through requiring productive playfulness and creativity in an encounter.[62] (3) Joy is not always a feeling of calm; instead, it can be exhilarating, invigorating, and potentially terrifying. Such can be the feeling, for example, of joyfully facing one's own open future. Thus, Beauvoir urges us to step with unease and joy into the messy and ambiguous possibilities of a life shared with multiple particular others. It is this complex notion of joy that is helpful for understanding the joy of existence that Beauvoir mentions is the result of living toward a concrete philosophy of life (and liberation).

Beauvoir, in the epigraph of this essay, urges us to get into the street again; the poster on my wall urges me to go for a walk together with others. This twofold advice reminds me of Lugones's thought-provoking suggestion to become a "streetwalker theorist" and hang out with others without mythifying "territorial enclosures and purities of peoples, languages, and traditions,"[63] which means that she urges us to find ourselves at "street-level, among embodied subjects, with ill-defined 'edges' ... without epistemological/political shortsightedness."[64] Most importantly, Lugones connects such streetwalking to becoming illegitimate: "The streetwalker theorist walks in illegitimate refusal to legitimate oppressive arrangements and logics."[65] Thus, to walk the street in a concrete coalition with others means to walk illegitimately. I suggest that this is the kind of collective walking that should be practiced by a philosophy that comes to life because this is a mobilization of the subject who precisely shifts out of place, moves incorrectly, uneasily, improperly, dis-com-fittedly, and disruptively, is engaged in a movement that limps, and is its virtue.[66]

But while the enlivened and complicated joy of such collective mobilization should be seen as a way toward coming closer together, experiencing this joy should not (at least not yet) be understood as the end of the struggle. Oppression, dominance, privilege, and complicity are not once and for all wiped out in a community gathering (not even in the marvelous coherent chaos of a casserole or the beauty of a round dance), but at least its participants might be given a temporary reprieve of having to swallow shock along with it, and at least we might catch a glimpse of the possibilities that lie ahead.

Conclusion: It's Not Philosophy, or Is It?

Traditional philosophy's main pillars of truth, essence, clarity, reason, totality, centrality, unity, etc., are reconceived and left behind when we begin to formulate marginal theories, or when philosophy proper is moved out of place to become philosophy *propre* or a philosophy that comes to life. A philosophy that comes to life is out of place in several senses: (1) It does not find its primary home in the quiet of impersonal libraries, but comes to life in the reality of this earthly life in the midst of living human beings. (2) It cannot be fixed in universal claims of truth, but instead it limps, walks, and shifts in response to the concrete situations it addresses. (3) It does not solely attend to reason and reflection, but instead is often no longer able to separate these reflections from affects of joy and pain. (4) It does not take a privileged place in theorizing because it needs other (social) sciences, humanities, poetry, social movements, walks, dances, and gatherings in order to be able to develop new *teorías*. (5) It does not speak with one voice, or one language, but is multilingual, and sometimes one might need to do extra work or practice an extraordinary patience in order to accommodate, receive, respond, and listen to the variety of voices speaking.

But then "it's not philosophy," is it?[67] So much is true: it is a philosophy that has precisely moved away from a traditional philosophical propriety and correctness and moved into the messy relationship between real flesh-and-blood human beings. And thus: "The conceptual explorations of Anzaldúa and other women of color [might] represent a new kind of philosophy, reunited to experience in the world."[68]

And then again, it is philosophy all over again, isn't it? By taking the borderlands as a better place from which to see and to theorize, are we not simply finding another foundation in which to ground our theories? So much is also true: it is indeed a philosophy that aims to find better places from which to see, listen, theorize, and speak. While as philosophers that come to life, we might no longer be positioning ourselves in the so-called universal gaze, we are still finding appropriate places, histories, and relationships in which to ground our shifting *teorías*. These philosophies that come to life are precisely not groundless, but instead seek out their foundation in, around, and beneath life.

Indeed, Merleau-Ponty was right to call a philosophy that is not situated above life a philosophy that *limps* between philosophy proper and non-philosophy. As I have suggested, Anzaldúa, Keating, and Beauvoir more concretely present such limping philosophy as philosophies that come to life by crossing borders between worlds, communities, and disciplines, by taking place between academy and activism, between joy and discomfort, between struggling for liberation and finding space for oneself, between stumbling over the lives of others and joining them in solidarity.

So, let's go for a walk, shall we? Or better, let's shift out of place.

NOTES

1 Beauvoir, *The Ethics of Ambiguity*, 159.
2 Merleau-Ponty, *The Visible and the Invisible*, 266.
3 Anzaldúa, *The Gloria Anzaldúa Reader*, 137.
4 Beauvoir, *The Ethics of Ambiguity*, 158–9.
5 Merleau-Ponty, *Visible and Invisible*, 266.
6 Nye, "It's Not Philosophy," 108.

7 Merleau-Ponty, "Philosophy and Non-philosophy since Hegel," 9. Also in Carbone, *The Thinking of the Sensible*, 14–15.

8 Anzaldúa, *Reader*, 3.

9 Ibid., 137.

10 Ibid., 144.

11 Sharp, "Is It Simple to Be a Feminist in Philosophy?," 20.

12 Merleau-Ponty, *Visible and Invisible*, 266.

13 Ibid., 113.

14 Merleau-Ponty, *In Praise of Philosophy and Other Essays*, 48.

15 Ibid., 58.

16 Ibid., 61.

17 Ibid., 63.

18 Merleau-Ponty, *Phenomenology of Perception*, 149.

19 Carbone, *Thinking of the Sensible*, 27.

20 Merleau-Ponty, "Philosophy and Non-philosophy," 9.

21 Carbone, *Thinking of the Sensible*, 47.

22 Ibid.

23 Butler, *Bodies That Matter*, 6 (italics added).

24 "However, the gift is snatched back when what appeared to be an ordinary stone is revealed as a diamond in the rough or something that could pass for one." Le Doeuff, *The Sex of Knowing*, 17.

25 See Le Doeuff on "How Intuition Came to Women," *Sex of Knowing*, 3–10.

26 For example, hooks, in "Eating the Other," worries about those white subjects who engage with the "exotic" in order to add spice to their lives, but who are not themselves open to being significantly changed by this encounter.

27 Keating, *Women Reading Women Writing*, 60.

28 Sharp, "Is It Simple to Be a Feminist?," 20

29 Gloria Anzaldúa, *Borderlands / La Frontera*, 42.

30 Anzaldúa, *Reader*, 115.

31 Anzaldúa, *Borderlands*, 104.

32 Anzaldúa, *Reader*, 144.

33 Anzaldúa, *Reader*, 136; Keating, *Women Reading*, 11.

34 Keating, *Women Reading*, 75.

35 Ibid., 76.

36 Anzaldúa, *Reader*, 115; Keating, *Women Reading*, 62.

37 Keating, *Women Reading*, 92.

38 "One always talks about the problem of 'the other,' of 'intersubjectivity,' etc. ... in fact what has to be understood is, beyond the 'persons' ... It is between them ... as their common level. It is the *Urgemeinshaftung* of our intentional

life, the *Ineinander* [in-one-another] of the others in us and of us in them."
Merleau-Ponty, *Visible and Invisible*, 180.

39 Merleau-Ponty, *Phenomenology*, 367–9.

40 Merleau-Ponty writes that we "slip into each other." *Phenomenology*, 369.

41 A "1,950 mile-long open wound / dividing a pueblo, a culture, / running down the length of my body, / staking fence rods in my flesh, / splits me splits me." Anzaldúa, *Borderlands*, 24.

42 Koshy, "Nepantlera-Activism in the Transnational Momenta," 151.

43 The borderlands and the multiple worlds we live in differ depending on our own particular situations. It requires that I adopt a double consciousness, that is, that I acknowledge the "historic legacy of white identity construction" and colonialism while simultaneously remembering and anticipating the "building of an inclusive human community." Alcoff, *Visible Identities*, 223.

44 Anzaldúa, "Haciendo caras, una entrada," xxv; Keating, *Women Reading*, 11 (italics added).

45 Beauvoir, *Ethics*, 134.

46 Anzaldúa, *Reader*, 140–56; Anzaldúa, "Now Let Us Shift … The Path of Conocimiento … Inner Work Public Acts."

47 Lugones and Spelman, "Have We Got a Theory for You!," 580.

48 Cadwallader, "Stirring up the Sediment."

49 Al-Saji, "When Thinking Hesitates."

50 "Staking fence rods in my flesh, / splits me splits me." Anzaldúa, *Borderlands*, 24.

51 Anzaldúa, *Reader*, 146.

52 Beauvoir, *Ethics*, 159.

53 Anzaldúa, *Reader*, 154.

54 For example, patriarchal structures are reinforced in explicitly reenacted wedding ceremony rituals, such as the giving away of the bride.

55 Sharp, *Spinoza and the Politics of Renaturalization*, 14.

56 Ibid. Note that here again the notion of pregnancy is invoked, but this time this pregnancy is described as facing an unknown (open) future and thus it is not an uncomplicated, compliant, and passive pregnancy.

57 For more on this account of liberation, see Beauvoir's *Ethics of Ambiguity*.

58 Beauvoir, *The Second Sex*, 16.

59 Beauvoir, *Ethics*, 135.

60 Ibid., 17.

61 For example as a white ally in the Black Lives Matter movement.

62 The disability activist Taylor writes: "Part of my favorite thing is being completely confused about how to greet someone. Not knowing how to give that

physical contact or how to even say hi ... and I think that those experiences are just so important, almost as a reminder of all the walls we have built." Butler and Taylor, "Interdependence," 194.

63 Lugones, *Pilgrimages/Peregrinajes*, 220.

64 Ibid., 209.

65 Ibid., 221.

66 To engage in such illegitimate walking, one also needs to be aware of the needs that each one of us might have to successfully move her or his body through space. Taylor and Butler take up the notion of movement through space in relation to our spatial dependence and social interdependence. Taylor says, "well ... I always tell people I am going for walks – I use that word even though I can't physically walk," and Butler responds, "nobody goes for a walk without something that supports that walk ... and maybe we have a false idea that the able-bodied person is somehow radically self-sufficient ... and that means we get to rethink what a walk is in terms of all the things that power our movement, all the conditions that support our mobility ... what does the environment have to be like in order to support your mobility?" Butler and Taylor, "Interdependence," 186, 187–8.

67 Nye, "Not Philosophy," 107.

68 Ibid., 112–13.

8

Surviving Time

Kierkegaard, Beauvoir, and Existential Life

ADA S. JAARSMA

Fickle adulterers, numbers make love with the generations
who move through them.
— *S. Lochlann Jain*[1]

The seductive appeal of numbers, as S. Lochlann Jain describes so compellingly in the above epigraph, is a phenomenon that was predicted in the mid-nineteenth century by Søren Kierkegaard. This portrayal of numbers as somehow animate and lively, making love to whole groups of individuals, emerges out of Jain's ethnographic research into cancer culture. The numbers that Jain refers to here are the statistical prognoses physicians hand out to individuals: the percentage chance of living to or beyond a moment in time with a particular form of cancer. Although this statistic is imminently personal (it is *my* life and, more specifically, my death that this number hails), it is also impersonal, based on the aggregate of many different individuals, grouped together by statisticians, and converted into the power of scientific data.

These numbers work through a kind of erotic fickleness, Jain writes, because of the subjective hold that they proffer, tantalizing the individual with promises about a knowable future but undercutting any real solidarity between persons with cancer. Statistics like prognoses, after all, measure one person's hopes for vitality over and against everyone else's similar chances in the same statistical aggregate. A prognosis speaks to the prowess of medical research, hiding from view the environmental conditions that, while responsible for vast numbers of cancer deaths, are not considered to be within the purview of cancer research.[2] This unwillingness of oncology researchers to conduct studies on the causal conditions of cancer is no neutral fact. An exclusive focus on survival rates impairs the ability of patients to cultivate skepticism toward the mechanisms of medical science, but it also undercuts solidarity among patients – solidarity sorely needed as a way to organize political action against ongoing environmental devastation and the inequitable distribution of toxicity.

The erotic fickleness of statistics is only one aspect, however, of an almost ubiquitous cultural sickness, to use one of Kierkegaard's terms for existential ailments. Kierkegaard calls this cultural sickness "levelling," describing a certain draining out of passion through abstractions like statistical aggregates.[3] Levelling *externalizes* existence, eliminating the otherness of singularity into the shared blandness of averages. In this way, our shared world becomes "a negatively leveled world, a common world that is no one's," as Alastair Hannay puts it,[4] a world in which "nothing has essential meaning" because "everything has so little meaning."[5]

While Kierkegaard's diagnosis focuses on the dangers of levelling in his own rapidly modernizing Danish society, its account of life captures pressing dilemmas of contemporary existence as well. Levelling deserves to be called seductive because of its subjective appeal to the self. On Kierkegaard's terms, though, it also deserves to be called self-deceptive, and this is an especially challenging point since it begs the question of how individuals might even acknowledge the subjective appeal of numbers or other abstractions when these cultural forces actually intensify an individual's fidelity to the governing logics of the age.[6]

In this essay, I bring Kierkegaard's existential insights to bear upon our own context, particularly in terms of pressing feminist questions about the subjective lure of numbers, progress narratives, and ideological scripts about time. As Kierkegaard and his pseudonyms insist across a wide range of texts, anxiety is a constitutive dynamic of selfhood. Put most simply, I can act this way or this way, and this very *possibility* of choice means that

I exist in anxiety. Possibility refers to the capacity to make a choice, to choose something in the face of nothing. However, as the lure of statistical numbers demonstrates, individuals confront anxiety as embodied selves in their own particular "age." And so reflections on the existential challenges of life need to consider the seductions or illusions of a given age. While not facing anxiety simply intensifies its force, succumbing to anxiety *in the wrong way* is also enervating, and endangers the life of impassioned selfhood. I am interested, in this essay, in drawing out the feminist implications of this Kierkegaardian critique of the right and the wrong way to engage anxiety.

As Simone de Beauvoir wrote in the mid-twentieth century, every individual is – always and unavoidably – caught up in the dramas of embodiment. Beauvoir's feminist existentialism invites us to recognize and live out what she calls the ambiguity of existence: "Let us try to assume our fundamental ambiguity. It is in the knowledge of the genuine conditions of our life that we must draw our strength to live and our reason for acting."[7] While the ambiguity of existence refers to the unavoidable fact that I am both body and embodied body – I am subject/object to myself and to others – it also refers to the meaning of existence itself: "To say that [existence] is ambiguous is to assert that its meaning is never fixed, that it must be constantly won."[8] The meaning of existence is never fixed, but must be constantly won, because of the tension between lived experience and the body. As Emily Anne Parker explains: "Lived experience is necessarily fraught. No record of lived experience is possible without a body, and yet no record of lived experience is capable of a finished account of oneself as a body, because this body is both lived and for-others."[9]

Beauvoir's insistence that we recognize the ambiguity of existence, not in the abstract but in our lived experiences, gives a retrospective explanation for Kierkegaard's insistence that an individual must express passion in the terms of that individual's present age.[10] Rather than taking up the drama of embodiment, in which the meaning of existence is always at stake, individuals who succumb to levelling disavow the ambiguity of existence. Conversely, though, individuals who embrace ambiguity are able not only to deepen the passion of their own existence but also to expand the freedoms available to others.

The feminist ramifications of Kierkegaard's account of levelling have rarely been discussed by scholars, despite its importance for explaining and confronting the embodied dynamics of bad faith. Kierkegaard's contribution here has to do with his claim that meaning-making is *qualitatively* particular.[11] One can make meaning in ways that are shallow, impoverished, and all too reflective of the prevailing ideals of one's community. One can also make meaning in ways that involve risky and self-disorienting choices. Ideology can have differing degrees of impassioned force, in other words. This point is under-emphasized within critical theory, but, as one of Kierkegaard's core insights, it has enormous value for thinking about resistance. While passion is the resource by which we take up our freedom, according to both Kierkegaard and Beauvoir, the very qualities that animate passionate existence are impoverished by the social and cultural phenomena of levelling.[12]

Invoking the ambiguity of an impassioned life, Beauvoir asks how we might exist in relation to a "living and finite future."[13] This invocation of a future that is both living and finite seems to highlight what is most at stake in the quandaries that arise from levelling. The future might become alive and finite, but the "future" might also convert into the abstracting terms of levelling, foreclosing such becoming. Beauvoir's emphasis on the future seems to sync exactly with Kierkegaard's critique of the present age. As we place hope in ambiguity, we also need to attend critically to the *proxies* of freedom or choice proffered by abstractions like statistical aggregates.

In order to affirm the edifying dimensions of time, while also undermining the deceptive version of temporality that saturate existence in late capitalism, I focus on the twofold critique that we find in Kierkegaard and Beauvoir. In the first section below, I identify the ideological predicaments of levelling, and in the second I elaborate the hope of existential resistance. In the conclusion, I reflect on the feminist ramifications of this twofold critique.

Levelling and the Evasion of Anxiety

Beauvoir names one of the quandaries that preoccupies existential philosophy when she points out, "but one can choose not to will himself free."[14] This recognition that one *can* choose not to will freedom is a claim about ontological freedom, but it opens up complicated questions about why and how, exactly, individuals bind themselves in unfreedom. Beauvoir asks: "If man has one and only one way to save his existence, how can he choose not to choose it in all cases? How is a bad willing possible?"[15]

How is a bad willing possible? This question, a sincere one for Beauvoir as well as for Kierkegaard, issues a challenge to feminist philosophy because it signals the ineffectiveness of methods that deny the possibility of "bad willing."[16] By admitting there is something called bad willing, or the self-deception of bad faith, Beauvoir and Kierkegaard before her imply that any consideration of freedom must involve ideology critique.[17] As Beauvoir asks in *The Second Sex*: Whence this complicity of women (and men) with bad faith?[18] How is it that individuals themselves uphold the very ideological scripts that undermine their own and others' freedom? As Bonnie Mann puts it: "If one's very consciousness is formed in the fire of one's value-laden prejudices, one can't, by an act of conscious determination, put them out of play."[19]

Kierkegaard provides a robust answer to these questions in his account of levelling. Bad willing, on these terms, manifests the "spiritlessness" of levelling, summed up by Kierkegaard's pseudonym Haufniensis as the evasion of anxiety.[20] Since anxiety is constitutive of selfhood, such evasions are doomed to fail, but the very resources of emancipation – spirit, passion, ambiguity – are essentially threatened in the process of levelling. This is a first existential predicament of levelling: the impoverishment of passion. A second predicament is that levelling leads to self-deception because it is impressively persuasive.[21] It is difficult to dislodge bad willing because ideology is essentially convincing to the self who has internalized its scripts. Common sense is impoverished by bad faith.

Cancer culture, as Jain's recent ethnography demonstrates, is one site in which we can think through these impoverishing effects of levelling. As Kierkegaard predicts and Jain documents, numbers in particular act as existential proxies in the present age. Jain's descriptions of cancer research point to this contradiction at the heart of levelling: "Actual individuals do not matter to the population-based basic science."[22] Individuals in the present age preoccupy themselves with "counting and counting,"[23] Kierkegaard explains, resulting in aggregates that alienate them. Levelling collapses the very meaning of "individual" into calculations of quantity: "Today the coinage standard has been changed so that about so and so many human beings *uniformly* make one individual; thus it is merely a matter of getting the proper number – and then one has significance."[24] Numbers mitigate anxiety because they stand as simulations of choice, while at the same time reinforcing the seeming legitimacy of statistics and opinion polls.[25]

Numbers act as proxies for particular bodies. As Jain explains, medical research protocols require bodies to be essentially equatable so that differences can be averaged out, aggregated, and cancelled. The resultant *non-referential* character of statistics, as Jain puts it,[26] contrasts with the fleshly referential and temporal nature of embodied lives. The existential confusion lies here, at this intersection of embodied life and abstracting universals.[27] We must, and yet cannot, exist in relation to statistical aggregates that specify the terms of our individual hopes for survival.[28] Statistics, including prognoses about the course of diagnoses, proffer a seemingly concrete trajectory within which to imagine one's self, securing certainty against uncertain risk. Moreover, survival, pitched as a battle against the odds rather than a battle against other people, positions an individual in relation to statistical aggregates, "as if one's own survivorship were somehow contingent, itself, on the statistics and those who are contained within them."[29] Statistical prognoses are both "stunningly specific" – here is the precise percentage that marks the likelihood that you will be alive in five years – and "bloodlessly vague."[30] Upon being diagnosed, I receive a number, which marks my own path toward the time-boundary between life and death; this number, though, arises out of the statistical analysis of many nameless deaths, counted for their mathematical relevance rather than for their singular and embodied lives.

Bodies and lives are of course not exchangeable, even though the statistical aggregate depends upon abstracting away differences in order to produce legible numbers. Many gruesome deaths are presupposed by the notion of "survival." I might survive cancer, for example, likely through painful treatments, but only by outliving vulnerable collectivities whose early deaths are sanctioned but not mourned in the name of profitable medical research. As Jain puts it, survival prognoses (e.g., I have 70 per cent chance of living) "require deaths to predict lives."[31] "Bodies lent to science suffer," Jain explains, "and in many cases greatly, from cancer treatments, both standard and experimental."[32]

Because numbers stand in as proxies for particular embodied lives, such suffering goes unrecognized, in practice but also in principle, as standard research methods do not involve attending to the fleshy specifics of individuals. While research trials presuppose and depend upon the deaths of many people, commercial culture insists on celebrating the progress of science through tropes like the pink ribbon for breast cancer.[33] Progress narratives that justify and make invisible the suffering that characterizes cancer culture powerfully block awareness of the fact that there has been very little progress in survival rates. Jain points out that, despite the ubiquity of pink ribbons, there has been a mere 6 per cent increase in those rates since 1975.[34]

The deceptive lures of levelling affect our ability to see through these kinds of ideological misrepresentations. Statistics, in the context of capitalist research production and commercialized medical practice, render violence by abstraction, as Jain puts it,[35] and also by exclusion. While the timeline of progress hides from view the countless embodied injuries that cancer treatment causes, it also hides the vast numbers of individuals who are disallowed access to insurance and treatment all together. Angela Mitropolous describes insurance, for example, as "the dream of inoculation,"[36] a dream dependent upon exclusionary mechanisms. Those individuals with access to such inoculations require the uninsurable to bear the burden of testing out the vaccines: "The actuarial requires uninsurable risk as its precondition."[37] What gets reinforced, in turn, is a naturalized timeline for those who are included in the progress story. After all, prognoses like that of cancer are legible only against a horizon in which disease is a tragic exception to the "natural" life course that is promised to healthy citizens.

The danger of levelling, according to Kierkegaard, is that while it undermines our capacity for risky choices, through *proxies* of risk, we delude ourselves into bad faith. Evasion is the mechanism by which individuals bind themselves in self-deception, and levelling works through the equivocation, evasion, and refusal of risk.[38] This might take the form of evading action in favour of inertia,[39] evading individuality in favour of abstraction,[40] or evading decisions by placing bets on those who actually do will something.[41]

The violence caused by levelling, described vividly in Jain's ethnography of cancer culture, demonstrate that the evasions proffered by proxies like statistics have profoundly ethical implications. Bad faith is ideological, as Beauvoir's analysis in *The Second Sex* makes evident, because it corrupts the self's relation to others; bad willing compromises the very sense of solidarity by which we cultivate responsibility for each other in the world. According to both Kierkegaard and Beauvoir, then, impassioned risk-taking offers not only the best resource for undermining levelling, but also secures a route toward ethical living. Beauvoir explains, for example, that impassioned risk-taking by definition works for the freedom of others: "The precept will be to treat the other ... as a freedom so that his end may be freedom; in using this conducting-wire one will have to incur the risk, in each case, of inventing an original solution."[42] In contrast to levelling, which involves evasion, Beauvoir declares, "existentialism proposes no evasion. On the contrary, its ethics is experienced in the truth of life."[43] Similarly, Kierkegaard explains, "fundamentally, essential passion is its own guarantee that there is something sacred."[44]

By pointing to ambiguity and passion as resources for resistance, Beauvoir and Kierkegaard are both tasked with the challenge of conceptualizing how individuals in bad faith might awaken from the lures of levelling. Kierkegaard warns, for example, that an individual who lacks "essential enthusiasm in his passion" will never discover the very disjunctions of choice that enable meaning to emerge in life.[45] Next, I look at the methodological propositions for such awakening advanced by Beauvoir and Kierkegaard, thinking in particular about the extent to which these two projects ultimately do align with each other.[46] By reading Kierkegaard through Beauvoir, the embodied nature of passion becomes more apparent and therefore also Kierkegaard's relevance to feminist thought. As I explore below, by reading Beauvoir through Kierkegaard, in turn, we find an emphasis on the singularity of selfhood that proffers a methodological challenge to feminist commitments.

Anxiety and the Intensification of Life

At first glance, the methods put forward by Beauvoir and Kierkegaard for overcoming bad faith might seem at odds. Throughout his writings and especially in his essay on the present age, Kierkegaard emphasizes that individuals are lost, or liberated, only ever by themselves and that therefore sociality cannot save us: "Every individual either is lost or, disciplined by the abstraction, finds himself religiously."[47] The forces of levelling can be halted "only if the individual, in individual separateness, gains the intrepidity of religiousness."[48] We can only help each other indirectly, on these terms.[49] The risk of doing otherwise, Kierkegaard warns, is that the medicine becomes incomparably worse than the sickness.[50]

In contrast, Beauvoir's discussions of ambiguity emphasize the existential importance of sociality. As Stacy Keltner points out, "the ambiguity diagnosed by Beauvoir has implications for how the social bond is to be thematized."[51] Keltner goes on to explain that "the initial formulation of ethical sociality is not that I *must* will the freedom of others for my own freedom, but that to will my own freedom *is* simultaneously to will the freedom of others."[52] On Beauvoir's account, the constitutive freedom of individuals is integrally tied up with the freedom of others, which is why *assuming* ambiguity is itself an ethical action. Instead of accepting this seeming contradiction between Kierkegaard's solitary self and Beauvoir's social self, though, I want to propose that Kierkegaard's insights into anxiety help us understand why singularity is a key concept for existential critique. In turn, I argue that Beauvoir's emphasis on the shared nature of ambiguity foregrounds the critical import of singularity.

By indicting the evasion of anxiety as the central mechanism of levelling, Kierkegaard affirms encounters with anxiety that prompt the "right way" to learn.[53] The age of levelling *can* be actually "genuinely educative,"[54] he explains, but only through the workings of anxiety. A confrontation with anxiety awakens the self to the impassioned riskiness of freedom because anxiety pulls the self toward a future marked by uncertainty. "What is anxiety? It is the next day,"[55] he writes, explaining, "anxiety always contains a reflection on time."[56]

Of course, reflections on time also saturate the scripts of bad faith, as demonstrated by the logic of prognosis time that we find in cancer culture. By pointing to "educative" anxiety, Kierkegaard refers to a more originary force of temporality that actually undoes the hold of such levelling. He names this originary force "the instant." Whereas levelling wards off anxiety, Kierkegaard's pseudonymous author Haufniensis asserts that "anxiety is the instant."[57] Anxiety is interruptive, disorienting, and terrifying. Through anxiety, the instant discloses nonbeing or the abyss of freedom. Rather than signifying a synthesizing present, the instant is "what originally allows the present at all," as David J. Kangas explains.[58] The instant both enables self-consciousness and precedes it; it is nothing and nowhere, reflecting "no-time-lapse."[59]

On Kierkegaard's account, then, projected time (the timelines by which we set up the categories of present, past, and future) is essentially different from originary time (the flux of temporality that makes possible but always exceeds our representative efforts). Our consciousness of time will never coincide with time, despite our representative efforts, because we cannot locate the beginning *while we stand in it*.[60] While we might procure temporal timelines through representations about "past" and "future," he explains, we hold nonsynthesizing relations to temporality. Kierkegaard looks to the leap of faith, ultimately, as the essentially risky disruption of determinant timelines. The leap of faith means opening oneself to uncertainty and indeterminacy. As another pseudonym, Johannes de Silentio, explains, "the outcome cannot help a person either in the instant of action or with respect to responsibility"[61] because the leap of faith marks the anarchic nature of beginning.[62] As this account of the instant demonstrates, there is a formal nature to the riskiness of passion. Through the instant, anxiety is a constitutive aspect of selfhood, evaded only at the peril of impassioned subjectivity.

Beauvoir agrees with Kierkegaard that such passion needs to be made to appear and cannot simply be assumed as given.[63] One's loves and desires and goals become certain through one's own drive,[64] Beauvoir writes, because "the result is not external to the good will which fulfills itself in aiming at it."[65] The crucial point, however, is that what Beauvoir calls *attachment* and what Kierkegaard calls *passion* are qualitatively distinctive. One can be more or less attached; one can become a self through lesser or more degrees of passion. This is why Kierkegaard, across his writings, addresses the reader as the "single individual." Each person must find themselves, in and through embodied dramas that take place through their own life-view: "Every life-view knows the way out and is cognizable by the way out that it knows."[66] Describing these life-views as aesthetic, ethical, and religious, Kierkegaard lays out a typology of the qualitatively different dimensions of selfhood.

The passion of risky choice cannot be generalized because passion takes the form of different degrees of vitality. This insight animates Kierkegaard's critical analysis of levelling. One individual's confrontation with the *either/or* might awaken an impassioned discomfort with the limits of consumer life, propelling them from an aesthetic to an ethical life. Another individual's *either/or* might disorient the ways in which they sync selfhood with social norms, propelling them from an aesthetic to a religious life.[67]

Especially given the fact that the instant is going to awaken individuals differently, because the qualitative degrees of passion differ from self to self, Kierkegaard is adamant that each individual ultimately faces their freedom alone: "There is nothing to do here but split [the crowd] apart, get the single individual aside, and place him existentially under the ideal. This is my work."[68] This is a useful point for feminist thinkers because it challenges us to parse our methods of critique. Rather than generalizing passion as a resource for resistance, Kierkegaard prompts us to recognize the many different expressions of ideology and bad faith.

In addition, what Beauvoir offers to Kierkegaard's existentialism is an emphasis on the corrective force of ambiguity. One's life is commensurate with one's attachment to existence, Beauvoir explains: "It will justify itself *to the extent that* it genuinely justifies the world."[69] I justify myself through the ideals and values by which I construct myself and live out my freedom. At the same time, I participate in the very production of our shared world, as I live out my ambiguity as subject/object and relate to others in their ambiguity. Self-deception is ultimately doomed, in other words, because it comes up against the workings of ambiguity. All liberation is brought about through the resistance of facticity, Beauvoir explains[70]: this lived embodiment, this body, and this body's relations to these others in this world, this situation, this age. It is the "contingent facticity of existence," she writes, that proffers the resources for emancipating us from bad faith.[71] The ethics of ambiguity is not solipsistic, in principle but also pragmatically, Beauvoir explains,[72] because one's freedom only emerges through relations to the world and to others.

Conclusion

We might ask, based on these reflections, what kind of feminism emerges from this encounter between Kierkegaard and Beauvoir. One answer has to do with the challenge to humanism that emerges from the critique of levelling. Basic ideals of humanism – ideals like choice, freedom, individualism – are all on the hook when we begin to read the symptoms of levelling as self-deceptive. The scripts that govern our present age, scripts that offer simulations of choice and individuality and even freedom, result so easily in the exclusionary logics of capitalist life. There is a real provocation here about the extent to which our own appeals to choice or freedom succumb to the forces of levelling.

Kierkegaard's methods exemplify this kind of self-reflexive attentiveness to one's own degrees of bad faith. Just as individuals live out their dramas through specific life-views, Kierkegaard explains that we can find various life-views at work in literary and philosophical texts. Praising the anonymous author whose novel he is reviewing, for example, Kierkegaard explains: "We gladly pick it [the novel] up to read, knowing in advance that there is the trustworthiness of a life-view; we are not disturbed by the vacillations of a straying star but are under the protection of a guiding star."[73] The guiding star of a reliable text "is an occasion for inwardness," he continues, implying that textual productions can be edifying resources for others. While each reader, on his terms, must be addressed as a "single individual," authors must also aspire to become singular selves.[74]

This point opens up another answer to the question about what kind of feminism results from these existential methods. Kierkegaard's emphasis on the singularity of selfhood, combined with Beauvoir's prediction that ambiguity itself reveals and corrects our expressions of freedom, suggest that the very adjective "feminist" might be understood as an emergent quality. Parker arrives at this insight from her reading of Beauvoir, explaining that feminist subjectivity is always to come, only ever in relation to ambiguity. Parker points out that such feminist emergence "will also require discussion of the ways in which this dialectic preempts the other's other: marked as raced, intersexed, queer or transgendered."[75] In other words, the precise dimensions of ambiguity continue to emerge in and through the work of existential resistance. Beauvoir affirms this intuition in *The Ethics of Ambiguity*, and explains: "The Other is multiple, and on the basis of this new questions arise."[76] Just as Kierkegaard places hope in the emergence of passion, Beauvoir places hope in the emergence of ambiguity.

Beauvoir proposes a limit to an alliance between her existentialist ethics and that of Kierkegaard at the end of *The Ethics of Ambiguity*: "If it came to be that each man did what he must, existence would be saved in each one without there being any need of dreaming of a paradise where all would be reconciled in death."[77] By affirming that existence might be saved without recourse to religiousness, she offers a gentle rejoinder to

Kierkegaard's insistence that ethical life, with its own specific limitations, might leap into religious life. By reading Kierkegaard in light of Beauvoir, though, I wonder if the resonances of passion with ambiguity invite us to see Kierkegaard's leap of faith as an immanent endeavour of the self in the world. Rather than a "dream of paradise," in other words, this leap intensifies the very relations of everyday life, while raising the stakes for all of us about how we live out our freedoms and mobilize for the freedom of others. While it is true that Kierkegaard ultimately points toward a religious account of freedom, the critique that he offers of the present age is a very this-worldly diagnosis of the ideological effects of levelling. Kierkegaard, read in conversation with Beauvoir, enables us to indict bad faith as spiritually enervating, and my own sense is that this kind of indictment intensifies, rather than brackets, our responsibility for the quality of life in the present age.

NOTES

1 Jain, *Malignant*, 34. I presented an early version of this paper at the meetings of *philo*SOPHIA in Banff in May 2013. I thank the reviewer of this paper for compelling and illuminating comments.

2 Jain, "The Mortality Effect." The "relentlessly future-oriented" paradigm of medical research, Jain explains, is almost completely hegemonic. This means that what *doesn't* get to count as oncology – as important or worthwhile cancer research – includes the analysis of early detection, past misdiagnoses, or – perhaps most obviously, and therefore most problematically – the environmental causes of cancer (101). In other words, cancer research – in order to count as cancer research – does not involve attentiveness to the past, retroactive analyses of specific cases, or examination of the material conditions within which cancer diagnoses emerge.

3 Kierkegaard, *Two Ages*. Kierkegaard elaborates his account of levelling in the present age in a book review, written as an affirmation of a novel, *Two Ages*, which he praises as an ethically robust engagement with social life. Kierkegaard's commendation of this novel hinges on his description of the anonymous author's consistent life-view, an attribute that Kierkegaard contrasts with literary perspectives that are "unstable," "a wandering star," wanting to capture "the changeable by means of changeableness" (8). This constitutes one of the complexities of Kierkegaard's essay: as he explores the problem of how one can or cannot be faithful to one's age, by advancing his own reading of

the novel *Two Ages*, he also implicitly enacts his own theories of literary writing. "*The author has been faithful to himself*," he explains, and this faithfulness secures the novel's import as a site of critical reflection (13). While *Two Ages* was published anonymously, its author was the popular novelist Thomasine Christine Gyllembourg-Ehrensvärd.

4 Hannay, "Levelling and *Einebnung*," 174.

5 Kierkegaard, *Two Ages*, 66. Battersby sums up the effects of levelling, as Kierkegaard describes, beautifully: "This 'public' is a kind of non-existent and abstract community that 'alienates' individuals from each other through a process of 'levelling' that treats each human being as simply a number or a unit." "Kierkegaard, the Phantom of the Public and the Sexual Politics of Crowds," 34.

6 Ibid. In his descriptions of levelling, Kierkegaard employs a similar metaphor to Jain's metaphor of adultery: "What is *philandering*? It is the annulled passionate distinction between essentially loving and being essentially debauched. Neither the essential lover nor the essential debauchee is guilty of philandering, which dallies with possibility. Thus philandering is a form of indulgence that dares to touch evil and refrains from actualizing the good" (102–3). Rather than a moralizing judgment about erotic behaviour, this description undermines the symptoms of levelling as actually *amoral*: "It vitiates moral action to the point of abstraction" (103).

7 Beauvoir, *The Ethics of Ambiguity*, 9. Beauvoir continues: "It was by affirming the irreducible character of ambiguity that Kierkegaard opposed himself to Hegel." Her recognition here of the resonances between how she and Kierkegaard affirm ambiguity is the guiding theme of this essay. Sonia Kruks points out that assuming ambiguity in this passage means to "assume a debt" or "assume responsibility" but also means "the taking up as one's own of the 'already-given' aspects of one's existence." *Simone de Beauvoir and the Politics of Ambiguity*, 33. This is a dual meaning that aligns closely with the account of selfhood advanced especially by Kierkegaard's pseudonym Anti-Climacus in *The Sickness unto Death*.

8 Beauvoir, *Ethics of Ambiguity*, 129.

9 Parker, "Singularity in Beauvoir's *The Ethics of Ambiguity*."

10 As Conway points out, this insistence by Kierkegaard might make us wonder if he is inadvertently limiting the very freedom that, across his writings, Kierkegaard wants to affirm for every individual. "Modest Expectations: Kierkegaard's Reflections on the Present Age," 23, 31. One way to understand the competing tensions of possibility and necessity is through the concept of ambiguity. While I advance a reading of Kierkegaard through Beauvoir here, feminist scholars point out Beauvoir's own interest in Kierkegaard's writings

for her exploration of ambiguity. For more on Beauvoir's indebtedness to Kierkegaard, see Heinämaa, *Toward a Phenomenology of Sexual Difference*; Heinämaa, "The Sexed Self and the Mortal Body"; and Green and Green, "Simone de Beauvoir."

11 Carlisle points out that the very movement of becoming, according to Kierkegaard, is marked by differing degrees of passion. "Kierkegaard's *Repetition*," 528. I am struck by the import of this claim for feminist continental philosophy, especially for how we think about and engage with debates about "life," choice, and desire.

12 For an essay that helpfully explores the relations between Kierkegaard's theory of existence-stages, implied in my description of the qualitative differences in meaning, and Kierkegaard's broader critique of the present age, see Wolstenholme, "Kierkegaard's 'Aesthetic' Age and its Political Consequences."

13 Beauvoir, *Ethics of Ambiguity*, 128.

14 Ibid., 25.

15 Ibid., 32.

16 One such denial can be found in liberal accounts of voluntarism, which over-emphasize each individual's autonomy at the expense of accounting for ideology. Beauvoir calls out the Kantian framework, for example, as impeding the recognition of bad willing in this way: "Moreover, in Kantian ethics, which is at the origin of all ethics of autonomy, it is very difficult to account for an evil will." *Ethics of Ambiguity*, 33.

17 In "Kierkegaard, Biopolitics and Critique in the Present Age," I explore the ways in which Kierkegaard's critique of the present age aligns with contemporary feminist critiques of biopolitics. The twofold dynamics of *assujetisee-ment* – the subjection of individuals to surveillance and the subjectification of individuals to ideological prescriptions – suggests that existentialism proffers valuable resources by which to undermine biopolitical forms of injustice and exclusion. As I write there: "A person's very sense of self is caught up in complicity with capitalist dictates while – and this is the pressing problem – they feel free in such expressions of obedience" (851).

18 Beauvoir asks: "Why do women not contest male sovereignty? ... Where does this submission in woman come from?" *Second Sex*, 7.

19 Mann, *Sovereign Masculinity*, 26.

20 Kierkegaard, *The Concept of Anxiety*, 157.

21 Referring to the technological achievements of mass media and the press, for example, Kierkegaard identifies "its inventiveness and technical skill in contriving spellbinding mirages and the rashness of its flares of enthusiasm." *Two Ages*, 69.

22 Jain, "Mortality Effect," 115.

23 Kierkegaard, *Two Ages*, 92.

24 Ibid., 85. Throughout his essay on the present age, Kierkegaard indicts the role of numbers in the force of levelling. Levelling itself, for example, can be understood as the ascendancy of generations over individuals (84): individuals get lost as such in herds, groups, and generations. Along similar lines, Kierkegaard explains that the whole age becomes a committee, another way in which individual action dissipates in favour of the simulation of action through committee meetings (78).

25 In *Søren Kierkegaard's Journals and Papers*, for example, Kierkegaard explains that the abstraction and anonymity of levelling are reinforced by "the tyranny of the daily press, periodicals, brochures, which are written for 'the many,' who understand nothing, and by those who understand how to write – for the many."

26 Jain, "Survival Odds: Mortality in Corporate Time," 49.

27 Existing in relation to statistical prognoses involves essentially irresolvable confusions. Jain points out, for example: "Living in prognosis by definition belies prediction and explanation: you don't 70 per cent die; you live or die." "Survival Odds," 47.

28 Jain explains: "The prognosis offers an abstract universal, moving through time at a level of abstraction that its human subjects cannot occupy, and in so doing it threatens to render us all (for we are all moving through the culture of cancer) inert." "Living in Prognosis," 79.

29 Jain, "Survival Odds," 47.

30 Ibid., 78.

31 Jain, "Mortality Effect," 90.

32 Ibid., 103.

33 For a feminist philosophical analysis of the pink ribbon, see Goldenberg, "Working for the Cure."

34 Jain, "Mortality Effect," 98.

35 Jain, *Malignant*, 34.

36 Mitropolous, "The Time of the Contract," 766.

37 Ibid., 776.

38 Kierkegaard, *Two Ages*, 69, 170. On these terms, Kierkegaard explains, the present age can be summed up as an age of "tergiversation," the Latin term for equivocation, evasion, and refusal.

39 Ibid., 69.

40 Ibid., 84.

41 Ibid., 105. Self-deception is the consistent symptom across these various examples: "Although we deceive ourselves, we know clever ways of avoiding decision" (76).

42 Beauvoir, *Ethics of Ambiguity*, 142.

43 Ibid., 159.

44 Kierkegaard, *Two Ages*, 64. "But existence mocks the wittiness that possesses no assets, even though the populace laughs shrilly" (74). Existence itself, on Kierkegaard's terms, can be a robust resource for critique, but only if its qualities align with how Beauvoir describes ambiguity: the disclosure of the world through subjective attentiveness to one's own becoming, as well as the becoming of others.

45 Kierkegaard, *Two Ages*, 67.

46 See n44 pointing to Beauvoir's own recognition that Kierkegaard's emphases on passion and faith ultimately align with her own emphasis on ambiguity.

47 Kierkegaard, *Two Ages*, 106. Similarly, Kierkegaard writes: "But through the leap out into the depths one learns to help himself, learns to love all others as much as himself" (89).

48 Ibid., 86.

49 Ibid., 109.

50 Ibid., 74.

51 Keltner, "Beauvoir's Idea of Ambiguity," 205.

52 Ibid., 208.

53 Kirkegaard, *Concept of Anxiety*, 155.

54 Kierkegaard, *Two Ages*, 88.

55 Kierkegaard, *Either/Or*, 78.

56 Ibid., 143.

57 Kierkegaard, *Concept of Anxiety*, 81.

58 Kangas, *Kierkegaard's Instant*, 181. "Originary time," Kangas writes, "breaks through to consciousness only in suffering" (116). My analysis here is indebted to Kangas's book on Kierkegaard's "instant," which lays out a deconstructive reading of Kierkegaard's reflections on time.

59 Derrida, *The Gift of Death*.

60 In an 1843 journal entry, Kierkegaard explains: "Philosophy is perfectly right in saying that life must be understood backwards. But then one forgets the other clause – that it must be lived forwards. The more one thinks through this clause, the more one concludes that life in temporality never becomes properly understandable, simply because never at any time does one get perfect repose to take the pose: backwards." In Eriksen, *Kierkegaard's Category of Repetition*, 11. Self-consciousness, as Kangas puts it, "does not know itself in its beginning" because "in the very act of thinking a process as complete, one steps beyond it." *Kierkegaard's Instant*, 75.

61 Kierkegaard, *Fear and Trembling*, 111.

62 In his own readings of Kierkegaard, Derrida reminds us, "a decision always takes place beyond calculation." *Gift of Death*, 95.

63 Beauvoir, *Ethics of Ambiguity*, 155. Beauvoir writes: "In setting up its ends, freedom must put them in parentheses, confront them at each moment with that absolute end which it itself constitutes, and contest, in its own name, the means it uses to win itself" (134).

64 Ibid., 159.

65 Ibid.

66 Kierkegaard, *Two Ages*, 15.

67 Across Kierkegaard's texts, we find this leap at work in the movement from one existence-stage to the other (the aesthete becomes ethical; the ethicist becomes Socratic; the Socratic becomes Christian). This point is somewhat controversial within Kierkegaardian scholarship, since how we characterize the nature of the leap has ramifications for how we conceptualize the relations between the existence-stages. I am partial to Westphal's account of the leap as *formal* in nature, meaning that there are similar dynamics at work for the aesthete, the ethicist, and the Socratic. "Kierkegaard's Teleological Suspension of Religiousness B," 113. This line of interpretation emphasizes the immanence of values and choices to the existence of each individual; there is no outside to which we can appeal in order to destabilize the subjective force of our own set of meanings. There is only the offense, encountered by the self, which cannot be mediated by others. What seems useful about this Kierkegaardian framework is that it enables us to reflect on the qualitatively different nature of impassioned lives.

68 Kierkegaard, *Søren Kierkegaard's Journals and Papers*, 18.

69 Beauvoir, *Ethics of Ambiguity*, 158, italics added.

70 Ibid., 141.

71 Ibid., 156.

72 Ibid.

73 Kierkegaard, *Two Ages*, 16.

74 Kierkegaard, in *Two Ages*, affirms his own role in this way (93). We could see his entire literary production, though, as a sustained exploration of the very endeavour of authors to become single individuals, as Kierkegaard's pseudonyms reflect on each other's life-views and as Kierkegaard, at various points, purports to undo the authority of his different texts.

75 Parker, "Rereading Beauvoir on the Question of Feminist Subjectivity," 127.

76 Beauvoir, *Ethics of Ambiguity*, 144.

77 Ibid., 159.

9

Beauvoir and the Meaning of Life

Literature and Philosophy as Human Engagement in the World

CHRISTINE DAIGLE

> It has gradually become clear to me what every great philosophy
> up till now has consisted of – namely, the confession of its originator,
> and a species of involuntary and unconscious auto-biography.
> — *Nietzsche*[1]

In this essay, I examine Simone de Beauvoir's answer to the question of the meaning of existence. Literature on the *Sinnfrage* overlooks what Beauvoir has to say about the matter, and if she is mentioned at all it is in conjunction with other atheistic existentialist thinkers who claim that life in itself is meaningless; it is up to the human being to render it meaningful. While this general claim may apply to what Beauvoir offers as an answer to the question of meaning, I show that her views are sophisticated and intricate as they intertwine with her views on philosophy and the task of a writer.

In order to demonstrate this, I first expose her treatment of the question of meaning as she elaborates it in *Pyrrhus and Cinéas*.[2] I then discuss Beauvoir's methodological choices; it is important to understand her views on philosophy since they are connected to her answer to the question of the meaning of existence. This in turn relates to the different modes of expression that she favours. From there, I demonstrate that Beauvoir's use of nonsystematic philosophizing alongside literature and autobiographical writings is her way to perform her own moral and political commitments. In the process, I show how these relate to her understanding of the meaning of human existence as transcendence, i.e., the movement of the individual toward one's self-assigned project(s).

Pyrrhus and Cinéas on the Meaning of Life

It is in her first published work on ethics, *Pyrrhus and Cinéas* (1944), that Beauvoir tackles the question of meaning.[3] The book opens with a dialogue between the king Pyrrhus and his adviser Cinéas. Pyrrhus is devising plans for conquests. He declares that he wants to subjugate Greece, to which Cinéas asks: "And after that?" Pyrrhus gives a series of other locations he wishes to conquer as Cinéas keeps asking the same question until finally Pyrrhus answers: "I will rest." Cinéas's following question then serves as the trigger for Beauvoir's investigation in the book. Cinéas asks: "Why not rest right away?"[4] Indeed, why not? The final outcome will be the same regardless: rest.

Cinéas is really asking: What is the meaning of human existence? He is questioning whether and in what way human action is meaningful. The question is pressing in a secular world devoid of a maker with a grand design. Beauvoir champions this existentialist world. In this world, however, it is essential to address the question of meaning, to determine what, if anything, can render human existence and action meaningful. Beauvoir refuses the potential nihilism that is the inherent risk of an atheistic point of view. She puts it very clearly in *The Ethics of Ambiguity*: "The notion of ambiguity must not be confused with that of absurdity. To declare that existence is absurd is to deny that it can ever be given a meaning; to say that it is ambiguous [Beauvoir's claim] is to assert that its meaning is never fixed, that it must be constantly won."[5] The problem for each individual human being is to justify human existence if there is no a priori meaning to it. The leading questions in *Pyrrhus and Cinéas* are a variation on Kant's questions guiding philosophy: "What, then, is the measure of a man? What goals can he set for himself, and what hopes are permitted him?"[6]

Kant's questions were: "What can I know? What ought I do? For what may I hope?" In a sense, Beauvoir's questions are the same. According to the editors of "Pyrrhus and Cinéas," the question "what is the measure of a man?" is a play on Protagoras's claim that man is the measure of all things. As a phenomenologist, Beauvoir would indeed consider the human being to be the measure of all things. As an intentional consciousness, I constitute the world and objects within it; I measure things and myself. Epistemologically, then, to ask what the measure of a man is amounts to asking what one can know. Beauvoir, however, is not so concerned with the epistemological question itself, but with the impact it has for the ethical flourishing of the individual. What matters ethically is for the individual to be able to determine her own measure.

Beauvoir starts by affirming her phenomenological stance. She deems superfluous Candide's advice to cultivate one's own garden: the world is always what I make it. Therefore, I am always cultivating my own garden. The world is not ready-made for us; it is constituted through our projecting and our doing. Beauvoir argues: "Each man decides on the place he occupies in the world, but he must occupy one. He can never withdraw from it."[7] One will take one's place through one's projects. This amounts to justifying one's existence. It is through one's projects that justification of one's existence is secured. Justification is thus "performed" through transcendence. By moving toward a goal that then becomes a new starting point toward another goal, a human life is justified as a project: "A project is exactly what it decides to be. It has the meaning that it gives itself. One cannot define it from the outside. It is not contradictory; it is possible and coherent as soon as it exists, and it exists as soon as a man makes it exist."[8] According to Beauvoir, then, human existence is given meaning by the goals an individual freely sets herself. However, and very importantly, each of our freedoms is tied to that of the Other.

She concludes the first part of the essay with this oft-quoted passage: "A man alone in the world would be paralyzed by the manifest vision of the vanity of all his goals. He would undoubtedly not be able to stand living. But man is not alone in the world."[9] The human being is an embodied consciousness that is a being-in-the-world and this world is populated by others. Thus the human being is always a being-with-others. Indeed, Beauvoir, along with Merleau-Ponty, conceives of consciousness as a fold of being.[10] As such, the Other, objects, and the world permeate it. This is what allows Beauvoir to claim in the opening pages of *The Second Sex*, "the category of *Other* is as original as consciousness itself."[11]

We exist for ourselves but also and always in the presence of others. I perceive the Other and this perception, phenomenologically and following Merleau-Ponty,[12] is both communication and communion. As a fold that perceives objects, consciousness also enfolds these objects, that which it perceives. The objects are thus constitutive of intentional consciousness that constitutes them. The same goes for the Other I meet in the world. My perception of the Other is thus necessarily also a bonding. However, I experience the Other's presence ambiguously since I feel objectification at her hand and put myself at risk while I interact with her. Indeed, "I am the facticity of [her] situation"[13] in virtue of being there in the world, but the same is true of the Other for me. She is the facticity of my situation.

The encounter with the Other generates an uncertain relationship because the Other as free may opt to engage with me as a free being or not. We always run the risk of being objectified and oppressed by the Other. But this uncertain and risky relation can be transformed into a positive collaborative relationship. In fact, this is a fundamental need for each individual. We must seek to have our being as well as the objects we create, the things we value, or the projects we make objectified and valued by the Other in order for anything to have meaning. Beauvoir explains:

> Only the other can create a need for what we give him; every appeal and every demand comes from his freedom. In order for the object that I founded to appear as a good, the other must make it into his own good, and then I would be justified for having created it. The other's freedom alone is capable of necessitating my being. My essential need is therefore to be faced with free men ... Thus it is not for others that each person transcends himself; one writes books and invents machines that were demanded nowhere. It is not for oneself [*soi*] either, because "self" [*soi*] exists only through the very project that throws it into the world. The fact of transcendence precedes all ends and all justification, but as soon as we are thrown into the world, we immediately wish to escape from the contingence and the gratuitousness of pure presence. *We need others in order for our existence to become founded and necessary.*[14]

This passage sums up very clearly Beauvoir's position on the question of the meaning of existence. I am the creator of my own meaning but I do need the validation that only the Other can give. Therefore, the justification of one's existence can only be achieved through the Other. For this to be possible, the Other must be free.

Beauvoir's answer to the question of meaning leads her to an argument for liberation. I need the Other to justify my projects. To do so, the Other must be free or, as Beauvoir puts it, must be made into a neighbour. She says: "I can concretely appeal only to the men who exist for me, and they exist for me only if I have created ties with them or if I have made them into my neighbors."[15] Considering Beauvoir's Catholic upbringing, the choice of the word "neighbor," *prochain* in French, is important. The Other is not just any other human being whom I recognize as a human being, but one for whom I must care. Therefore, I must acknowledge the Other as free, as a project, as a transcendence engaged in her own existential project of giving meaning to her own existence. If the Other is free, my appeal can resonate with her. This is key, since "my essential need is therefore to be faced with free men."[16] This remains a risky business given that "Our being realizes itself only by choosing to be in danger in the world, in danger before the foreign and divided freedoms that take hold of it."[17] However, we have no other choice.

Freedom, as well as the necessity to promote one's freedom and the freedom of Others, forms the ground for ethics. Beauvoir claims: "Our freedoms support each other like the stones in an arch."[18] This statement reiterates that the answer to the question of meaning is human-made and rests on no metaphysical ground. Beauvoir's answer to the question of meaning is that a human being has an ethical duty to make herself through her own committed projects. Only then will existence have meaning. To let oneself merely exist without a firm commitment to one's own flourishing is not acceptable. Further, a commitment to the flourishing of Others is tied to one's own, since one's projects must be validated by the Other. This view underlies Beauvoir's discussions in *The Ethics of Ambiguity* as well as in *The Second Sex*. Indeed, the reason why the latter book needs to be written is that women have historically been denied access to transcendence and have been relegated to the role of the inessential Other, one whose existential project does not matter. Women have thus been put in a position where they cannot have a meaningful human life. Oppression of any kind must be combatted for individuals to flourish through a meaningful life.

Beauvoir's Methodological Choices

Beauvoir's own existential project is to be a committed writer. As such, she appeals to her readers to take on her project of communication – to recognize it and to value it. Writing is not merely an aesthetic endeavour, but also an ethical and political gesture. She conceives of it as a powerful tool to combat the oppression discussed above and to help generate conditions for freedom to flourish. Not just any writing will do, and Beauvoir holds to certain methodological choices to convey her philosophy as well as to enact her own existential project.

There is no denying that Beauvoir was a philosopher, though she herself denied it for a long time.[19] However, as a philosopher she engaged in diverse modes of expression. There are important reasons why she chose not only philosophical and phenomenological essays, but also literary and autobiographical writing, which serve a function that the philosophical essay may fail to carry out.

She first discusses her views on the role of literature in the essay "Literature and Metaphysics." She proposes that novels should convey metaphysical ideas without being didactic. In a metaphysical novel, the philosophical and the literary intertwine and serve to expose various facets of the human experience. It is the best tool one can employ to unveil the human as the multifaceted, situated, historical, embodied being that she is. Beauvoir considers novelistic writing to be an antiuniversalist method that can evoke the upsurge of existence better than any other mode of expression. She summarizes her position:

> A metaphysical novel that is honestly read, and honestly written, provides a disclosure of existence in a way unequalled by any other mode of expression ... insofar as it is successful, it strives to grasp man and human events in relation to the totality of the world, and since it alone can succeed where pure literature and pure philosophy fail, i.e., in evoking in its living unity and its fundamental living ambiguity, this destiny that is ours and that is inscribed both in time and in eternity.[20]

In this passage, Beauvoir evokes the notion of pure philosophy. Pure philosophy is one that is expressed in systematic treatises by system-builders. Beauvoir is a philosopher, but one who does not engage in pure philosophy. In interviews, she repeatedly claims that she was not a philosopher because of the very narrow view she holds of philosophy. She explains: "For me, a philosopher is someone like Spinoza, Hegel, or like Sartre: someone who builds a great system ... someone who truly constructs a philosophy."[21] However, she also defines philosophy elsewhere as a way of life: "There is no divorce between philosophy and life. Every living step is a philosophical choice and the ambition of a philosophy worthy of the name is to be a way of life that brings its justification with itself."[22] Sara Heinämaa sees Beauvoir's philosophy as a questioning rather than a systematic construction of the world.[23] It is because it questions and unveils that Beauvoir's thought needs to be expressed in a variety of modes of expression.

Ulrika Björk offers an interesting analysis of the nonsystematicity of Beauvoir's philosophy. She suggests that it is nonsystematic in a Kierkegaardian sense.[24] As she puts it, the conceptual language of systematic philosophy "is capable of expressing only what is universal in character. It therefore fails to account for human existence in its pregnant sense, that is, as a universal *and* singular reality."[25] This is why Beauvoir is critical of pure philosophy and why she is interested in different modes of philosophizing, similarly to Kierkegaard. Björk adds: "While direct communication 'speaks' its meaning abstractly and by means of conceptual language, indirect communication does not speak. Rather, it 'shows' or makes meaning manifest by the presence of contingent details and the use of different narrative voices."[26] This is the disclosure of existence, the task of metaphysical literature as identified by Beauvoir.

Beauvoir's methods of inquiry are diverse: philosophical essays, interdisciplinary phenomenological inquiries, one play, many novels, and numerous autobiographical writings. Even at her philosophical best, Beauvoir does not offer what she qualifies as pure philosophy, nor does she aim to. Because her philosophy is existential and phenomenological, it avoids the traps that pure philosophy inevitably encounters. It "shows" rather than merely "speaks." In *The Second Sex*, a combination of speaking and showing allows Beauvoir to better communicate with her reader. By refusing to systematize human experience and dwell in the realm of abstract principles and by focusing on the concrete ambiguous experiences of human beings, Beauvoir's works all provide a "disclosure of existence." Furthermore, this disclosure appeals to the reader to act. This is true not only of her literature, but also of her other writings. Beauvoir's philosophy is a philosophy of the appeal.[27] I need the Other to be free so that she may validate my project; therefore, I appeal to the Other. I disclose existence in my writings, enacting the project of disclosure as a writer. Doing so is a political gesture because the appeal aims to disclose the world in which oppression exists. The appeal consists in exposing that world to the reader so the reader can undertake to change the world. When communication happens between writer and reader, an act of liberation can be undertaken. In this way, literature can be committed to and serve as a political function.[28]

However, we must ask ourselves whether there is a clear advantage to literary writing as opposed to more direct forms of speech. Erika Ruonakoski suggests: "The role of literature is to facilitate communication within separation, or, in other words, grant us access to the other's world, to the first-person perspective of the other."[29] Again, literature discloses and unveils, and in so doing bridges the gap between consciousnesses. Ruonakoski adds: "All literary works are essentially a search, which – in opposition to scientific writing – operates on the level of non-knowledge and communicates the meaning of lived experience to the readers."[30] By offering those lived experiences, the work of literature proceeds to its unveiling of existence without being didactic or, even worse, dogmatic. Phenomenology is a type of philosophy that explores lived experience in a way unparalleled by systematic pure philosophy. *The Second Sex*, replete as it is with first-person accounts, certainly serves the same function as literature I describe here.[31]

Nevertheless, it appears that literary writing holds an advantage over other modes of expression. Björk points out that literary works mediate between the "uniqueness of one's singular life and the shared, universal structures of human existence."[32] In this sense, novels and autobiographies, which focus on the singular experience, are "privileged places of intersubjectivity."[33] The advantage of the novel over autobiographical writing is that it can offer a multiplicity of perspectives while the autobiography provides just one. But what, besides its "truth value," is the advantage of autobiographical writing? I believe that in autobiographical writing, the writer can make the case that one's philosophy can be enacted and incorporated into one's own life project. Beauvoir's autobiographical writings are crucial to and constitutive of an application of her overall philosophical stance. For her, memoirs serve to explore the life of single individuals from a subjective point of view. They are a means to test the applicability of a philosophy.

Beauvoir's Autobiographical Writings: Remaking, Rewriting, Rediscovering Oneself[34]

A large portion of Beauvoir's works took the form of autobiographical writing. Beauvoir wrote a total of four volumes of memoirs, *Memoirs of a Dutiful Daughter, The Prime of Life, Force of Circumstance*, and *All Said and Done*. She also wrote a vivid account of Sartre's last years in *Adieux: A Farewell to Sartre*, as well as an account of her mother's struggle with disease and death in *A Very Easy Death*. The problems she tackles in her theoretical writings as well as in her novels and play are all problems that emerge in the course of her life and the lives of those close to her. However, it is really the exploration conducted in the autobiographical writings that serves to illustrate the enactment of her life project.

Writing on Sartre's *Les Mots*, Michel Contat suggests, "Existentialism is an autobiographism."[35] Contat explains: "The autobiographical project co-incides with the existential project which is to give an account of oneself, to give a narrative or dramatic form to one's experience of the world, to give to the other a truth about oneself which can point to that of all."[36] The point is to present one perspective on the world, the disclosure of existence as experienced by one individual. Contat indicates that there is a universal aim to such an exercise. However, and taking into considera-tion what Beauvoir says about autobiographical writing, the point is not to unveil one's experience and claim that this is how each individual experi-ences the world; rather, the point is to share one's experience and offer it as a singular way to deal with the world. That experience is presented as an alternative to the reader's own experience and is an appeal to the reader to acknowledge and validate the existential project presented. The urge to give an account may be universal, but the accounts and experiences them-selves are not. If existentialism is an autobiographism, as Contat suggests, it is such because it posits that the individual is both the subject of per-ception and the subject of action, and because the act of giving an account of oneself, narrating one's experience as such a subject, helps to unveil a "truth" about human beings and our role and place in the world. It unveils the fact that the human being is in charge of disclosing existence and rendering it meaningful. The act of disclosure is a constituting act and, furthermore, the autobiographical account appeals to the reader to validate it as such.

Autobiographies present the author's point of view on reality. They have truth-value since the one who speaks, the author, is the one who has the experiences and recounts them. This is different from a novel wherein author and fictional character are two different persons and, even in cases where the narrator is the fictional character, the distinction holds. If we grant truth-value to the story told by the author of an autobiography, it is because we believe that the autobiographical pact is operative.

In his book, Philippe Lejeune discusses the notion of an autobiographical pact.[37] This pact amounts to an implicit contract between writer and reader according to which the writer promises to tell the truth about herself. While this seems rather straightforward, many questions arise if we consider the fact that autobiographical writing is, first and foremost, a form of *authoring*. Every form of writing is mediation, and this necessarily calls into question the problem of interpretation. Can the author give a purely objective account of the truth? Can the author take the necessary distance from herself to be able to give an account of the truth? Is there anything qualitatively or substantially truer about a subjective truth about oneself? If so, can it be told? And, importantly, is authoring not always fictionalizing, at least to some degree?

I think that the truth of autobiographical writing is qualitatively the same as the truth of novels and philosophical essays. The autobiographical account may give the illusion of a privileged standpoint and a higher truth-value, but in fact there is no more truth to it than to fiction.[38] This, however, does not make autobiographical writing any less valuable and important for Beauvoir. What she seeks in her philosophy as well as in her autobiographical writings is a disclosure of existence and an appeal to the Other. For her, to disclose existence is not to offer any epistemologically true statements about it; rather, the point is to establish an existential truth thanks to the enactment of an existential project that the Other validates.

Beauvoir's autobiographical writings accomplish this task. She tells her readers the story of her own becoming as a human being who undertook to disclose existence through her project to be a writer. For example, in *Memoirs of a Dutiful Daughter*, Beauvoir says that writing her memoirs was as much a creative act as it was a mnemonic act. This type of account is everything but objective, which is precisely why the exercise is valid. She says, in her *prière d'insérer*: "It is my past that made me, so much that in interpreting it today, I bear witness to it."[39] It is interesting to note that Beauvoir does not claim to give a true account of her past. Instead, she says very bluntly that she is "*interpreting* it today." In her autobiographies, she narrates and thus recreates her own self-constitution, making use of some genetic myths.

Éliane Lecarme-Tabone explains this in her book on *Memoirs of a Dutiful Daughter*.[40] She points out that a few myths underlie the storytelling about one's own life. The most important one for Beauvoir is the genetic myth of the writer. Thus, while revisiting her childhood, Beauvoir tells the story of how the little girl Simone became Beauvoir, the writer and philosopher who is writing her memoirs. This storytelling amounts to myth creating. Beauvoir tells the story of her conversion to atheism, her liberation from conventions, and her dedication to literature. Everything in her past is reinterpreted through the looking glass of these genetic myths. The autobiography illustrates that one can make a choice of oneself and live one's life according to that choice. In Beauvoir's case, the choice is to be a writer. This existence that revolves around the existential choice of oneself is thus justified and grounded in the freedom of the individual and may qualify as authentic. Autobiographical writing is a meta-performance of the performance of the project of oneself.

Lecarme-Tabone notes that the *Memoirs* go well beyond the individual – the singular concrete individual – to address the universal. She says that the book exceeds the sociological perspective in addressing the generality of childhood and woman's condition.[41] She also remarks that little Simone's development follows the same steps as the ones Beauvoir describes in *The Second Sex*. This, to her, is another indication that autobiographical writing reconstitutes the self, since the treatise was published earlier than the memoirs. If Lecarme-Tabone is correct, and I think she has an excellent point, then this further reinforces my interpretation of autobiographical writings as a way to illustrate how one must give meaning to one's own existence by embracing an existential project.

For Beauvoir, autobiographical writing is the occasion of mythologizing about her own authorial becoming. She presents her life as the coherent unfolding of an original choice of herself as writer. While she does not believe in a permanent self that endures over one's life, she does believe that one's existential choice permeates one's whole life and gives it meaning. There might not be a persistence of the self, but there is a coherence of the self.

While autobiographical writings may do something special, and while literary texts, novels, and plays may have an advantage over others insofar as they provide a plurality of perspectives, I think that Beauvoir's use of all forms of expression positions her as an extraordinary thinker, one who cannot be surpassed by the system-builders whose myopia she criticizes. According to her view of literature and what it can and ought to do, their views are too narrow and fail to encompass the many complexities of human life. Their appeal to their readers may still be effective, but is necessarily limited. Her view is far more inclusive and, furthermore, it brings to life the ethical prescription to make of one's life a project: to make one's life meaningful.

Beauvoir takes herself and Sartre as existential/phenomenological case studies. For her, the autobiographical writings are the occasion to remake, rewrite, and thereby rediscover herself. The act of telling one's story to oneself – and most importantly to others, her readers – reinforces the existentialist imperative to make oneself and to give meaning to one's existence. Autobiographies help show that one makes oneself through one's deeds, one's writings, and one's appeal to the Other. For Beauvoir, to exist as a committed individual is to exist as a committed writer, *un écrivain engagé*, who appeals to her readers by unveiling the world, herself, and her own activity of meaning generation. This project binds the reader to the project and to incite the reader to act. The aim that permeates this endeavour is to make the world one in which every individual may freely make oneself and thereby give meaning to one's own existence.

NOTES

1 Nietzsche, *Beyond Good and Evil*, §6.

2 Beauvoir, "Pyrrhus and Cinéas."

3 This essay was only very recently translated into English and thus made accessible to Anglophone audiences. By contrast, Beauvoir's later contribution to ethics, *The Ethics of Ambiguity*, was translated only one year later. For a long time, it was deemed to encompass her whole thinking on ethical matters. A lot of readers did not pay much attention to the earlier essay, deeming it immature. Further, a lot of scholars interpret *The Ethics of Ambiguity* as the missing Sartrean ethics. Indeed, for those interested in Sartre's ethics and who see Beauvoir as Sartre's disciple, *The Ethics of Ambiguity* is a resource in the absence of the ethics promised at the end of *Being and Nothingness*. This, however, fails to appreciate the originality of Beauvoir's thought. I discuss this in "The Ambiguous Ethics of Simone de Beauvoir," in *Existentialist Thinkers and Ethics*. For more on the question of influence between Beauvoir and Sartre, see Daigle and Golomb, *Beauvoir and Sartre*.

4 Beauvoir, "Pyrrhus and Cinéas," 90.

5 Beauvoir, *The Ethics of Ambiguity*, 129.

6 Beauvoir, "Pyrrhus and Cinéas," 91.

7 Ibid., 100. She says something similar in "A Review of *The Phenomenology of Perception* by Maurice Merleau-Ponty": "One understands that we could never be out of place [*dépaysés*] in the world. The most savage desert, the most hidden cave still secrete a human meaning. The universe is our domain."

8 Beauvoir, "Pyrrhus and Cinéas," 100.

9 Ibid., 115.

10 At the time of writing "Pyrrhus and Cinéas," Beauvoir has not yet theorized on this. I am thus using the concept of fold anachronistically. However, I believe it is fair to say that what she claims about the individual and the other is merely awaiting the phrase as she will find it in Merleau-Ponty. In her review of *The Phenomenology of Perception* published in *Les Temps Modernes* in 1945, Beauvoir is very enthusiastic about the concept of fold. She finds that it replaces advantageously the concept of pure for itself that Sartre proposes in *Being and Nothingness* and of which she was critical. See Beauvoir, "A Review of *The Phenomenology of Perception*," 163.

11 Beauvoir, *The Second Sex*, 6.

12 She explains that according to Merleau-Ponty, "perception is not a relationship between a subject and an object foreign to one another; it ties us to the

world as to our homeland, it is communication and communion." "A Review of *The Phenomenology of Perception*," 162.

13 Beauvoir, "Pyrrhus and Cinéas," 126.

14 Ibid., 129, italics added.

15 Ibid., 135. The last part of the French reads "si j'ai fait d'eux mon prochain." Beauvoir, *Pour une morale de l'ambiguïté suivi de Pyrrhus et Cinéas*, 303.

16 Beauvoir, "Pyrrhus and Cinéas," 129.

17 Ibid., 133.

18 Ibid., 140.

19 Consult Simons's works on this issue, as well as Daigle and Golomb, *Beauvoir and Sartre*.

20 Beauvoir, "Literature and Metaphysics," 276. I argue elsewhere that Beauvoir neither offers nor aims to offer anything like pure literature or pure philosophy. She is critical of pure philosophy. What follows is a short discussion of what I analyze in depth in "Making the Humanities Meaningful."

21 Simons, "Beauvoir Interview (1979)," 11.

22 Beauvoir, "Existentialism and Popular Wisdom."

23 Heinämaa, *Toward a Phenomenology of Sexual Difference*, 4–6.

24 Björk, "Reconstituting Experience," 74. Heinämaa also suggests this in her book. She sees Kierkegaard's questioning as well as his critique of Hegel as influential on Beauvoir. Further, she thinks that Husserl's critical phenomenology was an important influence. She points out that Husserl made room for fiction in his philosophical method, although he himself did not write it. See Heinämaa, *Phenomenology of Sexual Difference*, 14–15.

25 Björk, "Reconstituting Experience," 75.

26 Ibid., 85.

27 I discuss this in greater detail and as it relates to the philosophy of ambiguity in my essay "*The Second Sex* as Appeal."

28 This is something about which she agrees with Sartre. Sartre expresses this view of literature as committed in *What Is Literature?*

29 Ruonakoski, "Literature as a Means of Communication," 254. Ruonakoski focuses on Beauvoir's later talk, "My Experience as a Writer," from 1965. While it is a much later expression of her views, I contend that they amount to the same as those presented in "Literature and Metaphysics." What differs is the vocabulary Beauvoir uses, leaving out "metaphysical."

30 Ruonakoski, "Literature as a Means of Communication," 255–6.

31 I have explained this in more detail in "*The Second Sex* as Appeal."

32 Björk, "Reconstituting Experience," 88.

33 Ibid.

34 The following is a summary of what I have argued in the context of comparing Beauvoir's and Sartre's use of autobiographical writing in "L'(la ré-)écriture de soi-même."

35 This is a pun on the title of Sartre's famous essay "Existentialism Is a Humanism." See Contat, "Introduction: une autobiographie politique?," 2.

36 My translation of: "Pour une conscience de ce type, le projet autobiographique coïncide avec le projet existentiel: rendre compte de soi, donner une forme narrative (ou dramatique), par une écriture communicative, à sa propre expérience du monde, donner à autrui une vérité de soi qui puisse indiquer celle de tous." Contat, "Une autobiographie politique?," 2.

37 Lejeune, *Le Pacte autobiographique*.

38 In an essay on autobiography and philosophy, Genevieve Lloyd suggests: "My subjectivity seems to give me a special status in the world. But it is difficult to see how that special status is to be reconciled with ideals of objective knowledge." "The Self as Fiction," 168. It is on that count that autobiographical writing is interesting, namely as a type of writing that gives access to a subjective truth that a self possesses about herself.

39 My translation of "mais c'est mon passé qui m'a faite, si bien qu'en l'interprétant aujourd'hui je porte témoignage sur lui." Quoted in Lecarme-Tabone, *Mémoires d'une jeune fille*, 218.

40 Lecarme-Tabone, *Mémoires d'une jeune fille*.

41 Lecarme-Tabone says: "La perspective sociologique se trouve elle-même dépassée par la généralité de l'enfance et de la condition feminine." *Mémoires d'une jeune fille*, 173.

PART THREE

Precarious Lives

10

Defining Morally Considerable Life

Toward a Feminist Disability Ethics

STEPHANIE C. JENKINS

Disability theorists distinguish between two dominant models of disability: the medical model and the social model. While the medical model locates the problem of disability in individuals (deviation from species-typical norms marks bodies and minds as *being* disabled), the social model identifies the problem of disability in social practices, environments, and institutions that exclude and stigmatize certain kinds of difference. In the social model, it is social practices that disable certain kinds of subjects, not their bodies. More recently, a number of critical disability theorists – including feminist scholars Shelley Tremain and Margrit Shildrick – have challenged both the social and medical models of disability, arguing that impairment as well as disability is culturally constructed. Such critical disability theorists have begun to develop a third approach to disability, sometimes called the impairment model.

These different models for understanding disability – on which I elaborate below – result in different ethics. While the medical model corresponds with a "bioethics of disability," the social model corresponds with "disability bioethics." Advocating for more recent ontological approaches to disability, which move beyond both the medical and social models, in this essay I propose a corresponding ethics, or what I call a "disability ethics." This disability ethics challenges the negative ontology of disability, the "framing" of morally considerable life, and the naturalization of impairment.

Bioethics of Disability and the Predominance of the Medical Model

Mainstream bioethics has paid significant attention to disability-related ethical issues, as demonstrated, for example, in research on end-of-life decisions, genetic interventions, and reprogenetic technologies. Because such work applies preexisting moral frameworks to disability topics, Jackie Leach Scully calls such mainstream bioethical approaches to disability the "bioethics of disability."[1] The bioethics of disability is the "systematic reflection on morally correct ways to behave toward disabled people" in biomedical practice and research.[2] Mainstream bioethicists adhere to the medical model, which assumes a "negative ontology of disability,"[3] and often explicitly reject the disability rights movement's theoretical advances. To say that disability is ontologically negative means that it is inherently a "harmed condition ... [that we] have a strong rational preference not to be in."[4] Or, in other words, to consider a life as disabled is "to see something wrong with it."[5] In short, a negative ontology of disability assumes that "to be disabled is inherently bad in virtue of being a state of suffering, neediness, or dependence."[6]

Though bioethicists of disability may offer guidelines for patient treatment and principles for determining how medical goods ought to be distributed, they do not challenge the medical categories of health, illness, and impairment that determine who and what conditions will be treated. Therefore, these approaches rely on the medical descriptions of disability as pathology for understanding atypical bodily variation. Bioethical tools are brought to bear on disabilities when new technologies create opportunities to prevent (e.g., prenatal genetic diagnosis), treat (e.g., normalizing surgery), or terminate (e.g., euthanasia) disabled lives. The medical model characterizes disability with four main attributes: negation, pathological deprivation, modulation, and homogeneity. These four features define the negative ontology of disability; they describe how disability, from the perspective of the medical model, appears as inherently "bad."[7]

To illustrate these four points, I will provide examples from *From Chance to Choice: Genetics and Justice*.[8] This book is one of the best examples of a mainstream bioethical engagement with criticism coming from disability advocates, because Buchanan et al. frame the project as responding to the disability rights movement's rejection of the medical model.[9] Yet, even though the authors concede that the extent to which a disability is "disabling" depends on social context, they still conclude that disabilities are natural disadvantages that health professions must cure or prevent when possible.

The first component of the medical model of disability is that disability is seen not as constitutive of experience, but only as the absence of typical human experience. Scully argues that disability is a unique form of bodily difference, because the concept is unavoidably negative. The word disabled linguistically implies the privation of natural abilities. The prefix "dis" indicates that the negative of disability is not just a lack, but that something has been taken away, whether a physical capacity, mental ability, or sensory experience.[10] Disability as the negation of normal experience is a guiding theme in *From Chance to Choice*, because Buchanan et al. argue that the moral ground for medical intervention is equality of opportunity. From their perspective, disability, or "adverse departures from normal species function,"[11] limits affected individuals' life opportunities.

Second, the medical model views disability as pathological deprivation – that is, as an individual rather than social concern. Disability is cast not only as a lack, but also as a harmful one; as deprivation, the "something taken away" is understood as a loss of essential human experience. Because this deprivation is believed to cause physical and emotional suffering, disability is characterized as medical pathology. Like an illness, it is undesirable and therefore must be treated and cured. While people with disabilities do not always experience their bodily variation as unambiguously negative, medical discourse casts disability as ontological error or pathology. According to Buchanan et al., medicine's aim is to cure or prevent disease and disability. Although they admit that a disability's severity depends on social expectations (for example, learning disabilities are significant only in highly literate cultures), they still view disabilities as natural errors that medical professionals are obligated to restore to normalcy when possible. Moreover, the assumed pathology of disability in this work can be seen in the authors' contention that the biomedical sciences objectively determine the line between impaired and normal functioning.[12] A central component of the medical model is that the solution to the limitations of disability is understood to be individual and not social in nature; the "problem" is eliminated by curing the disability rather than by reorganizing social arrangements. For example, while Buchanan et al. recognize that it is possible to equalize opportunities for disabled individuals through social interventions, they conclude that justice does not require rearranging social conditions, because curative and preventative techniques are available and the status quo is beneficial to the majority of (able-bodied) individuals.[13]

Third, disability is divided into physical and mental disabilities, a division that Edwards calls the "modularity thesis."[14] The mind/body division is recast within the realm of disability so that physical and mental disabilities are seen as ontologically distinct. Within disability theory, this often plays out as a privileging of physical over mental disabilities.[15] In *From Chance to Choice*, the modulating of disability is found in the authors' use of the term disability to stand in for physical abnormality. Their overwhelming focus is physical disability; mental disabilities are offered as special cases, for example, in the case of learning or cognitive disability.[16]

Finally, although there are distinct kinds of disability, the disabled tend to be treated as a homogeneous group. Disability is a nominal concept defined in opposition to ability norms; the term awkwardly lumps together diverse phenotypic variations of dissimilar etiologies, cultural responses, and degrees of impairment. Disability is hypostatized as a stable referent. However, the social processes unifying this heterogeneous assemblage must be understood in reference to the norms from which disability deviates. For example, the phrases "severely disabled" or "severely retarded [sic]" often replace the specifics of particular disabilities.[17] As Lennard Davis argues, the problem of disability is not persons with disabilities, but the "way that normalcy is constructed to create the 'problem' of the disabled person."[18] Additionally, disability is taken as self-evident, meaning that we can easily distinguish between abled and disabled bodies.

This last component of the medical model is most clearly seen in Buchanan et al.'s interchangeable use of disease, disability, and impairment.[19] As is common in the bioethics of disability literature, they do not distinguish impairment from disability, as this is a distinction introduced by the social model, discussed below. When they do distinguish between the terms, impairment/disease identifies a physiological condition, while disability names the limitations resulting from the condition. Impairment and disability are *causally related*; the limitations (disability) of impairment (disease) are biological in nature, but become more or less relevant in varying social contexts. In either case, disability clearly and objectively names a wide range of embodiments for which the common denominator is deviation from normal species functioning.

Another example of the medical model can be found in the work of bioethicist John Harris, who advocates the "harmed condition" model of disability. His harmed model makes explicit the negative ontology inherent to the medical model. Through this framework, Harris seeks to understand "what might be harmful about conditions variously described as disability, handicaps or impairments."[20] Arguing that there are no significant conceptual differences between these terms, he lumps them together as "disabilities," defined as conditions that someone has "a strong rational preference" to avoid. This is because Harris views disabilities as obstacles to freedom, and states: "To be disabled in any sense is not the same as being differently abled. Being deaf for example is not simply a 'dimension of human experience not available to hearing people ... ' but a condition which harms the individual relative to freedom from deafness."[21] Given that disability is seen as a source of immense suffering, it is no wonder that, as Simo Vehmas describes, "the relationship between bioethics and disability has traditionally focused on killing."[22] Traditional bioethical literature concerning people with disabilities focuses almost exclusively on the ethics of ending or preventing their existence, as seen in debates about euthanasia, selective abortion, and preimplantation genetic diagnosis.[23] In other words, many bioethicists advocate values that presuppose that disabled lives are not worth living, despite theoretical commitments to the equality of humanity. At minimum, the bioethics of disability assumes that species-typical embodiments are preferable to disabled existence (even in the case of "minor" disabilities), and that medical technology ought to be deployed to cure or prevent disability when possible.

Disability Bioethics: A Disability Rights Intervention in Bioethics

While the medical model predominates bioethical discussions about disability, a growing body of literature influenced by the disability rights movement advocates the rejection of the medical model. Most work in disability bioethics offers a competing ontological framework for understanding disability as "neutral," what Michael Oliver calls the "social model"[24] of disability. While this second model has received little uptake in mainstream bioethics,[25] it is ubiquitous in disability advocates' interventions in this discipline. Here, I highlight the major components of the social model, as well as the problems that "social modelists" identify within the medical model of disability.

As the "leading theoretical achievement of the disability rights movement,"[26] the social model of disability is the starting point for most work in disability bioethics. Debates between mainstream bioethics and disability bioethics typically focus, directly or indirectly, on the opposition between the ontologies of the medical and social models of disability.[27] The latter's central aim is to disrupt the negative ontology of the medical model. For example, Asch contends that the main difficulty with the medical model is its necessary assumption that disability harms affected individuals: "[The] medically oriented understandings of impairment contain two erroneous assumptions. First, the life of someone with a chronic illness or disability ... is forever disrupted, as one's life can be temporarily disrupted by the flu or a back spasm. Second, if a disabled person experiences isolation, powerlessness, poverty, unemployment, or low social status, these are inevitable consequences of biological limitation."[28] The social model of disability, which is the predominant alternative to the medical, proposes a neutral ontology of disability. In other words, social model advocates argue that disability possesses neither inherently bad nor inherently good value.

The move from a negative to neutral ontology of disability that characterizes the social model is supported by differentiating disability from impairment. Impairment, proponents argue, is defined as "lacking part of or all of a limb, or having a defective limb, organism or mechanism of the body."[29] It is understood as a biological aberration from species-typical functioning. Disability, however, is the social stigmatization of impairment, but there is not a necessary, causal relationship between impairment and disability according to this model.[30] The social construction of disability is imposed upon the natural foundation of impairment. As Oliver notes, the main issue at stake in these two ontological models is causation: whether the disadvantage of disability stems from an individual's biological pathology or from oppressive social organization.[31] According to this second model, impairment does not cause disability (which is not to say they are not correlated).

From the perspective of the social model, disability is ontologically neutral because its "harm" results not from physical necessity, but from systemic barriers to social participation such as prejudice, inequities in built environments, and lack of social support for disabled individuals.[32] For instance, although deafness may be a natural impairment, it only becomes a disability that inhibits communication in a society in which speaking, rather than signing, defines language. Disability, therefore, is understood as produced according to contingent social arrangements. In this sense, the impairment/disability dichotomy plays a similar role in disability studies as the sex/gender division in many feminist theories; while impairment names a biological embodied difference, disability identifies the meaning physical variation takes on in a cultural context.

The hallmark of the social model – the separation of disability from impairment – enables a pointed criticism of the medical model's basic assumptions. Most notably, the limitations and hardships associated with disability become social, rather than individual, problems. Because medical techniques prefer to eliminate the harm of disability at an individual level over reorganizing social institutions for maximum accessibility, the cultural obsession with curing or preventing disability is revealed to be a component of the widespread and systemic oppression of people with disabilities. Just as feminists and gay activists argue that attempts to "cure" individuals of their queerness reinforce rather than alleviate homophobia, disability advocates contend that medical treatments for disability seek to eliminate the victims, rather than the causes, of disability prejudice. As Silvers argues: "The social model of disability usefully reminds us that it is not the individual but the environment that is defective ... [It] directs us to address the suffering of people with disabilities by eliminating or reforming the external circumstances that contribute to it rather than by eliminating or revising the people themselves."[33] Shifting the focus of disability analysis away from the "personal tragedy theory of disability"

to a "social oppression theory,"[34] proponents of the social model introduce a much-needed analytics of power into debates about the bioethics
of disability.

The move from a negative to a neutral ontological model of disability
that constitutes the theoretical buttress for the social model is most clear
in the work of Anita Silvers. In the essay "On the Possibility and Desirability of Constructing a Neutral Concept of Disability," she identifies the
central conflict between traditional bioethics and disability bioethics as
the "meta-question"[35] concerning the valuing of disability. Disability, she
argues, is an "essentially contested concept"[36] that functions as an obstacle
to meaningful debate on ethical issues. This means that disability is a term
that operates with radically different meanings and background assumptions that inevitably prevents dialogue between advocates of the medical
and social models. To resolve this conflict, she advocates the adoption of
a neutral concept of disability, or a framework that tables the assumption
of disability's inherent "badness."[37] Although Silvers states that such an
approach "will impose neither the social nor the medical model of disability,"[38] her proposal exemplifies the social model's separation of impairment from disability. This is because the main aim of a neutral concept of
disability is to disrupt the causal relationship between impairment and
disability. As Silvers puts it: "One point of adopting a neutral framework
is not to deny that disabilities can be health issues, but instead to acknowledge they are neither necessarily nor mainly so."[39]

Disability bioethics' social model has advantages over the medical
model entrenched in the bioethics of disability. Perhaps most significantly, it empowers individuals with disabilities to identify and condemn
oppressive social forces as the cause of their suffering. Liz Crow, for example, describes this difference: "The social model of disability ... gave
me an understanding of my life ... what I had always known, deep down,
was confirmed ... It wasn't my body that was responsible for all my difficulties, it was external factors, the barriers constructed by the society in
which I live."[40] Another advantage is that disability bioethics is better able
to address the everyday needs of people with disabilities. Much bioethical
work is removed from the daily needs, concerns, and experience of such
people because disability is medicalized as an illness or impairment that
requires a cure. Rather than asking when and how disability can be prevented, cured, or normalized, disability bioethics addresses questions of

justice, discrimination, care, and/or health care access. Yet, while the social model offers a significant advancement beyond the medical model, it is not without its flaws. I address these difficulties in the following section.

Disability Ethics: Beyond Negative Ontology

While the social model explicitly rejects the negative ontology of the medical model, in practice this second framework reinforces the invalidation of disability through the category of impairment. This is because the conceptual apparatus of the social model hinges on a division between nature and culture in order to break the causal relation between impairment and disability within the medical model. From this new perspective, the natural body becomes the raw material and limit of the social construction of disability. Mapping the impairment/disability dichotomy onto the nature/culture split simultaneously enables an examination of the role of social forces in disability oppression and relegates impairment to the realm of natural physiology. This latter move – which is essential to the social model but not always acknowledged – does not entirely disrupt the medical model, but rather relocates it in the physiology of impairment. The concept of impairment, defined as biological limitation resulting from atypical embodied variation, is experienced as restriction and harm the natural body itself produces.

The social model naturalizes the biomedical understanding of impairment, which obscures the direction of the causal relation between disability and impairment and reinforces the negative ontology of impairment.[41] The negative ontology of impairment is evidenced by the social model's acceptance of the idea that impairment is inherently defective, whether as operating assumption or explicit definition. From this perspective, impairment is always limiting in comparison to species-typical abilities, though the severity and relevance of physiological disadvantages depend on social context. The limits deafness places on symphony-listening are commonly referenced examples.[42] For social modelists, the inability to listen to symphonies may not be relevant to someone who is not a music lover, whether their hearing is impaired or not. Deafness becomes disability, along these lines, within societies organized around verbal communication. In the same manner, deafness is not a disability in signing communities. What is relevant to this second criticism, however, is that impairment within even the most sophisticated accounts of the social model is understood as incapacity or defect in relation to normal embodiments; deafness describes the inability to hear and is therefore not a neutral variation.

This acceptance of impairment as natural defect distances disability as social phenomenon from its inherent "badness." One consequence of this distinction is that the negative ontology of the medical model is pushed to a biologically "deeper" theoretical space. Impairment becomes the natural substrate and prerequisite for disability oppression. This obscures the parts of the medical model that are essential to the social model. Additionally, understanding impairment as defect naturalizes the distinction between impaired/unhealthy and normal/healthy bodies. Limited by what Foucault calls a juridical model of power, the social model lacks the capacity to address ableism's productive power to not only invalidate abnormal bodies but also construct normalcy itself.[43] In doing so, social modelists miss the significance of the causal relation between impairment and disability.

Developing a Foucauldian approach to disability, Shelley Tremain inverts the relationship between impairment and disability.[44] Impairments can only be recognized as such in the context of historico-politically specific requirements concerning bodies' capacities: what functions they ought to be able to perform, what physical structure they are expected to take, what variations are recognized as disease, and so forth. Therefore, the mechanism of inclusion/exclusion (disability) must precede the identification of any particular "physical" impairment. Impairment is consequently an effect, and not a cause, of disability.[45] Simply stated, bodily variation can only be characterized as an inherently limiting impairment after the establishment of the expectations for species-typical norms as well as criteria for evaluating those impairments as negative. The social model's naturalization of impairment as physiological limitation legitimizes the constitutive power relations of ableism that materialize atypical embodied difference as natural defect and produce the very standards of normality and ability through which those differences are invalidated.

The oppositions between the medical and social models of disability are predominately ontological in nature. Although these conflicts are not explicitly characterized as ontological debates, they hinge on disagreements about the nature of disability and what makes a life livable. As Bill Hughes describes in regard to developments within disability studies,

"ontological arguments are implicit and sometimes explicit in the literature that describes the 'othering' of disabled people ... and the ways in
which these processes invalidate disabled lives."[46] Contemporary research
at the forefront of disability studies is characterized by an increasingly
"ontological turn"[47] that seeks an alternative to the near-uniform acceptance of the social model in disability studies and activism.[48] The social
model's effectiveness at representing disability is coming under increasing
question.[49] A number of ontological frameworks have been proposed, including "materialist ontology of impairment,"[50] Foucauldian genealogy,[51]
"postmodern"[52] deployments of Foucault, Derrida, and Deleuze's works,
"affirmative" ontology,[53] phenomenology,[54] "feminist disability studies,"[55]
and "critical social ontology."[56]

Some disability scholars have begun to examine the implications of
new ontologies for disability ethics – most notably Margrit Shildrick, Tom
Shakespeare, Shelley Tremain, and Jackie Leach Scully.[57] Their efforts highlight the need to do more than extend existing bioethical frameworks to
increase their coverage of disability-related topics. From the perspective of
disability ethics, apparent differences between these bioethical traditions
such as consequentialism, deontology, and virtue ethics are merely super-
ficial; each replicates the hierarchy of mind over body found in liberal
humanism and the medical model's invalidation of abnormal bodies. As
Shildrick points out: "The discipline has effectively duplicated master discourses and maintained the split between a secure sense of transcendent
self as moral agent, and a more or less unruly body that must be subjected
to its dictates."[58] Feminist interventions within bioethics mark a significant exception to the ableist themes within traditional bioethics through
a revaluation of dependency and care.[59] However, disability ethics differs
from these approaches in its rejection of a humanist framework that cam-
ouflages species-typical capacities as moral aims, principles, and criteria.

Debates between traditional bioethicists and disability advocates still
pivot on the ontological valuation of disability and conflicting understandings of moral personhood. If disability is rendered a harmed condition, the ethical imperative to cure disabling conditions becomes clear.
Until disability ethics can account for the political constitution of impairment, we will be unable to counter the biomedical and common sense
presumption that disability is a "harmed condition," as it will always be
analyzed through an ableist lens. To move beyond the negative ontology

of disability, disability ethics must challenge the moral anthropology that determines who counts in the moral community.

Disability ethics introduces a new moral boundary that makes the invalidation of embodiments as disabled, impaired, or diseased an ethico-political valuation open to reformulation. Judith Butler's work helps to clarify the boundaries of livable life and is thus useful for a disability ethics. In *Precarious Life* and *Frames of War,* she attempts to understand how social norms and political contexts portray others' lives as "grievable" or not.[60] Her examination of the production of moral "recognizability" reveals how relations of power, regimes of knowledge, and modes of subjectivation differentially value some lives as worthy of moral attention, concern, and protection. A "tacit interpretive scheme" governs standards for inclusion in the moral community and "maximize[s] precariousness for some and minimize[s] precariousness for others."[61] For Butler, humanity operates as a normative frame, rather than simply as a biological or morphological concept. The essential human capacities that earn moral status for some animate beings "deprive certain other individuals of the possibility of achieving that status, producing a differential between the human and the less-than-human."[62]

By moving ethics to the question of "who counts as a 'who,'"[63] Butler makes explicit how moral decisions and theories conceal the boundary between moral subjects and nonsubjects. Butler's work is significant to disability ethics not just because it addresses the "who" rather than the "what," of ethics, but also because it explicates the role of normalization in distinguishing between moral and nonmoral subjects. The framing of moral considerability is a matter of life and death for individuals at the margins of recognizable life. For this reason, Butler proposes the need to reimagine the right to life through an analysis of what kinds of lives matter morally.[64]

Butler's question, "What makes a life livable?," cannot be answered without considering the moral cartography that distributes moral worth in accordance with ableist norms. Specifically, a disability ethics is needed to problematize what counts as a life worthy of moral attention, recognition, and protection. The study of disability demands a more explicit discussion of the who of ethics, in order to challenge how people with disabilities have been excluded from the moral community in ethical theory and action. The history of eugenic violence against people with disabilities, persistence of ableist discrimination, and inaccessibility of social environments demonstrate that not all individuals are treated as possessing equal moral worth. From the perspective of disability ethics, the who of moral considerability is far from self-evident. Asking "who counts as a 'who'"[65] problematizes the use of performance capacities for determining the boundaries of the moral community.

In order to account for how disability shapes the limits of moral consideration, the study of moral framing must clarify how the division between moral and nonmoral others is historically variable. Recognizing disability as a historical phenomenon is central to understanding its contingency and recognizing the potential for change. Specifically, this recognition situates the biomedical model for understanding disability within the rise of modern biopower in the late eighteenth and nineteenth centuries. From this perspective, the biological can no longer be regarded as natural or neutral; it is thoroughly and unavoidably politically and historically situated.

A historical ontology of disability accounts for the divisions between normal/abnormal, able-bodied/disabled, and diseased/healthy bodies as constructed and malleable rather than fixed. It also reveals the interconnection of ontological and ethical questions; how we understand the nature of disability determines a number of ethical questions, including the extent of – and limits to – disabled individuals' moral considerability. I contend that the examination of moral framing as an embodied practice must consider historical changes in patterns of moral consideration. Foucault's genealogical works demonstrate that what he calls the "political technology of the body"[66] has undergone several significant transformations over the course of Western history; what bodies are, how they are valued, and the activities they are expected to perform change over time. The scientific, political, and economic institutions of biopower normalize an understanding of the human body defined by its species-typical capacities. Contemporary quality-of-life measures descend from the conflation of the statistically average individual with normative ideals that accompanied the advent of biopower.[67] Individuals who cannot perform allegedly essential human functions are excluded from the moral values of humanism. Foucault's genealogy of biopower is therefore an effective tool for a disability-ethics-informed analysis of ableism because it explains how subjects are constituted through health assessments, economic and political institutions, moral theory, biological sciences, and statistical analysis.

Both the medical and the social model of disability rely on a negative ontology of disability, which is seen in the category of impairment as deviations from "species' typical functioning." This is because the production of a normal, abled-bodied subject necessarily entails the delimitation of the abnormal, disabled-bodied. As long as impairment is treated as a natural, prediscursive bodily dysfunction, the primacy of the able-bodied subject will continue in bioethical literature and practice through the category of species' typical functioning.[68] Moral considerability itself is a product of ableism as a biopolitical mechanism that differentially values atypical embodiments. This is because the human (often conflated with moral personhood) is defined by ableist "performance criteria,"[69] determined by an assessment of species-typical capacities. Ethical criticism that does not interrogate the boundaries of moral considerability as a distinct ethical question unproblematically imports politico-historically specific liberal humanist understandings of personhood.[70]

Ableism functions as an interpretative frame through which marginal others are excluded from the moral community. Because species-typical capacities (such as the ability to reason or speak) serve as prerequisites for moral consideration, the limits of moral response are maintained through the biopolitical mechanisms of ableism. Disability ethics elucidates how ableism produces a normalized understanding of the human that is defined in terms of performance criteria, or capacities that are considered essential to a meaningful human existence. As a result, a performance-driven conception of personhood underlies notions of moral status, even within models that strive to revalue attributes, like vulnerability, that oppose exclusionary standards. Given the way in which normalization functions, moral others are perceived through the frames of the historically produced normate human body. A normate, according to Rosemarie Garland-Thomson, identifies "the constructed identity of those who, by way of the bodily configurations and cultural capital they assume, can step into a position of authority and wield the power it grants them."[71] Standards of normalcy are constituted through what Robert McRuer calls "compulsory able-bodiedness."[72] Disabled people suffer the consequences of this exclusionary, performance-driven morality. The ubiquity of these criteria for moral standing inhibits the ability of moral theorists to fully contemplate the meaning of the indeterminacy inherent within the concept of moral standing, because they assume the very criteria for humanness that are under evaluation.

The classifications of disability, disease, and impairment are not objective descriptions of bodies; the boundaries between these terms and normal, healthy embodiments are historically variant invalidations of deviations from contingent species-typical norms. Directly challenging the negative ontology of disability, the historical ontology of a genealogical method demonstrates the productive power of ableism as a biopolitical apparatus in framing the invalidation of disability. This move is significant for bioethical inquiry because it exposes the contingency of ability norms, opening the seemingly natural divisions between impaired/disabled/diseased and healthy/normal bodies to ethical analysis.

Disability ethics holds the potential to challenge essentialist conceptions of the human and for articulating difference as productive variation, rather than as ontological deprivation. Problematizing the connection between moral considerability and species-typical performance criteria bridges the gap between a purportedly disembodied moral framework that applies to disability-related topics and an ethical perspective that emerges from and is imbued with bodily difference.

The aim of disability ethics is not to construct new criteria for moral standing or bioethical concepts, such as a new and improved quality of life measure, but rather to unsettle the very grounds upon which such concepts exist. It throws into question the basis for judgments about the moral status of disability: the binary between good and bad, quality of life assessments, the value of rationality, the impartiality of justice, the evil of pain, and so forth. No concept of personhood can resolve the "tensions and ambiguities" in moral criteria.[73] In the end, the boundaries of human life "remain shifting and uncertain."[74]

NOTES

1 Scully, *Disability Bioethics*, 11.
2 Ibid., 9.
3 Campbell, "Legislating Disability."
4 Harris, "Is There a Coherent Social Conception of Disability?," 97.

5 Engelhardt, *The Foundations of Bioethics*, 197.

6 Silvers, "Formal Justice," 85.

7 Silvers, "On the Possibility and Desireability of Constructing a Neutral Conception of Disability."

8 Buchanan et al., *From Chance to Choice*.

9 Ibid., 10.

10 Scully, "Disability Bioethics."

11 Buchanan et al., *From Chance to Choice*, 74.

12 Ibid., 121.

13 Ibid., 79.

14 Edwards, "The Body as Object Versus the Body as Subject," 47.

15 Corker, "Sensing Disability."

16 Buchanan et al., *From Chance to Choice*, 117.

17 Kuhse and Singer, *Should the Baby Live?*

18 Davis, *Enforcing Normalcy*, 25.

19 Buchanan et al., *From Chance to Choice*, 129.

20 Harris, "One Principle and Three Fallacies of Disability Studies," 383.

21 Ibid.

22 Vehmas, "Live and Let Die?," 146.

23 Scully, *Disability Bioethics*.

24 Oliver, *The Politics of Disablement*.

25 For discussions of the extent to which mainstream bioethicists and medical professions refuse to engage with the social model of disability, see Amundson and Tresky, "On a Bioethical Challenge to Disability Rights"; Asch, "Disability, Bioethics, and Human Rights"; Koch, "The Difference that Difference Makes"; Kuczewski, "Disability"; Newell, "The Social Nature of Disability, Disease, and Genetics"; Ouellette, *Bioethics and Disability*; Parens, "How Long Has This Been Going On?"; Scully, *Disability Bioethics*; Silvers, "Possibility and Desireability"; Swain and French, "Toward an Affirmation Model of Disability"; Wolbring, "Disability Rights Approach towards Bioethics?"

26 Amundson and Tresky, "Bioethical Challenge," 543.

27 See further Wolbring, "Disability Rights"; Ouellette, *Bioethics and Disability*; Asch, "Disability, Bioethics."

28 Asch, "Disability, Bioethics," 300.

29 UPIAS definition in Oliver, "Politics of Disablement," 11.

30 Amundson, "Disability, Ideology, and Quality of Life"; Amundson and Tresky, "Bioethical Challenge"; Wolbring, "Disability Rights."

31 Oliver, "Politics of Disablement," 11.

32 Silvers, "Formal Justice"; Morris, *Pride against Prejudice*; Oliver, "Politics of Disablement"; Koch, "The Difference"; Newell, "Social Nature of Disability."

33 Silvers, "Formal Justice," 94.

34 Oliver, "Politics of Disablement," 1; Wolbring, "Disability Rights."

35 Silvers, "Possibility and Desirability," 472.

36 Ibid., 473.

37 Ibid., 481.

38 Ibid., 477.

39 Ibid.

40 Liz Crow quoted in Silvers, "Formal Justice," 94.

41 Tremain, "The Biopolitics of Bioethics and Disability," 104.

42 Amundson, "Disability, Ideology, and Quality of Life."

43 Foucault, *The History of Sexuality*, vol. 1, 135–59.

44 Tremain, "Foucault, Governmentality, and Critical Disability Theory"; Tremain, "On the Subject of Impairment."

45 Tremain, "Biopolitics of Bioethics," 103; Tremain, "Reproductive Freedom, Self-Regulation, and the Government of Impairment in Utero," 39; Tremain, *Foucault and the Government*, 11; Tremain, "On the Government of Disability," 632.

46 Hughes, "Being Disabled," 674.

47 Ibid.

48 Silvers, "An Essay on Modeling."

49 Davis, *Enforcing Normalcy*; Shakespeare, *Disability Rights and Wrongs*; Shakespeare and Watson, "The Social Model of Disability"; Hughes, "Disability and the Body."

50 Thomas, "Disability and Impairments," 25.

51 Carlson, "Docile Bodies, Docile Minds," 149.

52 Shildrick, *Dangerous Discourses of Disability, Subjectivity and Sexuality.*

53 Campbell, *Contours of Ableism.*

54 Scully, *Disability Bioethics.*

55 Hall, *Feminist Disability Studies*; Garland-Thomson, "Feminist Disability Studies."

56 Hughes, *Being Disabled*, 680.

57 Shildrick, *Dangerous Discourses*; Scully, *Disability Bioethics*; Tremain, *Foucault and the Government*; Shakespeare, *Disability Rights.*

58 Shildrick, "Beyond the Body of Bioethics," 3.

59 See further Kittay, *Love's Labor.*

60 Butler, *Frames of War.*

61 Butler, *Precarious Life*, 12–13.

62 Butler, *Undoing Gender*, 2.

63 Butler, *Frames of War*, 163.

64 Ibid., 18.

65 Ibid., 163.

66 Foucault, *Discipline and Punish*, 30.

67 Tremain, *Foucault and the Government*; Tremain, "On the Subject of Impairment."

68 See Amundson, "Against Normal Function."

69 Bérubé, *Life as We Know It*.

70 Foucault, *The Order of Things*.

71 Garland-Thomson, *Extraordinary Bodies*, 8.

72 McRuer, "Crip Theory."

73 Connolly, "Beyond Good and Evil," 348.

74 Koch, *The Limits of Principle*, 33.

II

Life behind Bars

The Eugenic Structure of Mass Incarceration

LISA GUENTHER

In June 2014, the Center for Investigative Reporting broke a story about the unauthorized sterilization of women in California prisons.[1] Between 2006 and 2010, at least 148 women received tubal ligations that were not approved by a state health care review committee as required under California law.[2] Another ten prisoners were sterilized by other means. While the women had signed consent forms for the procedure, some said they felt pressured to sign, or that they did so under misleading and coercive circumstances. Moreover, whether or not written consent was obtained, the situation of imprisonment complicates issues of agency, choice, and consent for women behind bars, to the point where it isn't clear what a "consent form" could mean in this context.

Christina Cordero, age thirty-four, spent two years at what was then the Valley State Prison for Women on a conviction for auto theft. She reports being pressured by Dr James Heinrich, the prison's obstetrician-gynecologist, to undergo a tubal ligation after the birth of her son in 2006: "As soon as he found out that I had five kids, he suggested that I look into getting it done. The closer I got to my due date, the more he talked about it … He made me feel like a bad mother if I didn't do it."[3] Dr Heinrich denies having coerced the women in his care, but he does not deny his support for the sterilization of women in prison, and justifies the practice as "an important service to poor women who faced health risks in future pregnancies because of past cesarean sections," as well as a service to tax-payers who would "save in welfare paying for these unwanted children – as they procreated more."[4] He adds: "If [the women] come a year or two later saying, 'Somebody forced me to have this done,' that's a lie. That's somebody looking for the state to give them a handout. My guess is that the only reason you do that is not because you feel wronged, but that you want to stay on the state's dole somehow."[5] Dr Heinrich's support for the sterilization of women in prison follows upon a century of formal and informal eugenics projects in the United States that target poor women, women of colour, women with disabilities, and women whose sexual practices were considered "deviant" by doctors and policy-makers. In addition to coercive sterilization, the history of American eugenics includes anti-miscegenation laws, selective immigration policies, state-funded research and records offices, targeted social welfare policies, and uneven access to birth control based on one's perceived race, class, ability, and sexuality.

The recent sterilization of women in California prisons represents another chapter in the history of explicit and implicit eugenics programs in the United States. But it also calls for a broader analysis to connect the dots between racism and class oppression, reproductive injustice, mass incarceration, and the hyperincarceration of poor people and people of colour. In this essay, I argue that the current US prison system is implicated in eugenics not just at particular moments, such as when a woman behind bars is sterilized without proper authorization, but also throughout the multiple interlocking structures that criminalize and incarcerate certain groups of people at disproportionate rates, both implicitly and explicitly controlling their power to have and raise children. In other words, the structure of the current US prison system is *fundamentally eugenic*. It systematically prevents certain groups of people – primarily poor people and people of colour, who are targeted for police surveillance, arrest, and incarceration – from making basic decisions concerning their own reproductive capacity. There need not be an explicit, or even an implicit, eugenic *intention* behind this structure for it to function as a eugenic structure; and yet, as Dr Heinrich's remarks suggest, there is no shortage of people who are ready and willing to lend their own voices to support the control of other people's reproductive capacities.

By "reproductive capacities," I mean both the *biological capacity* to become pregnant or impregnate someone, to gestate a fetus, to give birth, and to support the physical growth of a child, and also the *social capacity* to raise a family and to reproduce certain ways of being, including the capacity to inherit and bequeath languages, cultures, knowledges, technologies, habits, gestures, ways of desiring, and other patterns of embodied social existence. Biological and social reproduction are not separate processes but rather are intertwined and mutually implicating. There is no biological reproduction without a social context in which someone's sperm fertilizes someone's egg under certain conditions that involve at least two people intimately, as well as families, communities, technologies, institutions, ethnic or cultural groups, and species at various levels of particularity and generality. Likewise, there is no social reproduction without bodies that emerge from other bodies and grow more or less independent, connecting with other bodies in ways that mark them, sometimes temporarily and sometimes irreversibly. We are engaged in social reproduction – in other words, we propagate, modulate, resist, and reject the patterns of others – both in particular moments of biological reproduction and in our everyday lives more generally.

Both biological and social reproduction are especially difficult for people in US prisons. Only five states currently permit conjugal visits, and given the prevalence of extremely long sentences in the United States, even for nonviolent crimes, many people who do not already have children upon entering prison will lose the chance to have them.[6] Women who give birth in prison are typically separated from their newborn babies within several days of giving birth and, as I detail below, are at high risk of permanently losing custody of their children. Only nine states have prison nursery facilities where babies may remain with their mothers for up to a year or, in some cases, eighteen months.[7] High phone rates, limited visitation schedules, and many prisons' location far from urban centres and public transportation grids make it difficult for families to stay connected and to engage in processes of social reproduction with one another.[8]

One might acknowledge that such conditions are difficult, and that they put a strain on the reproductive lives of people in prison, without necessarily concluding that they form part of a eugenic structure. One might even argue that such conditions are the unfortunate side effect of otherwise reasonable limitations on the freedom of people who have been convicted of a crime. What evidence is there to suggest that mass incarceration is eugenic in structure? And if we are convinced by the evidence, what would it take to resist and dismantle this structure?

The Structure of Eugenics

The American Bioethics Advisory Commission defines eugenics as "the study of methods to improve the human race by controlling reproduction."[9] There are two mutually reinforcing approaches to eugenics: *positive eugenics*, or the promotion of reproduction for groups of people thought to possess desirable traits, and *negative eugenics*, or the restriction, discouragement, and prevention of reproduction for groups thought to possess undesirable traits. These approaches reflect a key structural element of eugenics: the opposition between the fit and unfit, the normal and abnormal, the valued and devalued. While negative and positive eugenics programs differ in their emphasis, they also imply one another. The more abnormal groups reproduce, the less favourable the environment becomes for normal groups to live, thrive, and reproduce; likewise, the greater and stronger the normal population is, the lower the chances of abnormality taking root and proliferating. This mutual opposition is key for understanding the structure of eugenics, and for following this structure beyond the projects that are explicitly carried out under its name.

From the beginning, eugenics was tied to issues of race, class, ability, addiction, and sexuality. Francis Galton, who coined the term "eugenics" in 1883, opposed charity and other social welfare support for the poor on the grounds that it created an environment for the unfit to reproduce themselves rather than being weeded out by natural selection.[10] A wide range of people faced coercive sterilization and other forms of reproductive control through negative eugenics movements in the early twentieth century. These included (in the language of the time) imbeciles, morons, the feebleminded, cripples, drunkards, paupers, and criminals, as well as people who were racialized as nonwhite or perceived as sexually deviant, such as sex workers, women who were sexually active outside of the marriage relation, and women who failed to display "the normal aversions of a white girl to a coloured man who was perhaps nice to her."[11]

Over 65,000 people were sterilized in thirty-three states under official, state-run eugenics programs in the United States between 1907 and 1974.[12] California led the way, with around 20,000 compulsory sterilizations between 1909 and 1964; that's nearly a third of all eugenic board sterilizations in the country.[13] But these numbers pale in comparison with the impact of public health and social welfare policies targeting poor people and people of colour. By 1980, an estimated 700,000 people had been sterilized through such policies; that's more than ten times the number of people who were sterilized by state eugenics boards.[14] Medically unnecessary hysterectomies became so common for Black women in 1970s Mississippi that they were nicknamed "Mississippi appendectomies."[15] A federally funded campaign in Puerto Rico offered women hysterectomies for free or at very low cost in the 1950s, which led to an almost unthinkable situation in 1968 where "more than one-third of the women of childbearing age in Puerto Rico had been sterilized, the highest percentage of women in the world at the time."[16] In addition to the targeting of Black and Puerto Rican women, more than 3,000 indigenous women were sterilized without adequate consent between 1973 and 1976. This left more than a quarter of Native American women infertile by the end of the 1970s.[17] One doctor reported: "All of the pureblood women of the Kaw tribe of Oklahoma have now been sterilized. At the end of the generation the tribe will cease to exist."[18] In Canada, Alberta and British Columbia were the only provinces to pass legislation permitting coercive sterilization. In Alberta, nearly 3,000 procedures were performed between 1928 and 1972 under the Sexual Sterilization Act, which targeted people with mental and physical disabilities, as well as indigenous people, Métis, and immigrant groups such as Ukrainians. In British Columbia, eugenic board records have been lost or destroyed, but it is estimated that several hundred people were sterilized between 1933 and 1973 under the province's own version of the Sexual Sterilization Act.[19]

At the same time that racialized groups of women were targeted for sterilization, white middle-class women found it nearly impossible to obtain a voluntary hysterectomy. The "120 formula" was selectively applied to those whose reproductive capacities were valued by doctors and public health officials: "If a woman's age multiplied by the number of children she had totaled 120, she was a candidate for sterilization."[20] Following this formula, a woman with one child or no children would never become eligible for a voluntary hysterectomy, a woman with two children would become eligible at age sixty, when she is unlikely to have more children anyway, and a woman with three children would become eligible at forty.

Because white women's lack of access to sterilization was seen as an obstacle to their own right to a full range of reproductive choices, the American Civil Liberties Union, NARAL Pro-Choice America, and Planned Parenthood attempted to block a proposal by the Committee to End Sterilization to end coercive sterilization, an issue that affected almost exclusively poor women and women of colour.[21] Here again we see the inadequacy of middle-class, white-centred pro-choice frameworks for addressing issues of reproductive justice issues, especially as they disproportionately affect poor women and women of colour. We also catch a glimpse of how feminist reproductive politics may unwittingly perpetuate the structure of eugenic policies, which pit the interests of a valued and normalized group against the survival of the devalued and abnormalized.

Eventually, antisterilization activists did manage to pass legislation banning coercive sterilization, but the practice of controlling the reproductive capacities of poor women and women of colour through social welfare policies continues to this day. The 1990s were a particularly intense time for welfare reform in the United States. In 1996, Bill Clinton fulfilled his promise to "end welfare as we know it" by passing the Personal Responsibility and Work Opportunity Reconciliation Act, which replaced welfare with Temporary Assistance for Needy Families and introduced workfare, family caps on welfare payments, and a five-year lifetime limit for people on social assistance. New and controversial birth control methods such as Norplant (which prevents pregnancy for five continuous years through the implantation of pellets under the skin) were promoted for women on welfare, and especially for women who were found to use drugs during their pregnancy.[22]

These programs continue to be funded by state and federal incentives, and also by nonprofits such as Project Prevention (formerly known as CRACK: Children Requiring a Caring Kommunity). Project Prevention is a nonprofit organization that pays drug users $300 cash to undergo permanent or temporary sterilization.[23] Its mission statement is to "reduce the burden of this social problem on taxpayers, trim down social worker caseloads, and alleviate from our clients the burden of having children that will potentially be taken away."[24] Rather than supporting women to retain custody of their children and/or to access treatment for addiction, Project Prevention aims to "alleviate ... the burden" of losing children by reducing or removing a woman's reproductive capacity altogether. While the program presents itself as a service to women as "clients," as well as to taxpayers and social workers, the founder's unofficial comments in media interviews devalue and dehumanize the women targeted by the program, pitting their own rights and interests against the health of children and of society at large. In a 2010 interview with *Time* magazine, founder Barbara Harris asked, "What makes a woman's right to procreate more important than the right of a child to have a normal life? ... Even if these babies are fortunate enough not to have mental or physical disabilities, they're placed in the foster-care system and moved from home to home."[25] In a 1998 interview with *Marie Claire*, her comments were even more frankly eugenic: "We don't allow dogs to breed. We neuter them. We try to keep them from having unwanted puppies, and yet these women are literally having litters of children."[26]

Originally based in California but now operating out of North Carolina, Project Prevention has funded sterilization procedures for over 4,000 people in the United States since it began in 1997. In 2010, it expanded to the United Kingdom, where it offers drug addicts £200 for sterilization, and to Kenya, where it offers HIV+ women forty US dollars in small business start-up funds if they agree to have an intrauterine device implanted.[27] Needless to say, the use of an intrauterine device does not prevent the transmission of the virus to adult sexual partners, but only prevents the potential birth of a child who is HIV+, and the latter risk could be addressed through antiretroviral treatment and ongoing health care for both women and children.

Project Prevention emerged in a climate of widespread moral panic in the 1990s in response to the spectre of so-called crack babies. While long-term studies have found no significant differences in developmental outcomes for children exposed to crack or other forms of cocaine in the womb, and have pointed instead to poverty as the decisive factor in fetal and early childhood development, this research comes too late for the many women who were singled out for drug testing, arrest, criminal prosecution, incarceration, and sterilization on the basis of their perceived status as a crack users – which is to say, on the basis of their devalued race and class.[28]

Together, these official and unofficial eugenic policies constitute what Ladelle McWhorter, following Foucault, calls "racism against the abnormal."[29] It targets, and arguably produces, "individuals who, as carriers of a condition, stigmata, or any defect whatsoever, may more or less randomly transmit to their heirs the unpredictable consequences of the evil, or the non-normal, that they carry within them."[30] The "defect" that Dr Heinrich identified in the women he sterilized in California prisons was, by his own account, their poverty. This a frank, if also unintentional, admission that the US prison system functions not only to punish people who have been convicted of a crime, but also to manage and control the reproductive policies of poor and otherwise "unfit" or "abnormal" populations. To what extent can a eugenic structure be discerned in the US prison system more broadly, especially in a situation of mass incarceration?

The Eugenic Structure of Mass Incarceration

The United States has the largest prison population and the highest incarceration rate in the world. Sociologist Loïc Wacquant goes so far as to call the United States "the first genuine prison society in history."[31] He proposes the term "carceral-assistential complex" to account for the interlocking systems of punishment and "care" that target poor people for disproportionate surveillance and control, in both prisons and social welfare systems. He argues that the term "prison industrial complex" is inadequate to account for the radical expansion of the US prison system in a time of post-industrial or deindustrializing economic reform. The carceral-assistential complex functions "to surveil, train and neutralize the populations recalcitrant or superfluous to the new economic and racial regime according to a gendered division of labor, the men being handled by its penal wing while (their) women and children are managed by a revamped welfare-workfare system designed to buttress casual employment."[32] In other words, it aims to preside over the social reproduction of surplus populations whose productive capacities have been rendered superfluous by neoliberal economic reforms. Wacquant calls this "the penalization of social insecurity" or "mass incarceration as a masked antipoverty policy."[33] The poor are both excluded from the legal wage economy and punished for their survival skills; they are both denied supportive social services and also targeted for "punitive services" that undermine their productive and reproductive capacities, whether in prison or in prisonized social housing complexes. These services include the sterilization of women in prison, whether or not they have signed a legal consent form.

Wacquant's analysis of the carceral-assistential complex is helpful for articulating the role of prisons in managing and controlling the poor; but his account of the gendered division of carceral-assistential labour, whereby the women get welfare and the men get prison, is increasingly becoming outdated. In the United States, Black women are more than three and a half times more likely to be behind bars than white women, and they represent the fastest-rising prison population in the country.[34] Between 1980 and 2010, the number of women behind bars increased 646 per cent – one and a half times greater than the rate of increase for men in the same period.[35] In Canada, indigenous women are the most disproportionately incarcerated group, representing 4 per cent of the population and 34 per cent of the federal inmate population; these numbers have increased by 86.5 per cent in the past ten years.[36]

The war on drugs, along with increasingly punitive sentencing structures, have been largely responsible for the dramatic increase in the US prison population over the past thirty years.[37] Over a quarter of the women behind bars are serving time for drug-related offenses; together with nonviolent property crimes, these account for two-thirds of incarcerated women. Until very recently, drug offenses involving crack cocaine were punished at a weight ratio of 100:1 with powder cocaine under the Rockefeller drug laws; they are still punished at a ratio of 18:1. This disproportionately affects poor people of colour, who are more likely to use crack than other more expensive or less accessible drugs.

Once convicted of a drug felony, a person can be permanently disqualified from housing assistance, food stamps, and other social welfare programs.[38] This is especially punitive given the high rates of unemployment for formerly incarcerated people. Even before going to prison, almost 40 per cent of incarcerated women and 30 per cent of incarcerated men lived in poverty prior to their arrest, with monthly incomes of less than $600.[39]

Many of these people are parents of young children, and given the unequal gender distribution of responsibility for children across the social spectrum of race and class, many women behind bars are the primary or sole caregivers of these children. Of women in prison, 75 per cent are mothers, and two-thirds of these women have children under the age of eighteen.[40] Of adult women in prison, 25 per cent were pregnant at the time of their arrest, or gave birth within the year prior to their arrest.

Widespread public support for the criminal prosecution of women who used drugs such as crack during their pregnancy, combined with a severe and chronic shortage of drug rehabilitation programs for pregnant women and mothers with small children, led to skyrocketing arrest and incarceration for poor women of colour in the 1990s.[41] These women were charged under laws that were designed to protect children but were expanded to include fetuses, such as laws against child abuse or distributing drugs to a minor. The enthusiasm for protecting the fetus, both against the woman who bears it and in spite of her, led to the rise of myriad fetal protection laws and fetal homicide laws, which punish violence against the fetus in addition to or separately from violence against pregnant women.[42] This rhetoric is bolstered by the pro-life movement, and more recently by the personhood movement, which seeks to redefine a legal person to include a fertilized egg cell and to invest the zygote with the full rights of a citizen.

But the rhetoric of fetal protection rarely, if ever, translates into a commitment to improve the material conditions for emerging life, and even more rarely translates into social support for children once they are born. Prenatal and postnatal care in prison is notoriously insufficient.[43] In all but eighteen states, women who give birth in prison are shackled with heavy chains that severely restrict their movement, apparently to discourage escape attempts while in hospital.[44] Within two to four days of giving birth, women are returned to prison and separated from their newborn babies. If they are unable to find a friend or family member to assume temporary custody of their children (whether newborn or grown), or if their chosen guardian is not approved by the state, their children are put in foster care. If the child remains in foster care for fifteen of the most recent twenty-two months, parental rights are automatically terminated under the federal Adoption and Safe Families Act of 1997.[45] Given that most prison sentences, even for nonviolent offenses, are longer than fifteen months, this can result in the permanent loss of a parent's access to their children.[46]

There need not be an explicit, or even an implicit, eugenic *intention* behind this structure for it to function as such. Modifying Wacquant's analysis to account for the hyperincarceration of women of colour, I propose to call this a *carceral-eugenic complex*: it not only manages populations rendered unproductive by neoliberal economic reforms, but also controls their reproductive capacities, focusing most intensely on poor women of colour, both on the streets and behind bars. Apologists for the carceral-eugenic complex include right-wing criminologists and political scientists such as Richard Herrnstein and Charles Murray, co-authors of *The Bell Curve*. In a single-authored article on "Criminogenic Traits," Herrnstein makes a eugenic argument for the genetic transmission of criminality: "Inasmuch as criminal behavior is associated with [inferior] intelligence and [antisocial] personality, and inasmuch as personality and intelligence have genetic influences on them, then it follows logically, as night follows day, that criminal behavior has genetic ingredients."[47] Note how this "argument" reduces social reproduction to biological reproduction, and even reduces biological reproduction to the transmission of genetic traits, as if they were essences that are magically passed down independent of any social or even physiological context. In the same volume, Brennan, Mednick, and Volacka make a similar argument in an article titled "Biomedical Factors in Crime": "Criminal behavior in parents increases the likelihood of nonviolent crime in the offspring. This relationship is due, in part, to genetic transmission of criminogenic characteristics. This genetic effect is stronger for females and is especially important for recidivistic crime."[48] If criminal behaviour has genetic ingredients, and if these ingredients are stronger in the females of criminal(ized) populations, then it follows logically, as night follows day, that the management and control of certain women's reproductive capacities will reduce the crime rate and (factoring in Dr Heinrich's point) save taxpayers money.

These right-wing proponents of eugenic responses to social problems find an unlikely companion in Margaret Sanger, founder of Planned Parenthood. While Sanger was initially motivated by a desire to support the reproductive autonomy of poor and working-class women, she also advocated for the limitation and control of reproduction for Black people and otherwise "unfit" people on the grounds that "we are paying for and even submitting to the dictates of an ever-increasing, unceasingly spawning class of human beings who never should have been born at all."[49] To what extent has the pro-choice movement, and mainstream feminism, remained complicit with the eugenic structure of mass incarceration long after Sanger's explicit endorsement of eugenics has faded from white feminist memory?[50] And what would it take to dismantle the structural coupling of hypervalued and hyperdevalued lives in a way that benefits all women – even if it also entails a loss of privilege for white women?

White Feminist Complicity with the Carceral-Eugenic Complex

Consider the statement of Daun Martin, the top medical manager at California's Valley State Prison for Women from 2005 to 2008. When asked to comment on recent reports of unauthorized sterilizations of women prisoners under her watch, Martin readily acknowledged that she collaborated with Dr Heinrich to facilitate the sterilization of prisoners by manipulating the prison's rules and authorization structures, such as by documenting their situation as a medical emergency in order to fast-track procedures.[51] While Martin does not explicitly identify herself as a feminist, she defends the sterilization of women in prison in the language of mainstream feminism, "as an empowerment issue for female inmates, providing them the same options as women on the outside."[52]

Presumably, she means that access to sterilization in prison could translate into greater reproductive freedom for women post-release; they would no longer have to worry about pregnancy, birth control, or access to abortion. In other words, incarcerated women would benefit from being relieved of the burden of having to manage their own reproductive capacity. This thinking assumes, of course, that incarcerated women are so powerless and ill-equipped to make responsible choices about their own reproductive lives that the permanent elimination of their capacity to get pregnant and give birth counts as a lifestyle improvement: one less thing to worry about. It also assumes that reproductive liberty can be equated with reproductive choice, which in turn is equated with the choice to avoid pregnancy and birth. Otherwise, it's hard to imagine how sterilization could be construed as "having the same options as women on the outside."

The conflation of reproductive liberty with freedom from pregnancy and motherhood reflects a dominant assumption of the pro-choice movement, to the extent that it is based on the right to privacy and structured around the interests of young, white, middle-class women. The slogan "My body, my choice!" implies an investment in the body as a type of private property, or even as the quintessence of private property, which has historically marginalized the concerns of poor women and women of colour who may not have the wealth, the social standing, or even the desire to mobilize a property interest in their own bodies.[53]

But the problem goes deeper. The carceral-eugenic structure of mass incarceration produces two classes of people: normal and abnormal, valued and devalued, product and waste. While some women find themselves caught in a tight network of racism, poverty, and criminalization, others are offered a seemingly endless array of consumer and technological options for getting pregnant, giving birth, breastfeeding, and raising children. Not only do white, middle-class women benefit symbolically from the hypervaluation of their lives and the lives of their children, but many also benefit materially from the availability of low-wage domestic workers — many of whom are women of colour — to clean their houses and take care of their children while they engage in more "productive" and lucrative work. Furthermore, many feminist antiviolence groups continue to advocate for increased police surveillance, arrest, and long-term incarceration as responses to violence against women, even though poor women and women of colour are less likely to be protected or supported by the police or the courts, and more likely to be arrested or sexually and physically abused by police even when they have called them for help.[54]

White middle-class women have multiple incentives to comply with or even intensify the eugenic structure of mass incarceration, which affects poor women and women of colour in disproportionately negative ways. And yet, it's not clear that this structure is "good" even for the women it most directly benefits. The white, middle-class, able-bodied, gender-normative, and sexually acceptable beneficiaries of positive eugenics may be valued, but they are not for this reason respected or recognized as singular subjects with a life of their own. More insidiously, positive eugenics programs recruit white women as junior partners in negative eugenics campaigns against devalued others.[55] As such, they undermine solidarity among women by obscuring the common interest of white women and women of colour in resisting reproductive injustice and developing a relational, socially contextualized sense of the right to make decisions concerning our own reproductive capacity.

The reproductive choices of all women are increasingly constrained by pro-life strategies that limit access to abortion, birth control, and women's health services through legal reform, administrative management, and social pressure.[56] It is up to white women to struggle against our own complicity in the carceral-eugenic complex, but (as a white women myself) I think we can learn a lot from the reproductive justice movement developed by women of colour activists and scholars.

Dismantling Eugenic Structures: The Reproductive Justice Movement

The reproductive justice movement emerged in the mid-1990s as a critical response to the mainstream pro-choice movement's narrow focus on the priorities of young, white, middle-class women. Influenced by the human rights discourse of postcolonial feminists, a Black women's caucus convened at the Illinois Pro-Choice Alliance conference in 1994 to develop a conceptual and political framework for reproductive *justice* that moved beyond the reproductive choice framework and connected reproductive rights to broader struggles for social justice.[57] This group was called Women of African Descent for Reproductive Justice; in 1997, its members joined with other women of colour and indigenous women to form the SisterSong Women of Color Reproductive Justice Collective. SisterSong defines reproductive justice in terms of "the right to have children, not have children, and to parent the children we have in safe and healthy environments."[58] Note the breadth of this definition; it includes not only the right to reproductive "choice" in the sense of a range of options for preventing pregnancy and birth, but also the right to have children and raise them in a way that supports the mutual flourishing of parents and children.

The affiliated organization, Trust Black Women, identifies this cluster of rights as the *human* rights of *women of colour*.[59] In other words, they make a universal claim to human rights that remains rooted in the particular situations and standpoints of women of colour. Simply by making a rights claim, Trust Black Women may seem to operate within a liberal political framework, but a closer examination proves otherwise. In the words of

SisterSong: "Human rights provide more possibilities for our struggles than the privacy concepts the pro-choice movement claims only using the US Constitution."[60] The reproductive justice movement refuses to presuppose the legitimacy, or even the continued existence, of the United States as a nation founded on native genocide and the enslavement of Black people. In light of this, I interpret the demand for Black women's human rights as a counterhegemonic claim from the particular to the universal – not in order to seek inclusion in the circle of privilege, but to provoke a radical restructuring of the human, of rights, and of the racist logic that continues to structure the particular social landscapes that women of colour inhabit, including the prison system.[61]

Scholar-activist Dorothy Roberts makes a similar counterhegemonic claim for universal liberation rooted in the particular struggles of women of colour when she claims that "Black women's reproductive autonomy can transform the meaning of liberty for everyone."[62] Why? Because the eugenic structure of past and present reproductive policies does not just *disadvantage* black reproduction; it also *advantages* and incentivizes white reproduction through everything from tax credits for middle-class families (and welfare cuts for indigent families) to expensive in vitro fertilization services marketed toward white women. Again, the challenge is not to expand the circle of privilege, as if hypervaluation were an uncomplicated good, and as if it could ever take place without a correlative hyperdevaluation of another group; rather, the challenge is to transform the eugenic structure of reproductive injustice by centring the perspectives of those who are most directly affected by it and dismantling those structures under their leadership.

This final point is crucial. The activist group EMERJ (Expanding the Movement for Empowerment and Reproductive Justice) situates the reproductive justice movement within an explicitly intersectional framework that centres the concerns of those who are directly affected by reproductive injustice: "Reproductive Justice aims to transform power inequities and create long-term systemic change, and therefore *relies on the leadership of communities most impacted by reproductive oppression.* The reproductive justice framework recognizes that all individuals are part of communities and that our strategies must lift up entire communities to support individuals."[63] The subject of the reproductive justice movement is therefore not an isolated, rights-bearing individual – although her rights to have children, to not have children, and to raise the children she has are nevertheless a key point of the movement's legal and political struggle. But these rights must be understood and embodied within an intersectional context in which relational subjectivity is shaped and reshaped by mutually defining formations of race, class, gender, sexuality, and ability. Since the carceral-eugenic complex is an intersectional form of violence, targeting subjects on the basis of their race, class, gender, sexuality, and ability, only an intersectional critique and an intersectional social movement can dismantle it.

Moreover, the negative or critical work of dismantling eugenic structures of valuation must be complemented by a positive movement of affirmation and support for the relational (inter)subjectivity of women and girls, understood as members of a community and political actors in a common world. In "A New Vision," Asian Communities for Reproductive Justice, now known as Forward Together, defines reproductive justice as "the complete physical, mental, spiritual, political, economic, and social well-being of women and girls."[64] It argues:

> We need a movement with a vision of addressing women wholly and comprehensively so that we do not single out pieces of a woman's body but see their bodies as whole. Similarly, we cannot focus solely on one aspect of a woman's life, whether at work, at school, at home, or on the streets. We need to understand how reproductive oppression may exist in all arenas of her life, and recognize that she may have to walk through all of these arenas in a single day.[65]

The reproductive justice framework developed by SisterSong, Asian Communities for Reproductive Justice, and other women of colour activists and scholars helps to navigate the issues raised by the recent sterilization of women in California prisons, and to connect these issues to broader social struggles that affect all women and all human beings, whether or not they have been incarcerated and whether or not they have considered having children of their own. Their affirmation of women of colour's collective and individual power of self-organizing and self-determination is rooted in a radical critique of oppression and in a commitment to social transformation, which recognizes both the strategic position of women of colour in eugenic campaigns and also the power of women of colour to analyze, resist, and transform these structures. But they cannot accomplish this transformation alone. It is the responsibility of white women, especially white feminists, to educate ourselves about the history of eugenics, its contemporary legacy, and its underlying logic in order to resist the structures that undermine the possibility of reproductive justice for all.

NOTES

1 Johnson, "Female Inmates Sterilized in California Prisons without Approval."
2 State of California, *California Code of Regulations*, title 15, div. 3, ch. 1, art. 8, sec. 3350.1.
3 Ibid. See also the excellent analysis of reproductive injustice in California prisons, including coercive sterilization, in the testimony of Justice Now, *Testimony on Budget Issues Related to Conditions of Confinement and Illegal Sterilizations*.
4 Johnson, "Female Inmates Sterilized."
5 Ibid.
6 "Conjugal Visits." The official policy of Correctional Service Canada grants many, but not all, prisoners a seventy-two-hour private family visit every two months. "Private Family Visiting," Correctional Service of Canada.
7 Women's Prison Association (Institute on Women and Criminal Justice), "Mothers, Infants and Imprisonment."
8 For more than ten years, private phone contractors have charged exorbitant rates for calls to and from prisons, offering kickbacks to state correctional departments in exchange for a monopoly on the market. Dannenberg, "Nationwide PLN Survey Examines Prison Phone Contracts, Kickbacks." In August 2013, the Federal Communications Commission put a cap of twenty-five cents per minute on interstate calls, but intrastate calls remain unregulated. Reardon, "FCC Puts Cap on Prison Phone Rates." This situation forces many families to choose between phone calls and basic living expenses. New York Campaign for Telephone Justice, "Pay or Be Silent."
9 "Eugenics," American Bioethics Advisory Commission.
10 Galton, *Inquiries into Human Faculty and Its Development*.
11 Aptheker, "Sterilization, Experimentation, and Imperialism," 45, quoted in Roberts, *Killing the Black Body*, 69.
12 Bruinius, *Better for All the World*; see also Davis, "Racism, Birth Control and Reproductive Rights," 9.

13 For an official apology by the state of California, see "Governor Davis Makes Statement on Eugenics," and "Untitled" from State of California Office of the Attorney General.

14 Roberts, *Killing the Black Body*, 90.

15 Ibid.

16 Ibid., 94.

17 Ibid., 95; see also Smith, *Conquest*.

18 Uri, quoted in May, *Barren in the Promised Land*, 119, as quoted in Roberts, *Killing the Black Body*, 95.

19 For more information, see Harris-Zsovan, *Eugenics & the Firewall*; Grekul, "A Well-Oiled Machine." The policy of "killing the Indian in the child," which underwrote Canada's residential school system, is arguably also a policy of cultural genocide with a carceral-eugenic structure. For more on residential schools, see Milloy, *A National Crime*, and the Truth and Reconciliation Commission of Canada.

20 May, *Barren in the Promised Land*, as quoted in Roberts, *Killing the Black Body*, 95.

21 Roberts, *Killing the Black Body*, 95–6.

22 Ibid., 104–49.

23 Bickman, "Should Addicts Be Sterilized?"

24 Project Prevention, "Objectives."

25 Bickman, "Should Addicts Be Sterilized?"

26 Ibid. Compare this statement by Andre Bauer, lieutenant governor of South Carolina from 2003 to 2011, in a town hall meeting in January 2010, during his unsuccessful bid for the Republican nomination for state governor: "My grandmother was not a highly educated woman, but she told me as a small child to quit feeding stray animals. You know why? Because they breed. You're facilitating the problem if you give an animal or a person ample food supply. They will reproduce, especially ones that don't think too much further than that. And so what you've got to do is you've got to curtail that type of behavior. They don't know any better." Bauer offered this anecdote in support of his view that the parents of children who receive free lunches or lunch subsidies should be subject to mandatory drug testing and required to attend parent-teacher association meetings and parent-teacher interviews. He added: "I can show you a bar graph where free and reduced lunch has the worst test scores in the state of South Carolina." When the scandal broke nation-wide, Bauer insisted that he did not mean to imply that people who receive social assistance "were animals or anything else." He clarified, "he would penalize only adults and that he never advocated taking away a child's

free or reduced-price lunch." Montopoli, "S.C. Lt. Gov. Andre Bauer Compares Helping Poor to Feeding Stray Animals."

27 Clark, "IUDs to Prevent HIV in Kenya?"

28 FitzGerald, "'Crack Baby' Study Ends with Unexpected but Clear Result." Furthermore, cocaine use (in any form) has been found to be less prevalent and less harmful for fetal and early childhood development than the use of other controlled substances such as alcohol, cigarettes, marijuana, and pharmaceutical drugs such as Oxycontin. Roth, *Making Women Pay*, 141–5; Roberts, *Killing the Black Body*, 150–201; Maia Szalavitz, "Are Oxycontin Babies the New Crack Babies?"

29 McWhorter, *Racism and Sexual Oppression*, 28–32.

30 Foucault, *Abnormal*, 316–17, as quoted in McWhorter, *Racism and Sexual Oppression*, 32.

31 Loïc Wacquant, "Deadly Symbiosis," 120.

32 Ibid., 97. See also Wacquant, *Prisons of Poverty*, 83.

33 Wacquant, "Deadly Symbiosis," 98; Wacquant, *Prisons of Poverty*, 71.

34 Public Safety Performance Project, "One in 100: Behind Bars in American 2008." See also Ritchie, *Arrested Justice*; Davis, *Are Prisons Obsolete?*

35 The Sentencing Project, "Incarcerated Women."

36 Tefft, "Canadian Justice System Failing Aboriginal People"; Gartner, Webster, and Doob, "Trends in the Imprisonment of Women in Canada."

37 Alexander, *The New Jim Crow*.

38 Ibid.

39 INCITE! Women of Color Against Violence, "Women of Color & Prisons."

40 Arkansas Educational Television Network, "Mothers in Prison, Children in Crisis."

41 Roberts, *Killing the Black Body*, 150–201; Roth, *Making Women Pay*, 135–83; Levi et al., "Creating the Bad Mother."

42 As per the National Conference of State Legislatures:
Currently, at least thirty-eight states have fetal homicide laws. The states include: Alabama, Alaska, Arizona, Arkansas, California, Colorado, Florida, Georgia, Idaho, Illinois, Indiana, Iowa, Kansas, Kentucky, Louisiana, Maine, Maryland, Massachusetts, Michigan, Minnesota, Mississippi, Nebraska, Nevada, North Carolina, North Dakota, Ohio, Oklahoma, Pennsylvania, Rhode Island, South Carolina, South Dakota, Tennessee, Texas, Utah, Virginia, Washington, West Virginia and Wisconsin. At least twenty-three states have fetal homicide laws that apply to the earliest stages of pregnancy ("any state of gestation," "conception," "fertilization" or "post-fertilization").

These laws have names such as the Fetal Protection Act, the Preborn Victims of Violence Act, and the Unborn Victim of Violence Act. "Fetal Homicide Laws."

43 For more details on the insufficiency of prenatal and postnatal care for women in prison, see Levi et al., "Creating the Bad Mother"; Roth, *Making Women Pay*.

44 Nation Inside, "Birthing behind Bars."

45 Adoption and Safe Families Act of 1997, Pub. L. no. 105–89, 111 Stat. 2115 (1997)., sec. 103 (a)(3).

46 Roberts, *Shattered Bonds*.

47 Herrnstein, "Criminogenic Traits," 114.

48 Brennan, Mednick, and Volacka, "Biomedical Factors in Crime," 87–98, quoted in Wacquant, *Deadly Symbiosis*, 126.

49 Sanger, *The Pivot of Civilization*, 187, quoted in Roberts, *Killing the Black Body*, 74; see also Roberts, *Killing the Black Body*, 56–103; Davis, "Racism, Birth Control and Reproductive Rights."

50 By "mainstream feminism," I mean an approach to feminism that centres on the interests of white middle-class women and focuses on building collaborative relationships with dominant power rather than with grassroots movements. Ritchie, "How We Won the Mainstream but Lost the Movement."

51 Johnson, "Female Inmates Sterilized." Johnson further reports:

After learning of the restrictions, Martin told CIR that she and Heinrich began to look for ways around them. Both believed the rules were unfair to women, she said. "I'm sure that on a couple of occasions, (Heinrich) brought an issue to me saying, 'Mary Smith is having a medical emergency' kind of thing, 'and we ought to have a tubal ligation. She's got six kids. Can we do it?'" Martin said. "And I said, 'Well, if you document it as a medical emergency, perhaps.'"

52 Ibid.

53 Silliman and Bhattacharjee explain: "This conception of choice is rooted in the neoliberal tradition that locates individual rights at its core, and treats the individual's control over her body as central to liberty and freedom. This emphasis on individual choice, however, obscures the social context in which individuals make choices, and discounts the ways in which the state regulates populations, disciplines individual bodies, and exercises control over sexuality, gender, and reproduction." *Policing the National Body*, x–xi. See also Smith, *Conquest*; Davis, "Racism, Birth Control and Reproductive Rights."

54 Ritchie, *Arrested Justice*; INCITE! Women of Color Against Violence, *Color of Violence*; Conrad, *Against Equality*.

55 Wilderson, in "The Prison Slave as Hegemony's (Silent) Scandal," argues that white women are positioned as "civil society's junior partners" (20). He asks whether and how "the production and accumulation of junior partner social capital [is] dependent upon an anti-Black rhetorical structure and a decomposed Black body" (20). In other words, the upward mobility of white women is based upon the civil, social, and rhetorical death of Black women and men: "There is something organic to Black positionality that makes it essential to the destruction of civil society ... Blackness is a positionality of 'absolute dereliction' (Fanon), abandonment, in the face of civil society, and therefore cannot establish itself or be established, through hegemonic interventions. Blackness cannot become one of civil society's many junior partners: Black citizenship, or Black civic obligation, are oxymorons" (18). Any meaningful resistance to white supremacy would have to break this dependence of white women's social and political advancement on the incapacitation of Black women and men, whether in prison or in other sites of inclusive exclusion.

56 Deprez, "Abortion Clinics Close at Record Pace after States Tighten Rules."

57 Asian Communities for Reproductive Justice, "A New Vision for Advancing Our Movement for Reproductive Health, Reproductive Rights and Reproductive Justice." According to Loretta Ross, one of the caucus participants:

> We were dissatisfied with the pro-choice language, feeling that it did not adequately encompass our twinned goals: To protect the right to have – and to not have – children. Nor did the language of choice accurately portray the many barriers African American women faced when trying to make reproductive decisions. Perhaps because we were just returning from the International Conference on Population and Development in Cairo, Egypt in 1994, we began exploring the use of the human rights framework in our reproductive rights activism in the United States, as many grassroots activists do globally. We sought a way to partner reproductive rights to social justice and came up with the term "reproductive justice." (5)

58 SisterSong, "What Is RJ?"

59 SisterSong, "Trust Black Women."

60 SisterSong, "What Is RJ?"

61 See also Asian Communities for Reproductive Justice's commitment to radical social transformation: "For reproductive justice to become a reality, we must undergo a radical transformation; change must be made on the individual, community, institutional, and societal levels to end all forms of oppression so that women and girls are able to thrive, to gain self-determination, to exercise control over our bodies, and to have a full range of reproductive

choices. The control and exploitation of women and girls through our bodies, sexuality, and reproduction is a strategic pathway to regulating entire populations that is implemented by families, communities, institutions, and society." "A New Vision," 1.

62 Roberts, *Killing the Black Body*, 7.

63 EMERJ, "Core Aspects of Reproductive Justice" in "Three Applications of the Reproductive Justice Lens." Emphasis added. This approach is affirmed by SisterSong in "What Is RJ?" and is linked to an engagement with lived experience: "Reproductive justice emerged as an intersectional theory highlighting the lived experience of reproductive oppression in communities of color. It represents a shift for women advocating for control of their bodies, from a narrower focus on legal access and individual choice (the focus of mainstream organizations) to a broader analysis of racial, economic, cultural, and structural constraints on our power."

64 Asian Communities for Reproductive Justice, "A New Vision," 1.

65 Ibid., 9.

12

Fetal Life, Abortion, and Harm Reduction

SHANNON DEA

Despite the ubiquity of the word "life" in the abortion debate, I propose that both sides pay too little attention to fetal life.[1] Irrespective of whether pro-choice advocates feel concern for the lives of fetuses, they rarely express it, and instead typically emphasize concern for women's choice and autonomy.[2] On the other side, while pro-life advocates invoke the sanctity of life, they oppose mechanisms empirically shown to reduce the loss of fetal (and maternal) life. They are ideologically pro-life, but in practice careless with actual lives.[3]

I wish here to make two broad, mutually supporting points: first, that those who theorize about and research abortion, and who advocate for or against limits on access to abortion, ought to show serious concern for both the lives and the quality of life of both women and fetuses; and second, that a harm reduction model is the best approach available to us to act on such concern, and in so doing to reduce suffering, morbidity, and death among women, their families, and fetuses.

These claims are likely to be controversial to anyone involved in the abortion debate. The first claim will be controversial for reasons that I suggested at the outset: pro-choice advocates shrink from addressing fetal life, and pro-life advocates are stubbornly indifferent to the real mechanisms associated with preserving fetal life. With respect to my second claim, many pro-choice proponents reject in principle the idea that abortions cause or constitute harms. Pro-life proponents, by contrast, regard abortions as both causing and constituting harms. However, the laws and policies for which they advocate do nothing to reduce those harms. Thus, on both the importance of the life of the fetus and on the harmfulness of abortion, my view might be said to align in principle with the pro-life position, but in practice with the pro-choice position. In short, I argue that pro-life principles are best supported by pro-choice practices (and, crucially, by pro-choice laws and policies). In a very robust sense, then, I propose a life-centred approach to abortion. It is life-centred both because it attends unflinchingly to the lives – and the quality of life – of fetuses and women (and the children of those women), and because it offers the best strategy we have for reducing loss of life and for supporting quality of life.

First, I argue that we ought to show concern for the lives of both fetuses and women, and that such concern is consistent with the view that abortions ought to be safe and accessible. Pro-choice proponents, I argue, have no reason to shrink from attending to questions about fetal life. Second, I elaborate the public health approach termed "harm reduction," and suggest three principles that help determine whether a harm reduction approach is appropriate. Finally, I show that abortion satisfies all three criteria, and thus is a suitable target for harm reduction interventions.

Thinking about the Fetus

I have for years now been an active advocate of abortion access – even serving as a fairly high-profile regional Planned Parenthood president. In that role, I have uttered the standard pro-choice phrases, but for some time the notion of choice as the conceptual basis for abortion access has sat uneasily with me. In the context of the abortion debate, appeals to choice privilege the woman[4] and ignore (*inter alia*) the fetus.[5] While recent legislative attacks on women's reproductive autonomy make salient the need to attend to women in particular when thinking about abortion, I reject the idea that attending to women means disregarding fetuses.

Indeed, it has always struck me as deeply unsatisfying that when someone expresses concern for aborted fetuses, many pro-choice supporters reply with assertions about women's rights. Consider, for example, the

"How to Think about the Fetus" poster used by the Abortion Rights Coalition of Canada. The poster asks, "Are these the key questions in the abortion debate? When does life begin? Is a fetus a person? Is abortion murder?" The poster goes on to diagnose the foregoing questions as examples of "the fetus focus fallacy," and retorts, "No, here's [sic] the REAL questions: Should we let women suffer and die from unsafe, illegal abortions? Should we force women to bear children against their will? Should we force unwanted children to be born? Ultimately, it doesn't matter what the fetus is, how valuable we think it is, or whether it has any rights. True justice demands that women not be compelled to bear children they don't want."[6] The Abortion Rights Coalition of Canada does excellent, evidence-based work, and its rhetorical emphasis here on women rather than fetuses is understandable, given the neglect of women's health and autonomy in much pro-life propaganda. Nonetheless, the Abortion Rights Coalition of Canada's "REAL questions," while important, are orthogonal to the question of whether or not we should be concerned about fetuses.

The belief that fetuses deserve our concern sits uneasily with the view that women have the right to do with their bodies as they will. It is, in some respects, easier to maintain one of these views and reject the other than it is to hold both of them at once. However, while there are empirical and ethical difficulties inherent in acting on concern for fetuses while supporting women's autonomy, there is at least no *logical* obstacle to maintaining both beliefs at once. Thus, it is irrelevant to answer questions about fetuses with facts about women. To do so is to change the subject.[7]

To change the subject when someone raises a genuine worry about the lives of aborted fetuses not only fails to show adequate attention to the person posing the worry and to the content of her concern, but also fosters the impression that it is impossible to answer the fetus worry square on without undercutting the view that abortions should be legal and accessible. This impression is mistaken. It is possible to admit that fetuses deserve concern, and to show such concern, while at the same time supporting abortion access.

In my association with Planned Parenthood, I have both directly and indirectly sought to assist women who have decided to have abortions procure safe, affordable ones. Throughout that time, I have always regarded fetuses as warranting moral concern. This is not to say that I regard them as persons.[8] Indeed, I do not think that our moral concern should be reserved exclusively for persons. I feel moral concern for a range of nonhuman animals as well as for human fetuses who are not yet – and indeed may never become – persons. This concern eventuates in a range of large and small acts. Here is a small act: when I walk down the street after a rainfall and see earthworms on the pavement, I remove them to a bit of grass so that they are not trod upon. I do not regard earthworms as having a right to life. However, I am moved by sympathy for them as living creatures. Here is a larger act: for all of my adult life, I have been some kind of vegetarian or other because I believe that it is morally unjust of me to contribute unnecessarily to the loss of life of nonhuman animals.

I do not regard all lives as equally deserving of moral consideration. I eat plants, even though they are alive, and I do not feel guilty about doing so. I sometimes eat bivalves such as mussels because their simple neuro-anatomy means that they are far less likely to experience suffering than a nonhuman animal in possession of a large, complex brain. For the same reason, I feel more moral concern for neurologically complex animals such as cetaceans, cephalopods, and primates[9] than I do for less neurologically complex ones such as insects and gastropods. I regard harms to the former as more morally troubling than harms to the latter.

It would be very odd indeed if someone like me, who had long allowed her moral concern about nonhuman animals to influence her conduct in a variety of ways, showed no such concern for human fetuses. As in the case of nonhuman animals, I do not wish to contribute to loss of life or vitiation of quality of life among human fetuses. All other things being equal, I would rather that fewer rather than more fetuses died. And again, all other things being equal, I would especially prefer to reduce suffering and loss of life of gestationally older fetuses, who are more neurologic-ally complex.[10]

My point here is not psychological, but moral. I do not merely claim that, as a descriptive fact, I happen to feel concern for fetuses. Rather, I claim that I (and others) *ought* to feel such concern, and that such con-cern ought to guide action. That is, I think that our actions toward fetuses can be morally blameworthy or praiseworthy, and I think this is true even though I do not regard fetuses as persons.

I suspect that the vast majority of pro-choice supporters privately share the views that I have just expressed. However, the long-polarized and heavily politicized contest between two alleged rights – a woman's right to choose and a fetus's right to life – has, I think, inclined many otherwise vocal pro-choice advocates to silence on the matter of fetal life. The perception that we face a zero-sum game between the two supposed rights discourages taking seriously the right championed by "the other side." Advocates on both sides worry that any evidence in favour of one right may be used, however misleadingly, to undermine the other.[11] The dichotomous character of the debate explains pro-choice advocates' silence about the life of the fetus and their evasiveness when asked about fetal life.

Fortunately, the choice between showing moral concern for fetuses or women is one we need not make since it rests upon a false dichotomy. On my view, anyone genuinely concerned with avoiding the loss of life – and in particular loss of life of women and fetuses – as well as with supporting quality of life, ought to support safe, accessible abortions. Indeed, the very best way to act on appropriate concern for fetal and maternal lives is to adopt a harm reduction approach to abortion.

Harm Reduction

Harm reduction (hereafter, HR) is the name given to the public health approach that seeks to reduce the harmful effects of usually stigmatized behaviours. The approach emerged in Merseyside, UK, in the mid-1980s in response to rampant HIV infection among intravenous drug users.[12] HR has since often been applied in the contexts of drug use[13] and sex work. Unlike abolitionists, who seek to eliminate intravenous drug use or sex work by criminalizing them, HR proponents accept that the behaviours in question can cause harms, but argue that abolitionism is not effective in reducing those harms and indeed may exacerbate them. When sex work is criminalized, HR proponents argue, sex workers are afraid to go to the police when they are in danger; this leads to increased risks to these workers. Conversely, a HR approach to harm-associated behaviours can substantially reduce the risk to individuals who exhibit those behaviours. For instance, making clean needles and other supplies available to injection drug users has been shown to reduce the incidence of blood-borne illnesses such as hepatitis and HIV among populations of drug users (and, hence, among their families and communities).

To adopt HR, one must agree that the targeted behaviours are causally associated with harms. However, HR proponents think that even greater harm is done by refusing to provide support for safe sex work, safe injection, etc., than would otherwise occur.[14] Some HR proponents harbour the secondary goal of reducing the underlying behaviours. However, the primary goal is the reduction of ancillary harms, not the cessation of the underlying behaviour.

Since the 1980s, HR has been the subject of much empirical study by social scientists, but has received very little theorization by humanists. Because HR is so undertheorized by value theorists, little scholarly attention has been paid to the consideration of under what circumstances HR is appropriate. In a 2013 lecture, Daniel Weinstock offered general praise for HR, but wondered whether it would be appropriate to apply it to such phenomena as state interrogation methods involving torture and female genital mutilation (FGM).[15]

The question of whether there are some phenomena that are so wrong that it would be inappropriate to adopt HR toward them is a difficult one. If there are, then certainly acute other-directed harmful behaviours like FGM are intuitively the likeliest candidates. Moreover, the idea of, for instance, providing surgical training and sterile conditions for individuals who perform FGM may seem to condone an abhorrent practice. On the other hand, if an abhorrent practice is going to occur with or without our approval, then it is presumably better that it causes less rather than more harm.

I cannot here decisively settle the question of whether some behaviours are just objectively wrong and thus inappropriate targets for HR. That is a much larger project than is possible in a single essay.[16] However, let me propose two separate, complementary considerations that help us to move closer to answering the question. First, I wish to suggest that we should not in principle rule out the appropriateness of HR for other-directed harmful behaviours such as FGM. In the case of the most acute harms occasioned by such behaviours, we may not have the luxury of standing on deontological principle. If we can see no ready way to prevent a wrong with acutely harmful consequences from occurring, then while it is not obvious that we ought to seek to reduce the harms associated with the wrong, it is no more obvious that we ought *not* to do so. That is, where prevention of the wrong is highly unlikely, there is no *prima facie* reason to oppose reducing the harms associated with the wrong. Thus, some proponents of animal rights work to improve the conditions in factory farms and abattoirs, even though they would on the whole prefer that such places not exist at all. This means though – and this is the second consideration that I promised – that if HR is appropriate in cases of other-directed harmful behaviours, then it is most obviously appropriate where such behaviours cannot easily be eliminated, but where there are available mechanisms to reduce the harms attendant on them.

Taking the second consideration as inspiration, we can, I think, isolate three principles that should guide the decision about whether or not HR is in the instance appropriate. I propose that HR is appropriately directed:

1 Toward behaviours that are (more or less) ubiquitous or intractable (or, at least, tenacious) rather than toward those that are rare or terminable;
2 Toward behaviours that commonly produce a range of harms that can be reduced even though the primary behaviours persist; and
3 Toward behaviours whose attendant harms may be exacerbated by attempts to abolish the primary behaviours.

These three principles are admittedly not sufficient conditions for HR approaches to behaviours that are themselves wrong. However, (1) and (2) are, at least, jointly necessary to establish the appropriateness of HR in such cases, and (3), while not necessary, lends extra force to the decision to employ HR. Thus, it is only appropriate to employ HR to FGM in contexts in which FGM would be difficult to prevent, and if there are mechanisms available to reduce the harms caused by it even though it persists. Moreover, if attempting to abolish FGM caused an increase in FGM-related harms – perhaps by serving as a disincentive for families to seek emergency medical care for their daughters following unintended FGM-related injuries – this fact would lend weight to the suggestion to use HR.

Interestingly, the three principles I propose not only serve as a useful heuristic when considering controversial cases such as FGM and torture, but also help us to understand the now-widespread application of HR to less morally fraught phenomena such as drug use and sex work.[17] They also help us to weed out some phenomena as inappropriate sites for HR. As an example of the latter, let us consider genocide, both because HR is pretty clearly inappropriate for genocide and because it has become a trope for pro-life organizations to characterize abortion as a variety of genocide.[18] Let us apply the three principles to each of these examples.

With respect to ubiquity and tenacity, drug addiction and sex work are transcultural and transhistorical phenomena, occurring almost everywhere and everywhen (as is implied by joking references to prostitution as "the world's oldest profession").[19] While the incidence of both phenomena vary considerably between socioeconomic contexts, both occur in every socioeconomic context. Moreover, prohibiting these behaviours does not eliminate or even substantially reduce them. By contrast, genocide is neither ubiquitous nor intractable. Admittedly, genocide had a very good run in the twentieth century, and we are sufficiently in the shadow of the twentieth century that it would be premature to suppose that the age of genocide is behind us. However, unlike sex work and drug use, which are never altogether eliminated, genocides end. Thus, it would be false, and horrifically complacent, to say of genocide, "Some things just never change. No matter what you do, there's always going to be genocide."

Sex work and drug use are not only ubiquitous and intractable, they also (absent appropriate supports) can result in serious harms. Illegal sex work can lead to (inter alia) human trafficking, the spread of sexually transmitted infections, and violent assaults on sex workers. Injection drug users frequently suffer from not only intoxication and addiction but also infections, abscesses, cotton fever, and such blood-borne illnesses as hepatitis B and C and HIV. In both cases, HR has been remarkably effective in reducing the incidence of the secondary harms associated with those behaviours. By contrast, the chief harms associated with genocide are genocide itself, not secondary harms attendant upon genocide. Plausibly, the chief secondary harm of genocide is the trauma and post-traumatic stress survivors experience. However, it is almost inconceivable that one could effectively reduce this secondary harm by focusing on it alone, rather than by addressing the primary harm – the genocide. A truth and reconciliation commission (TRC) approach to genocide may seem like a possible counterexample to this claim. TRCs might be seen as adopting HR in that they emphasize reducing the secondary harms (the survivors' trauma and the perpetrators' feelings of guilt, for instance) rather than criminally prosecuting the perpetrators of the primary behaviours. However, while TRCs are increasingly common national responses to war, violence, and historic injustices, they are much less common as a response to genocide than are tribunals and criminal courts.[20]

Moreover, TRCs are established once the relevant conflict or injustice has ended. Even if one were to use TRC as an HR response to a genocide, it is implausible that a TRC could begin to address the secondary harms associated with the genocide were the genocide still underway. So, genocide clearly fails to satisfy the third criterion, which stipulates that HR is appropriate in cases where harms may actually be exacerbated by attempts to abolish the underlying behaviours. The opposite is true with respect to sex work and drug use. Many of the serious harms associated with sex work and drug use are exacerbated in abolitionist contexts. When sex work is decriminalized, sex workers can seek protection from the law, and law enforcement agencies can remain in friendly communication with sex worker communities to ensure that their members are adults and working in the industry by choice. Public health agencies can mandate regular testing and certification, and appropriate use of condoms, etc., to reduce the spread of sexually transmitted infections. Similarly, where drug use is decriminalized,[21] injection drug users can obtain clean needles and sterilization materials and can safely dispose of their sharps, as well as receiving hepatitis B vaccinations, regular testing for other blood-borne illnesses, and other health supports such as regular check-ups and education on safe injection. Harms to drug users, and to the broader community, are concomitantly reduced.

So, sex work and drug use are both good candidates for HR; genocide isn't. However, we saw above that HR might under some circumstances be appropriate for FGM – like genocide, an acute other-directed harmful behaviour. This result suggests that the inherent wrongness of a behaviour does not determine whether or not HR is an appropriate response.

Harm Reduction and Abortion

What about abortion? Let us again apply the three criteria. First, abortion is ubiquitous and intractable. Legal and court records from as early as the Code of Hammurabi (1760 BCE) discuss abortion, and there is good reason to believe that people used a variety of nonsurgical abortion methods long before these practices were encoded in law. Today, abortion is an international phenomenon. The only state in the world in which abortions do not routinely occur is the Vatican. Despite deep cultural, legal, and economic differences between countries, a statistically significant proportion of women in every country on Earth undergo abortions each year. Regionally, the abortion rate[22] ranges from about seventeen in Western Europe and Oceania to thirty-two in Latin America, and this despite the fact that Latin America has the world's strictest anti-abortion laws.[23] In rich countries and poor, in religious states and secular, whether legal or harshly criminalized, abortion happens everywhere on Earth. It is ubiquitous and intractable.

What about the second criterion – that HR is appropriate if it is possible to reduce the harms associated with an underlying behaviour without eliminating the behaviour? In order to address this criterion, we must first identify the harms associated with abortion. The chief harms associated with abortion are death to fetuses, pain suffered by gestationally older fetuses during abortions, and injury or death to women who undergo unsafe abortions. Abortions also harm the 220,000 children who are orphaned each year when their mothers die as a result of unsafe abortions.[24] This last harm is especially acute in developing nations.[25] In addition to the above harms, pro-life materials often list depression, increased risk of breast cancer, and difficulty conceiving or bearing children in the future. However, there is no empirical evidence to support the first two claims.[26] The risk of infertility varies according to the safety of the abortion. Abortions performed using modern methods and sterile equipment are not associated with infertility because with such abortions the risk of infection is low. However, there is a risk of infertility when women undergo illegal, unsafe abortions.[27] Plausibly, then, the main harms associated with abortion are fetal suffering and death, maternal morbidity (including infections resulting in infertility) and death, and orphanage. Additional harms include social stigma, costs to the health care system, and so on. Is it plausible that we can reduce these harms without abolishing abortion? In a word: yes.

Indeed, the data show that, internationally, the lowest abortion rates – and the lowest rates of morbidity and death associated with abortion – correlate with the most liberal abortion laws. Moreover, access to abortion earlier in pregnancy prevents the abortion of gestationally older fetuses and the increased risk of maternal injury or death associated with late-term abortions. A 2012 study concluded that, worldwide, "the proportion of women living under liberal abortion laws is inversely associated with the abortion rate."[28] The same study found sharp drops in abortion-related injuries in countries that legalized the procedure.[29] However, the authors argue that legalization alone cannot explain either lower abortion incidence or lower rates of morbidity associated with abortion. Just as crucial is access to quality abortion aftercare, available contraception, and adequate sexual health education.[30] In short, the best approach to reducing the harms associated with abortion is a systemic one that combines safe, legal, accessible abortion services with a wider array of sexual health and education services. More strongly though, the abortion-related harms that are demonstrably reduced by a nonabolitionist HR approach skyrocket under abolition. Not only is prohibition ineffective in eliminating abortion, it also correlates with an increase in abortion-related harms, especially in developing nations.[31] In other words, banning abortion does not reduce its incidence, but it does increase the incidence of abortion-related harms. Thus, abortion satisfies my third proposed principle – that HR is appropriately directed toward behaviours whose attendant harms may actually be exacerbated by attempts to abolish the primary behaviours.

In summary, then, not only is abortion a plausible candidate for application of HR; it is arguably already the site of such an approach. While abortion and sexual health providers seldom deploy the language of HR,[32] the very best approaches to abortion-related health services, law, and policy are those that employ a broad range of services geared toward reducing the harms associated with abortion without seeking to abolish abortion. What is striking is that a holistic approach involving good quality all-round sexual health services, both clinical and educational, as well as legal access to abortions, reduces all of the harms we have considered. Moreover, such an approach strongly correlates to reductions in the incidence of abortion itself. That is, for those who regard abortion as itself constituting a harm and who therefore wish to reduce the incidence of abortion, the most effective mechanism combines liberal abortion laws, access to safe abortions, and a broad suite of sexual health services.

Among feminist pro-choice proponents, it is controversial to claim, as I do, that abortions often cause or constitute harms. I am willing to bite this bullet. However, not all harms are equal. Poorly seasoned food may cause or constitute a harm, but that harm is nowhere near as acute as the harm of having no food at all. Death to a nine-week embryo may constitute a harm[33] but, if so, it is a less acute harm than the suffering and death of a thirty-two-week fetus. It is also arguably less of a harm than that occasioned by undermining a woman's bodily autonomy by forcing her to remain pregnant against her wishes.[34] And, of course, while harms are associated with abortion, harms are also associated with being unable to have an abortion. These include (*inter alia*) financial hardship, delays to education and career, and health risks associated with pregnancy and childbirth.[35]

Finally, when thinking about the HR landscape, and about abortion in particular, it is worth remarking that there is no way to altogether prevent harm from occurring. In "War and Massacre," Thomas Nagel observes that the world is such that moral agents often, sometimes by no fault of their own, find themselves in situations where there is no available course of action that is not wrong – where there is literally no chance of doing a right thing.[36] Similarly, when we attend to harms and their underlying causes in an evidence-based way, we are often forced to deliberate between two harms rather than between a good and a harm. It is often (perhaps always?) impossible to prevent harms. I noted above that there are harms associated with both having and not having an abortion. As they say, "Sometimes, you can't win for losing." However, the HR proponent has at least the following advantage over Nagel's tragic moral agent: while for Nagel the world is a bad – perhaps evil[37] – place in which there is often no right thing to be done, for the HR proponent there is usually, if not always, a way to reduce harms, even if they cannot be altogether prevented. HR proponents, then, can focus on attaining modest, practical, measurable, repeatable victories rather than on fighting grand moral battles[38] and banging their heads against the stone wall of a universe in which such battles are unwinnable. Thus, harm reduction may be not only an appropriate approach to the harms occasioned by such phenomena as abortion, drug use, and sex work. It is also perhaps an antidote to quietism and despair.

NOTES

1 I am most grateful to Katharine Jenkins, Tim Kenyon, Jenny Saul, Hasana Sharp, Mark Stephenson, Chloë Taylor, and members of the University of Sheffield Centre for Gender Research for their comments on earlier drafts of this essay.

2   See, for instance, Superson, "The Right to Bodily Autonomy and the Abortion Controversy," who argues that restrictions on abortion violate women's bodily autonomy.

3   Throughout, I use the familiar terms "pro-choice" and "pro-life" precisely because they are familiar, not because they are particularly apt.

4   Of course, not all people who can become pregnant are women, and not all women can become pregnant. Throughout, I use "woman" as a linguistic convenience to refer to anyone who may become pregnant. However, my arguments also apply to trans men and to others who might become pregnant whether or not they identify as women.

5   The argument from choice also fails to engage the (it seems to me) legitimate question of whether abortion is morally wrong, which in turn blocks any possible rapprochement between pro-choice and pro-life proponents, who are quick to point out that the appeal to choice does not justify wrong actions such as murder or theft. A distinct worry I have about the language of choice is that it is grounded in liberal individualism, a view that I find metaphysically implausible and politically harmful. However, that issue is beyond the scope of this essay. See Jaggar, *Feminist Politics and Human Nature*, 15–36, for good elaborations of this worry.

6   Arthur, "How to Think about the Fetus."

7   To be clear, pro-life supporters who answer questions about women's rights with facts about fetuses commit the same logical/rhetorical error as the one I identify above. Indeed, that error is arguably the more blameworthy of the two, given human beings' long history of ignoring women's rights.

8   My position is in some sense the converse of Judith Jarvis Thomson's. Where Thomson argues in "A Defense of Abortion" that even if fetuses are persons, their mothers are not morally obliged to carry them to term, I hold that even if (as I believe) fetuses are not persons, we may still have moral obligations to them. I here remain agnostic on the exact character of those moral obligations.

9   I am not alone, as is evidenced by the movement currently afoot among activists and scholars to regard some nonhuman animals, in particular the most intelligent ones, as persons. See, for instance, Francione, *Animals as Persons*.

10 The best evidence we have today indicates that fetuses do not have the neurological capacity to feel pain before twenty-nine to thirty weeks. See Derbyshire, "Can Fetuses Feel Pain?"; Lee et al., "Fetal Pain." Moreover, late-term abortions are extremely uncommon. In Canada, of the 27,576 abortions performed in 2010 for which detailed data is available, only 537, or 1.9 per cent, were performed on fetuses at twenty gestational weeks or older. This proportion is skewed by the fact that in Canada late-term abortions are only per-

formed at hospitals, not clinics. If we include in the total 2010 abortion count abortions performed at clinics, the total number swells to 64,641, meaning that late-term abortions constitute a mere .83 per cent of all abortions performed in the country. The rate for third-trimester abortions is considerably lower than even this. Canadian Institute for Health Information, "Induced Abortions Performed in Canada in 2010."

11   Among scholars who write on abortion, Shrage notably seeks to avoid either pole. In *Abortion and Social Responsibility*, she argues that abortion ought to be legal and unrestricted in the first trimester and restricted afterward, a solution she regards as addressing concerns and values on both sides of the abortion debate. See also Kenyon's illuminating discussion in "False Polarization" of the abortion debate as an example of false polarization.

12   Riley and O'Hare, "Harm Reduction," 3–4.

13   Throughout, I variously mention "drug use," "intravenous drug use," and "injection drug use." Internationally, there are a range of harm reduction programs that focus on different types of drug use, and different populations of drug users. I do not here intend to pick out, for instance, injection opiate users in particular. Nor do I intend to exclude the harmful use of such legal drugs as alcohol and pharmaceuticals.

14   By contrast, some critics of HR argue that it misleadingly suggests that dangerous, stigmatized behaviours are in fact safe and acceptable, and that, in so doing, they encourage such behaviours. Pope Benedict XVI, for instance, famously claimed on just this basis that the distribution of condoms "can even increase the problem" of HIV/AIDS in Africa. BBC News, "Pope Tells Africa 'Condoms Wrong.'"

15   Weinstock "So, Are You Still a Philosopher?"

16   It is, however, a project I have begun. This essay constitutes some of the initial spadework.

17   I do not intend to suggest that sex work or drug use are morally comparable to FGM or torture. I use these behaviours as examples because they are common sites of the HR approach, not because I wish to suggest that they are morally blameworthy.

18   My thanks to Kasia Narkowicz for this example.

19   Both sex work and drug use are transhistorical only in the thin sense of occurring in every historical period. Crucially, however, they have not always occurred in the same way. Both practices are constructed and understood in very different ways in different cultures. Historically, they have run the gamut from being strongly stigmatized to being honoured and associated with religious practices. So, while the practices of sex work and drug use are transhistorical, the perception that they cause or constitute harm is not.

20 For instance, following the 1994 Rwandan genocide, the Rwandan government opted against a truth and reconciliation approach, despite Bishop Desmond Tutu's 1995 advice that "unless you move beyond justice in the form of a tribunal, there is no hope for Rwanda." TRC of SA Report, vol. 5, 351, quoted in Gruenbaum, *Memorializing the Past*, 39.

21 This sometimes amounts to a kind of de facto decriminalization by local law enforcement agencies.

22 Abortions per 1,000 women aged fifteen to forty-four.

23 In El Salvador, for instance, all abortions are illegal, with both doctors and patients serving prison time for performing/procuring the procedure. Notoriously, El Salvador even imprisons some women who have had miscarriages or stillbirths on suspicion of having undergone an abortion. Nonetheless, legal and health scholars agree that the abortion rate in El Salvador likely remains on par with the rest of Latin America. On worldwide abortion rates, see Sedgh et al., "Induced Abortion"; Berer, "Making Abortions Safe." On El Salvador, see Oberman, "Cristina's World," 9; Lakhani, "El Salvador"; "Miscarriages of Justice."

24 Vlassoff et al., "Assessing Costs and Benefits of Sexual and Reproductive Health Interventions."

25 One thing that rings clear in the literature on worldwide abortion practices is that risks are less risky and harms less harmful for the rich than for the poor. This is true of both rich individuals and rich nations.

26 Munk-Olsen et al., "Induced First Trimester Abortion and Risk of Mental Disorder," 264; Major et al., "Abortion and Mental Health"; Lea et al., "Breast Cancer and Abortion," 491.

27 A report on complications associated with Canadian abortions performed in 2010 found that, of the 27,576 abortions for which detailed reports were available, infections occurred in only 107 cases, or 0.38 per cent, Canadian Institute for Health Information, "Induced Abortions." See also Royal College of Obstetricians and Gynaecologists, "Induced Termination of Pregnancy and Future Reproductive Outcomes."

28 Sedgh et al., "Induced Abortion," 631; Berer, "Making Abortions Safe," 580.

29 Sedgh et al., "Induced Abortion," 631.

30 Ibid.

31 Ibid.

32 The so-called Uruguay Model, founded in 2001 by Iniciativas Sanitárias, wherein physicians provide women who are ineligible for abortions with evidence-based information about medical abortions (specifically, the use of misoprostol as an abortifacient), is explicitly cast as a harm reduction approach. However, it is less thoroughgoing than what I describe above. In-

spired by the Uruguay Model, Erdman is doing important work on abortion and harm reduction. See Erdman, "Access to Information on Safe Abortion"; Erdman, "Harm Reduction, Human Rights, and Access to Information on Safer Abortion."

33 I here remain agnostic on this point. See Harman, "Creation Ethics," for an interesting argument that two early fetuses at the same stage of gestational development do not necessarily have the same moral status.

34 There may be individual instances in which one might intuitively support the idea of preventing a woman from having an abortion, such as the much storied third trimester pregnant woman who capriciously seeks an abortion in order to fit into a bikini. Even if there were evidence that such cases occurred, to limit the capricious woman's choices in this way would occasion harm for other women. After all, laws that permitted the undermining of some women's autonomy in this way would have the systemic effect of limiting or blocking other women's access to abortion.

35 My thanks to Meredith Schwartz for raising this point.

36 Nagel, "War and Massacre," 143.

37 Ibid., 144.

38 Throughout, I have remained silent on whether there is a moral fact of the matter about abortion. In fact, I think that some abortions are moral and some are immoral. I do not have space here to discuss this demarcation. However, the question of abortion's morality is a matter for individual agents. I am here concerned not with the morality of individuals, but with approaches to public health and law as they bear upon entire populations. On my view (a view that I develop further in a work still in progress), legalizing all abortions and ensuring that all women, regardless of circumstances, can affordably access safe abortions is good policy, even if some of those abortions are immoral.

13

Beyond Bare Life

Narrations of Singularity of Manitoba's Missing and Murdered Indigenous Women

JANE BARTER

> In Isleta the rainbow was a crack
> in the universe. We saw the barest
> of all life that is possible.
> Bright horses rolled over
> and over the dusking sky.
> —*Joy Harjo*[1]

For more than eight years, the Osborne family of Winnipeg has been waiting for news of their sister, mother, and daughter, Claudette. Claudette Osborne, a mother of four, disappeared from the streets of Winnipeg in July 2008. "The not knowing, that's the hardest part," said her sister, Bernadette Smith. "We've gone searching; she's not laid to rest."[2] Brenda Osborne, Claudette's mother, says: "It's like screaming from the deepest hole, and no one can hear ... how long will it be before somebody rescues us?"[3] Why do these screams generally go unheard in public consciousness? In this essay, I argue that the "deepest hole" in which victims and their family members are trapped is not only that of colonial and patriarchal violence against indigenous women, but also represents a new form of sovereign power – a *biopower* through which the missing women were violated not only by their assailants, but also through their *abandonment* by the colonial society itself.

The question of missing and murdered indigenous women[4] has not gone unnoticed by feminist theorists. Andrea Smith, for example, tirelessly draws attention to how violence against indigenous women is linked to colonial violence, and has made a convincing case – now commonly adopted by indigenous activists – that society's obliviousness to this linkage is the very obstacle to justice in the cases of the murdered and missing women.[5] Other theorists consider the vulnerability that these women faced when they were uprooted from their communities and living in cities. The specific space that some indigenous women occupy within cities is recognized as often a characteristic feature of the type of violence that befell them. In her analysis of the case of Pamela George, a sex-trade worker who was raped and beaten to death by two suburban white males, Sharene Razack argues that the power to control and dehumanize indigenous women is part and parcel of the lingering colonial geography of Canada. Such is the power of male settlers to be free citizens within a colonial culture, and the power that relegates indigenous women like George to the Stroll:

> Two white men who buy the services of an Aboriginal woman in prostitution, and who then beat her to death, are enacting a quite specific violence perpetrated on Aboriginal bodies throughout Canada's history, a colonial violence that has not only enabled white settlers to secure the land but to come to know themselves as entitled to it. In the men's encounter with Pamela George, these material (theft of the land) and symbolic (who is entitled to it) processes shaped both what brought Pamela George to the Stroll and what white men from middle-class homes thought they were doing in a downtown area of prostitution on the night of the murder. These processes also shaped what sense the court made of their activities.[6]

These tacit processes of ongoing colonial violence conspire to delimit the victim's standing under the law, and also grant the perpetrators the authority to use and dispose of her with relative impunity. As the judge presiding over the case, Justice Malone, reminded the jury as he asked it to determine whether she was (capable of being?) sexually assaulted, George was "indeed a prostitute."[7]

Similarly, recent cases within Winnipeg speak to the abject places missing and murdered women occupy in the ongoing colonial violence of Canadian cities. In June of 2012, Shawn Cameron Lamb, a fifty-two-year-old Winnipeg man, was charged with second-degree murder in the cases of three indigenous women – Lorna Blacksmith, eighteen, Carolyn Sinclair, twenty-five, and Tanya Nepinak, thirty-one. The bodies of Blacksmith and Sinclair were discovered wrapped in plastic near city garbage bins. Nepinak's remains have not been found. Nepinak was last seen in September 2011 and it is believed that her body was put in a garbage bin that was taken to a landfill.[8]

In the midst of such horror, family members continue to hold regular vigils[9] and marches in memory of the missing and murdered women. These gatherings are generally accompanied by family members' testimony about their relatives. "I'm always amazed by the resilience and strength of our people," says Winnipeg activist Nahanni Fontaine. "I am in awe of the mothers who continue to go to the vigils, continue to speak out. It's the courage of our women and our girls that is the beautiful piece of this story. Not that we're less-than, not that we're savages. We're not whores, we're not prostitutes … We're there to shed the light."[10]

In this essay, I aim to investigate the manner in which the family members shed the light on the identity of their daughters and sisters who are missing and murdered. And, specifically, I consider how their witness is a political act of renarration of their identities.[11] Such work is done, I argue, both by protesting ascriptions of their identity that would link them to what philosopher Giorgio Agamben calls "bare life" (life outside the realm of political activity and speech), and also by renarrating their identities as indigenous women, women who deserve to be "remembered" – not only within their households, but also within settler colonial consciousness in Canada, and particularly the juridical system.[12] In turning to the question of narrating lives, I engage feminist philosopher Adriana Cavarero's work. In my view, both the protest and counternarrative rely also on contesting the place from which the stories of indigenous women emerge. Rather than silencing these voices within an apolitical zone, counternarratives and other practices of resistance allow family members to reclaim missing and murdered women as subjects belonging specifically to indigenous communities. Thus, through the family members' testimony, the women are retrieved from the landfills and the dumpsters and restituted into "Indian country," an imaginative space – a place and a collectivity that insists that they be remembered. This final aspect of my analysis is informed by the theoretical and literary work of indigenous scholar Craig S. Womack.

Beyond Bare Life

Like Smith and Razack, I believe that the sexual violence that has disproportionately befallen indigenous women in Canada is colonial violence through and through, but I argue that it is colonial violence of a different order from the original violence of colonial conquest. While both are forms of sovereign power – power that was used to create and sustain Canadian colonial dominance – contemporary colonial domination is far more subtle and far-reaching, and therefore more difficult to resist or even to identify as colonial in nature. What is peculiar to these cases is the manner in which the missing and murdered indigenous women in Canada are indicative of a new form of sovereign power – not simply through the imposition of colonial rule upon indigenous peoples' lives, but also through their abandonment by the colonial society itself, which renders the women especially vulnerable to its lack of protection.

Giorgio Agamben argues that sovereign power has always structurally rested on the power to distinguish bare life from political life, and thereby to exclude certain life from the polis, by creating a sphere of life that is deemed an "exception." However, what is distinctive about contemporary sovereign power – what Agamben, following Foucault, deems biopower – is its capacity to create an ever-expanding realm of exceptionality. As Agamben puts it: "In Western politics, bare life has the peculiar privilege of being that whose exclusions found the city of men."[13] Whereas ancient sovereign power has had the power to kill and let live, today's biopower is the power to let die and make live. In the case of letting die, biopower creates bare life; that is, life is deprived of political capacity or significance, and therefore of speech.

For Agamben, the paradigmatic form of biopower is the camp. A concentration or prisoner-of-war camp forms the unseen structure of our society, as prisoners are irremediably reduced to bare life stripped of any possibility of citizenship or belonging. Within such "zones of indifference" – such as Guantanamo or Auschwitz – prisoners live a life between life and death, a life that is virtually impossible to narrate because the existence of its members is cut off from witnesses and from the conditions for discursive speech that might be heard beyond the camp's boundaries.

Several postcolonial theorists take up Agamben's analysis and apply it to colonial power.[14] Although critical of Agamben's general neglect of colonization as a form of biopower, such thinkers nevertheless find his analysis congenial to analyzing the contemporary situation of indigenous peoples in settler society. Mark Rifkin analyzes the reservation system in the United States as a "zone of indifference" that exposes indigenous peoples to the arbitrarily shifting machinations of colonial power, thus rendering them increasingly dependent upon that power. Further, biopower tacitly extends its reach over all aspects of indigenous life in order to ensure conformity to colonial standards. Projects aimed at assimilation, in Canada most notoriously the Indian residential schools, controlled each aspect of the physical lives of the children from their dress to the scrutiny of hygiene, sexuality, and health. Preeminently, residential schools systematically banned children from speaking their language and thus thwarted their capacity to discuss their experiences in the schools with their families back home. While residential schools sought to gain increasing control over the biological life of these children, they were markedly silent about their deaths.[15] Leaving to die (abandonment) was the corollary to the power of increasing and invasive control over their biological life. As Rifkin discusses, those political subjects who did not fit the ideal of the state apparatus of assimilation were "left abandoned by it, exposed and threatened on the threshold of the political order that [was] made possible by their exception."[16]

Applied to the cases of missing and murdered indigenous women, this analysis accounts for their exclusion from visibility before the law, as their absence has seldom been recognized or investigated, and when investigated, as in the George case, has been naturalized because she was, after all, "indeed a prostitute." Located in geographies outside the bounds of civil society, the women too have been situated as exceptions so that their protection or the investigation of their disappearances have been matters of juridical and political indifference. Winnipeg's inner city serves as a zone of indifference where the disappearance of indigenous women – who are considered unworthy or deviant subjects – is considered "normal" or not newsworthy, and their abandonment upholds the very appearance of security beyond its boundaries.[17]

In contrast to the silence of colonial society with respect to the missing women, family members refuse to remain silent. In a society predicated upon the silencing of indigenous peoples, these family members bear witness to the lives of the women who have disappeared. In this sense, they enable to women to "appear" within public consciousness through the determined and deliberate acts of renarrating their life stories. In witnessing to their lives and the irreducible loss of their disappearances and death, they refuse either to forget them or to consign them inevitably to death.

Thus the witness of family members of the missing and murdered women are politically effective in ways that go beyond – and also critique[18] – the abjected silent witness of Agamben's survivors. While Agamben's *Muselmann* bears mute witness in the grey zone of the camps, here family members speak into such zones and offer (albeit imperfect) testimony to the living. So although modern sovereign/colonial power has the capacity to produce bare life and thus silence persons as political agents, this capacity is not a total one, for, as I show below, new forms of agency – and of speech – can emerge even within zones of indifference to challenge sovereign power's totalizing hold and to restore life to its context.

The Work of Remembering

If the work of sovereign power is to uncouple bare life from its cultural and political context, then part of the task of those who seek to resist it is to reconnect life to its home, its place of origin, which is always linguistic and discursive. This is precisely what is done as the women's lives are reclaimed from the zone of indifference of settler colonials to a place where they are reconnected to a community, a culture, a narrative. This testimony is the fundamental political work that the family members are engaged in as they narrate the lives of their sisters and daughters: not as bare life, but as lives that are singular and situated within a form-of-life that challenges their abandonment within colonial discourses and practices. In this sense, they can be said to achieve what Cavarero seeks to enable: to speak of the self not as a *what* – an instance of a generic ontology of the human – but as a *who* – a singularity that is unique and irreducible.[19] For Cavarero, unlike Agamben, life – no matter how abjected and violated – can never be entirely bare, for all persons are singularities by virtue of their relationships to others. Even the degradation of the various biopolitical projects that contemporary sovereign power offers up cannot eliminate ontological singularity or "who-ness."

Cavarero sees identity or who-ness as inscribed upon individuals' very birth. According to Cavarero, birth itself confers a singular identity, a vulnerability that is at its very basis an exposure to another – specifically to a mother. Cavarero sees this vulnerability as the precondition for politics; the life exposed to others is a life that longs to be exposited, to be told in narrative form. The narration of the singular subject without abstraction and in resistance to violence is for Cavarero the very essence of the political work of remembering. It is also a distinctly feminist task, because women family members – mothers, grandmothers, aunts – are generally privy to the stories of a person's life since birth, and because these women are also those who are able to identify the damaging force of patriarchal violence upon girls' and women's lives. As Cavarero describes: "If everyone is who is born, from the start – and with the promise of unity that the story inherits from the start – then no recounting of a life-story can in fact leave out this beginning with which the story itself began. The tale of her beginning, the story of her birth, nevertheless can only come to the existent in the form of a narration told by others."[20] We rely from the moment of our births upon others to narrate our stories.[21] The singular self "shines forth" most powerfully in the self's expression or evocations.[22] Such evocations compel the conferring of an account of that life; a story of this life's singularity.[23]

A poignant example of this in the case of murdered and missing indigenous women is Bernadette Smith's narration of her baby sister, Claudette Osborne. Smith's recounting is a reflection on Osborne's singular capacity (even when unaware) to evoke happiness, and perhaps even (if I am reading the story correctly) to teach her teenaged sister about a love more powerful than the usual patriarchal romantic kind:

I remember one time when Claudette was just a baby... *My boyfriend and I broke up. I was really sad and emotional. Dad asked if I'd*

come over and babysit you and the other girls. I didn't want to but he
came and picked me up. When I arrived, there you were in your jolly
jumper with your big beautiful smile. You were so excited to see me.

I felt so good inside. I knew somebody loved me unconditionally and
everything was going to be okay. I sit here in tears writing this because
I may never see your big beautiful smile or feel that unconditional love
from you again. Please come home so we can make more memories
together.[24]

Often the storytelling of the family members is a multilayered form of resistance. Not only is it a lament of their deaths, but it is also a resistance to ascriptions of identity that reduce the victims and their female family members themselves from the status of a who to a what. Precisely in their deliberate public remembering do the family members effectively counter the forces that would relegate them eternally to the what of the inner city garbage bins. Here, a politics that is not reducible to soundbites or stereotypes is displayed. Here, the sometimes-lengthy stories of loved ones become a powerful counternarrative to the years of representations of them that depict them, if at all, as merely runaways, addicts, and prostitutes. This is done not through the overcoming of their desubjectification (or by the forgetting of instances of the subject's violation), but by bearing witness to a life marred by exploitation. Such testimony is often done best by survivors themselves. For narration, too, is an act of survival; not just survival of the memory of loved ones, but, in a colonial context in which indigenous women are telling the stories of other women, their own survival. Family members' testimonies seek thus to shed the light – to remember the missing and murdered women in their irreducible singularity, but just so to narrate common experiences as indigenous women within colonial society.

Yet Cavarero is cautious about any ascription of identity that would subsume the singular into a collective social identity. In her challenge to modern ontologies of the human, she offers a picture of the subject that is not prescribed by discourse of collective identity:

The ontology of the *who* does not do away with cultural identities and community belonging, but it does keep them from becoming the foundation of politics. The who, in fact, underscores the primary value of an existent without qualities, memberships, cultural identities ... Politics is therefore a relational space – contextual, contingent and groundless – that opens everywhere for everyone. The permit for entry into this space does not require membership in a group that share an identity. Identity, in fact, must be left behind or subordinated to the genuine political character of mere relation.[25]

As much as Cavarero is congenial to a feminist project that wishes to acknowledge the profoundly political nature of narrating women's identities, her assertion that any conception of shared identity must be left behind in order to preserve singularity chafes against indigenous conceptions of the self. Here, identity includes the narration not only of singularities but also of a people, and of the shared narratives and place that constitute such a people. Are there ways, then, of thinking about collective belonging that do not evade Cavarero's chief concern; that is to enable the appearance of women's singularity? Further, is it possible to speak of a shared experience of oppression in such a narration? Is it possible to think about the self in ways that recognize precarity as central, but that also account for the manner in which precarity is variously dispersed according to race, gender, and colonialism?

This exploration of recent work on sovereignty and narratival resistance by two Italian philosophers, Agamben and Cavarero, affirms the precisely political significance of the missing and murdered women's family members as they refuse to abandon their sisters and daughters to the further violence of being forgotten or remembered poorly. However, the renarration of their lives depends not only upon a dwelling upon their singularity, nor even upon their singularity in relation to a mother, but also upon a narration of their singularity within a community, namely a community that resides within a larger narrative, a history, and a space resistant to the colonial project. While philosophy takes us so far in understanding the contemporary colonial violence and the significance of narratives of resistance, I would be remiss in my exploration of the significance of the family members' testimony if I did not seek to understand (albeit briefly) the significance of a larger narrative and theoretical frame in constituting such resistance. Indigenous theory and storytelling are abidingly helpful in understanding not only the importance of witnessing as an anticolonial act, but also the importance of witness through indigenous self-understanding.

Shared Narratives and Remembering

At the very beginning of his novel *Drowning in Fire*, Muscogee (Creek) critic and novelist Craig Womack gives narration a prominent place in shaping and healing his young protagonist, Josh. The story opens with Josh as a young boy seeking comfort in his aunt's generous lap as she breathes smoke into his throbbing ear and tells him the stories of his clan: "I felt her legs, so much bigger than mine; her muscles relaxed beneath my finger-tips as she began to speak. Lucy pulled me closer, deeper into her lap until I could feel her breathing in and out, each exhalation in rhythm with her voice. The smoke floated with her words through the kitchen, and a cloud settled around an old tube radio on a high shelf above her head."[26] Lucy proceeds to tell Josh two stories that will shape his self-narration through-out the novel. The first is the Muskogee creation story, in which clans and animals stumble in darkness until their animal name is disclosed through the clearing of the thick fog that envelops them. The second is a recent story of exile and return of the remnants of Josh's clan from Oklahoma to California, where exile means their silencing by the ascription of a foreign and demeaning identity, while return means the reinstatement of their voice: "They wanted to take away the one thing they hate the most – the fact that we exist as a nation of people, the Creek nation."[27] Womack's char-acters, as with his literary theory, root their speaking voice within both a collective voice and a space – within a narratival and embodied world – where bodies dwell in relation to each other and the land that precedes them. It is from the theatre of Oklahoma that Josh learns at once to ar-ticulate his singular narrative (the novel is also a coming out story of a young gay man), and to appropriate the ancient stories of his people and the land, its "turtle voices."

Narrative Sovereignty

Womack thus seeks to identify the manner in which the individual in-digenous subject is narrated – not merely by colonial power, but also by locality and an inalienable relation to "Indian country." The meaning of Indian country here is not sharply defined territoriality, or the possession or occupation of a distinct space, so much as it is a belonging to what indigenous philosopher Anne Waters calls "mind space-place occupied by an American Indian orientation."[28] This mind space-place corresponds to what Womack understands as sovereignty. Sovereignty is above all an imaginative orientation that affirms the innate integrity both of self and of Indian country. Although altogether wary of Western conceptions of the sovereign and autonomous subject or state predicated on sovereign right, Womack nevertheless affirms indigenous conceptions of sovereignty as those that both predate contact[29] and undermine rather than commit the violence of exclusion endemic to Western sovereign power.

Not everyone shares Womack's optimism about sovereignty. Most notably indigenous theorist, Taiaiake Alfred, argues that discourses of indigenous sovereignty reproduce the exclusionary politics of colonialism that render indigenous people dependent on Eurocentric political programs aimed at recognition. According to Alfred, recognition is likely to set firm and violent parameters around definitions of who is Indian, an ascription that colonial forces once again set.[30] Other critics note how vacuous and shifting the term sovereignty is within contemporary settler states. According to Mark Rifkin, sovereignty "functions as a placeholder that has no determinate content":

> From that perspective settler-state sovereignty can be viewed as less
> an expression of the nation's rightful control over the land within
> its boundaries than the topological production of the impression
> of boundedness by banning – rendering "peculiar," "anomalous,"
> "unique," "special" – competing claims to place and collectivity. This
> line of thought further suggests that if the validity of national policy
> is presented as being derived from the underlying fact of sover-
> eignty, such a claim to legitimacy itself relies on the promulgation
> of an exception that rests on nothing more than the absoluteness
> with which it is articulated and enforced.[31]

Indigenous sovereignty all too often is forced to rely upon state apparatuses of power in order to discern who is in and who is out. For the missing and murdered indigenous women, both the sovereign power of nationalism and indigenous attempts at self-governance in a colonial setting conspired to allow their cases to fall between the cracks as overlapping and unclear jurisdiction complicated the investigation in several instances. Once again, their occupancy within a "zone of indifference" thwarted their protection under the law. Indigenous sovereignty, at least as it is currently permitted within a colonial context, may be ill-equipped to resolve this.[32]

Yet, according to Womack, indigenous sovereignty is not so much the immediate right to seize jurisdictional control as it is a prior capacity to determine the content and the meaning of indigenous histories and narratives. This is done not in order to include some and exclude others so much as it is to acknowledge the distinctiveness of "worldviews that deserve to be taken seriously."[33] While this is indeed a distinction, it is not a final one because sovereignty in this case does not work through the straightjacket of the law, but through the flexible and generous power of imagination and of stories that have the power to transform territoriality into Indian country and subjects into singularities.

Thus, while the narratabilty of a singular life is central also to Womack, such narrations cannot be abstracted from the narrations of a people who seek to inscribe individuals into a story so that they are not constrained but set free. Such narration enables an alternative account, an alternative imaginative universe, where dominant narratives no longer determine indigenous self-understanding. As Alexander Hollenberg puts it: "Womack makes use of his model of imaginative sovereignty by constructing a liberated space on his own terms. Moreover, it is a nonassimilated space, one that does not exist wholly within the dominant order but parallel to it. As a subject who disidentifies, Womack asserts himself and his community as voices that can more effectively and equally communicate through their own worldview."[34] Narrative sovereignty thus construed offers the possibility of an imaginative space that is freed from colonial authority and its manifold forms of violence (including its replication within indigenous communities as indigenous women are desubjectified).[35] This alternative view of sovereignty is not predicated by the violence of exclusion, but connects life to form within communities, narratives, and place. Yet that form of life, like the individual herself, is not simply an individual subsumed within a fixed collective. Like Indian country itself, she has open borders and crosses over into stories that are not yet spoken as "language and stories ... are born out of that landscape."[36]

In this respect, the family members of the missing and murdered indigenous women are engaged in the political activity of reconstituting their loved ones and themselves as subjects of this nonassimilated space. Their insistence that the landfills and dumpsters be searched so that their loved ones might rest is both practical and symbolic. By locating these bodies and restoring them to Indian country, they at once affirm the inherent inviolability of their daughters and sisters, and also make a collective sovereign claim: indigenous family members and friends have a particular "right" to narrate these women's stories. Although this right may give rise to political and territorial claims, it is foremost not a discourse of birthright, but an imaginative and spiritual capacity – born of community, story, and place – that serves precisely to uproot dominant stories that would conceal or violate these women once again.

What to make of this conversation between these vastly different thinkers? And why seek to apply so theoretical a discussion to the proximate and pained voices of family members in the inner city of Winnipeg? I have argued that what occurs in my city in vigils and testimonies is an alternative politics, and that it arises from voices that are rarely listened to in a world given over to stereotypes and dehumanizing ascriptions of identity to indigenous women. While Agamben provides an account of their abjection as indigenous women from dominant settler society through the tacit forces of biopower, Cavarero shows that the narrations of family members are a protest against the narrow *what* of such abjection. Womack shares with Cavarero an awareness that the work of faithful narration is a central political activity – indeed, *the* central political activity. However, he captures better the family members' insistence that the missing and murdered women were not just singular, but singular precisely in and through their communities and their stories. Thus he allows us to see that the political work of family members is their recounting of singular lives that were lost to violence and to distorted narratives imposed upon them, but also that they do so by bringing them home, by situating them within a story and within a place that bears their own histories. If the murdered and missing women occupied an abject space in our cities and our psyches, we find in the testimonies of family members a setting free of them as irreducible and sovereign members of Indian country.

Claudette Osborne hailed from Norway House Cree Nation. She was the second cousin of Helen Betty Osborne, an indigenous student who was raped and murdered in The Pas, Manitoba, in 1971 by four white men. Each year, Claudette's family endures an 800-kilometre walk from Norway House to the Manitoba legislature to raise awareness about her and other missing indigenous women and to protest their absence. When interviewed recently, Claudette's mother, Brenda, said that she wanted people to know that while her daughter was "a sex-trade worker and a drug addict, she was still loved by her family and *that they must locate her*."[37]

NOTES

1 Harjo, "Vision," 36.

2 Pauls, "Missing Aboriginal Women a Priority."

3 Turner, "On the Front Lines of the Missing and Murdered Tragedy, Pain Never Ends."

4 According to *Missing and Murdered Aboriginal Women*, a recently published report by the Royal Canadian Mounted Police: "Aboriginal female homicides and unresolved missing Aboriginal females ... total 1,181. This number includes 1,017 Aboriginal female homicide victims between 1980 and 2012, and 164 Aboriginal women currently considered missing. Of these, there are 225 unsolved cases of either missing or murdered Aboriginal women."

5 See, for example, Smith's landmark study *Conquest*.

6 Ibid., 128–9.

7 The issue of consent was key to the trial because it determined whether the perpetrators, Kummerfeld and Ternowetsky, would be convicted of the lesser charge of manslaughter rather than first-degree murder. Kummerfeld was granted full parole after only four years of his sentence. Ternowetsky was granted day parole three years after his conviction.

8 Although Winnipeg police searched the landfill site for several days, they were unable to find Nepinak's remains.

9 Some of the vigils in Winnipeg are spontaneous gatherings in response to local events; others are organized on a regular basis, such as the Sisters in Spirit walk on Mother's Day (an event originally initiated by the Native Women's Association of Canada and local churches).

10 Fontaine, "On the Front Lines of the Missing and Murdered Tragedy."

11 Sources on missing and murdered women in Manitoba include national documents and national and local press coverage. Knowledge of the narration of identity of family members is also drawn from my experience as a volunteer and attendee at the marches and gatherings.

12 For several years, family members have called for a national inquiry on murdered and missing indigenous women. In April 2013, nine of the ten provinces joined their voices to the family members, indigenous leaders, and human rights groups who called for such an inquiry. So far, the Government of Canada has appointed a special committee on the matter, while it has claimed to address this issue under its revisions to the justice system.

13 Agamben, *Homo Sacer*, 7.

14 See Svirsky and Bignall, *Agamben and Colonialism*. See also Mbembe, "Necropolitics."

15 According to recent research in Canada, at least 3,000 indigenous children died in residential schools. Canadian Press, "At Least 3,000 Died in Residential Schools, Research Shows."

16 Rifkin, "Indigenizing Agamben," 98.

17 According to Kristin Gilchrist's research in "Newsworthy Victims?," the difference between news coverage of the disappearances of white women as opposed to indigenous women is stark:

> When the number of articles mentioning the White and Aboriginal women in any capacity were counted, it was found that the White women were mentioned in the local press a total of 511 times compared with only eighty-two times for the Aboriginal women; more than six times as often ... When this analysis was broken down to include only articles discussing the missing/murdered women's cases specifically, disparities remained. The Aboriginal women garnered just fifty-three articles compared with 187 articles for the White women; representing three and a half times less coverage overall for the Aboriginal women.

18 See Lisa Guenther's critique of Agamben on precisely this issue in "Resisting Agamben": "As Levi, Antelme and Blanchot teach us, life is never bare – not because bios cannot be separated from zoe, but because the relation to the Other cannot be destroyed. Even when reduced to a 'naked relation to naked existence,' even when exposed to an unimaginable extremity of need and affliction, even when forced to steal from others in order to secure one's own survival, the subject retains a relation to alterity which provides a starting-point, however minimal, for resistance."

19 Cavarero, *Relating Narratives*, 63.

20 Ibid., 39.

21 "The point is that ... the life-story that memory recounts is not enough for the narratable self. Not so much because the memory proceeds like a voluble and discontinuous narration, or because the demon of self-interpretation produces mythological-biographical texts, but rather because memory claims to

see that which was instead revealed only through the gaze of another." Cavarero, *Relating Narratives*, 40.

22 I am grateful to an anonymous reviewer for this way of describing the nature of singularity.

23 Or, as Agamben puts it: "Exposition is the location of politics … Human beings … separate images from things and give them a name because they want to recognize themselves, that is, they want to take possession of their own very appearance. Human beings thus transform the open into a world, that is, into the battlefield of political struggle without quarter. This struggle, whose object is truth, goes by the name of History." Agamben, *Means without End*, 93.

24 Native Women's Association of Canada, *Voices of Our Sisters in Spirit*, 68.

25 Cavarero, "Politicizing Theory," 521.

26 Womack, *Drowning in Fire*, 4.

27 Ibid., 7.

28 Waters, "'Indigeneity, Self-Determination, and Sovereignty,'" 11.

29 Womack, "Theorizing American Indian Experience," 361–3.

30 Alfred, "Sovereignty."

31 Rifkin, "Indigenizing Agamben," 91, 98.

32 See Native Women's Association of Canada, *What Their Stories Tell Us*: Finally, NWAC has found that overlapping and unclear jurisdictional areas of RCMP, First Nations, municipal and provincial police forces has impeded effective resolution of some cases. Family members have shared stories about jurisdictional conflicts when attempting to file a missing persons report outside their community of residence. For example, while one police service says the report needs to be filed in the city where their loved one went missing, the other maintains the report should be filed with police in her home community. Jurisdictional issues such as this act as a tremendous barrier to families and loved ones who try to make a missing persons report, but also to the investigation into a case. Jurisdictional conflicts also impact families' access to victim services.

33 Womack, *Red on Red*, 29.

34 Hollenberg, "Speaking with the Separatists."

35 According to the Dakota-based national American Indian Resource Center for domestic and sexual violence's publication, *Sovereign Women Strengthen Sovereign Nations*, women's sovereignty must parallel tribal sovereign claims to Native women's assertion of sovereignty: "As relatives of women who have been victimized, it is our right and responsibility to be advocates supporting

every woman's right to power and control over her body and life – personal sovereignty." Cited in Smith, "Native American Feminism, Sovereignty and Social Change," 101.

36 As Womack writes in "Theorizing American Indian Experience," 368: "The idea of presence and nonpresence ... is a spiritual matter, especially if one argues, as I do, for the possibility of presence, of inerrancy. To argue for presence, however, or a metaphysical dimension of language, does not cancel out the way language is also socially constructed. These two phenomena are not mutually exclusive."

37 Reynolds, "Family Prays for Missing Daughter."

14

Endangered Life

Feminist Posthumanism in the Anthropocene?

HASANA SHARP

In her provocative introduction to the interdisciplinary collection *Extinction*, Claire Colebrook diagnoses posthumanism as "delusional," "symptomatic," and "psychotic." Now that we live in what geologists informally call the "anthropocene" – a new epoch in which a preponderance of the earth's systems are irreversibly altered by human activity – she claims that it is dangerous, insane even, to imagine that the traditional, "Cartesian" idea of man as master of nature is invalid.[1] The declaration of the death of man betrays a willful denial of humanity's destructive capacity. The dream that man is disappearing like a "face drawn in the sand at the edge of the sea"[2] is a symptom of a psychosis that protects us from the truth of man's irretrievable imprint: eroding coral reefs, melting glaciers, gaping ozone, thousands of extinct species, and so much more. Colebrook's is not only an indictment of French post-structuralism. She issues no less a challenge to feminist posthumanisms, which have launched influential assaults against the Cartesian figure of the self-possessed subject (who, we must admit, has few defenders in Continental philosophy generally). Does the heralding of the anthropocene demand a critical revival of Cartesian humanism? Must we affirm that humans are exceptional after all? Must we acknowledge that even if the cosmos was not designed with man at its centre, man has made himself, through his destructive activities, its centre? Is the masculinist model of man as lord and possessor of nature an ugly truth?

Colebrook's challenge appears untimely because developments in ethological and environmental sciences make posthumanism increasingly attractive to critical theorists today. Posthumanism is a complex family of discourses that shares a critical posture toward Enlightenment humanism, according to which humanity is a distinctive mode of being, uniquely capable of moral agency.[3] Humans alone can become "persons," because we are the only beings who can determine ourselves to act according to a (or "the") moral law and thereby to free ourselves from brute natural determination. Feminists, as well as anticolonial and antiracist thinkers, have long been suspicious of such humanism, since it is women, children, and non-Europeans who have historically functioned as the many exceptions that prove the rule of man's unique metaphysical privilege. The esteemed humanist canon is littered with testimony that women and non-Western peoples never free themselves from the brute determination appropriate to brutes. Today, critical discourse can draw also from ethological and brain sciences, which pose increasingly serious challenges to philosophical anthropologies that maintain human exceptionalism – nonhuman animals are much more intelligent than imagined, and the human mind appears to be much less autonomous than many theories of moral agency presuppose. Likewise, the threat of ecological catastrophe binds our fates palpably to nonhuman beings and powers, which puts increasing pressure on the human provincialism that has reigned for millennia in mainstream ethics and politics in the Western world.

Yet Colebrook claims that it is precisely anthropogenic climate change that exposes posthumanism as an escapist fantasy of human continuity with nature. Just as human agency becomes a geological force in its own right, posthumanists aspire to undermine the image of "sovereign man," calling attention to the role that nonhuman powers – such as impersonal social structures, technologies, nonhuman animals, and physical systems – play in enabling and constraining our capacities. As a feminist and posthumanist, I am provoked by Colebrook's polemical intervention. Could the ecological posthumanist subject serve as a mere alibi for ecological destruction? Is posthumanism a "reaction formation" obscuring our responsibility for the current horizon of mass extinction?

Although I think Colebrook identifies some worrisome features of posthumanist discourses, I do not find her claim that the anthropocence exposes the truth of Cartesianism to be persuasive. Indeed, in line with ecofeminists, I believe that climate change can better be understood as humanity's failure to master nature. Having unintentionally altered the earth's ecosystems so as to bring about the destruction of many species, including quite possibly our own, climate change reveals the self-undermining effects of treating other beings as instruments and resources for human use. Surely, human beings frequently act *as if* we are lords and masters of nature, but the effects of our actions both exceed and undermine our intentions. Anthropocentrism and humanism belong to the ideologies that contribute to the irreversible transformation of the earth's ecosystems and the reckless disregard for other intelligent and sensitive life, but such destruction is not done by a Cartesian subject endowed with a transparent will. Isn't the anthropocene better understood as exposing the manly project of mastery as a failure?

Feminists have advocated posthumanism not merely to deny the validity of the description of man as lord and master of nature but also to challenge its normative force. Posthumanism does not merely name an ontological project or a deconstructive exercise. It expresses the desire for an alternative to society organized by the ideas of human exceptionalism, anthropocentrism, and the masculinist models of man they entail. Even if there may not be any humans to witness the epoch after the anthropocene, ecological catastrophe will soon require that we find new ways to live. Feminist posthumanism has a role to play in imagining how to live amidst the destruction wrought by masculinist humanism. I briefly develop each of these points in what follows.

Descartes in the Anthropocene?

The anthropocene is an informal term for a new geological epoch marked, first and foremost, by anthropogenic environmental change. Reputable earth scientists largely agree that, since the Industrial Revolution, human activity has had a sufficient impact on the earth's systems to justify a formal shift in how we study, name, and understand those systems.[4] To underscore how monumental the introduction of a new geohistorical boundary is, consider that the Holocene epoch dates 10,000 years before the Common Era calendar used in the study of human history, and the Pleistocene epoch prior to that lasted more than 2.5 million years. Human beings have left "a global stratigraphic signature distinct from that of the Holocene or of previous Pleistocene interglacial phases, encompassing novel biotic, sedimentary, and geochemical change,"[5] in a *very* short period of time, geologically speaking.[6] Anthropogenic changes are so potent that 300 years of industrialization may be all it takes for our children and grandchildren to find themselves by 2100 CE "on a 'different planet' than the one on which human civilization has evolved."[7] Now that the collective effects of human activity are thought to be the dominant agent of geological transformation, critics must reckon with the fact that "the wall between human and natural history has been breached,"[8] if it ever existed.

In light of this reality, Colebrook finds that the generalized disrepute of Cartesianism across disciplines and subfields is not only misplaced but also indicative of a "reaction formation." In her words: "Cartesian man (the subject detached from the world who pictures and masters a world of dead matter) is diagnosed as the error of modernity from which life now saves us ... On the other hand, and at the same time, there is widespread evidence of the truth of Cartesianism, a truth that is intoned everywhere and yet never heard, witnessed but not recognized."[9] She elaborates on the truth of Cartesianism in her recent obituary for the "posthuman": "Can we say that the Cartesian figure of disembodied life is really a mistake, or is it not a more accurate picture of 'man' in the anthropocene era? This, I think, suggests that we need to consider the future that this non-organic, non-relational, rigidly disembodied life has allowed to occur."[10] Posthumanist critics announce the error of the dualist portrait of man, while humanity persistently and ruthlessly subordinates anything nonhuman to its own ends. Rather than appreciating our fragile community with other beings, the cumulative effects of human activity[11] since the industrial era threaten to destroy it.[12] Even if we might not represent any and all nonhuman phenomena as "dead," encoded in our law and reflected in our behaviour is the view that we need only consider the independent purposes of current and potential "persons." As Descartes might have hoped, there is nothing illegitimate, juridically speaking, in our ambition to become "lords and masters of nature."[13]

Although diverse forces have collaborated in the institution of the anthropocene, Cartesian subjectivity aptly describes an orientation to the world that has contributed to climate change. We – or at least those born into national, racial, socioeconomic, and/or gender privilege – have been able to treat nonhuman nature as a mere resource for human projects. The near limitless exploitation and instrumentalization of nonhuman nature is supported by the metaphysical portrait of ourselves as uniquely minded, distinctively sensitive, and fundamentally different in kind from all other beings in nature.[14] We have, either consciously or unconsciously, individually or collectively, acted as though we are the centre of the cosmos and as though the fulfillment of human ambition justifies just about anything.[15] Moreover, the humanist tradition, for which Descartes has come to stand, considers the mastery of nature to be not only justifiable but also imperative. When Descartes announces the ambition to "make ourselves, as it were, lords and masters of nature," he identifies its virtues as follows: "This is desirable not only for the invention of innumerable devices which would facilitate our enjoyment of the fruits of the earth and all of the goods we find there, but also, and most importantly, for the maintenance of health, which is undoubtedly the chief good and the foundation of all the other goods in this life."[16] Thus Descartes presents mastery of nature, especially the internal frontier of the human body, as necessary for the acquisition of that chief temporal good: human survival. Indeed, the subordination of everything to the human will to survive is precisely the orientation toward the biosphere that has ushered in the anthropocene. While history shows that this subordination of everything to "humanity" is highly selective and includes primarily those human owners of the means of production,[17] there is no denying that the Cartesian outlook has been efficacious and describes a mode of experience that can now be understood not only as a cultural but also as a geological force.

If our unparalleled destructive power is legible in ice cores, is the rejection of Cartesianism mere wish fulfillment? The aspects of Cartesianism that have come under attack by posthumanists include, broadly speaking, dualism and atomism, but I fail to see how climate change confirms either of these metaphysical presuppositions. If mastering nature involves the subordination of other beings to human projects, climate change is evidence that such a disregard for the complex web of relationships by virtue of which we exist, rather than guaranteeing our survival in the long term, is fatal. Acting as though the laws of nature do not apply to us is what enables us to deplete the biosphere's resources, poisoning and annihilating many living beings and eventually undermining the habitability of the planet for humanity. The fantasy that human ingenuity can figure its way out of any problem – colonize space! – reflects the Cartesian optimism that planetary systems are fully knowable and manipulable. The anthropocene is precisely what reveals that these systems have a logic of their own and that, once sufficiently altered, they are not susceptible to any interventions that would guarantee our survival. Moreover, if we want to do anything more than diagnose the pathologies of the anthropocene, we need to fight the human exceptionalism it presupposes.

Indeed, it is only because we are part of nature that terms like "environment" become senseless. We are not surrounded by other kinds of reality. We are actors within a single, albeit infinitely complex, forcefield of powers *and* counterpowers. It is our ineluctable involvement with other beings that unites our fates and redirects our aims well beyond our intentions. It is because we are connected that we are both dangerous and endangered. Thus Colebrook is right to be wary of the romantic strain in some posthumanisms that underappreciates the importance of counterpowers, the antagonisms among various parts of nature, and replicates, albeit in a cosmological mode, humanism's failure to attend to differences among our kind. But to fight this we do not need Colebrook's polemic; we need *feminist* posthumanism.

Feminist Posthumanism in the Anthropocene

Posthumanism is more than antihumanism. It includes the antihumanist critique of the Cartesian man as the spontaneous centre of volition, thoughts, and feelings, but it insists also on turning our theoretical and political attention to nonhuman powers – animal, vegetable, mineral, electric, structural, atmospheric, and so on. Posthumanism insists on what is sometimes called an "ecological" analysis, which must take into account relations of dependence, community, material, and even spiritual involvement among members of the biosphere. In contrast to several of the posthumanist thinkers Colebrook targets in her critique, the feminist tradition entails attention to inequalities, power relations, and the different capacities and vulnerabilities proper to differently situated subjects.

But, with the exceptions of ecofeminism (including those who focus on the suffering of nonhuman animals) and (some) recent new materialist feminisms, feminist criticism is not especially attentive to either our domination of or our dependence on nonhuman nature. In the age of the anthropocene, a position that is equally posthumanist and feminist alerts us to how the "human activity" that has reconfigured the earth's systems in devastating ways has never been human activity *simpliciter*. It has been suggested that the anthropocene is more aptly called the "Eurocene" because the preponderance of industrial activity and carbon emissions since the industrial revolution has come from the region that we now call Europe.[18] Likewise, the "Capitalocene" has been proposed to emphasize the economically driven development of agriculture, migration patterns, and trade relations without focusing narrowly on industrial pollution.[19] We might also call it the "Androcene," to emphasize the extent to which the epoch of climate change has been patriarchal. Considering these modifications together, we point to the reality that the agents and beneficiaries of resource colonization and extraction have been and remain overwhelmingly male owners of the means of production in the developed world. A full, critical diagnosis of the anthropocene entails attention to Europe as a patriarchal and colonial power. Colonialism under industrial capitalism has been motivated, in significant part, by the appropriation of natural resources and the exploitation, trade, and trophy killing of nonhuman animals. Feminist posthumanism needs to draw upon a multiplicity of critical resources to discern how capitalism, patriarchy, and colonialism, among other systemic forces, have driven anthropogenic transformation, while striving for a new appreciation of scale, temporality, and impact on nonhuman beings and ecosystems.

A feminist stance helps us remain alert to the unavoidable risks of theorizing in a geohistorical mode. As we strive to think in terms of geological time, the interconnections of ecosystems, geopolitics, and the myriad effects of economies over time in different regions – the differences upon which feminist theory insists – may become more imperceptible than ever. But we know that those who have contributed least to climate change are those who are most vulnerable to its effects – future generations, of course, but also other species and the world's poor (the overwhelming majority of whom are women and children). The regions likely to be most affected in

the short term, the far north and the Global South, are the least responsible for warming the planet.[20] If Colebrook, for example, is concerned
to reckon with human extinction, we should appreciate the fact that, if
indeed this is our horizon, we will not go extinct all at once. Devastation
will first – and perhaps very soon – be felt by those in poor, highly populated coastal communities below the equator and the mostly indigenous
communities in and near the Arctic. These communities bear very little
responsibility for the changes that may soon devastate their land and food
sources. So, how do we begin to reckon with species domination in a way
that genuinely appreciates the differences within our species?

The anthropocene reveals the historical emergence of what we might call,
prompted by Dipesh Chakrabarty's analysis, "the species effect."[21] Chakrabarty argues that the concept of the anthropocene urges us to reckon with
our historical emergence as a species. With the dawn of industrialization,
we became the kinds of beings that could impose "a signature" upon the
entire biosphere. The industrial infrastructure developed in Europe in the
eighteenth century intensified colonialism and myriad forms of human
industry, rapidly transforming social and natural life on a global scale. As
Marx and Engels memorably put it: "The need for a constantly expanding market for its products chases the bourgeoisie over the whole surface
of the globe. It must nestle everywhere, settle everywhere, establish con-
nexions everywhere."[22] Industrialization was fuelled by capitalist social
organization, in which the quest for profit sharpens the instruments of our
species signature. We developed the ability to act as a species, as a collective author of legible effects on the biosphere, only at a certain point in history and only by virtue of structures that exceed our intention and control.

To identify capitalism as a primary force driving anthropogenic change,
however, is not to minimize differences among human beings. Capitalism correlates with an ideology that negates fixed, natural differences,[23]
but, at the same time, requires a stable and capacious gap between prop-
ertied capitalists and propertyless workers.[24] As Marxist feminists have
long pointed out, although humanity may appear to be "more and more
splitting up into two hostile camps,"[25] this appearance conceals those who
labour to feed, clothe, and reproduce the proletariat.[26] It conceals both
the unwaged reserve army of domestic labour as well as the differences
among the working proletariat, marked by race, gender, religion, and

ethnicity, the vastly different working conditions in different nations and industries, as well as the persistence of slave labour within the capitalist mode of production.[27]

The ecological emphasis upon our ineluctable involvement with non-human nature, allied with critical race feminism's appreciation of structural domination among human beings, joined to anticolonial Marxism: these must all be among the crucial resources for reckoning with the anthropocene. The species effect is a historical phenomenon, driven by capitalism, industrialization, colonial expansion, and expropriation. These structures continue to be major features of our social organization. The drive for profit maximization, for example, compels oil and gas companies to settle the far reaches of the Arctic, threatening to displace indigenous communities and wreaking havoc on particularly fragile ecosystems.[28] The more we warm the climate, the more quickly and deeply the wealthiest and most militarily endowed countries and corporations will be able to inscribe the "human" signature, erasing those of other beings and peoples.[29]

Although I have barely pointed out the resources necessary, it is imperative to gather our tools to diagnose and combat the forces of anthropogenic climate change. Even if climate change is irreversible, it might be slowed down and we might direct our resources to the most vulnerable populations. Our struggle is to assess, concomitantly, the effects of centuries of unintended collective action while acknowledging the diverse and fractured character of this collective. The anthropocene signals the simultaneous triumph and decline of industrial man. Colebrook is right to reject, in the moment of climate change and on the horizon of extinction, posthumanist celebrations of universal connection and continuity between humans and nature. Nevertheless, Cartesianism fails to grasp how human vulnerability to extinction is an expression of our mutual dependency. Likewise, it does not begin to apprehend the unequal distribution of vulnerabilities and harms, human and nonhuman. Surviving in the anthropocene, even if we do not live to see the next epoch, calls for thought about which humans, practices, and institutions most urgently require transformation. As Colebrook emphasizes, our extinction, however grim the prospect, would not be the end of life itself. However, this does not mean that we should ignore the question of how the actions and institutions that define the twilight of our species might affect the evolution of the life that will persist beyond us.[30] Rather than come to grips with humanity's "mastery of nature," we ought to mobilize against anthropogenic destruction to whatever extent we are able. Our critical tools will help us in our striving to understand the forces most necessary to combat, the alternatives we might institute, and the webs of life that most urgently need mending.

NOTES

1 Colebrook, "Introduction," 18.
2 Foucault, *The Order of Things*, 387.
3 For a comprehensive overview of feminist posthumanism, see Braidotti, *The Posthuman*.
4 Zalasiewicz et al., "Are We Now Living in the Anthropocene?"
5 Ibid., 4.
6 Dahr Jamail, "We're Looking at the End of Humanity – And It Might Happen Sooner Than You Think," notes that a report in *Science* in August 2013 "revealed that in the near-term Earth's climate will change ten times faster than at any other moment in the last 65 million years."
7 Gardiner, *The Perfect Moral Storm*, 229. According to Jamail's reporting cited above, a number of serious scientists believe that catastrophic changes will occur well before 2100 and as early as 2035.
8 Chakrabarty, "The Climate of History," 221.
9 Colebrook, "Introduction," 19.
10 Colebrook, *Death of the Posthuman*, 95.
11 "Human activity," of course, is a very blunt phrase that fails to identify that in fact a relatively small proportion of humanity is responsible for the greatest destruction. I will say more on this below.
12 There is a great deal of fascinating debate about the dating of the Anthropocene. See Luciano, "The Inhuman Anthropocene."
13 Cottingham, Stoothoff, and Murdoch, *Philosophical Writings of Descartes*, vol. 1, 142–3.
14 See Francione for a humanist objection to excluding the personhood of animals from our legal system, *Animals as Persons*.
15 This ambition is ostensibly limited by the harm principle, which bars us from harming other "persons" but leaves it open to the law to determine to what extent various biological humans count as persons. The imperative not to harm persons has proven to be highly flexible and does not exclude the ruthless exploitation of human labour, among other kinds of damage.

16 Cottingham et al., *Philosophical Writings of Descartes*, vol. 1, 142–3.

17 Just as many people live in abject poverty so that a few people can live a life of opulence, the rich are already planning to safeguard themselves from the ill effects of climate change. See Lukacs, "New, Privatized African City Heralds Climate Apartheid."

18 Caluya, "Fragments for a Postcolonial Critique of the Anthropocene," 35.

19 Moore, "The Capitalocene, part 1."

20 See Cook, "Those Who Contribute the Least to Greenhouse Gases Will Be Most Impacted by Climate Change."

21 This term came to me upon reading the following: "Climate change is an unintended consequence of human actions and shows, only through scientific analysis, the effects of our actions as a species. Species may indeed be the name of a placeholder for an emergent, new universal history of humans that flashes up in the moment of the danger that is climate change." Chakrabarty, "The Climate of History," 221.

22 Marx and Engels, *The Communist Manifesto*, 65.

23 Although feminists still have to work very hard to demonstrate how power and status differences among men and women continue to be naturalized, capitalism, with its rapid transformations and continual revolutionizing of the means of production, tends to destabilize fixed differences. Likewise, technology, the exchange of cultural products, and the domination of multinational companies bring more and more peoples into contact and communication.

24 See Marx, part 7 of *Capital*, vol. 1.

25 Marx and Engels, *The Communist Manifesto*, 62.

26 See, for example, Dallacosta and James, *The Power of Women and the Subversion of the Community*.

27 See, for example, James, *Sex, Race, and Class*.

28 Klare, *The Race for What's Left*, chapters 1 to 3.

29 Ibid., chapter 8.

30 This is how Elizabeth Kolbert explains the ambition of her book. Kolbert, *The Sixth Extinction*, 268–9.

Bibliography

Agamben, Giorgio. *Homo Sacer: Sovereign Power and Bare Life*. Translated by Daniel Heller-Roazen. Stanford: Stanford University Press, 1998.
– *Means without End: Notes on Politics*. Translated by Vincenzo Binetti and Cesare Casareino. Minneapolis: University of Minnesota Press, 2000.
– *State of Exception*. Translated by Kevin Attell. Chicago: University of Chicago Press, 2005.
Ahmed, Sara. "Imaginary Prohibitions." *European Journal of Women's Studies* 15, no. 1 (2008): 23–39.
Alaimo, Stacy. *Bodily Natures: Science, Environment, and the Material Self*. Bloomington: Indiana University Press, 2010.
Alcoff, Linda. *Visible Identities: Race, Gender and the Self*. Oxford: Oxford University Press, 2006.
Alexander, Michelle. *The New Jim Crow: Mass Incarceration in the Age of Colorblindness*. New York: New Press, 2010.
Alfred, Taiaiake. "Sovereignty." In *A Companion to American Indian History*, edited by Philip J. Deloria and Neil Salisbury, 460–74. London: Blackwell, 2002.
Al-Saji, Alia. "When Thinking Hesitates: Philosophy as Prosthesis and Transformative Vision." *Southern Journal of Philosophy* 50, no. 2 (2012): 351–61.
Althusser, Louis. *Lenin and Philosophy and Other Essays*. Translated by Ben Brewster. London: New Editions Press, 1971.
Amundson, Ron. "Against Normal Function." *Studies in History and Philosophy of Science* part C31, no. 1 (2000): 33–54.
– "Disability, Ideology, and Quality of Life." In *Quality of Life and Human Difference*, edited by David Wasserman, Robert Wachbroit, and Jerome Bickenbach, 101–24. New York: Cambridge University Press, 2005.

Amundson, Ron, and Shari Tresky. "On a Bioethical Challenge to Disability Rights." *Journal of Medicine and Philosophy* 32, no. 6 (2007): 541–61.

Anzaldúa, Gloria. "Haciendo caras, una entrada." In *Making Face, Making Soul/Haciendo Caras*, edited by Gloria Anzaldúa, 142–8. San Francisco: Aunt Lute, 1990.

– "Now Let Us Shift ... the Path of Conocimiento ... Inner Work Public Acts." In *This Bridge We Call Home*, edited by Gloria Anzaldúa and Analouise Keating, 540–78. New York: Routledge, 2002.

– *The Gloria Anzaldúa Reader*. Edited by Analouise Keating. Durham: Durham University Press, 2009.

– *Borderlands / La Frontera*. San Francisco: Aunt Lute, 2012.

Aptheker, Herbert. "Sterilization, Experimentation, and Imperialism." *Political Affairs* 53, no. 2 (1974): 46–59.

Arthur, Joyce. "How to Think about the Fetus." Poster presented at the Third International Congress on Women's Health and Unsafe Abortion, Bangkok, Thailand, 26–9 January 2016. Abortion Rights Coalition of Canada. http://www.arcc-cdac.ca/presentations/fetusposter.pdf.

Åsberg, Cecilia. "The Timely Ethics of Posthumanist Gender Studies." *Feministische Studien* 31, no. 1 (2013): 7–12.

Asch, Adrienne. "Disability, Bioethics, and Human Rights." In *Handbook of Disability Studies*, edited by Gary Albrecht, Katherine Seelman, and Micheal Bury, 297–326. Thousand Oaks: Sage, 2001.

Asian Communities for Reproductive Justice. "A New Vision for Advancing Our Movement for Reproductive Health, Reproductive Rights and Reproductive Justice." 2005. http://forwardtogether.org/assets/docs/ACRJ-A-New-Vision.pdf.

Barad, Karen. "Posthuman Performativity." *Signs: Journal of Women in Culture and Society* 28, no. 3 (2003): 801–31.

– *Meeting the Universe Halfway: Quantum Physics and the Engtanglement of Matter and Meaning*. Durham: Duke University Press, 2007.

– "'Matter Feels, Converses, Suffers, Desires, Yearns and Remembers': Interview with Karen Barad." *New Materialism: Interviews and Cartographies*, edited by Rick Dolphijn and Iris Van der Tuin, 48–70. Ann Arbor: Open Humanities Press, 2012. http://hdl.handle.net/2027/spo.11515701.0001.001.

Battersby, Christine. "Kierkegaard, the Phantom of the Public and the Sexual Politics of Crowds." In *Kierkegaard and the Political*, edited by Alison Assiter and Margherita Tonon, 27–44. Newcastle upon Tyne: Cambridge Scholars Publishing, 2012.

BBC News. "Pope Tells Africa 'Condoms Wrong.'" 17 March 2009. http://news.bbc.co.uk/go/pr/fr/-/1/hi/world/africa/7947460.stm.

Beauvoir, Simone de. *Pour une morale de l'ambiguïté* suivi de *Pyrrhus et Cinéas*. Paris: Gallimard, 1947.

– "My Experience as a Writer." (1965). In *Simone de Beauvoir, "The Useless Mouths" and Other Literary Writings*, edited by Margaret A. Simons and MaryBeth Timmermann, 282–301. Champaign: University of Illinois Press, Beauvoir Series, 2011.

– *The Prime of Life*. London: Penguin Classic, 1965.

– *Force of Circumstance*. London: Penguin Classic, 1968.

– *The Ethics of Ambiguity*. New York: Citadel Press, 1976.

– *All Said and Done*. London: Penguin, 1977.

– *Adieux: A Farewell to Sartre*. New York: HarperCollins, 1984.

– *A Very Easy Death*. New York: Pantheon, 1985.

– "Existentialism and Popular Wisdom." In Simons, Timmermann, and Mader, *Simone de Beauvoir*, 203–20.

– "Literature and Metaphysics." In Simons, Timmermann, and Mader, *Simone de Beauvoir*, 269–77.

– "Pyrrhus and Cinéas." In Simons, Timmermann, and Mader, *Simone de Beauvoir*, 89–149.

– "A Review of *The Phenomenology of Perception* by Maurice Merleau-Ponty." In Simons, Timmermann, and Mader, *Simone de Beauvoir*, 159–64.

– *Memoirs of a Dutiful Daugther*. New York: Harper Perennial Modern Classics, 2005.

– "Conditions of Servitude: The Peculiar Role of the Master-Slave Dialectic in Simone de Beauvoir's *The Second Sex*." In Simons, *The Philosophy of Simone de Beauvoir*, 276–93.

– *The Second Sex*. Translated by Constance Borde and Sheila Malhovany-Chevallier. New York: Knopff, 2010.

Bekoff, Marc, ed. "A Gentle Heart." In *The Smile of a Dolphin: Remarkable Accounts of Animal Emotions*. Ludlow: Discovery Books, 2000.

– *The Emotional Lives of Animals*. Novato, CA: New World Library, 2007.

Bennett, Jane. *Vibrant Matter: A Political Ecology of Things*. Durham: Duke University Press, 2010.

Benjamin, Adam. *Making an Entrance: Theory and Practice for Disabled and Non-disabled Dancers*. London: Routledge, 2002.

Berer, Marge. "Making Abortions Safe: A Matter of Good Public Health Policy and Practice." *Bulletin of the World Health Organization* 78, no. 5 (2000): 580–92.

Bergson, Henri. *Matter and Memory*. Translated by Nancy Margaret Paul and W. Scott Palmer. Brooklyn: Zone Books, 1988.

Bérubé, Micheal. *Life as We Know It: A Father, a Family, and an Exceptional Child*. New York: Vintage Books, 1998.

Bickman, Jed. 2012. "Should Addicts Be Sterilized?" *Salon*, 2 May 2012, http://www.salon.com/2012/05/02/should_addicts_be_sterilized_salpart.

Björk, Ulrika. "Reconstituting Experience: Beauvoir's Philosophical Conception of Literature." *Sapere Aude* 3, no. 6 (2012): 73–95.

Bradshaw, G.A. *Elephants on the Edge*. New Haven: Yale University Press, 2009.

Braidotti, Rosi. *Metamorphoses: Towards a Materialist Theory of Becoming*. Cambridge: Polity Press, 2002.

– "Affirming the Affirmative: On Nomadic Affectivity." *Rhizomes* 11/12 (2005).

– "The Politics of 'Life Itself' and New Ways of Dying." In *New Materialisms: Ontology, Agency, and Politics*, edited by Diana Coole and Samantha Frost, 201–18. Durham: Duke University Press, 2010.

– *The Posthuman*. Cambridge: Polity Press, 2013.

Bréhier, Émile. *The Hellenistic and Roman Age*. Translated by Wade Baskin. Urbana: University of Chicago Press, 1971.

Brennan, Patricia, Sarnoff A. Mednick, and Jan Volacka. "Biomedical Factors in Crime." In *Crime*, edited by James Q. Wilson and Joan Petersilia, 65–90. San Francisco: ICS Press, 1995.

Bruinius, Harry. *Better for All the World: The Secret History of Forced Sterilization and America's Quest for Racial Purity*. New York: Vintage Books, 2007.

Buchanan, Allen, Dan W. Brock, Normal Daniels, and Daniel Wikler. *From Chance to Choice: Genetics and Justice*. New York: Cambridge University Press, 2001.

Butler, Judith. *Gender Trouble*. New York: Routledge, 1990.

– *Bodies That Matter: On the Discursive Limits of Sex*. New York: Routledge, 1993.

– *The Psychic Life of Power: Theories in Subjection*. Stanford: Stanford University Press, 1997.

– *Precarious Life: The Powers of Mourning and Violence*. New York: Verso, 2004.

– *Undoing Gender*. New York: Routledge, 2004.

– *Giving an Account of Oneself*. New York: Fordham University Press, 2005.

– *Frames of War: When Is Life Grievable?* New York: Verso, 2009.

– *Parting Ways: Jewishness and the Critique of Zionism*. New York: Columbia University Press, 2013.

Butler, Judith, and Sunaura Taylor. "Interdependence." In *Examined Life: Excursions with Contemporary Thinkers*, edited by Astra Taylor, 185–213. New York: New Press, 2009.

Cadwallader, Jessica. "Stirring up the Sediment: The Corporeal Pedagogies of Disabilities." *Discourse: Studies in the Cultural Politics of Education* 31, no. 4 (2010): 513–26.

Caluya, Gilbert. "Fragments for a Postcolonial Critique of the Anthropocene: Invasion Biology and Environmental Security." In *Rethinking Invasion Ecologies from the Environmental Humanities*, edited by J. Frawley and I. McCalman, 31–44. New York: Routledge, 2014.

Campbell, Fiona Kumari. "Legislating Disability: Negative Ontologies and the Government of Legal Identities." In *Foucault and the Government of Disability*, edited by Shelley Lynn Tremain, 108–31. Ann Arbor: University of Michigan Press, 2005.

— *Contours of Ableism: The Production of Disability and Abledness*. New York: Palgrave Macmillan, 2009.

CARA (Communities against Rape and Abuse). "Taking Risks: Implementing Grassroots Community Accountability Strategies." In *The Color of Violence: The INCITE! Anthology*, edited by INCITE!, 250–66. Cambridge, MA: South End Press, 2006.

Carbone, Mauro. *The Thinking of the Sensible*. Evanston: Northwestern University Press, 2004.

Carlisle, Clare. "Kierkegaard's *Repetition*: The Possibility of Motion." *British Journal for the History of Philosophy* 13, no. 3 (2005): 521–41.

Carlson, Licia. "Docile Bodies, Docile Minds: Foucauldian Reflections on Mental Retardation." In *Foucault and the Government of Disability*, edited by Shelley Lynn Tremain, 133–52. Ann Arbor: University of Michigan Press, 2005.

Cavarero, Adriana. "Politicizing Theory." *Political Theory* 30, no. 4 (August 2002): 506–32.

— *Relating Narratives: Storytelling and Selfhood*. Translated by Paul Kottman. New York: Taylor and Francis, 2006.

Chakrabarty, Dipesh. "The Climate of History: Four Theses." *Critical Inquiry* 35 (Winter 2009): 197–222.

Chandler, Mielle, and Astrida Neimanis. "Water and Gestationality: What Flows beneath Ethics." In Chen, MacLeod, and Neimanis, *Thinking with Water*, 61–83.

Chanter, Tina. *Ethics of Eros*. New York: Routledge, 1995.

Cheah, Pheng. "Mattering." *Diacritics* 26, no. 1 (Spring 1996): 108–39.

Cheah, Pheng, and Elizabeth Grosz. "The Future of Sexual Difference: An Interview with Judith Butler and Drucilla Cornell." *Diacritics* 28, no. 1 (Spring 1998): 19–42.

Chen, Cecilia, Janine MacLeod, and Astrida Neimanis, eds. *Thinking with Water*. Montreal: McGill-Queen's University Press, 2013.

CIHI. "Induced Abortions Performed in Canada in 2010." Canadian Institute for Health Information, 2010. http://www.cihi.ca/CIHI-ext-portal/pdf/internet/TA_10_ALLDATATABLES20120417_EN.

Colebrook, Claire. "Is Sexual Difference a Problem?" In *Deleuze and Feminist Theory*, edited by Ian Buchanan and Claire Colebrook, 110–27. Edinburgh: Edinburgh University Press, 2000.

– "Feminist Extinction." In *Undutiful Daughters: New Directions in Feminist Thought and Practice*, edited by Henriette Gunkel, Chrysanthi Nigianni, and Fanny Soderback, 71–83. New York: Palgrave MacMillan, 2012.

– "Introduction." In *Extinction*, 9–28. Ann Arbor: Open Humanities Press, 2012.

– *Death of the Posthuman: Essays on Extinction*. Vol. 1. Ann Arbor: Open Humanities Press, 2014.

Connolly, William. "Beyond Good and Evil: The Ethical Sensibility of Michel Foucault." *Political Theory* 21, no. 3 (1993): 365–89.

Conrad, Ryan. *Against Equality: Prisons Will Not Protect You*. Oakland: AK Press, 2012.

Contat, Michel. "Introduction: une autobiographie politique ?" In *Pourquoi et comment Sartre a écrit* Les Mots?, edited by Michel Contat, 1–41. Paris: PUF, 1996.

Conway, Daniel W. "Modest Expectations: Kierkegaard's Reflections on the Present Age." In *Kierkegaard Studies Yearbook*, edited by Niels Jørgen Cappelørn, Hermann Deuser, Alastair Hannay, and Christian Fink Tolstrup, 21–49. New York: Walter de Gruyter, 1999.

Cook, John. "Those Who Contribute the Least to Greenhouse Gases Will Be Most Impacted by Climate Change." *Huffington Post*, 16 March 2011, http://www.huffingtonpost.com/john-cook/those-who-contribute-the-_b_835718.html.

Coole, Diana, and Samantha Frost, eds. *New Materialisms: Ontology, Agency, and Politics*. Durham: Duke University Press, 2010.

Coombes, Muriel. *Gilbert Simondon and the Philosophy of the Transindividual*. Translated by Thomas LaMarre. Boston: MIT Press, 2012.

Cooper Albright, Ann. *Choreographing Difference: The Body and Identity in Contemporary Dance*. Middletown: Wesleyan University Press, 1997.

Corker, Mairian. "Sensing Disability." *Hypatia* 16, no. 4 (2001): 34–52.

Cottingham, John, Robert Stoothoff, Dugald Mudroch, eds. and trans. *The Philosophical Writings of Descartes*. Vol. 1. Cambridge: Cambridge University Press, 1984.

Cruikshank, Julie. *Do Glaciers Listen? Local Knowledge, Colonial Encounters, and Social Imagination*. Vancouver: UBC Press, 2005.

Cuomo, Chris. *Feminism and Ecological Communities: An Ethics of Flourishing*. New York: Routledge, 1998.

Daigle, Christine. "The Ambiguous Ethics of Simone de Beauvoir." In *Existentialist Thinkers and Ethics*, edited by Christine Daigle, 120–41. Montreal: McGill-Queen's University Press, 2006.

– "L'(la ré-)écriture de soi-même: de l'utilisation de l'autobiographie et des mémoires dans les oeuvres de Beauvoir et Sartre." In *L'écriture et la lecture: des phénomènes miroir? L'exemple de Sartre*, edited by Natalie Despraz and Noémie

Parant, 55–63. St Aignan: Publications des Universités de Rouen et du Havre, 2011.

– "*The Second Sex* as Appeal: The Ethical Dimension of Ambiguity." *philoSOPHIA: A Journal of Continental Feminism* 4, no 2 (2014): 197–220.

– "Making the Humanities Meaningful: Beauvoir's Philosophy and Literature of the Appeal." In *Simone de Beauvoir: A Humanist Thinker*, edited by Tove Pettersen and Annlaug Bjørnøs, 15–28. Rodopi: Value Inquiry Book Series, 2015.

Daigle, Christine, and Jacob Golomb, eds. *Beauvoir and Sartre: The Riddle of Influence*. Bloomington: Indiana University Press, 2009.

Dallacosta, Maria, and Selma James. *The Power of Women and the Subversion of the Community*. Bristol: Falling Wall Press, 1975.

Dannenberg, John. "Nationwide PLN Survey Examines Prison Phone Contracts, Kickbacks." *Prison Legal News*, 15 April 2011, https://www.prisonlegalnews.org/news/2011/apr/15/nationwide-pln-survey-examines-prison-phone-contracts-kickbacks.

Davis, Angela Y. "Racism, Birth Control and Reproductive Rights." In *Women, Race, and Class*, 202–21. New York: Vintage Books, 1983.

– *Are Prisons Obsolete?* New York: Seven Stories Press, 2003.

Davis, Lennard J. *Enforcing Normalcy: Disability, Deafness, and the Body*. New York: W.W. Norton, 1995.

– ed. *The Disability Studies Reader*. 2nd ed. New York: Routledge, 2006.

Delanda, Manuel. *Intensive Science and Virtual Philosophy*. New York: Continuum, 2002.

Deleuze, Gilles. *Negotiations, 1972–1990*. Translated by Martin Joughin. New York: Columbia University Press, 1988.

– *Spinoza: Practical Philosophy*. Translated by Robert Hurley. San Francisco: City Lights, 1988.

– *Expressionism in Philosophy: Spinoza*. Translated by Martin Joughin. Brooklyn: Zone Books, 1990.

– *The Logic of Sense*. Translated by Mark Lester with Charles Stivale. New York: Columbia University Press, 1990.

– *The Fold, Leibniz and the Baroque*. Translated by Tom Conley. Minneapolis: University of Minnesota Press, 1992.

– *Difference and Repetition*. Translated by Paul Patton. New York: Columbia University Press, 1994.

– *Desert Islands and Other Texts, 1953–1974*. Edited by David Lapoujade. Translated by Michael Tormina. Los Angeles: Semiotext(e), 2004.

Deleuze, Gilles, and Félix Guattari. *Anti-Oedipus, Capitalism and Schizophrenia*. Vol. 1. Translated by Robert Hurley, Mark Seem, and Helen Lane. Minneapolis: University of Minnesota Press, 1983.

- *A Thousand Plateaus*. Translated by Brian Massumi. Minneapolis: University of Minnesota Press, 1987.
- *What Is Philosophy?* Translated by Hugh Tomlinson and Graham Burchell. New York: Columbia University Press, 1994.

del Lucchese, Filippo. *Conflict, Power, and Multitude in Machiavelli and Spinoza*. London: Continuum, 2009.

Derbyshire, Stuart. "Can Fetuses Feel Pain?" *BMJ* 332, no. 7546 (April 2006): 909–12.

Derrida, Jacques. "Geshlecht: Sexual Difference, Ontological Difference." Translated by Ruben Berezdivin. *Research in Phenomenology* 13 (1983): 65–83.
- "Women in the Beehive: A Seminar with Jacques Derrida." *Differences: A Journal of Feminist Cultural Studies* 16, no. 3 (2005): 139–57.
- *The Gift of Death*. Translated by David Wills. 2nd ed. Chicago: University of Chicago Press, 2007.

Deutscher, Penelope. "Animality and Descent: Irigaray's Nietzsche, on Leaving the Sea." In *Thinking with Irigaray*, edited by Mary Rawlinson, Serene Khader, and Sabrina Hom, 55–74. Albany: SUNY Press, 2011.

de Waal, Frans. *Primates and Philosophers*. Princeton: Princeton University Press, 2006.

Dolphijn, Rick, and Iris van der Tuin, eds. *New Materialism: Interviews and Cartographies*. Ann Arbor: Open Humanities Press, 2012. http://hdl.handle.net/2027/spo.11515701.0001.001.

Donaldson, Sue, and Will Kymlicka. *Zoopolis: A Political Theory of Animal Rights*. Oxford: Oxford University Press, 2013.

Dussel, Enrique. *Ethics of Liberation*. Edited and translated by Alejandro A. Vallega. Durham: Duke University Press, 2013.

Economist. "Miscarriages of Justice: A Brutal Farce in El Salvador Highlights a Regional Failing." 8 June 2013, http://www.economist.com/news/americas/21579065-brutal-farce-el-salvador-highlights-regional-failing-miscarriages-justice.

Edwards, Stephen D. "The Body as Object Versus the Body as Subject: The Case of Disability." *Medicine, Health Care and Philosophy* 1, no. 1 (2008): 47–56.

EMERJ: Expanding the Movement for Empowerment and Reproductive Justice. "Core Aspects of Reproductive Justice." In Asian Communities for Reproductive Justice, "Three Applications of the Reproductive Justice Lens." 2009, http://forwardtogether.org/assets/docs/ACRJ-Three-Applications-of-the-RJ-Lens.pdf.

Engelhardt, H. Tristram. *The Foundations of Bioethics*. Oxford: Oxford University Press, 1996.

Erdman, Joanna. "Access to Information on Safe Abortion: A Harm Reduction and Human Rights Approach." *Harvard Journal of Law and Gender* 34 (2011): 413–62.

– "Harm Reduction, Human Rights, and Access to Information on Safer Abortion." *International Journal of Gynecology and Obstetrics* 118 (2012): 83–6.

Eriksen, Niels Nymann. *Kierkegaard's Category of Repetition: A Reconstruction.* New York: Walter de Gruyter, 2000.

Fausto-Sterling, Anne. *Sexing the Body: Gender Politics and the Construction of Sexuality.* New York: Basic Books, 2000.

Fielding, Helen. "Questioning Nature: Irigaray, Heidegger and the Potentiality of Matter." *Continental Philosophy Review* 36, no. 1 (2003): 1–26.

Foucault, Michel. *Les mots et les choses: Une archéologie des sciences humaines.* Paris: Gallimard, 1966.

– *The Order of Things: An Archaeology of the Human Sciences.* New York: Random House, 1970.

– *Discipline and Punish: Birth of the Prison.* Translated by Alan Sheridan. New York: Vintage Books, 1977.

– *The History of Sexuality.* Vol. 1, *An Introduction.* Translated by Robert Hurley. New York: Random House, 1978.

– *The History of Sexuality.* Vol. 2, *The Use of Pleasure.* Translated by Robert Hurley. New York: Vintage Books, 1985.

– "The Ethics of the Concern for Self as a Practice of Freedom." In *Essential Works of Foucault, 1954–1984,* vol. 1, *Ethics: Subjectivity and Truth,* edited Paul Rabinow, 281–302. New York: New Press, 1997.

– "Lives of Infamous Men." In *Essential Works of Foucault, 1954–1984,* vol. 3, *Power,* edited by James D. Faubion, 157–75. New York: New Press, 2000.

– *Abnormal: Lectures at the Collège de France, 1974–1975.* Translated by Graham Burchell. New York: Picador, 2003.

– *History of Madness.* Translated by Jonathan Murphy and Jean Khalfa. London: Routledge, 2006.

– *Speech Begins after Death.* Edited by Phillippe Artières. Translated by Robert Bononno. Minneapolis: Minnesota University Press, 2013.

Francione, Gary. *Animals as Persons: Essays on the Abolition of Animal Exploitation.* New York: Columbia University Press, 2008.

Galton, Francis. *Inquiries into Human Faculty and Its Development.* London: MacMillan, 1883.

Garland-Thomson, Rosmarie. *Extraordinary Bodies: Figuring Physical Disability in American Culture and Literature.* New York: Columbia University Press, 1997.

– "Feminist Disability Studies." *Signs* 30, no. 2 (2005): 1557–87.

Gartner, Rosemary, Cheryl Marie Webster, and Anthony N. Doob. "Trends in the Imprisonment of Women in Canada." *Canadian Journal of Criminology and Criminal Justice* 51, no. 2 (April 2009): 169–98.

Gilchrist, Kristen. "'Newsworthy' Victims?" *Feminist Media Studies* 10, no. 4 (2010): 373–90.

Goldenberg, Maya. "Working for the Cure: Challenging Pink Ribbon Activism." In *Configuring Health Consumers: Health Work and the Imperative of Personal Responsibility*, edited by Roma Harris, Nadine Wathen, and Sally Wyatt, 140–59. London: Palgrave Macmillan, 2010.

Goodall, Jane "Primate Spirituality." In *The Encyclopedia of Religion and Nature*, edited by B. Taylor, 1303–6. New York: Thoemmes Continuum, 2005.

Graeber, David. *Debt: The First 5,000 Years*. Brooklyn: Melville House, 2011.

Green, Ronald M., and Mary Jean Green. "Simone de Beauvoir: A Founding Feminist's Appreciation of Kierkegaard." In *Kierkegaard and Existentialism*, edited by Jon Stewart, 1–22. Burlington, VT: Ashgate, 2011.

Grekul, Jana Marie. "A Well-Oiled Machine: Alberta's Eugenics Program, 1928–1972." *Alberta History* 59, no. 3 (Summer 2011): 16–23.

Grosz, Elizabeth. *The Nick of Time*. Durham: Duke University Press, 2004.

– *Time Travels: Feminism, Nature, Power*. Durham: Duke University Press, 2005.

– *Becoming Undone: Darwinian Reflections on Life, Politics, and Art*. Durham: Duke University Press, 2011.

– "Irigaray and the Ontology of Sexual Difference." In *Becoming Undone: Darwinian Reflections on Life, Politics and Art*, 99–112. Durham: Duke University Press, 2011.

Grunebaum, Heidi. *Memorializing the Past: Everyday Life in South Africa after the Truth and Reconciliation Commission*. New Brunswick, NJ: Transaction, 2011.

Guenther, Lisa. "Resisting Agamben, the Biopolitics of Shame and Humiliation." *Philosophy and Social Criticism* 38 (January 2012): 59–79.

Hall, Kim Q. *Feminist Disability Studies*. Bloomington: Indiana University Press, 2011.

Hannay, Alastair. "Levelling and *Einebnung*." In *Kierkegaard and Philosophy: Selected Essays*, 163–78. New York: Routledge, 2003.

Haraway, Donna. "Situated Knowledges: The Science Question in Feminism and the Privilege of Partial Perspective." *Feminist Studies* 14, no. 3 (1988): 575–99.

– "A Cyborg Manifesto: Science, Technology, and Socialist-Feminism in the Late Twentieth Century." In *Simians, Cyborgs and Women: The Reinvention of Nature*, 149–81. New York: Routledge, 1991.

– "The Promises of Monsters: A Regenerative Politics for Inappropriate/d Others." In *Cultural Studies*, edited by Lawrence Grossberg, Carey Nelson, and Paula Treichler, 295–337. New York: Routledge, 1992.

- *The Companion Species Manifesto: Dogs, People, and Significant Otherness.* Chicago: Prickly Paradigm Press, 2003.
- "Otherworldly Conversations, Terran Topics, Local Terms." In *Material Feminisms,* edited by Stacy Alaimo and Susan Hekman, 157–85. Bloomington: Indiana University Press, 2008.

Harjo, Joy. "Vision." In *She Had Some Horses: Poems.* New York: W.W. Norton, 2008.

Harman, Elizabeth. "Creation Ethics: The Moral Status of Early Fetuses and the Ethics of Abortion." *Philosophy and Public Affairs* 28, no. 4 (1999): 310–24.

Harris, John. "Is There a Coherent Social Conception of Disability?" *Journal of Medical Ethics* 26 (2000): 95–100.
- "One Principle and Three Fallacies of Disability Studies." *Journal of Medical Ethics* 27, no. 6 (2001): 383–7.

Harris-Zsovan, Jane. *Eugenics & the Firewall: Canada's Nasty Little Secret.* Winnipeg: J. Gordon Shillingford Publishing, 2010.

Heidegger, Martin. *Basic Writings.* Edited by David Farrell Krell. New York: HarperCollins, 2008.

Heinämaa, Sara. *Toward a Phenomenology of Sexual Difference: Husserl, Merleau-Ponty, Beauvoir.* Lanham: Rowman & Littlefield, 2003.
- "The Sexed Self and the Mortal Body." In *Birth, Death, and Femininity: Philosophies of Embodiment,* edited by Robin May Schott, 73–97. Bloomington: Indiana University Press, 2010.

Herman, Amanda, and Steven Chatfield. "A Detailed Analysis of DanceAbility's Contribution to Mixed-Abilities Dance." *Journal of Dance Education* 10 (2010): 41–55.

Herrnstein, R.J. "Criminogenic Traits." In Wilson and Petersilia, *Crime,* 39–64.

Hird, Myra. *Sex, Gender and Science.* New York: Palgrave Macmillan, 2004.
- "Digesting Differences: Metabolism and the Question of Sexual Difference." *Configurations* 20, no. 3 (Fall 2012): 213–37.

Hird, Myra, and Noreen Giffney, eds. *Queering the Non/Human.* Hampshire: Ashgate, 2008.

Hollenberg, Alexander. "Speaking with the Separatists: Craig Womack and the Relevance of Literary History." *Studies in American Indian Literatures* 21, no. 1 (2009): 1–17. http://search.proquest.com/docview/210681453?accountid= 15067.

hooks, bell. "Eating the Other: Desire and Resistance." In *Feminist Approaches to Theory and Methodology,* edited by Sharlene Hesse-Biber, Christina Gilmartin, and Robin Lydenberg, 179–94. New York: Oxford University Press, 1999.

Houle, Karen. "Making Animal Tracks: Asking the Animal Question: Is the Fetus (in) Question?" *PhaenEx* 2, no. 2 (Fall 2007): 239–59.

Hubbard, Ruth. "Abortion and Disability: Who Should and Who Should Not Inhabit the World." In Davis, *The Disability Studies Reader*, 93–104.

Huffer, Lynne. *Mad for Foucault: Rethinking the Foundations of Queer Theory*. New York: Columbia University Press, 2010.

Hughes, Bill. "Disability and the Body." In *Disability Studies Today*, edited by Colin Barnes, 58–76. Cambridge: Polity Press, 2002.

– "Being Disabled: Towards a Critical Social Ontology for Disability Studies." *Disability and Society* 22, no. 7 (2007): 58–76.

INCITE! Women of Color Against Violence. *The Color of Violence: The INCITE! Anthology*. Cambridge, MA: South End Press, 2006.

– "Women of Color and Prisons." Accessed 21 July 2014, http://www.incitenational.org/page/women-color-prisons.

Irigaray, Luce. *Speculum of the Other Woman*. Translated by Gillian C. Gill. Ithaca: Cornell University Press: 1985.

– *This Sex Which Is Not One*. Translated by Catherine Porter. Ithaca: Cornell University Press, 1985.

– *Marine Lover of Friedrich Nietzsche*. Translated by Gillian C. Gill. New York: Columbia University Press, 1991.

– *Elemental Passions*. Translated by Joanne Collie and Judith Still. New York: Routledge, 1992.

– *An Ethics of Sexual Difference*. Translated by Carolyn Burke and Gillian C. Gill. Ithaca: Cornell University Press, 1993.

– *Je, Tu, Nous: Toward a Culture of Difference*. Translated by Alison Martin. New York: Routledge, 1993.

– *Sexes and Genealogies*. Translated by Gillian C. Gill. New York: Columbia University Press, 1993.

– *Thinking the Difference: For a Peaceful Revolution*. Translated by Karin Montin. New York: Routledge, 1994.

– *I Love to You: Sketch of a Possible Felicity in History*. Translated by Alison Martin. New York: Routledge, 1995.

– "The Question of the Other." Translated by Noah Guynn. *Yale French Studies*, no. 87 (1995), 7–19.

– "The Envelope: A Reading of Spinoza's *Ethics*, 'Of God.'" In *The New Spinoza*, edited by Warren Montag and Ted Stolze, 37–45. Minneapolis: University of Minnesota Press, 1997.

– *The Forgetting of Air in Martin Heidegger*. Translated by Mary Beth Mader. London: The Athelone Press, 1999.

– "From *The Forgetting of Air* to *To Be Two*." In *Feminist Interpretations of Martin Heidegger*, edited by Nancy Holland and Patricia Huntington, 309–15. University Park: Pennsylvania State University Press, 2001.

– *To Be Two*. Translated by Marco Cocito-Monoc and Monique Rhodes. New York: Routledge, 2001.

– *Between East and West: From Singularity to Community*. Translated by Stephen Pluhacek. New York: Columbia University Press, 2002.

– *In the Beginning, She Was*. London: Bloomsbury, 2013.

Jaarsma, Ada S. "Kierkegaard, Biopolitics and Critique in the Present Age." *European Legacy* 18, no. 7 (2013): 850–66.

Jaggar, Alison. *Feminist Politics and Human Nature*. Totowa, NJ: Rowman & Allenheld, 1983.

Jain, S. Lochlann. "Living in Prognosis: Toward an Elegiac Politics." *Representations* 98 (2007): 77–92.

– "The Mortality Effect: Counting the Dead in the Cancer Trial." *Public Culture* 22, no. 1 (2010): 89–117.

– "Survival Odds: Mortality in Corporate Time." *Current Anthropology* 52, no. 3 (2011): 45–55.

– *Malignant: How Cancer Becomes Us*. Berkeley: University of California Press, 2013.

Jamail, Dahr. "We're Looking at the End of Humanity – and It Might Happen Sooner Than You Think." *Alternet*, 17 December 2013, http://www.alternet.org/were-looking-end-humanity-and-it-might-happen-sooner-you-think.

James, Selma. *Sex, Race, and Class – the Perspective of Winning*. Oakland: PM Press, 2012.

Johnson, Corey G. "Female Inmates Sterilized in California Prisons without Approval." Center for Investigative Reporting, 7 July 2013, http://cironline.org/reports/female-inmates-sterilized-california-prisons-without-approval-4917.

Justice Now. *Testimony on Budget Issues Related to Conditions of Confinement and Illegal Sterilizations*. 2012. http://www.jnow.org/downloads/JusticeNow.3.15.BudgetTestimony.FemaleOff.pdf.

Kangas, David J. *Kierkegaard's Instant: On Beginnings*. Bloomington: Indiana University Press, 2007.

Keating, Analouise. *Women Reading Women Writing*. Philadelphia: Temple University Press, 1996.

Kelly, Daniel. *Yuck! The Nature and Moral Significance of Disgust*. Cambridge, MA: MIT Press, 2011.

Keltner, Stacy. "Beauvoir's Idea of Ambiguity." In Simons, *Philosophy of Simone de Beauvoir*, 201–13.

Kenyon, Tim. "False Polarization: Debiasing as Applied Social Epistemology." *Synthese* 191, no. 11 (July 2014): 2529–47.

Kierkegaard, Søren. *Søren Kierkegaard's Journals and Papers*. Edited and translated by Howard V. Hong and Edna H. Hong. Vol 1. Bloomington: Indiana University Press, 1967.

- *Søren Kierkegaard's Journals and Papers.* Edited and translated by Howard V. Hong and Edna H. Hong. Vol. 4. Bloomington: Indiana University Press, 1975.
- *Two Ages: The Age of Revolution and the Present Age.* Edited by Howard V. Hong and Edna H. Hong. Princeton: Princeton University Press, 1978.
- *The Sickness unto Death: A Christian Psychological Exposition for Upbuilding and Awakening.* Edited by Howard V. Hong and Edna H. Hong. Princeton: Princeton University Press, 1980.
- *The Concept of Anxiety.* Edited and translated by Reidar Thomte with Albert B. Anderson. Princeton: Princeton University Press, 1981.
- *Fear and Trembling.* Edited and translated by Howard V. Hong and Edna H. Hong. Princeton: Princeton University Press, 1983.
- *Either/Or.* Edited by Howard V. Hong and Edna H. Hong. Vol. 1. Princeton: Princeton University Press, 1987.

Kirby, Vicki. *Telling Flesh: The Substance of the Corporeal.* New York: Routledge, 1997.
- *Quantum Anthropologies: Life at Large.* Durham: Duke University Press, 2011.

Kittay, Eva. *Love's Labor: Essays on Women, Equality and Dependency.* London: Routledge, 1998.

Kittay, E., and L. Carlson. "Introduction: Rethinking Philosophical Presumptions in Light of Cognitive Disability." *Metaphilosophy, Special Issue: Cognitive Disability and Its Challenge to Moral Philosophy* 40 (2009): 307–30.

Klare, Michael. *The Race for What's Left: The Global Struggle for the World's Last Resources.* New York: Picador, 2012.

Koch, Tom. *The Limits of Principle: Deciding Who Lives and What Dies.* Westport, CT: Praeger, 1998.
- "The Difference That Difference Makes." *Journal of Medicine and Philosophy* 29, no. 6 (2004): 697–716.

Kolbert, Elizabeth. *The Sixth Extinction: An Unnatural History.* New York: Henry and Holt, 2014.

Koshy, Kavitha. "Nepantlera-Activism in the Transnational Moment: In Dialogue with Gloria Anzaldúa's Theorizing of Nepantla." *Human Architecture: Journal of the Sociology of Self-Knowledge* 4, no. 3 (2006): 147–61.

Krause, Sharon. "Bodies in Action: Corporeal Agency and Democratic Politics." *Political Theory* 39, no. 3 (2011): 299–324.

Kruks, Sonia. *Simone de Beauvoir and the Politics of Ambiguity.* Oxford: Oxford University Press, 2012.

Kuczewski, Mark. "Disability: An Agenda for Bioethics." *American Journal of Bioethics* 1, no. 3 (2001): 36–44.

Kuhse, Helga, and Peter Singer. *Should the Baby Live?: The Problem of Handicapped Infants.* London: Oxford University Press, 1985.

Lakhani, Nina. "El Salvador: Where Women May Be Jailed for Miscarrying." *BBC News Magazine*, 18 October 2013, http://www.bbc.co.uk/news/magazine-24532694.

Lea, Robert, Diane Provencher, John F. Jeffrey, Amit Oza, Robert Reid, and Kenneth Swenerton. "Breast Cancer and Abortion." SOGC/GOC Joint Committee Opinion, *Journal of Obstetrics and Gynaecology Canada* 27, no. 5 (2005): 491.

Le Doeuff, Michèle. *The Sex of Knowing*. Translated by Kathryn Hamer and Lorraine Code. New York: Routledge, 2003.

Lee, Susan, Henry Ralston, Eleanor Drey, John Partridge, and Mark Rosen. "Fetal Pain: A Systematic Multidisciplinary Review of Evidence." *Journal of the American Medical Association* 294, no. 8 (2005): 947–54.

Lejeune, Philippe. *Le Pacte autobiographique*. Paris: Seuil, 1996.

Leslie, John. *The Historical Development of the Indian Act*. 2nd ed. Ottawa: Department of Indian Affairs and Northern Development, Treaties and Historical Research Branch, 1978.

Levi, Robin, Nerissa Kinakemakorn, Azadeh Zohrabi, Elizaveta Afanasieff, and Nicole Edwards-Masuda. "Creating the Bad Mother: How the US Approach to Pregnancy in Prisons Violates the Right to Be a Mother." *UCLA Women's Law Journal* 18, no. 1 (2010): 1–78.

Lingis, Alfonso. *Foreign Bodies*. New York: Routledge, 1994.

Linton, Jamie. *What Is Water: The History of a Modern Abstraction*. Vancouver: UBC Press, 2010.

Lloyd, Genevieve. "The Self as Fiction: Philosophy and Autobiography." *Philosophy and Literature* 10 (October 1986): 168–85.

Lloyd, Margaret. "The Politics of Disability and Feminism: Synthesis or Discord?" *Sociology* 35, no. 3 (2001): 715–28.

Long, A.A., and D.N. Sedley. *The Hellenistic Philosophers*. Cambridge: Cambridge University Press, 1987.

Lorde, Audre. *Sister Outsider*. Freedom, CA: Crossing Press, 1984.

Lorraine, Tamsin. *Irigaray and Deleuze: Experiments in Visceral Philosophy*. Ithaca: Cornell University Press, 1999.

Luciano, Dana. "The Inhuman Anthropocene." *Los Angeles Review of Books*, 22 March 2015. http://avidly.lareviewofbooks.org/2015/03/22/the-inhuman-anthropocene.

Lugones, María. *Pilgrimages/Peregrinajes: Theorizing Coalition against Multiple Oppressions*. Lanham: Rowman & Littlefield, 2003.

Lugones, María, and Elizabeth Spelman. "Have We Got a Theory for You! Feminist Theory, Cultural Imperialism, and the Demand for 'The Woman's Voice.'" *Hypatia* 1 (1983): 573–82.

Lukacs, Martin. "New, Privatized City Heralds Climate Apartheid." *Guardian*, 21 January 2014, http://www.theguardian.com/environment/true-north/2014/jan/21/new-privatized-african-city-heralds-climate-apartheid.

MacLeod, Janine. "Water and the Material Imagination: Reading the Sea of Memory against the Flows of Capital." In Chen, MacLeod, and Neimanis, *Thinking with Water*, 40–60.

Mader, Mary Beth. *Sleights of Reason: Norm, Bisexuality, Development*. Albany: SUNY Press, 2011.

Major, Brenda, Mark Appelbaum, Linda Beckman, Mary Ann Dutton, Nancy Felipe, and Carolyn West. "Abortion and Mental Health: Evaluating the Evidence." *American Psychologist* 64, no. 9 (2009): 863–90.

Mann, Bonnie. *Sovereign Masculinity: Gender Lessons from the War on Terror*. Oxford: Oxford University, 2014.

Margulis, Lynn, and Dorion Sagan. *Origins of Sex: Three Billion Years of Genetic Recombination*. New Haven: Yale University Press, 1986.

– *What Is Sex?* New York: Simon & Schuster, 1997.

Marx, Karl. *Capital*. Vol. 1. Translated by Ben Fowkes. London: Penguin, 2004.

– *The Communist Manifesto*. Edited and translated by L.M. Findlay. Peterborough: Broadview Press, 2004.

May, Elaine Tyler. *Barren in the Promised Land: Childless Americans and the Pursuit of Happiness*. Cambridge: Harvard University Press, 1997.

Mbembe, Achille. "Necropolitics." Translated by Libby Meintjes, *Public Culture* 15, no. 1 (2003): 11–40.

McMahan, Jeff. *The Ethics of Killing: Problems at the Margins of Life*. New York: Oxford University Press, 2002.

McMenamin, Mark, and Dianna McMenamin. *Hypersea*. New York: Columbia University Press, 1994.

McRuer, Robert. *Crip Theory: Cultural Signs of Queerness and Disability*. New York: New York University Press, 2006.

– "Crip Theory. Cultural Signs of Queerness and Disability." *Scandinavian Journal of Disability Research* 10, no. 1 (2008): 67–9.

McWhorter, Ladelle. *Racism and Sexual Oppression in Anglo-America: A Genealogy*. Indianapolis: Indiana University Press, 2009.

– "Darwin's Invisible Hand: Feminism, Reprogenetics, and Foucault's Analysis of Neoliberalism." *Southern Journal of Philosophy* 48, Spindel supplement (2010): 43–63.

Merleau-Ponty, Maurice. *The Visible and the Invisible*. Edited by Claude Lefort. Translated by Alphonso Lingis. Evanston: Northwestern University Press, 1968.

– *In Praise of Philosophy and Other Essays*. Translated by John Wild, James Edie, and John O'Neill. Evanston: Northwestern University Press, 1988.

– "Philosophy and Non-philosophy since Hegel." In *Philosophy and Non-philosophy since Merleau-Ponty*, edited by Hugh Silverman, 9–83. Evanston: Northwestern University Press, 1988.

– *Phenomenology of Perception*. Translated by Donald A. Landes. New York: Routledge, 2012.

Milloy, John S. *A National Crime: The Canadian Government and the Residential School System*. Winnipeg: University of Manitoba Press, 2011.

Mitropolous, Angela. "The Time of the Contract: Insurance, Contingency, and the Arrangement of Risk." *South Atlantic Quarterly* 111, no. 4 (2012): 763–81.

Montopoli, Brian. 2010. "S.C. Lt. Gov. Andre Bauer Compares Helping Poor to Feeding Stray Animals." CBS *News*, 25 January 2010, http://www.cbsnews.com/news/sc-lt-gov-andre-bauer-compares-helping-poor-to-feeding-stray-animals.

Moore, Jason. "The Capitalocene, Part I: On the Nature and Origins of Our Ecological Crisis." June 2014, http://www.jasonwmoore.com/uploads/The_Capitalocene__Part_I__June_2014.pdf.

Morris, Jenny. *Pride against Prejudice*. London: Women's Press, 1991.

Munk-Olsen, Trine, Thomas Munk Laursen, Carsten B. Pedersen, Øjvind Lidegaard, and Preben Bo Mortensen. "Induced First Trimester Abortion and Risk of Mental Disorder." *New England Journal of Medicine* 364 (2011): 332–9.

Nagel, Thomas. "War and Massacre." *Philosophy and Public Affairs* 1, no. 2 (Winter 1972): 123–44.

National Cancer Institute. "Summary Report: Early Reproductive Events and Breast Cancer Workshop." Updated March 2010, http://www.cancer.gov/cancertopics/causes/ere/workshop-report.

National Geographic Live. "Face-off with Deadly Predator." Accessed 10 October 2013, http://www.youtube.com/watch?feature=player_embedded&v=Zxa6P73Awcg#t=11.

Native Women's Association of Canada. *What Their Stories Tell Us: Research Findings from the Sisters in Spirit Initiative, 2010*. Accessed 3 June 2013, http://www.nwac.ca/sites/default/files/reports/2010_NWAC_SIS_Report_EN.pdf.

Neimanis, Astrida. "Bodies of Water, Human Rights and the Hydrocommons." *TOPIA: Canadian Journal of Cultural Studies* 21 (2009): 161–82.

– "On Collaboration (for Barbara Godard)." *NORA: Nordic Journal of Feminist and Gender Research* 20, no. 3 (2012): 1–7.

Newell, Christopher. "The Social Nature of Disability, Disease, and Genetics." *Journal of Medical Ethics* 25 (1999): 172–5.

Newmark, Kevin. *Irony on Occasion: From Schlegel and Kierkegaard to Derrida and de Man*. New York: Fordham University Press, 2012.

Nietzsche, Friedrich. *The Will to Power*. Translated by Walter Kaufmann. New York: Vintage Books, 1968.

Nye, Andrea. "It's Not Philosophy." *Hypatia* 13, no. 2 (Spring 1998): 107–15.

Oberman, Michelle. "Cristina's World: Lessons from El Salvador's Ban on Abortion." *Stanford Law and Policy Review* 24 (2013): 1–38.

Oliver, Kelly. *Womanizing Nietzsche: Philosophy's Relation to the "Feminine."* New York: Routledge, 1995.

– *Animal Lessons: How They Teach Us to Be Human*. New York: Columbia University Press, 2009.

Oliver, Michael. *The Politics of Disablement*. Basingstoke: Palgrave Macmillan, 1990.

Ouellette, Alicia. *Bioethics and Disability*. New York: Cambridge University Press, 2011.

Parens, Erik. "How Long Has This Been Going On? Disability Issues, Disability Studies, and Bioethics." *American Journal of Bioethics* 1, no. 3 (2001): 54–5.

Parisi, Luciana. "Event and Evolution." *Southern Journal of Philosophy* 48, Spindel supplement (2010): 147–64.

Parker, Emily Anne. "Rereading Beauvoir on the Question of Feminist Subjectivity." *Philosophy Today* 53 (2009): 121–9.

– "Singularity in Beauvoir's *The Ethics of Ambiguity*." *Journal of Southern Philosophy* 53, no. 1 (March 2015): 1–16.

Peers, Danielle, Melisa Brittain, and Robert McRuer. "Crip Excess, Art and Politics: A Conversation with Robert McRuer." *Review of Education, Pedagogy and Cultural Studies* 34 (2012): 148–55.

Piepmeier, Alison. "The Inadequacy of 'Choice': Disability and What's Wrong with Feminist Framings of Reproduction." *Feminist Studies* 39, no. 1 (2013): 159–86.

Puar, Jasbir K. "Prognosis Time: Towards a Geopolitics of Affect, Debility and Capacity." *Women and Performance: A Journal of Feminist Theory* 19, no. 2 (2009): 161–72.

Public Safety Performance Project. "One in 100: Behind Bars in America 2008." Washington, DC: Pew Center on the States, 2008. Accessed 23 June 2012, http://www.pewcenteronthestates.org.

Puig de la Bellacasa, Maria. "Ethical Doings in Naturecultures." *Ethics, Place and Environment* 13, no. 2 (2010): 151–69.

Pulitano, Elvira. *Native American Critical Theory*. Lincoln: University of Nebraska Press, 2003.

Razack, Sherene. "Gendered Racial Violence and Spatialized Justice: The Murder of Pamela George." In *Race, Space and the Law: Unmapping a White Settler Society*, edited by Sherene Razack, 121–56. Toronto: Between the Lines, 2002.

Rich, Adrienne. "Notes towards a Politics of Location." In *Feminist Theory Reader: Local and Global Perspectives*, edited by Carole R. McCann and Seung-Kyung Kim, 447–59. New York: Routledge, 2003.

Rifkin, Mark. "Indigenizing Agamben: Rethinking Sovereignty in Light of the 'Peculiar' Status of Native Peoples." *Cultural Critique* 73 (Fall 2009): 88–124.

Riley, Diane, and Pat O'Hare. "Harm Reduction: History, Definition, and Practice." In *Harm Reduction: National and International Perspectives*, edited by James Inciardi and Lana Harrison, 1–26. Thousand Oaks: Sage, 2000.

Ritchie, Beth E. *Arrested Justice: Black Women, Violence, and America's Prison Nation*. New York: New York University Press, 2012.

Roberts, Dorothy. *Killing the Black Body: Race, Reproduction, and the Meaning of Liberty*. New York: Vintage Books, 1997.

– *Shattered Bonds: The Color of Child Welfare*. New York: Basic Books, 2000.

Rose, Nikolas. *The Politics of Life Itself: Biomedicine, Power, and Subjectivity in the Twenty-First Century*. Princeton: Princeton University Press, 2007.

Roth, Rachel. *Making Women Pay: The Hidden Costs of Fetal Rights*. Ithaca: Cornell University Press, 2000.

Royal Canadian Mounted Police. *Missing and Murdered Aboriginal Women: A National Operational Overview*. 2014. http://www.rcmp-grc.gc.ca/pubs/mmaw-faapd-eng.pdf.

Royal College of Obstetricians and Gynaecologists. "Induced Termination of Pregnancy and Future Reproductive Outcomes – Current Evidence." 16 September 2009, http://www.rcog.org.uk/induced-termination-pregnancy-and-future-reproductive-outcomes-%E2%80%93-current-evidence.

Ruonakoski, Erika. "Literature as a Means of Communication: A Beauvoirian Interpretation of an Ancient Greek Poem." *Sapere Aude* 3, no. 6 (2012): 250–70.

Sanger, Margaret. *The Pivot of Civilization*. New York: Brentano's, 1922.

Sartre, Jean-Paul. *What Is Literature?* (1948). New York: Routledge, 2001.

– *Being and Nothingness*. New York: Routledge Classics, 2003.

Saxton, Marsha. "Disability Rights and Selective Abortion." In Davis, *The Disability Studies Reader*, 105–16.

Schwartzman, Lisa. *Challenging Liberalism: Feminism as Political Critique*. University Park: Pennsylvania State University Press, 2006.

Scott, Charles. *The Question of Ethics: Nietzsche, Foucault, Heidegger*. Bloomington: Indiana University Press, 1990.

Scully, Jackie Leach. *Disability Bioethics: Moral Bodies, Moral Difference*. Lanham: Rowman & Littlefield, 2008.

Sedgh, Gilda, Susheela Singh, Iqbal Shah, Elisabeth Ahman, Stanley Henshaw, and Akinrinola Bankole. "Induced Abortion: Incidence and Trends Worldwide from 1995 to 2008." *Lancet* 379, no. 9816 (February 2012): 625–32.

Shakespeare, Tom. *Disability Rights and Wrongs*. New York: Routledge, 2006.

Shakespeare, Tom, and Nicholas Watson. "The Social Model of Disability: An Outdated Ideology?" *Research in Social Science and Disability* 2 (2002): 9–28.

Sharp, Hasana. "'Is It Simple to Be a Feminist in Philosophy?': Althusser and Feminist Theoretical Practice." *Rethinking Marxism* (2000): 18–34.

– "Animal Affects: Spinoza and the Frontiers of the Human." *Journal for Critical Animal Studies* 9, no. 1–2 (2011): 48–68.

– *Spinoza and the Politics of Renaturalization*. Chicago: University of Chicago Press, 2011.

Shildrick, Margrit. "Beyond the Body of Bioethics: Challenging the Conventions." In *Ethics of the Body: Postconventional Challenges*, edited by Margrit Shildrick and Roxanne Mykitiuk, 1–28. Cambridge: MIT Press, 2005.

– *Dangerous Discourses of Disability, Subjectivity and Sexuality*. Basingstoke: Palgrave Macmillan, 2009.

Shildrick, Margrit, and Janet Price. "Deleuzian Connections and Queer Corporealities: Shrinking Global Disability." *Rhizomes* (2005): 11. http://www.rhizomes.net/issue11/shildrickprice.

Shotwell, Alexis. "Open Normativities: Gender, Disability, and Collective Political Change." *Signs: Journal of Women in Culture and Society* 37 (2012): 989–1016.

Shrage, Laurie. *Abortion and Social Responsibility: Depolarizing the Debate*. Oxford: Oxford University Press, 2003.

Silliman, Jael, and Anannya Bhattacharjee, eds. *Policing the National Body*. Cambridge, MA: South End Press, 2002.

Silvers, Anita. "Formal Justice." In *Disability, Difference, Discrimination: Perspectives on Justice in Bioethics and Public Policy*, edited by Anita Silvers, David T. Wasserman, and Mary Briody Mahowald, 13–146. Lanham: Rowman & Littlefield, 1998.

– "On the Possibility and Desireability of Constructing a Neutral Conception of Disability." *Theoretical Medicine* 26, no. 6 (2003): 471–87.

– "An Essay on Modeling." *Philosophical Reflections on Disability* 104, no. 1 (2010): 19–36.

Simms, Eva-Maria. "Eating One's Mother: Female Embodiment in a Toxic World." *Environmental Ethics* 31, no. 3 (2009): 263–77.

Simons, Margaret A. "Beauvoir Interview (1979)." In *Beauvoir and the Second Sex: Feminism, Race, and the Origins of Existentialism*, 1–21. Lanham: Rowman & Littlefield, 1999.

Simons, Margaret A., ed. *The Philosophy of Simone de Beauvoir: Critical Essays*. Bloomington: Indiana University Press, 2006.

Simons, Margaret A., with Marybeth Timmermann and Mary Beth Mader, eds. *Simone de Beauvoir: Philosophical Writings*. Translated by Veronique Zaytzeff. Urbana: University of Chicago Press, 2004.

Simondon, Gilbert. *L'individu et sa genese physico-biologique*. Paris: PUF, 1964.

— *Du mode d'existence des objets techniques*. Paris: Aubier, 1989.

— *L'indiviudation psychique et collective*. Paris: Aubier, 1989.

— "The Position of the Problem of Ontogenesis." Translated by Gregory Flanders. *Parhessia* 7 (2009): 4–16.

— *Two Lessons on Animal and Man*. Translated by Drew S. Burk. Minneapolis: Univocal Books, 2011.

SisterSong: Women of Color Reproductive Justice Collective. "What Is RJ?" Accessed 15 October 2013. http://www.sistersong.net/index.php?option= com_content&view=article&id=141&Itemid=81.

Smith, Andrea. *Conquest: Sexual Violence and American Indian Genocide*. Cambridge, MA: South End Press, 2005.

— "Native American Feminism, Sovereignty and Social Change." In *Making Space for Indigenous Feminism*, edited by Joyce Green, 93–7. Black Point: Fernwood Publishing, 2007.

Smith, Owen. "Shifting Apollo's Frame: Challenging the Body Aesthetic in Theatre Dance." In *Bodies in Commotion: Disability and Performance*, edited by Carrie Sandahl and Philip Auslander, 73–85. Ann Arbor: University of Michigan Press, 2005.

Smuts, Barbara. "Encounters with Animal Minds." *Journal of Consciousness Studies* 8 (2001): 293–309.

Snow, C.P. *The Two Cultures*. Cambridge: Cambridge University Press, 1998.

Snyder, Sharon L., and David T. Mitchell. *Cultural Locations of Disability*. Chicago: University of Chicago Press, 2006.

Spinoza, Benedict de. *The Chief Works of Spinoza*. Vol. 2, *On the Improvement of the Understanding; The Ethics; Correspondence*. Translated by R.H.M. Elwes. New York: Dover Publications, 1951.

— *Ethics*. Translated by E. Curley. New York: Penguin Classics, 1996.

— *Political Treatise*. Translated by S. Shirley. Indianapolis: Hackett, 2000.

Spivak, Gayatri S. *Death of a Discipline*. New York: Columbia University Press, 2003.

Stanescu, James. "Species Trouble: Judith Butler, Mourning, and the Precarious Lives of Animals." *Hypatia* 27, no. 3 (2012): 567–82.

State of California. *California Code of Regulations*. Accessed 21 July 2014, http://www.cdcr.ca.gov/Regulations/Adult_Operations/docs/Title15-2014.pdf.

Stone, Alison. "The Sex of Nature: A Reinterpretation of Irigaray's Metaphysics and Political Thought." *Hypatia* 18, no. 3 (2003): 60–84.

– *Luce Irigaray and the Philosophy of Sexual Difference*. Cambridge: Cambridge University Press, 2006.

Sullivan, Nicki. "The Somatechnics of Perception and the Matter of the Non/Human: A Critical Response to the New Materialism." *Journal of Women's Studies* 19, no. 3 (2012): 299–313.

Superson, Anita. "The Right to Bodily Autonomy and the Abortion Controversy." In *Autonomy, Oppression and Gender*, edited by Andrea Veltman and Mark Piper. Oxford: Oxford University Press, forthcoming.

Svirsky, Marcelo, and Simone Bignall. *Agamben and Colonialism*. Edinburgh: University of Edinburgh Press, 2012.

Swain, John, and Sally French. "Toward an Affirmation Model of Disability." *Disability and Society* 15, no. 4 (2000): 569–82.

Taylor, Chloë. "The Precarious Lives of Animals." *Philosophy Today* 52, no. 1 (2008): 60–72.

Taylor, Paul. "An Ethics of Respect for Nature." *Environmental Ethics* 3 (Fall 1981): 197–218.

Thomas, Carol. "Disability and Impairments." In *Disabling Barriers – Enabling Environments*, edited by John Swain, Sally French, Colin Barnes, and Carol Thomas, 21–7. Thousand Oaks: Sage, 2004.

Thomson, Judith Jarvis. "A Defense of Abortion." *Philosophy and Public Affairs* 1, no. 1 (Autumn 1971): 47–66.

Tremain, Shelley Lynn. "On the Government of Disability." *Social Theory and Practice* 27, no. 4 (2001): 617–36.

– "On the Government of Disability." In Davis, *The Disability Studies Reader*, 185–96.

– "On the Subject of Impairment." In *Disability/Postmodernity: Embodying Disability Theory*, edited by Marian Corker and Tom Shakespeare, 32–47. London: Continuum, 2002.

– ed. *Foucault and the Government of Disability*. Ann Arbor: University of Michigan Press, 2005.

– "Reproductive Freedom, Self-Regulation, and the Government of Impairment in Utero." *Hypatia* 21, no. 1 (2006): 35–53.

– "The Biopolitics of Bioethics and Disability." *Journal of Bioethical Inquiry* 5, no. 2 (2008): 101–6.

Union of the Physically Impaired against Segregation. "Fundamental Principles of Disability." Accessed 20 August 2014, http://disability-studies.leeds.ac.uk/files/library/UPIAS-fundamental-principles.pdf.

Van der Tuin, Iris. "Deflationary Logic: Response to Sara Ahmed's 'Imaginary Prohibitions': Some Preliminary Remarks on the Founding Gestures of the 'New
Materialism.'" *European Journal of Women's Studies* 15, no. 4 (2008): 411–16.

Van der Tuin, Iris, and Rick Dolphijn. "The Transversality of New Materialism."
Women: A Cultural Review 21, no. 2 (2010): 153–71.

Vehmas, Simo. "Live and Let Die? Disability in Bioethics." *New Review of Bioethics*
1, no. 1 (2003): 145–57.

Vlassoff, Michael, Susheela Singh, Jacqueline Darroch, Erin Carbone, and Sam
Bernstein. "Assessing Costs and Benefits of Sexual and Reproductive Health
Interventions." In *Occasional Report*, no. 11. New York: Alan Guttmacher Insti-
tute, 2004.

Wacquant, Loïc. "Deadly Symbiosis: When Ghetto and Prison Meet and Mesh."
Punishment and Society 3 (January 2001): 95–133.

– *Prisons of Poverty*. Expanded ed. Minneapolis: University of Minnesota Press,
2009.

Warren, Karen. "The Power and Promise of Ecological Feminism." *Environmental
Ethics* 12 (Summer 1990): 125–49.

Waters, Anne. "Indigeneity, Self-Determination, and Sovereignty." *American Philosophical Association Newsletter* 2, no. 1 (February 2002): 9–16.

Weinstock, Daniel. "So, Are You Still a Philosopher?" Big Thinking lecture at the
Congress of the Canadian Federation of Humanities and Social Sciences, University of Victoria, Victoria, Canada, 3 June 2013.

Westphal, Merold. "Kierkegaard's Teleological Suspension of Religiousness B." In
Foundations of Kierkegaard's Vision of Community, edited by George B. Connell
and C. Stephen Evans, 110–29. New Jersey: Humanities Press, 1992.

Wilderson, Frank B. "The Prison Slave as Hegemony's (Silent) Scandal." *Social Justice* 30, no. 2 (2003): 18–27.

Willett, Cynthia. *Maternal Ethics and Other Slave Moralities*. London: Routledge,
1995.

– *The Soul of Justice*. Ithaca: Cornell University Press, 2001.

– *Interspecies Ethics*. New York: Columbia University Press, 2014.

Williams, James. *Gilles Deleuze's Logic of Sense: A Critical Introduction and Guide*.
Edinburgh: Edinburgh University Press, 2008.

Wilson, Elizabeth A. "Gut Feminism." *differences* 15, no. 3 (2004): 66–94.

Wilson, E.O. *Biophilia*. Cambridge: Harvard University Press, 1984.

Wolbring, Gregor. "Disability Rights Approach towards Bioethics?" *Journal of Disability Policy Studies* 14, no. 3 (2003): 174–80.

Wolstenholme, Thomas. "Kierkegaard's 'Aesthetic' Age and Its Political Consequences." In *Kierkegaard and the Political*, edited by Alison Assiter and Mar-

gherita Tonon, 63–80. Newcastle upon Tyne: Cambridge Scholars Publishing, 2012.

Womack, Craig S. *Red on Red: Native American Literary Separatism*. Minneapolis: University of Minnesota Press, 1999.

– *Drowning in Fire: A Novel*. Tucson: University of Arizona Press, 2001.

– "Theorizing American Indian Experience." In *Reasoning Together: The Native Critics Collective*, edited by Craig S. Womack, Daniel Heath Justice, and Christopher B. Teuton, 353–410. Norman: University of Oklahoma Press, 2008.

Zalasiewicz, Jan et al. "Are We Now Living in the Anthropocene?" GSA *Today* 18, no. 2 (February 2008): 4–8.

Zourabichvilli, Francois. *Deleuze: A Philosophy of the Event: Together with the Vocabulary of Deleuze*. Edited by Gregg Lambert and Daniel W. Smith. Edinburgh: Edinburgh University Press, 2012.

Contributors

JANE BARTER is associate professor and chair of the Department of Religion and Culture at the University of Winnipeg. She has written and edited several books in theology, and also researches in feminist philosophy. Her work has appeared in *Canadian Woman Studies/cahiers de la femme*, the *Journal of the Motherhood Initiative for Research and Community Involvement*, and *Studies in Religion/Sciences religieuses*.

CHRISTINE DAIGLE is a professor of philosophy and chancellor's chair for research excellence at Brock University. She is the author of *Le nihilisme est-il un humanisme? Étude sur Nietzsche et Sartre* (Presses de l'Université Laval, 2005) and *Routledge Critical Thinkers: Jean-Paul Sartre* (Routledge, 2009). She edited *Existentialist Thinkers and Ethics* (McGill-Queen's University Press, 2006), to which she contributed a chapter on Simone de Beauvoir's ethics. She also coedited *Beauvoir and Sartre: The Riddle of Influence* (Indiana University Press, 2009) with Jacob Golomb and *Nietzsche and Phenomenology: Life, Power, Subjectivity* (Indiana University Press, 2013) with Élodie Boublil. She is the author of a number of articles on Nietzsche, Sartre, and Beauvoir.

SHANNON DEA is associate professor of philosophy and the former director of women's studies at the University of Waterloo. Her research spans the history of metaphysics, the scholarship of teaching and learning, and the philosophy of sex and gender. She is the author of *Beyond the Binary: Thinking about Sex and Gender* (Broadview Press, 2016). Dea's research on abortion is an outgrowth of her time as a local Planned Parenthood president, and later as the media spokesperson for that Planned Parenthood. She thinks you can tell a lot about people from their choice of companion animals; hers is an irascible rabbit named William.

LINDSAY EALES is a choreographer, instructor, performer, and scholar who explores integrated dance, disability, madness, and social justice. She is currently a PhD student in the Faculty of Physical Education and Recreation at the University of Alberta. Her work has been published in journals including *Adapted Physical Activity Quarterly*, *Leisure/Loisir*, and *Emotions, Space, and Society*. Her PhD work uses research-creation to explore mad politics, aesthetics, and mad-accessible practices through dance. She is supported by the Vanier Canada Graduate Scholarship (SSHRC). Eales is also a founder and co-artistic director of CRIPSiE (Collaborative Radically Integrated Performers Society in Edmonton).

ELIZABETH GROSZ is Jean Fox O'Barr Women's Studies Professor in Trinity College of Arts and Sciences at Duke University. She is the author of numerous books, including *Volatile Bodies: Toward a Corporeal Feminism* (Indiana University Press, 1994), *Space, Time, and Perversion: Essays on the Politics of Bodies* (Routledge, 1995), *The Nick of Time: Politics, Evolution, and the Untimely* (Duke University Press, 2004), *Time Travels: Feminism, Nature, Power* (Duke University Press, 2005), *Chaos, Territory, Art: Deleuze and the Framing of the Earth* (Columbia University Press, 2008), and, most recently, *Becoming Undone: Darwinian Reflections on Life, Politics, and Art* (Duke University Press, 2011). She is also the editor of several anthologies, including *Sexy Bodies: The Strange Carnalities of Feminism* (Routledge, 1995) and *Becomings: Explorations in Time, Memory, and Futures* (Cornell University Press, 1999).

LISA GUENTHER is associate professor of philosophy at Vanderbilt University. She is the author of *Solitary Confinement: Social Death and Its Afterlives* (University of Minnesota Press, 2013) and *The Gift of the Other: Levinas and the Politics of Reproduction* (SUNY, 2006), and the coeditor of *Death and Other Penalties: Philosophy in a Time of Mass Incarceration* (Fordham University Press, 2015). Her current book project is tentatively entitled *Life against Social Death: From Reproductive Injustice to Natal Resistance.*

LYNNE HUFFER is Samuel Candler Dobbs Professor of Women's, Gender, and Sexuality Studies at Emory University. She is the author of four books: *Are the Lips a Grave? A Queer Feminist on the Ethics of Sex* (Colombia University Press, 2013), *Mad for Foucault: Rethinking the Foundations of Queer Theory* (Colombia University Press, 2010), *Maternal Pasts, Feminist Futures: Nostalgia and the Question of Difference* (Stanford University Press, 1998), and *Another Colette: The Question of Gendered Writing* (University of Michigan Press, 1992). She currently serves as coeditor of *philoSOPHIA: A Journal in Continental Feminism*, and has published widely in academic, literary, and mass-media venues.

ADA S. JAARSMA is associate professor of philosophy in the Department of Humanities at Mount Royal University, where she teaches continental philosophy. She has published articles in *Hypatia, Constellations*, the *Journal for Cultural and Religious Theory, European Legacy*, and *Studies in Education and Philosophy*, and has edited two special journal issues. She is completing a book about the existential significance of evolutionary theory, epigenetics, and new materialist critical theory.

STEPHANIE JENKINS is assistant professor of philosophy in the School of History, Philosophy, and Religion at Oregon State University. Her research and teaching interests include twentieth-century continental philosophy, feminist philosophy, disability studies, critical animal studies, and ethics. She has a PhD in philosophy and women's studies from Pennsylvania State University. Her doctoral dissertation, "Disabling Ethics: A Genealogy of Ability," argues for a genealogy-based ethics that departs from traditional bioethical approaches to disability. Jenkins also served as a research assistant at the Rock Ethics Institute, where she wrote an extensive handbook on ethics pedagogy across the curriculum and organized workshops for faculty on incorporating ethics into their classrooms. She has published articles and book chapters on the philosophy of disability and animal ethics, and is currently completing a monograph on disability ethics.

LADELLE McWHORTER holds the Stephanie Bennett Smith Chair in Women, Gender, and Sexuality Studies, is a professor of environmental studies, and holds an appointment in the Philosophy Department at the University of Richmond in Richmond, Virginia. She is the author of *Bodies and Pleasures: Foucault and the Politics of Sexual Normalization* (Indiana University Press, 1999), *Racism and Sexual Oppression in Anglo-America: A Genealogy* (Indiana University Press, 2009), and more than three dozen articles on Foucault, Bataille, Irigaray, and race theory. With Gail Stenstad, she edited a revised and greatly expanded second edition of her 1992 anthology *Heidegger and the Earth: Essays in Environmental Philosophy* (University of Toronto Press, 2009). She is currently working on a book tentatively entitled *The End of Personhood on a Postmodern Planet.*

ASTRIDA NEIMANIS is a lecturer in gender and cultural studies at the University of Sydney. She writes primarily about water, weather, and other environmental matters and has published in journals such as *Hypatia, philoSOPHIA, TOPIA, feminist review,* and *Somatechnics.* She coedited the collection *Thinking with Water* (McGill-Queen's University Press, 2013). Her research and writing practice is strongly collaborative, including projects with bioartists, poets, designers, playwrights, filmmakers, ecologists, and pathologists. Her forthcoming manuscript is entitled *Bodies of Water: Feminist Phenomenologies for Posthuman Worlds* (Bloomsbury), while her most recent work explores invisible ecologies and water as a planetary archive of feeling. She is also a cofounder of the Swedish-based Environmental Humanities Collaboratory: The Seed Box.

DANIELLE PEERS is a queer-crip community organizer, artist, and scholar who engages sociocultural theory to study disability movements and the non-normative moving body. Peers was recently a Banting Postdoctoral Scholar in Communication Studies at Concordia University in Montreal, and is assistant professor in the Faculty of Physical Education and Recreation at the University of Alberta. Her work spans numerous fields, with publications, for example, in *Disability and Society,* the *Journal of Sport and Social Issues, Adapted Physical Activity Quarterly,* and the *Review of Education, Pedagogy and Cultural Studies.* Peers's work in her chapter was supported by both the Vanier Canada Graduate Scholarship (SSHRC) and the Trudeau Foundation Scholarship.

STEPHEN D. SEELY is a doctoral candidate in the Department of Women's and Gender Studies at Rutger's University. His dissertation, "A Technics of Sexual Difference," explores the relationship between sex/uality and technicity in philosophy, psychoanalysis, the biological and technosciences, and science fiction. His coauthored book with Drucilla Cornell, *In the Spirit of Revolution: Beyond the Dead Ends of Man* (Polity Press, 2015), rethinks the relationship between revolution, spirituality, and sexual ethics as they have been configured in queer and feminist theory and in various revolutionary movements in the Global South. Their article "There's Nothing Revolutionary about a Blowjob" was published in *Social Text* in 2014. Seely has also published work on queer becoming, affect theory, race and psychoanalysis, sexual difference, and biophilosophy.

HASANA SHARP is associate professor of philosophy at McGill University. Her work explores the affective constitution of social and political life as well as the consequences of the denial of human exceptionalism. She is author of *Spinoza and the Politics of Renaturalization* (University of Chicago, 2011) and the coeditor of *Between Hegel and Spinoza: A Volume of Critical Essays* (Continuum, 2012). Sharp has also published articles in journals such as *Journal of the History of Philosophy*, *History of Philosophy Quarterly*, *Hypatia*, and *Political Theory*. She lives with two small human animals, a not-so-small human animal, and two felines.

CHLOË TAYLOR is associate professor of women's and gender studies and philosophy at the University of Alberta. She is the author of *The Culture of Confession from Augustine to Foucault* (Routledge, 2008), and the coeditor of *Asian Perspectives on Animal Ethics* (Routledge, 2014). She is currently completing a *Routledge Guidebook to Michel Foucault and the History of Sexuality* and a monograph titled *Bucolic Pleasures? Foucault, Feminism, and Sexual Crime*. In addition to her work in feminist philosophy and Foucault studies, she has published in the area of animal and alimentary ethics, and is at work on a second monograph, titled *Abnormal Appetites: Foucault and Food Politics*. She lives with an ever-growing number of rescue companion cats.

FLORENTIEN VERHAGE is assistant professor of philosophy and core faculty member in the Women's and Gender Studies Program at Washington and Lee University. Her research is concerned with intersubjective encounters. In addition to exploring such encounters through a traditional phenomenological (Merleau-Pontian) framework, she lets this framework be challenged and unsettled by contemporary work in feminist phenomenology, chicana theory, critical race theory, and post-colonial theory. Her work on such unsettling encounters is expressed not only by letting these different theoretical fields encounter each other, but also in the theme of disorientation and discomfort that she addresses in several of her published and in-progress works. She has published articles in journals such as *Emotion, Space and Society* and *Symposium*, and book chapters in volumes such as *Understanding Maurice Merleau-Ponty*, *Understanding Modernism*, and *Coming to Life: Philosophies of Pregnancy, Childbirth, and Mothering*.

RACHEL LOEWEN WALKER (BA, MA) is the executive director of OUT-Saskatoon, a non-profit agency that supports Saskatoon's queer community through education, advocacy, and programming. She is also a sessional lecturer at the University of Saskatchewan, teaching classes on queer theory, philosophy of sexuality, feminist philosophy, and popular culture. Loewen Walker has published a number of articles in journals including *Hypatia*, *Women: A Cultural Review*, *Emotion, Space and Society*, the *Canadian Journal of Native Studies*, and *Pimatisiwin*.

CYNTHIA WILLETT teaches philosophy at Emory University. Her authored books include *Interspecies Ethics* (Cambridge University Press, 2014); *Irony in the Age of Empire: Comic Perspectives on Freedom and Democracy* (Indiana, 2008); *The Soul of Justice: Racial Hubris and Social Bonds* (Cornell University Press, 2001); and *Maternal Ethics and Other Slave Moralities* (Routledge, 1995). She edited the anthology *Theorizing Multiculturalism* (Oxford University Press, 1998) and is a coeditor for the *Symposia on Race, Gender, and Philosophy*. She is currently working on the ethics of music and comedy and coauthoring an essay on the sociality of cats.

Index

epistemology, 91; and existentialism, 173–4; posthuman, 44; postmodern, 93; mainstream, 228

feminist science studies, 4, 89, 108, 114

fiction, 38, 147, 190

flourishing, 14–16, 88–9, 185–6, 230

Fontaine, Nahanni, 257

fossils, 85–103

Foucault, Michel, 118, 156, 208–11, 224, 258; and contingency, 9, 85–103

framing, 6, 13, 129–44, 147; conceptual, 29, 43, 48, 263; epistemic, 85–103; normative, 200, 210–13; of recognition, 9, 11

freedom, 71–2, 78–82; and disability, 203; existential, 154–9, 163–75, 181–92; free will, 76–8; and incarceration, 220, 228–9; as invention, 91; reproductive, 12–15, 228–9

Freud, Sigmund, 94, 117

friendship, 74, 79, 81–2

future, 142, 163–75, 275, 278; becoming, 116–20; construction of, 39, 72; open, 156–9; potential, 44, 51–2; unknown, 56–7, 90–1

Galton, Francis, 220

games of truth, 86, 103

Garland-Thomson, Rosemarie, 212

gender: gendered bodies, 5; and culture, 92–6; and disabilities, 16; gendered division of labor, 224–6; inequality, 88; minorities, 9; performative, 109–10; sex/gender division, 205

genealogy: of biopower, 211; of life, 32, 96; as method, 87

generosity, 69, 82, 140–2

genetic: interventions, 199–213; material 117; myth, 191

genocide, 231, 245–7

God, 29–32

Goodall, Jane, 81

grievability, 6–12, 210

Grosz, Elizabeth, 16–17, 27–39, 70–5, 85–98, 111–15

Guattari, Félix, 35, 71

habit, 154–6

habitat, 54–61

Haraway, Donna, 4–5, 19, 45, 59, 70–1, 130

Harjo, Joy, 255

harm, 15, 200–9; reduction, 239–50

Harris, Barbara, 223

Harris, John, 203

health care, 4, 207, 217, 223, 248

Hegel, Georg Wilhelm Friedrich, 9, 69–82, 92–4, 146, 187

Heidegger, Martin, 108–20

Heinämaa, Sarah, 187

hesitation, 19, 154–5

heteronormativity, 108, 111

heterosexuality. See under sexuality

Hill Collins, Patricia, 70

Hird, Myra, 108–20

historicity; 17–18, 96, 99

HIV, 223, 243, 246

Hobbes, Thomas, 76

Hollenberg, Alexander, 266

Hughes, Bill, 208

human beings: and ethics, 71, 210, 228, 232; and existence, 181–92; and particularity, 155–9, 167, 188, 190

human exceptionalism, 76, 78, 80, 92, 272–81. See also anthropocentrism

humanism, 3, 8, 209; and the anthropocene, 272–81; challenges to, 90–103, 173; and ethics, 67–82

hybridity, 5, 60, 71

Hypersea, 54–61

ideas, 30–2, 142–4, 149–51

identity: constructed, 212; and intelligibility, 95, 99; masculine, 118; and singularity, 255–68; and stability, 139; struggle for, 28

ideology, 69, 166–73, 279

imagination, 5, 71, 75, 82, 266

immanence, 11, 38, 117

impairment, 199–213

incarceration, 217–33; carceral-assistential complex, 224–5; carceral-eugenic complex, 227, 232; hyperincarceration, 218, 227; mass incarceration, 223–33

movement: of bodies, 129–44; of differentiation, 90; social/political, 35, 78, 150, 200–4, 220, 226–33; theoretical, 150–9
multiplicity, 90, 136, 142, 278; of bodies, 48–51, 131, 134; of life, 85, 135; of others, 157, 174; of perspectives, 188; sexual, 111, 118–19
myth, 68, 117, 157, 191–2

Nagel, Thomas, 250
narrative, 260–8; counternarrative, 257; personal, 147, 189; progress, 164, 169; renarration, 257–63
natural history, 99, 275
natural selection, 90
nature: and culture, 44, 207; and humans, 5, 45, 47, 67–82, 272–81; philosophy of, 50; return to, 85–103; sex and, 108–20
neutrality, 148, 164, 204–11; neutralization, 34–7, 110–12, 117, 224
Nicklen, Paul, 81
Nietzsche, Friedrich, 30–5, 42, 51, 94, 181
nihilism, 111, 182
nonhuman, 3, 31–3, 44–8, 61; animals, 5, 11–15, 67–82, 85, 242; archive, 85–103; forces, 6, 112, 272–81; nature, 68, 72, 99, 102, 272–81
normativity; 3–7, 46, 76–80, 136–8, 210–11, 274; non-normativity, 133, 139
novel, 174, 186–92, 264

Oliver, Kelly, 73
Oliver, Michael, 204–5
ontic, 109–10
onto-epistemology, 9, 43–8, 57–60
ontogenesis, 113–20
ontology, 4–5, 42–61, 70, 75; and life, 27–39, 85–103; negative, 199–213; and sexual difference, 108–20; of the who, 260–2
oppression, 70, 78, 151–8, 186–8, 263; and disability, 205–8; intersectional, 218, racial, 4; reproductive, 231–2, sexist, 4, 61; structural, 137
organism, 13, 77, 92, 96, 115–20

organization: biological, 31; self, 74, 77, 79, 113; social, 205, 280
other, the, 7, 10, 69, 120; ethics and, 46, 73–4, 95; self and, 153, 170–4, 181–92. *See also* alterity

parenthood, 226–30
Parisi, Luciana, 111–15
Parker, Emily Anne, 165, 174
passing, 139
passions: and action, 77–82, 92; bodily, 30–9; elemental, 49; and existence, 163–75
past, 36–9, 85–103, 136, 172, 191
pathology; 21, 200–5; (de)pathologization; 98
Payne, Katy, 82
perception, 154, 184
performance: of able-bodiedness, 137; criteria, 211–13; of gender, 5, 110; of oneself, 191; performativity, 6, 92, 109–10, 155; of ritual, 155
phenomenology, 88, 181–92, 209
Planned Parenthood, 222, 227, 240–1
pleasure, 80–1, 97–103, 157
polemic, 272–5
politics: biopolitics, 86, 95, 109–11; of contestation, 28; cyborg, 5; disability, 133–41; feminist, 27–39, 92; geopolitics, 278; identity, 153; relational, 262–7; of renaturalization, 67–82; reproductive, 222; US, 6–8; of vulnerability, 11, 261; Western, 258, 273
possibility, 78, 135–42, 157, 164–7; conditions of, 87, 92, 100, 116–19; impossibility, 9, 57
posthumanism, 5, 43–52, 68, 86–99, 272–81
post-structuralism, 5, 44, 88, 133, 272
power, 156, 212–13, 232; biopower, 86, 96–103, 211, 256–68; colonial, 256–68; configurations of, 3, 8, 47, 59; of existing, 71–82; nonhuman, 273, 276–81; questions of, 12, 206; relations, 34, 208–10, 277; sovereign, 255–68